REFIGURING SPAIN

REFIGURING SPAIN

Cinema / Media / Representation

Marsha Kinder, Editor

Duke University Press   Durham and London

1997

© 1997 Duke University Press
All rights reserved. Printed in the United States of
America on acid-free paper ∞
Typeset in Garamond 3 with Frutiger display by
Keystone Typesetting, Inc.
Library of Congress Cataloging-in-Publication Data
appear on the last printed page of this book.
This book has been published with the aid of a
grant from the Program for Cultural Cooperation
between Spain's Ministry of Culture and Education
and United States's Universities.

This book is dedicated

to my husband, Nicolás Bautista,

and to our son, Victor Aurelio

CONTENTS

ACKNOWLEDGMENTS

Originally this volume was to be a book version of the special issue of *Quarterly Review of Film and Video* titled "Remapping the Post-Franco Cinema," which I edited in 1991. But because I increasingly wanted to add new, more up-to-date essays, I finally decided to abandon that project entirely and start a new anthology from scratch.

There are several individuals and institutions I want to thank for helping me with this process of transforming the volume: the Program for Cultural Cooperation between Spain's Ministry of Culture and United States' Universities, which supported this project with grants; the Instituto de la Cinematografía y las Artes Audiovisuales within the Ministerio de Cultura (particularly Carmelo Romero), the Filmoteca Española (particularly its director, José María Prado García, and its head librarian, Dolores Devesa), and the Academia de las Artes y las Ciencias Cinematográficas de España (particularly its current president, José Luis Borau), who have consistently supported my work and who helped me obtain the illustrations (unless otherwise specified, the source for the photographs was the Filmoteca Española); Dennis Bartok of the American Cinematheque and Block-Korenbrot (representing Sony Pictures Classics), who helped me obtain a few additional photographs and press kits; Ken Wissoker, my editor at Duke University Press, who helped to publish the volume; and my students in a graduate seminar on Spanish cinema at the University of Southern California School of Cinema-Television, who read the manuscript and offered helpful criticism.

Since the volume took a long time to assemble, it was essential to see many of the films again. Thus, I want to thank the organizers and sponsors of the Spanish Film Series, also called "Refiguring Spain," which I curated at the University of Southern California (January 20 through February 10, 1996). Containing twenty-one films (most of which are discussed in this anthology), the series was organized by the Oficina de Educación de España (particularly Miguel Lahoz, Enrique Contreras, and Begoña Aguado), and at USC by the Spanish Resource Center in the School of Education (particularly Margarita Ravera), the School of Cinema-Television (particularly Dana Knowles), and the Department of Spanish and Portuguese (particularly Ramón Araluce). The patrons and sponsors of this series were Victor Ibáñez-Martín, the cónsul general de España in Los Angeles; the Ministerio de Cultura; the Instituto Español de Comercio Exterior; Casa de España in Los Angeles; and the Federación de Sociedades Españoles in California.

Throughout the book, translations from Spanish to English are the work of the individual authors unless otherwise noted.

REFIGURING SPAIN

MARSHA KINDER

Refiguring Socialist Spain: An Introduction

Refiguring Politics

Spain is an ideal case study for exploring the process of redefining national, regional, and cultural identity over the past twenty years, primarily because its rapid transition from Francoism to democracy prefigured the sudden collapse of the entire cold-war paradigm. Beginning with the assassination of General Francisco Franco's hand-picked successor, Admiral Luis Carrero Blanco, by Basque terrorists in 1973 (two years before the death of the dictator), this transition involved several dramatic transformative events: the legalization of the Communist Party in 1977, the signing of a new constitution in 1978 that dismantled Franco's centralized state into seventeen autonomous regional communities, an abortive right-wing coup in 1981 that was thwarted by the liberal monarch Juan Carlos, and the election of the Socialists in 1982 as the ruling party of post-Franco Spain. The relatively peaceful nature of Spain's political metamorphosis now seems even more extraordinary when contrasted with the bloody ethnic wars that have subsequently erupted throughout post-Soviet Eastern Europe.

While international forces were pursuing the herculean task of keeping the peace in Bosnia, Spain, in the spring of 1996, experienced another major political reversal, one that received very little press coverage in the United States, primarily because it occurred during a time when other post-cold-war nationalist struggles were more violent and therefore deemed more newsworthy (Cuba's downing of an American plane flown by Cuban exiles, a series of terrorist bombings in Israel, and a Chinese military threat against their alleged renegade region of Taiwan).

In Spain's March 1996 general election, the right-wing Partido Pop-ular (PP) defeated the Partido Socialista Obrero Español (PSOE) of Felipe González, ending thirteen years of uninterrupted left-wing rule and inaugurating a new period of political uncertainty that seemed more characteristic of Italy than Spain.[1] Although the PP is historically linked to those who supported Franco, it has redefined itself as a center-right, reformist party that promises to eradicate the Socialist legacy of political corruption and high unemployment (which was 23 percent at election time). Although the PP won more parliamentary seats than the PSOE, they were twenty seats short of a majority, which meant that in order to form a government with their own leader José María Aznar as president they had to seek a coalition with other parties.

The issue of regionalism figured prominently within this new crisis, for the revelations that González's government had ordered the as-sassination of Basque terrorists was the last in a series of scandals that helped bring his party down. Yet since Aznar's centralist party had failed to offer any new powers to Spain's regional governments during his campaign and promised to be even tougher than González in crack-ing down on Basque separatists, the PP initially found little support for a coalition among nationalist parties in the Basque country and Cata-lonia. However, after two months of intensive negotiation with various regional parties, especially Catalonia's Convergence and Union Party (which also enabled González to stay in power when his party had failed to get a majority), Aznar succeeded in forming a broad coalition with the moderate nationalist parties that rule Catalonia, the Basque country, and the Canary Islands. In order to reach this accord, Aznar had to grant concessions to these regions, expanding their jurisdiction over areas of government formerly reserved for the central administration and mak-ing (as *El País* put it) "a revolutionary change in the formulas for financing those communities." On May 5, when sworn in as the new president of Spain's government, Aznar promised that these concessions would not sacrifice the "interterritorial solidarity of the regions" or the "universal character of education, health, pensions, and social welfare" and that they would not compromise Spain's movement toward con-vergence with Europe.

Although this move to the right was consistent with recent political developments in several other European nations and also could be inter-preted as merely another minor episode in the perpetual struggle between the "two Spains," many Spaniards read the 1996 general election (in which an impressive 78 percent of Spain's 32 million registered voters participated) not as an affirmation of the Conservatives and their right-wing ideology but as a rejection of the Socialist Party and their corruption. Yet ironically, for the voters to risk such a return to right-wing conservatism, there must have been a broad-based belief in the basic stability of a democratic Spain. This successful refiguring of Spain may ultimately prove to be the Socialists' most important accomplishment.

Cinematic Icons as Cultural Capital

What is striking in the case of Spain is the crucial role played by the mass media in this ongoing process of refiguring the nation—a subject that is the primary focus of this anthology. One of the most dramatic demonstrations of this role was the stunning global success of Pedro Almodóvar's movies during the 1980s and early 1990s, which enabled him to perform a radical sex change on Spain's national stereotype. Not only did his parodic melodramas pretend that the patriarchal Franco never existed, but they displaced the stereotypical macho matadors and gypsies of the Andalusian *españoladas* with an outrageous libertarian array of transgressive sexualities, including gay couples, transsexuals, bisexuals, lesbians, and liberated women—a substitution most explicit in *Matador* (1986). Building on earlier examples of such dynamics in works by such filmmakers as Jaime de Armiñán (*Mi querida señorita* [My Dearest Señorita, 1971], and *Al servicio de la mujer española* [At the Service of Spanish Womanhood, 1978]), Vicente Aranda (*Cambio de sexo* [Sex Change, 1977]), José Juan Bigas Luna (*Bilbao,* 1978, and *Caniche* [Poodle, 1979]), and Eloy de la Iglesia (*El diputado* [The Deputy, 1978]), Almodóvar succeeded in establishing a mobile sexuality as the new cultural stereotype for a hyperliberated Socialist Spain and thereby generated a strategic combination of historical recuperation, sexual reinscription, and marketing transfiguration—the three categories that structure this volume.

That is why Almodóvar's name runs like a thread through this anthology, even though only one essay is devoted exclusively to his work. Emerging as the self-appointed film laureate of the socialist era, Almodóvar was keenly aware of his historic role in this process of refiguring.

Pedro Almodóvar
poses as a model of
commercial success for
Spanish cinema. (Print
courtesy: Pedro
Almodóvar)

As he expressed it when I interviewed him in 1987: "I think my films . . . represent . . . this kind of new mentality that appears in Spain after Franco dies. . . . Everybody has heard that now everything is different in Spain . . . but it is not so easy to find this change in the Spanish cinema. I think in my films they see how Spain has changed, above all, because now it is possible to do this kind of film here, . . . a film like *La ley del deseo*."[2] When *La ley del deseo* (Law of Desire) received critical raves at the 1987 Berlin Film Festival and did well commercially in foreign markets, it was praised even by Spain's oldest conservative film journal, *Fotogramas y video,* as a model for Spain's cinema of the future, one that could arouse interest abroad "not only at the level of . . . cultural curiosity but as an exportable and commercially valid product."[3] This prediction proved valid, for by 1991 Almodóvar had directed six of Spain's all-time top thirteen film exports to the United States.

This model of commercial success was not lost on other Spanish filmmakers, who realized that Almodóvar's combination of historical recuperation and sexual mobility was transferable. Even if they were not consciously following his lead, his global success created a more hospitable environment for the reception of their films abroad—particularly if their representation of Spain was consistent with the way his films had refigured it.

We can see this effect if we compare the two Oscars Spain has thus far won for best foreign-language film, the first rewarding the peaceful settlement of Spain's violent past and the second celebrating the venturous transfiguration of Spain's anarchistic legacy for the future. In 1983 (shortly after the Socialists were voted into power) an Oscar was awarded to José Luis Garci's *Volver a empezar* (To Begin Again, 1982), a sentimental film about a middle-aged Nobel Prize—winning poet who has fled from Spain after the Civil War and who now returns from exile in the United States to his hometown so that he can stoically settle his affairs before dying. The second was awarded in 1994 to Fernando Trueba's *Belle Epoque* (which won over China's *Farewell, My Concubine*), a commercially successful romantic comedy about a young man's sexual adventures with four sisters from a free-thinking family in the early 1930s. This film figures Spanish history not as a noble object of tragic pity for complacent global spectators but as an enviable source of unrestrained pleasure for a world plagued by AIDS and by waves of neoconservative backlash. Thus, the so-called new liberated mentality of Socialist Spain is shown to have historic roots in the pre–Civil War era, a period recuperated as a utopian fantasy for the same global audience that made Almodóvar a star.

The transference effect of Almodóvar's global triumph can be demonstrated even more dramatically in the successful move of Antonio Banderas to Hollywood—the first Spanish actor to make the crossover since the silent era. Calling it a "new renaissance for Spanish cinema," *El País* reported that on October 9, 1996, at the Berlin Film Festival the Italian government, the Italian film industry, and the region of Apulia awarded both Almodóvar and Banderas the Rudolph Valentino Award.[4] Although supposedly the former received it for "his commitment to the Spanish subculture" (the new national stereotype I have been describing) and the latter for "his charm and charisma" and for being "considered the reincarnation of the famous Rudolph Valentino," I suspect it was really given to reward them for being, like Valentino, crossover heroes in the global market—an important model not just for Spain but for the entire European Union (EU). Although Banderas was at first restricted to playing a "generic Hispanic" in Hollywood who breathed new life into the Latin lover stereotype (as in *Mambo Kings* [1992], and *The House of Spirits* [1993], and even later in *Miami Rhapsody* [1995] and Trueba's *Two Much* [1995]), he also began to challenge a formidable "A" list of Anglo male stars in more venturesome films like *Interview with the Vampire* (1994) and *Philadelphia* (1993), where he played an Almodóvarian sexual shifter capable of transgressing borders of gender and sexuality.

This path was paved in Madonna's documentary *Truth or Dare* (1991), where the then reigning queen of global pop culture confesses that the only person in the world she ardently desires to meet is Banderas, the star of those Almodóvar movies she loves. She pointedly prefers him over members of two generations of Hollywood heartthrobs, Warren Beatty and Kevin Costner (just as Melanie Griffith was later to prefer him to Don Johnson off-screen). Banderas mediates between these super-straight actors-cum-directors, whom Madonna finds pompous and boring, and the "male" members of her own company whose mobile sexuality she plays with but without taking them seriously. And she has chosen him again to play Che to her Evita. Unlike the others, Banderas is presented as a challenge worthy of her own talents as a postmodernist shifter—partly because she had to poach him not only from the heterosexual clutches of his beautiful Spanish wife but also from the quintessentially "queer" discourse of his brilliant Spanish director, Almodóvar.

As several U.S. journalists have noted, in *Interview with the Vampire* it is precisely this subversive bisexual mobility that enabled Banderas to outperform both the heterosexual lead Tom Cruise and his androgynous costar Brad Pitt,[5] especially in making the ambiguity of vampiric eroticism convincing. Banderas had an even smaller role in *Philadelphia* (1993), in which he played the loyal lover of Tom Hanks. When Hanks accepted his Oscar for best actor, he gave special thanks to Banderas, joking that if he were not already in love with his wife, he would love this young Spaniard. Although Hanks gave an admirable performance as a homosexual lawyer with AIDS, he still seemed to need Banderas as his lover to make his own sexual mobility convincing. In all these discourses Banderas carries the trace of a desirable, liminal antihomophobia that is immune to ridicule and that makes him appealing to spectators across the full spectrum of sexualities—a trace he acquired in the performative space of Almodóvar's sexually mobile melodramas.

Yet, as Banderas moved toward Hollywood superstardom, he was refigured as exclusively heterosexual in the North American press. We can see this tension in a cover article on Banderas in *Movieline,* which was timed to anticipate his first starring role in *Desperado* (1995). When asked by a journalist about "the near-kiss with fellow vampire Brad Pitt in *Interview,*" Banderas responded provocatively: "It *was,* in a way, a kiss, a sad good-bye kiss. It was not in the script. Brad and I planned it. . . . We wanted to push a little more the feeling of the strange sexual relationship between these strange humans. I always feel that art in general and acting in particular should make the audience a little uncomfortable, to slap them and wake them up" (76). Yet as if to assuage any discomfort that this comment may have aroused and to "naturalize" his masculinity, he immediately disavowed his sexual mobility by implying it had all been an act. When asked directly whether he had "ever availed himself of a gay experience," he replied: "No, never have. . . . Nature made me different. . . . I've done gay characters several times in my life and I tried to do it in the most honest way. . . . I've never played a queen. I always played a guy who was comfortable with his problems, who reacts not so differently from a heterosexual guy" (76). Having deftly redefined himself as "one of the boys," he could kiss Almodóvar movies good-bye!

In Hollywood Banderas's deviance has been transferred to the register of violence, for in his most successful starring roles (in *Desperado* and *Assassins* [1995]) he has been recast as (in the words of one journalist) "a lovable maniac, an icy killer with fiery passion and a perceptible, Mel Gibson–like awareness of the manure he's spreading."[6] The comparison with Gibson is telling, for he also made the successful crossover to Hollywood from a prior minor-league stardom in a peripheral national cinema (Australian rather than Spanish).

Although this crossover process could be dismissed merely as cultural erasure, it also could be seen as a means of generating a kind of cultural capital, which Spaniards could draw on in future projects. That was probably the assumption of Spanish producer Andrés Vicente Gómez and his associates (Sogetel/Sogepaq, Polygram Films, Interscope Communications, Lola Films, and Touchstone Pictures), who financed *Two Much,* a screwball comedy directed by Trueba and shot in English with Banderas and Griffith (whose off-screen romance was still hot news in the tabloids). In the United States the film was both a critical and commercial flop (grossing under $2 million in contrast to *Belle*

Epoque, which grossed nearly $6 million). American spectators were probably disappointed to see their new demonic darling domesticated and few of them had ever heard of Trueba, despite his recent Oscar. But Spaniards flocked to *their* theaters to see the "Hollywood" reinscription of two of their most successful local heroes. *Two Much* took in $10 million in Spain, making it the top-grossing "Spanish" film of 1995 and establishing a new all-time box office record. This kind of reinscription has been resisted by Almodóvar, whose global star power has thus far remained firmly rooted in Spain and has been at least partially based on his ability to hispanize Hollywood conventions.

Refiguring Financing

Almodóvar's global success became even more crucial in the 1990s, as Spain moved toward convergence with other members of the EU, for he could be used by the governments (both of González and Aznar) to prove that it *is* possible for a Spanish cinema to succeed on its own in the market both at home and abroad without heavy government subventions.

To Spanish filmmakers in the 1990s, González was no longer the Socialist savior freeing them from the last vestiges of Franco with his promise of "100 years of honesty." He no longer was relying on a heavily subsidized cinema to popularize images worldwide of the new liberated Spain as he did in the early 1980s. Rather, by the mid-1990s he was the leader of an entrenched establishment increasingly charged with political stagnation and financial corruption. As champion of "el Euro" (the European common currency approved at the 1995 Consejo Europeo de Madrid and which supposedly is to be in circulation by 1999), he remained determined to make Spain one of the elite members of the EU (that is, one of those who could meet the strict economic criteria agreed on at Maastricht in December 1991). This commitment contributed to Spain's high unemployment rate and compromised his earlier support of Spanish cinema. Since there was increasing pressure to stop subsidizing industries that were losing money, the crucial question was whether the film industry should be exempt given that it manufactures for world consumption unique cultural products that construct images of national identity.

This problem was intensified by television, which increasingly rivaled the refiguring power of cinema in the 1990s. It was the medium that succeeded in making Barcelona the star of the 1992 summer Olympics and that was now being represented as "the bad object" by Spanish filmmakers from Almodóvar to Víctor Erice. As both Richard Maxwell and Iñaki Zabaleta explain, television provided an effective means of dramatically redefining Spanish culture and its communities—no matter whether the spectators identified with subnational regions such as Catalonia and the Basque country, with the Spanish nation, with the new macroregion of the EU, or with the global audience unified by satellite transmission. The dramatic decentering of television provided a powerful model for other forms of cultural production, such as art museums, as Selma Holo details. During the post-Franco period there was a rapid transformation of Spanish television from a national monopoly with two public stations in Madrid to the fastest-growing market in Europe, with seven new regional networks (broadcasting in regional languages and being run by provincial governments) and three new private networks at least partially controlled and financed by outside European and multinational interests. These changes led not only to a boom in global advertising revenues but also to a series of political crises during the Socialist era, for those running the public stations were accused of financial mismanagement, political favoritism, and personal corruption. Nevertheless, unlike Spanish cinema, the television industry was not threatened with extinction.

The situation was more dire for Spanish cinema, which had to find new ways to survive (a topic explored by Peter Besas). In June 1992, Spanish filmmakers held a three-day conference in Madrid (Audiovisual Español 93), in which professionals from the film industry urged the González government to introduce a new subvention law to protect Spanish cinema from Hollywood domination and from the "europuding" co-productions that threaten to erase the cultural specificity of Spain and its autonomous regions. It also urged the government to support the French resistance to the United States position of including movies and television programs within the free-trade agreement during the GATT negotiations. Audiovisual Español 93 ended with a dire prediction from Conference President Román Gubern, who warned that without government protection, "in 1995, instead of celebrating the centennial of Spanish cinema . . . we will celebrate its funeral."[7] The last-minute elimination of film and TV from the 1993 GATT agreements made such protection possible, and in 1995, as the nation celebrated "cien años de cine español," this grim scenario fortunately failed to materialize. But the looming crisis was only postponed, not resolved.

As the national imaginary of Spain continues to be challenged both at the microlevel of the autonomous regions and the macrolevel of the EU the funding sources and regulatory policies for Spanish cinema have also undergone change. While (as Peter Besas details) the state subventions at the national level continue to be the most important source of advance funding for Spanish features, several other sources emerged in the late 1980s and early 1990s: subventions from regional governments; advance sales of foreign distribution and broadcast rights to television networks (both national and regional, public and private); and grants from European commissions (such as the Media Program of the European Union and Eurimages, which supports films with producers from three participating countries). Since several films now receive advance funding from all four sources, any puristic notion of "national" cinema seems highly problematic.

There are also financial incentives for this kind of transnational cultural hybridity in the new regulations concerning screen quotas and dubbing licenses—the two mechanisms that historically have supported the system of subventions in protecting Spanish cinema against foreign imports. Although both can be traced back to the early 1940s and neither is unique to Spain, both mechanisms were recently modified to fit the political realities of the 1990s by making Spanish and European films interchangeable and by setting them in opposition to those made outside the EU. This "outsider" category refers primarily to films made in the United States given that "the EU takes 60 percent of US film exports and has a film trade deficit with the US of $4 billion a year."[8] The quota system in Spain now requires local exhibitors to screen at least one Spanish *or* European Union film for each two non-European Spanish-dubbed films in cities over 125,000; in smaller cities, the ratio is one-to-three. According to a new law passed in 1994, a distributor will be granted a dubbing license (for foreign imports) whenever a Spanish or EU film grosses 20 million pesetas; a second license can be granted on two conditions: the Spanish or EU film must bring in 30 million pesetas, and it must also be dubbed into another of Spain's official languages (such as Catalan).

A similar transnational hybridity can be found in the structure of private funding. To launch *Too Much*, Spain's most successful independent producer Vicente Gómez (Iberoamericana Films) gained funding first from Spanish conglomerate Sogetel/Sogepaq (the film production and distribution subsidiaries of Prisa, which also owns *El País*) before making additional distribution deals with Polygram Films and Canal Plus. Similarly, El Deseo, the production company of the Almodóvar brothers, has an ongoing alliance with CIBY 2000, a French "minimajor" that specializes in commercially viable art films, such as Jane Campion's *The Piano* (1992), Emir Kusturica's *Underground* (1995), and Mike Leigh's *Secrets and Lies* (1996), which each won a Palmes d'Or at the Cannes Film Festival. Together El Deseo and CIBY 2000 produced Almodóvar's three latest films—*Tacones lejanos* (High Heels, 1991), *Kika* (1993), and *La flor de mi secreto* (The Flower of My Secret, 1995).

No longer is it a matter of thinking of Spain as an isolated nation whose population cannot support a film industry but rather viewing it as an aggregate of autonomous microregions that is part of larger aggregates of European or Spanish-language communities vying with other macroregions such as North America or the Pacific Rim for a prominent position in the global political economy.

Apparently, these new measures and modes of thinking are paying off for Spanish cinema, at least for the moment. In contrast to 1994, when Spain produced only forty-one films, 1995 generated fifty-six Spanish features, twenty-three of which were international coproductions. In contrast to the early 1990s, 1995 also brought a 45 percent increase in the average film budget and a 50 percent increase in the investment in production. Perhaps most encouraging, in 1995 there was a reversal of the downward trend in Spain's share of the domestic film market, which went from 11.88 percent in 1991, to 9.32 percent in 1992, to 8.52 percent in 1993, to a dismal 7.12 percent in 1994, before bouncing back to 10.7 percent in 1995. This final year of Socialist rule proved to be a very good vintage for Spanish cinema, and despite the political change, the upswing continued in 1996 with an output of ninety-one films.

In August 1996 the Aznar government announced that it intended to abolish the protective policies of screen quotas and dubbing licenses. This position was supported by Miguel Angel Cortés, the Spanish Culture Secretary, who claims the last thirteen years under the Socialists "have been the worst in the history of Spanish cinema."[9] This attack was also supported by José María Otero, the director of the cinematographic and audiovisual institute, who claims that dubbing licenses never helped Spanish cinema. Yet most Spanish filmmakers were not convinced by these statements, particularly because 80 percent of all films shown in Spain are from the United States and Spain is now the fifth largest market for Hollywood movies. The announcement by the government elicited such strong reactions from the filmmakers that Aznar temporarily backed down. Echoing Gubern's earlier prediction, even Almodóvar prophesied: "If cinemas are not obliged to put on a Spanish film once in a while, Spanish cinema will die."[10]

Within this debate over government policy, the recent successes in 1995 were crucial. Whereas one side attributed them to increases in government protectionism, the other side pointed to the 1994 law that restricted advance subsidies to first- or second-time directors (who brought a new generation of spectators to Spanish movies) and that tied other subsidies more directly to box-office success and to the Europeanizing of the films. The Aznar government strongly favors cooperative ventures with other EU nations to build a European film industry that will compete successfully with Hollywood without relying so heavily on subventions and protectionist policies. One specific venture is a pan-European loan-guarantee fund, proposed by the European Commission, to support the production of 415 European films. Originally proposed by Polygram (which enjoyed a major box-office success with *Four Weddings and a Funeral* [1994], this plan is supported by Spain, Italy, and France. Yet it has been opposed by Germany and many European filmmakers on the grounds that it will benefit only big companies and encourage the production only of films with mass appeal—in other words, European films that imitate Hollywood blockbusters and that ignore the kind of cultural specificity that could be found in some of the most interesting Spanish films released in 1995.

Flowers, Beasts, and the Dead: Three Films from 1995

I want to look briefly at three popular Spanish films released in 1995 to see how they specifically addressed the political changes that were occurring in Spain and anticipated what was to follow in the 1996 general elections: Almodóvar's *La flor de mi secreto* (The Flower of My Secret); Alex de la Iglesia's *El día de la bestia* (The Day of the Beast), which won six Goyas (Spanish Oscars), including best director; and Agustín Díaz Yanes's debut feature, *Nadie hablará de nosotras cuando hayamos muerto* (Nobody Will Speak of Us When We're Dead), which won eight, including best picture, best new director, best screenplay, and best actress.

La flor de mi secreto could be read as Almodóvar's swan song to Felipe González and to his own contract as film laureate of the Socialist era. Although González was billed as the global star of a cosmopolitan Socialist Spain, the film shows student demonstrators accusing him of being a jerk—of cheating them out of a future and abandoning his Spanish loved ones for quixotic dreams of a unified Europe. The film calls for a recuperation of traditional images of Spain that are reinscribed to suit Almodóvar's ethos. In a stunning performance by a mother/son dance team (played by Manuela Vargas and Joaquín Cortés), flamenco is infused with incestuous overtones, making it compatible with Almodóvar's revisionist stereotype of transgressive sexuality (a strategy similar to the one used in *Matador* to recuperate bullfighting). The small Spanish village (where several of his characters are headed at the end of earlier films) is here presented as a potent source of renewal both for the nation and its depressed citizens (who are urged to celebrate novenas there even if they are nonbelievers). Yet the film is clearly not provincial: it implies an acceptance of global melodrama in place of multinational militarism, world-class flamenco instead of world cup soccer, commuting between metropolitan Madrid and the local villages of Extremadura rather than between Brussels and Bosnia. Almodóvar claims that this is his "most Manchegan film," one that lyrically celebrates "the fields of red earth . . . and ash colored olive trees" of La Mancha, the region where both he and Don Quixote were born. Yet instead of resorting to the traditional religious icon, he places a large "political map" of Spain over the bed of his heroine and her Europeanized husband who no longer loves her.[11] The film pointedly refigures the nation and its complex relations with the old regional village and the new European Union.

The villages of La Mancha are presented as the Motherland, for like *Mujeres al borde de un ataque de nervios* (Women on the Verge of a Nervous Breakdown, 1988) and *Tacones lejanos,* not only is this a woman's film that rejects men of power and treats all women sympathetically (even those who are demented or temporarily treacherous) but it is also one that celebrates mothers. In fact, Almodóvar call it a "neorealist" portrait of his own mother. Like all his previous films, it combines melodrama

In *La flor de mi secreto,* Leo (Marisa Paredes, left) accompanies her mother (Chus Lampreave, right) back to their home village. (Photo courtesy: Sony Pictures Classics)

and comedy but in a different proportion; the melodrama dominates and contains "bile instead of honey," yet it is neither humorless nor pessimistic. It is closest to *¿Qué he hecho yo para merecer esto?* (What Have I Done to Deserve This?, 1984), the woman's film that he also called "neorealist" and which put melodrama at the generic center of his work. It also established his international reputation, thereby inaugurating his contractual bond with the Socialists (who subsequently supported him with subventions).[12]

La flor de mi secreto tells the story of Leocadia (brilliantly played by Marisa Paredes), a writer who (like Almodóvar) has also outgrown a restrictive contract. In fact, in her case there are two: a marriage contract to her adulterous, absentee husband Paco (Imanol Arias), who is a military strategist for the Spanish contingent of the NATO special forces stationed in Brussels and who has now volunteered for a peace-keeping mission in Bosnia; and a literary contract that requires her to write three "pink" novels a year under the secret pen name of Amanda Gris. The novels are escapist romances contractually required to contain no politics, no social conscience, no unhappy endings, and no reality. Her real novel, *In Cold Storage* (which expresses her current emotional

Sent by his mother to console her abandoned lady Leo (Marisa Paredes), the sexy Flamenco dancer Antonio (Joaquín Cortés) offers to spend the night in *La flor de mi secreto.* (Photo courtesy: Sony Pictures Classics)

state with its twisted hyperplots, unsavory characters, black tone, morbid violence, and unhappy endings), is stolen by a young flamenco dancer (the son of her maid) to capitalize his artistic debut and sold to make a Bigas Luna movie (a director with whom Almodóvar has exchanged mutual accusations of poaching). Although Leo futilely clings to these contracts as if they were her brain-dead child (a trope introduced in the inset video that opens the film), she must break free if she is to save her sanity. She comes from a long line of female crazies that includes not only her own dotty mother and sister (played respectively by Almodóvar veterans Chus Lampreave and Rossy DePalma) and her aunt and grandmother (who are repeatedly mentioned in the film) but also a distinguished international list of her favorite subversive women writers (Djuna Barnes, Jean Rhys, and Janet Frame) who all explore madness imposed on women. Despite the film's brief references to such current social issues as unemployment, drugs, and racism, *La flor de mi secreto* focuses on the love story and its political implications.

As in *Tacones lejanos,* Leo must listen to her mother's voice (which literally saves her life) and she must renounce her cold, macho husband for a warm-hearted, feminized man. The latter is an editor named Angel (Juan Echanove). He works at *El País,* Spain's leading newspaper, which is owned by Prisa, the conglomerate whose film subsidiaries have made it a major player in the Spanish film industry. Like Almodóvar, Angel is an ardent fan of Madrid, of women's confessional literature, and of Hollywood melodramas. He is so crazy about women's literature that he adopts an elephantine female pseudonym, Paqui Derma, which is not only the feminized form of Paco, but also has the same initials as Patty Diphusa, the female persona (a porn-star turned diarist) with which Almodóvar launched his own artistic career in the early 1980s. Eventually Angel appropriates Leo's pen name to fulfill and thereby liberate her from the terms of her contract (a conflation that helps confirm Almodóvar's double identification with both writers). Instead of curtailing the love-starved Leo to suit himself, Angel hungrily plumbs the depths of her subjectivity, eager to see what he can absorb to expand his own.

This contrast is presented in multiple scenes using reflective imagery. The first occurs in Angel's office at *El País*, where he and Leo stand facing each other in front of a series of glass panels and their reflections overlap, his multiplied several times as if being amplified by their encounter. This image contrasts with a triptych of shots that deconstruct Leo's marriage. The first occurs in Leo's hallway, where she hungrily kisses Paco behind a glass wall composed of many small panes, which prevent us from seeing their lips and which create "a fragmented image of . . . a fragmented couple." The second occurs in the bathroom after Paco has rejected Leo sexually; confined within a small hand mirror, her face is dwarfed by his larger mirror reflection, but both are merely images. In the final scene Leo shatters the glass frame that held the false image of her and Paco as a couple; the frame is suddenly dismantled into several translucent glass balls that bounce onto the floor, rolling randomly in all directions. The image functions as a witty visual pun for the devastating effects this breakup has on her sanity, literally "losing her marbles." Like the opening mirror sequence in *La ley del deseo*, these scenes illustrate the process of changing one's "imaginary" by changing one's object of desire, which is the subversive power of romance.

Leo's object of desire changes from a lean, silent man of action like Paco to the fleshy, verbal, nurturing Angel, who is more like an alter ego

The segmented glass panes, in which the images of Leo (Marisa Paredes) and her husband Paco (Imanol Arias) are reflected, prefigure the wrenching separation they are about to experience in *La flor de mi secreto*. (Photo courtesy: Sony Pictures Classics)

than a lover. She herself goes from being a masculinized, masochistic, love-starved woman trapped "in cold storage" to a flowering independent woman capable of liberating *and* transcending her own closeted hyperfeminine Amanda. Her mother reminds her that she used to be a *gordita* like Angel and began going downhill as soon as she started to diet. While the disciplined, militaristic Paco gave her a pair of boots several sizes too small for her feet (an extended trope symbolic of their painful, restrictive marriage), her Almodóvarian Angel gives her an ample column in the cultural supplement of *El País,* where she can freely spawn new literary identities and fictions.

La flor implies that it is also time for Spain to change its imaginary. It must reject the quixotic European obsessions of men like Paco and Felipe (González) and find renewal by looking at the specificity of "el país" (the country itself) through new eyes—whether through the ocular windows of Angel's new *piso* that look out over the church domes and urban skyscrapers of Madrid's skyline or through the hand-embroidered curtains of Almagro village, "the cradle of Female crafts."

Though promoted as outrageous products of a "new generation" of Spanish filmmaking, *El día de la bestia* and *Nadie hablará de nosotras cuando hayamos muerto* go much farther than *La flor de mi secreto* in condemning the libertarian ethos of a Socialist Spain and in recuperating certain values from its conservative past. Although I am not suggesting that these films or their directors support Aznar and the PP, their severe attack on the widespread corruption in Madrid and their intense reengagement with Catholicism (however parodic) evoke the kind of mentality that made both González's defeat and Aznar's coalition possible.

Both are action films featuring an excessive use of graphic violence, which on the surface seems the kind of random postmodern massacre found in global hits by Quentin Tarantino and Richard Rodríguez but which ultimately proves to be a form of religious sacrifice that reaffirms traditional Spanish institutions. I am referring not only to the militant Cervantine idealism that drives *Bestia* and the bullfight ethos and left-wing political activism that lie at the heart of *Nadie,* but also to a born-again neo-Catholicism central to both films. Although the violent acts they depict (drug wars, death-metal thugs, armed robberies, and death squads exterminating the foreign and homeless) can unfortunately be found in many big cities worldwide, they are given a specific Spanish inflection.[13] Unlike the killers in Almodóvar's *Matador* and *La ley del deseo,* the murderous protagonists of these films are not passionate lovers killing in the throes of ecstasy but exterminating angels struggling to save their souls. Whereas *Bestia* depicts Almodóvar's beloved Madrid as the ultimate urban dystopia, *Nadie* displaces the corruption onto the New World capital of Mexico City. Yet in both films Madrid is the site of the final Manichaean struggle between the forces of good and evil.

Nadie begins like a conventional drug-thriller, with an explosive gun battle between two handsome young undercover cops and two middle-aged Mexican drug dealers. The only survivors are a silver-haired Mexican killer (Federico Luppi) and a frightened young Spanish prostitute named Gloria (brilliantly played by Victoria Abril). It is hard to think of a protagonist who has a more demeaning introduction: in her first appearance on screen we cannot see her face for she is on her knees giving blow jobs to all four male players, and at the end of the sequence she pathetically puts up her hands, pleading to the police who deport her, "I'm nobody, just a whore." Still, in between, there is something un-

In *Nadie hablará de nosotras cuando hayamos muerto,* Gloria (Victoria Abril, right) draws moral and physical strength from her mother-in-law, Julia (Pilar Bardem, left). (Print courtesy: The American Cinematheque)

canny in the way she handles the men's bodies—both the flaccid fat belly of the drug dealer as she undoes his pants before sex and the bleeding body of the handsome young narc whose wounds she binds before he dies in her arms. Her moves show a familiarity with the flesh that is more clinical and assured than erotic. We come to understand this quality once she is back in Madrid, reunited with her handsome young husband, a matador whom she abandoned three years ago after he had been gored by a bull and transformed into a human vegetable. Without flashbacks or monologues, we also understand that in the wake of this loss she suffered a long descent into poverty, drunkenness, prostitution, and despair. The film focuses only on her comeback—her struggle to survive and to regain her faith in herself and in a revitalized Spain, which she comes to symbolize.

The most important relationship in this process is with her mother-in-law Julia (Pilar Bardem), a strong woman who was a radical activist associated with La Pasionaria, Dolores Ibarruri (the former president of the outlawed Spanish Communist Party, PCE), whose picture prominently hangs on the wall of their piso. Gloria is redeemed by the legacy of courage she draws both from her husband's experience in the ring and from Julia's resistance against the police.

In one scene we watch Gloria literally change her imaginary by reappropriating the traditional mantle of the matador (the same cultural mantle that Almodóvar had reinscribed). This event initiates the process of her moral and spiritual regeneration. The cape is being borrowed by a young neighbor for his bullfighting debut. Although Gloria is suffering from a terrible hangover and from a humiliating defeat as a would-be burgular, she pulls herself together to demonstrate the proper way to wear the cape. As she stands before a mirror, ritualistically wrapping herself in the garment, she watches her body regain a dignity we have not previously seen. The Christian dimensions of the ritual and its purifying effects are emphasized by two subsequent shots—one of Gloria washing her face, a symbolic baptism; and a final close-up of a dead fish (which she is preparing for Julia and her political friends), an image evoking the resurrection. Believing in Gloria's courage and powers of regeneration and wanting to make it easier for her to start a new life, Julia also decides to perform a ritual—to kill her son and commit suicide. Julia's sacrifice is another means of passing the mantle on from bullfighting and political struggle to a new cultural icon of the 1990s.

As if that were not enough symbolic baggage, Julia's sacrifice is made analogous to that of the other survivor of the opening shootout—the silver-haired Mexican assassin, who has since been sent to Madrid by his matriarchal underworld boss to find and kill Gloria. What gives him pause is the realization that God is punishing him for his sins through his daughter's mysterious illness. Whenever he kills, his daughter gets worse. Thus, the destiny of his daughter is linked with that of Gloria. Both plots are dominated by women: the strong matriarchs from the past (whether good or evil) and the young survivors who embody hope for the future of their respective nations, Mexico and Spain, which share not only a common cultural legacy of Catholicism, bullfighting, and political struggle, but also widespread social and political corruption. In the face of yet another corrupt patriarchy, *Nadie* (like *La flor de mi secreto*) reaffirms the moral strength of women. Yet it also makes us reconsider the moral price Spain paid for replacing matadors and militants with hookers and dopers as the nation's privileged cultural icons.

El día de la bestia was even more successful than *Nadie* at the box office. Although it cost only 2 million dollars, it is an action film with impressive special effects and stunts (a rarity in Spain), which might warrant its being called an *acción mutante,* the title of Alex de la Iglesia's debut feature, which was produced by Almodóvar. It is this dimension— along with the film's commercial success in Spain—that helped de la Iglesia get a deal to make his next "Spanish" film in the United States.[14]

Although Almodóvar helped launch Alex de la Iglesia's career and although the latter's work is frequently aligned with the underground, *Bestia* renounces Almodóvar's celebration of the hyperliberated Madrid. Instead it depicts the demonic phase of the *movida madrileña,* the youth culture movement that emerged after the death of Franco, with an urban dystopia policed by a squad of murderous vigilantes ("Limpia Madrid") and colonized by former Italian Prime Minister Silvio Berlusconi's corrupt multinational media, signs that herald a revived threat of fascism. For all its violence (which relies more on a stylized melange of amplified thuds and whacks than on graphic visuals), *Bestia* returns to a moralistic discourse that condemns and implicitly conflates right-wing attacks against the homeless with the government's covert support of violence against Basque terrorists. Like Almodóvar, de la Iglesia draws on the Spanish tradition of *esperpento* to create a form of black comedy that wavers in tone, in this case wild swings between humor and horror. Instead of generating a destabilizing mobility on the registers of gender, sexuality, and pleasure, it reinstitutes a rigorous Manichaean morality worthy of the jesuitical past that de la Iglesia shares with Buñuel. De la Iglesia is a former philosophy student who studied with the Jesuits at the Basque University of Deusto, the same college from which his protagonist priest Angel (Alex Angulo) derives. The film reveals the reactionary potential of Basque nationalism with its historic leanings toward Catholic fanaticism, its violent resistance against centralization, and its persistent opposition to all outside forces—whether from Madrid, Moscow, or multinational media.[15] This insularity is evoked in the very opening shot, where we see the phrase "puerta d'Europa" written on a wall, a revelation that Madrid's corruption is inextricably linked with the drive toward European convergence.

For salvation de la Iglesia looks backward to Spain's own *Don Quixote.* Turning the Cervantine trope against the González government (which, according to Dona Kercher, has fully exploited it as cultural capital), *Bestia* reinscribes this Golden Age myth for the 1990s while reminding

In *El día de la bestia* the fanatical priest Angelo (Alex Angulo, left) murders José María's phallic mother (right); and . . . terrorizes a blond bourgeois "bimbo" (below). (Prints courtesy: The American Cinematheque)

us of its legacy of militant violence. The protagonist is a quixotic priest from the north who, after deciphering the Apocalypse, is determined to commit as many evil deeds as possible so that he can make a pact with the devil and save the world from the Antichrist. Although we begin by laughing at the absurd incongruity between his idealistic goals and ultraviolent means, as with Quixote, we end up seeing him as one of the few forces of resistance against a totally corrupt culture. After going to the satanic city of Madrid, he recruits José María, a dim-witted Sancho from the local music store, who is into death-metal and whose violent castrating mother Angel eventually murders. When combined with the ridicule and parodic blood-letting of a virgin and the terrorizing of a blond bourgeois "bimbo," this killing of the phallic mother signals a misogynistic return to female stereotypes (mother, virgin, and whore) that will not warm the hearts of women. Angel begins his quest totally ignorant of television but is soon captivated by an Italian TV guru named Professor Caván, who has a big photo of Berlusconi hanging in his office. Although he and his Sancho capture and then brutalize this fake parapsychologist, they ultimately convert him to their holy cause, implying that Italians must also fight against corruption and resist multinational convergence (as their own recent political upheavals confirm).

Different as they are, when read against the context of Spanish cultural specificity all three films from 1995 show a growing disillusionment with the libertarian ethos and an attempt to recuperate conservative traditions. Yet to maintain their global appeal, they retain a radical surface of outrageousness, consistent with the hyperliberated stereotype Almodóvar popularized during the Socialist era. It was this stereotype that helped initiate the financial recovery of a broad-based belief in the stability of a democratic Spain, one that could withstand an occasional swing to the right.

It remains to be seen whether Spanish cinema will continue to perpetuate that image, particularly since Aznar has combined the Ministry of Culture with the Ministry of Education, placing them both under the ultraconservative rule of Esperanza Aguirre, who is frequently compared to Margaret Thatcher. Yet, before spawning any more gloomy prophecies, we should recall that under Thatcher's rule, British cinema was energized by a new spirit of opposition—one almost as vibrant as the oppositional cinema under Franco.

Overview of the Essays

This volume explores the ongoing process of refiguring Spanish cultural identity through media representation in the post-Franco period (1975–95) and the impact this transformation has had on Spain's position in the world economy. With a few exceptions, most of these essays were written before the 1996 general election, still within the Socialist era. The collection emphasizes issues of historical recuperation, sexual reinscription, and the marketing of Spain's transfiguration—the three categories into which the essays are grouped. Although this combination of issues is addressed by most of the contributors, they do so with different goals and emphases.

Historical Recuperation

All four essays in part 1 examine textual strategies that have been used to recuperate earlier historical images as a means of reinscribing Spanish cultural identity in the present and renegotiating the nation's political and economic power. These strategies usually involve an intertextual engagement with texts generated outside of Spain, which serves to demonstrate the nation's full participation in the global sphere. They also include some form of transgression on the registers of sexuality and gender.

Kathleen Vernon's essay "Reading Hollywood in/and Spanish Cinema: From Trade Wars to Transculturalism" is concerned with the strategic uses of American films in constructing an alternative imaginary in opposition to Spain's dominant cultural practices. Revealing a process of "semiotic layering" that involves extratextual discourses as well as reception, she examines those meanings that adhere to the original text as well as those that emerge from their transmission across historical, national, and cultural boundaries. Her essay concentrates on three cases: first, a single film from the Francoist period, Luis García Berlanga's *Bienvenido, Mr. Marshall* (1952); second, the wide spectrum of Hollywood intertexts in the work of a single auteur, Pedro Almodóvar; and third, the functions of a single intertext, the Hollywood noir classic *Gilda* (1946), which is evoked in three Spanish films from the 1980s and 1990s, all using Rita Hayworth's transnational "star image" to destabilize notions of gender and national identity.

In my own essay "Documenting the National and Its Subversion in a Democratic Spain," I focus on the so-called marginal genre of documentary and its Spanish specificity, showing how it has reflexively performed the subversive refiguration of the nation at three crucial political stages: (1) the transition between 1975, when Franco died, and 1977, when the first free elections were held, (2) the mid-1980s, after the Socialists were voted into power, and (3) the early 1990s, when Spain celebrated the 500-year anniversary of 1492 and moved toward convergence with the EU. Selecting a few works from each period that play at the borders between documentary and fiction (*Canciones para después de una guerra* [Songs for after a War, 1971] and *La vieja memoria* [Old Memory, 1977] from the first period; *Vestida de azul* [Dressed in Blue, 1983] and *Madrid* [1986] from the second; and *Innisfree* [1990], *El sol del membrillo* [The Quince Tree Sun, released in the United States as *The Dream of Light*, 1991], *Después de tantos años* [After So Many Years, 1994] and *Flamenco* [1995] from the third), I show how they adapt a series of interrelated discursive strategies to their specific historical contexts.

In "The Marketing of Cervantine Magic for a New Global Image of Spain," Dona Kercher explores how the González government has marketed its cultural hegemony under the sign of Cervantes, not only as a powerful series of intertexts but also institutionally through an international network of Spanish cultural centers called the Instituto Cervantes. Explaining the new role that this world-renowned literary figure has played in the post-Franco reorganization of power, the essay focuses on three adaptations of his work by a single filmmaker, Manuel Gutiérrez Aragón: two daring films (*Maravillas,* [1980] and *La noche más hermosa* [The Most Beautiful Night, 1984]) that loosely play with several Cervantine works and themes, and a "faithful" adaptation of *Quixote,* produced for Spanish National Television (TVE) in the crucial year 1992. Although her essay does not treat the latest *Quixote* adaptations— Alex de la Iglesia's popular *El día de la bestia* and the proposed second part of Gutiérrez Aragón's *El Quixote* (which was supposed to have the late Marcello Mastroianni succeeding the late Fernando Rey in the title role), it does provide an illuminating context for understanding their cultural resonance.

In Nations, Nationalisms, and *Los últimos de Filipinas:* "An Imperialist Desire for Colonialist Nostalgia" the process of refiguring is performed by the essay's Filipino author, Roland Tolentino, who rereads a 1945 historical film from the Francoist period in light of postcolonial discourse. This essay explores how Spain and the Philippines have represented each other in their respective national projects—a subject that becomes increasingly important as the Pacific Rim rivals Europe as the primary regional force in postcolonial cultural production. Tolentino argues that Spain's ceding of the Philippines signaled the end of European colonialism and the beginning of the era of neocolonialism, with the United States leading the new world order. Not only did the exchange of the Philippines between an old colonial and a new imperialist order position the Philippines in a "feminine" space, but it also reaffirmed the masculine gendering of Spain despite its conspicuous loss. Arguing that this gendered disavowal of loss lies at the center of *Los últimos de Filipinas* (The Last from the Philippines/Last Stand in the Philippines), the essay critiques not only this historic Spanish film but also Western theories of nationalism that define all Third World national projects as derivative. Thus it interrogates some of the key theoretical premises of the whole volume as well as the binary concept of center/periphery.

Sexual Reinscription

All four essays in this second part analyze the political use of sexuality and gender in works by Spanish auteurs who achieved commercial success in the international market. They move from Eloy de la Iglesia's success with *Los placeres ocultos* (Secret Pleasures, 1976) and *El diputado* in the late 1970s; to two crossover films by Almodóvar in the mid-1980s, *Matador* and *La ley del deseo;* to Bigas Luna's commercial triumph in the 1990s with his trilogy of *retratos ibéricos* (Iberian Portraits)—*Jamón, jamón, Huevos de oro* (Golden Balls, 1993), and *La teta i la lluna* (The Tit and the Moon, 1994); to the regendering of Spain's political bodies in two films made by women in 1992, Pilar Miró's *El pájaro de la felicidad* (Bird of Happiness) and Arantxa Lazcano's *Urte ilunak* (*Los años oscuros*—The Dark Years). They also move in sexual orientation from a universalizing contextualization of male homosexuality in the de la Iglesia films, to a nostalgic suspension of sexual difference in Almodóvar, to an exogamous sexuality in Bigas Luna, to a negotiation of regional identity with issues of gender and lesbian desire in Miró and Lazcano.

In "Out of the Cinematic Closet: Homosexuality in the Films of Eloy de la Iglesia," Stephen Tropiano argues that de la Iglesia situated homosexual issues within a universalizing context of economic and political oppression that was consistent with the political strategies of the Spanish homosexual rights movement and that exposed the continued oppression of male homosexuals during Spain's democratic transition. Tropiano defends de la Iglesia's films against those gay critics who have accused them of diluting homosexual issues through this process of contextualization. Reading *Los placeres ocultos* and *El diputado* as homosexual variations of the Spanish oedipal narrative, Tropiano claims that this "oedipalization" demonstrates how homosexual desire continues to be constructed and controlled by patriarchal capitalism and the legacy of Spanish fascism.

In "Pornography, Masculinity, Homosexuality: Almodóvar's *Matador* and *La ley del deseo*," Paul Julian Smith argues that Almodóvar's films redefine sexualities primarily in two ways: by displacing the binaries of gendered spectatorship and by generating this displacement formally through a dislocation between dialogue and image. Drawing on three different theoretical strata that address cinema and sexuality (the psychoanalytically based feminism of Laura Mulvey; the revisionist accounts of that gendering by anticensorship feminists such as Linda Williams, Gaylyn Studlar, and Carol Clover; and the postmodernist psychoanalytic theory of Slavoj Žižek), Smith performs a close textual reading of the openings of both films. He concludes that whereas *Matador* leads toward an impossible, utopian bisexuality in which it is only momentarily possible to be both sexes, *La ley del deseo* points to the necessary insatiability and failure of all sexuality.

In "*La teta i la lluna:* The Form of Transnational Cinema in Spain," Marvin D'Lugo claims that this third film in the Bigas Luna trilogy is distinctive in the way it engages both Spanish and foreign audiences in a playful reflection on the clichés of Spanish cultural identity and how that identity is now being reshaped by a complex network of regional, national, and transnational forces. D'Lugo argues that the plot is constructed around a gendered opposition between two central images: the phallic castle, which is emblematic of Catalan regional identity, versus the female dancer, who embodies a desirable feminized Europe. The film presents a revisionist reading of the Spanish "national fiction," moving between *catalanitat,* through which the individual and the community must pass in the process of maturation, and a European identity, toward which Spain and its cinema must aspire if they are to survive in the 1990s.

In "Regendering Spain's Political Bodies: Nationality and Gender in the Films of Pilar Miró and Arantxa Lazcano," Jaume Martí-Olivella explores how discourses on national cinema and gender are renegotiated with cultural specificity in two films made in the crucial year of 1992 by two of the most talented female filmmakers currently working in Spain, both of whom vigorously reject any identification with feminism. *El pájaro de la felicidad* carries autobiographical traces of its powerful Castilian-born writer/director Pilar Miró, who is hardly a marginal figure, having served as the former general director of cinematography as well as the director of TVE under González. *Urte ilunak,* in contrast, is the debut feature of the young Basque director Arantxa Lazcano, who is doubly marginalized, by her gender and region. Yet both films show women being assaulted by men in private and public space and turning to relationships with other women as a way of remobilizing their own personal and cultural identity.

Marketing Transfiguration (Money/Politics/Regionalism)

Whereas the essays in the first two parts all come from within critical studies or Spanish studies and all basically share common poststructuralist assumptions and methodologies, the four chapters in this third part come from outside the field—from Hollywood journalism, international political economy, empirical communication studies, and art history and museum studies. They are therefore much more varied in their methodology, object of study, writing style, and basic assumptions. In this way they lead us to see how issues of cinema can be broadened when considered in light of other forms of cultural production such as television, newspapers, advertising, and art museums. Despite these differences, all four of these essays focus on issues of cultural survival within the political economy of Spain and its autonomous regions in the 1980s and early 1990s. They all move beyond specific texts to consider larger issues of government policy and economic structure at the regional, national, and global levels.

In "The Financial Structure of Spanish Cinema," Peter Besas explains how films are financed in Spain. Because of his position since 1969 as the Madrid bureau chief and film critic for *Variety,* he writes as an industry insider who shares Hollywood's commercial and aesthetic assumptions. Yet, as an American émigré living in Spain, he is still a cultural out-sider—a duality that gives his analysis a unique tension. Arguing that there is no such thing as a Spanish film industry (only "artisanry"), he briefly overviews how the process of financing has functioned for the past fifty years—explaining its subsidies, exhibit quotas, and dubbing licenses and the government policies on which this system was based, with special emphasis on the Miró Law of 1983. After surveying the current sources of funding and observing that profits are usually made on the financing of the film rather than its performance at the box office, he speculates on what effects this unusual dynamic has for Spanish culture both at home and abroad.

In "Spatial Eruptions, Global Grids: Regionalist TV in Spain and Dialectics of Identity Politics," Richard Maxwell analyzes the regional television experience in Spain and identifies several core policy events and social transformations that gave rise to its institutional framework. He claims that this case study of Spain has special significance for theorizing the political economy of international media, particularly with respect to three issues. First, it challenges the cultural hegemony of the nation-state and encourages international media theory to focus on a range of site-specific media practices and their implications for redefin-ing nationality. Second, it illustrates a need for a theory that can address regionalism as both a cause and effect of a new international cultural economy. Third, it leads us to perceive the contradictory links between global media space and one produced by the politics of nationality. Thus, even when television within the autonomous cultural community is built on an oppositional politics of regionalism, systematically it may function according to a global corporate logic whose primary goal is the expansion of profit rather than political change.

In "Private Commercial Television versus Political Diversity: The Case of Spain's 1993 General Elections," Iñaki Zabaleta presents an empirical study of how media coverage affected a key moment of polit-ical history, the general election that followed the economic crisis brought on by González's huge 1992 expenditures for the Olympics and Expo '92 (the world's fair in Seville). He claims that instead of being depicted as a choice among several parties representing the full political spectrum, the election was refigured into essentially a two-party race between the ruling Socialists (PSOE), who won the election but lost their absolute majority in Parliament, and the Conservative Center Right (PP), who lost the election but gained 3 million more votes than they had in 1989. Among the losing parties that had been largely excluded from media coverage, the moderate Basque and Catalan nationalists experienced particularly sharp declines. The study analyzes three kinds of data: special election TV coverage; newspaper advertisements for three media events; and other opinion pieces and editorials. Although one might have predicted that the public television stations would have been more biased, Zabaleta finds that it was actually the private commercial TV channels who more emphatically stressed the dualism and more strongly reinforced the hegemony of the nation-state. Although restricted solely to 1993, this study lays the groundwork for a better understanding of the outcome and aftermath of the 1996 general election.

In "The Art Museum as a Means of Refiguring Regional Identity in Democratic Spain" Selma Holo describes the emergence of regional art museums in Spain during the past twenty years and their strategies for negotiating the conflicting cultural demands for local, regional, national, European, and global identity both within the art world and the communities where they are located. While acknowledging the positive political role these museums have played in helping Spain move toward a democracy that validates cultural diversity, Holo also examines how they are now being threatened by having their administration and policies subject to the outcomes of political elections—an issue that becomes even more resonant in the context of the 1996 general election. Three case histories of museums from extremely dissimilar regions demonstrate diverse ways of negotiating the complex relations between center and periphery: the Museo Extremeño e Iberoamericano de Arte Contemporáneo, in the autonomous region of Extremadura; the Museo de Bellas Artes de Asturias, in Oviedo; and the Institut Valencia d'Art Modern (IVAM), in Valencia.

Holo's essay intersects significantly with all the other articles in this section: Like Besas, she deals with the triple address to local, national, and international audiences, yet her optimism about Spanish culture contrasts sharply with his pessimism. Like Maxwell, she is interested in the way politics functions in regional cultural production, both in encouraging diversity and restricting its operations. Like Zabaleta, she deals with concrete case studies and specific elections and uses these particulars to address larger political dynamics. Like both Maxwell and Zabaleta, she suggests a more complex theorization of these dynamics is needed, one that might help us understand a post-Socialist Spain. Most important, like most of the other essays in this volume, her concluding chapter demonstrates the generative power of the Spanish case study for refiguring cultural identity in the post-cold-war era.

Notes

1. In April 1996, Italy experienced an equally dramatic reversal in its general election but (in contrast to Spain) with the opposite ideological outcome. The Italian election brought a narrow victory for the Olive Tree Coalition, a center-left alliance led by the former Communist Party. Although this event represented the first time that the Left had been voted into power since World War II, it was interpreted (as in the case of Spain) primarily as a protest vote against those in power—the center-right Freedom Alliance led by former Prime Minister Silvio Berlusconi (whose allies included supporters of the Fascists), a coalition that had filled the vacuum left by the long-reigning Social Democrats, whose corruption (like that of Spain's PSOE) had finally brought their own demise.

2. Quoted by Marsha Kinder, in "Pleasure and the New Spanish Mentality: A Conversation with Pedro Almodóvar," *Film Quarterly* 35, no. 1 (1987): 37.

3. "Cine español: De lo particular a lo universal," *Fotogramas* (April 1987): 7.

4. José Comas, "El cine español triunfa en Berlín," *El País,* October 14, 1996.

5. For example, in a cover story on Banderas, Stephen Rebello claims, "he stole all his scenes not only in *Miami Rhapsody* but, more important in *Interview with the Vampire*. . . . Not even Brad Pitt or Tom Cruise could block his light." *Movieline* 6, no. 11 (1995): 36, 39.

6. Jack Mathews also writes: "Banderas has the same combination of looks, sex appeal and physical athleticism, plus the knack for spontaneous emotional eruptions that Gibson made his signature in the three Donner-directed *Lethal Weapon* movies." "Manly Men: It's Where the Action Is—Still: Stallone, Banderas Are on Target in Richard Donner's Assassins," *Los Angeles Times,* October 6, 1995.

7. Diego Muñoz, "Los cineastas españoles piden al Gobierno la creación de una ley del audiovisual," *El País,* June 4, 1992, 30.

8. Hilary Clarke, "Film Fund to Fight Hollywood," *The European,* Business Section, October 10–16, 1996.

9. As quoted in Bess Twiston-Davies, "Spain to Strip Its Cinema of State Aid," *The European,* August 1–14, 1996.

10. *Ibid.*

11. Unless otherwise specified, all of the quotes in this reading of *La flor de mi secreto* are taken from the press kit.

12. The working-class protagonist (played by Carmen Maura) of *¿Qué he hecho yo?*—who is doubly domesticated as housewife and maid, kills her husband with a ham bone, and loans her budding gay son to the pederastic dentist (to whom she is indebted)—is transformed in the subplot of *La flor* into the loyal gypsy housekeeper, a former flamenco star who loans her handsome bisexual son to her lady Leo to console her in her loneliness. In both films Chus Lampreave plays a dotty mother who longs to return to her village. The loving gay son from *¿Qué he hecho yo?,* who brings his mother back from the verge of suicide, is replaced in *La flor* by the feminized guardian Angel, both alter egos for Almodóvar. Despite the outrageousness of the hyperplotted narrative of *¿Qué he hecho yo?,* Almodóvar saw it as a form of Spanish neorealism—one (like Leo's novel *In Cold Storage*) that addressed contemporary social issues (poverty, drugs, unemployment, and corruption)—precisely the kind of work that Amanda Gris was not allowed to write. See the following discussion.

13. For a discussion of the cultural specificity of the representation of violence in Spanish cinema, see chapter 4 of Marsha Kinder, *Blood Cinema: The Reconstruction of National Identity in Spain* (Berkeley and Los Angeles: U of California P, 1993).

14. According to Iglesia, the new film is an adaptation of a novel by Brian Gifford, who also wrote *Wild at Heart.* In fact, Iglesia's film uses the same character played by Isabella Rossellini in *Wild at Heart,* but this time she is a Hispanic played by Victoria Abril, who, along with her companion (John Leguizamo, who is almost as short as she is) kidnaps and tortures two tall blond Anglos.

15. For a fuller discussion of these paradoxes of Basque nationalism, see chapter 18 of John Hooper's *The Spaniards: A Portrait of the New Spain* (Harmondsworth and New York: Penguin, 1986).

PART 1

Historical Recuperation

KATHLEEN M. VERNON

Reading Hollywood in/and Spanish Cinema:

From Trade Wars to Transculturation

When one talks of cinema, one talks of American cinema. The influence of cinema is the influence of American cinema. . . . For this reason, every discussion of
cinema made outside Hollywood must begin with Hollywood.—Glauber Rocha

Mixed in with 1993's steady stream of press reports on the resurgence of
nationalist aggressions in Eastern Europe and the former Soviet Union
came a series of news stories noting the outbreak of a less violent,
perhaps, but to some commentators equally troubling, form of Western
European *cultural* nationalism provoked by proposals to include the
audiovisual sector—that is, film, television, and radio productions—in
the upcoming international free trade accord known as GATT. Though
the talk of economic and artistic crises among European national cinemas was nothing new, the combined stimuli of the GATT threat to
eliminate various national subsidy policies and screen quotas that had
kept French, Italian, and Spanish cinemas (barely) afloat against the ever
rising tide of a U.S.-dominated multinational film industry and the
impending European release of the Spielberg behemoth *Jurassic Park*
provoked a vitriolic war of words between a number of influential
European directors and their American counterparts that spilled from
the pages of the trade publication *Variety* to the foreign affairs coverage
of the *New York Times*.[1]

Although this essay in some sense represents a response to the current
crisis as well as to its historical roots, it is by no means a study of the
influence or, rather, domination of Hollywood cinema over the European or Spanish film industries. In the case of Spain, that story has been
told in detailed economic and political terms in books such as Santiago

Pozo's *La industria del cine en España,* Manuel Vázquez Montalbán's *La penetración americana en España* and, most recently, in the epilogue to Marsha Kinder's *Blood Cinema.*[2] Nor is it, strictly speaking, a study of the influence of the representational modes of Hollywood, understood somewhat monolithically as "classic narrative cinema," on both cinematic creation and reception in Spain. Rather than the "real" of American cultural-economic hegemony, I am interested here in the strategic uses of American film in constructing an alternative "imaginary" in opposition to dominant cultural practices in Spain.

Thus, I base my study in the analysis of the intertextual presence of Hollywood cinema, in the form of "direct quotations" or film clips, in a selected number of Spanish films. I will argue that these transnational juxtapositions have provided a space in which to construct an oppositional imaginary of resistance, initially against attempts by an official Francoist cinema to impose a self-serving national imaginary modeled by the repressive religious and militaristic values of the regime, and that later, after Franco's death, this interface of cultures and discourses continues to offer an opportunity to speak from (and listen to) the margins, to question the dominant fictions that have shaped Spaniards' views of their present as well as their past. The potential repertory of Spanish films that employ these intertextual quotes includes, surely not coincidentally, some of the most historically and aesthetically significant films made in Spain since the end of the Civil War: from Lorenzo Llobet Gràcia's *Vida en sombras* (Life in Shadows, 1947–48), Luis García Berlanga's *Bienvenido, Mr. Marshall* (Welcome, Mr. Marshall, 1952), and Víctor Erice's *El espíritu de la colmena* (The Spirit of the Beehive, 1973) and *El sur* (The South, 1983) to Pedro Almodóvar's *¿Qué he hecho yo para merecer esto!* (What Have I Done to Deserve This!, 1984), *Matador* (1986), *Mujeres al borde de un ataque de nervios* (Women on the Verge of a Nervous Breakdown, 1988), Manuel Gutiérrez Aragón's *Demonios en el jardín* (Demons in the Garden, 1982), Pilar Miró's *Beltenebros* (1992), and Francisco Regueiro's *Madregilda* (Mother Gilda, 1993). And their respective American intertexts, *Rebecca* (Alfred Hitchcock, 1941), genre films (Western and film noir), *Frankenstein* (James Whale, 1931), *Shadow of a Doubt* (Alfred Hitchcock, 1943), *Splendor in the Grass* (Elia Kazan, 1961), *Duel in the Sun* (Charles Vidor, 1946), *Johnny Guitar* (Nicholas Ray, 1954), and *Gilda* (Charles Vidor, 1946), for their part, provide a cannily representative roster of classic Hollywood film history.

One possible, and intended, consequence of this type of approach to what have generally been treated as closed systems, discreet national cinemas—Spanish versus American—is to challenge our understanding of the way global mass culture operates today and thus to restructure the terms of the debate. Whereas trade war rhetoric reaffirms the center-periphery model of American cultural colonialism, the focus I am proposing seeks to foreground a process of transcultural exchange, producing new readings that question the underlying ideological assumptions of both cultures. My intention is to read these films in their intertextuality as instances of a process of "semiotic layering," a concept I borrow from Maureen Turim, who defines it as "the accrual and transformation of meaning associated with an artifact as it passes through history, or as it is presented in different versions."[3] The advantage of this notion of semiotic layering over more familiar accounts of literary and filmic intertextuality is that the former explicitly allows for the intervention of extratextual discourses and effects of reception, some of which adhere to the original text and others that result from their transmission through history, and, in this case, across national/cultural boundaries. Thus I seek to recover the meaning and function of the Hollywood intertexts in their original cultural, historical, and generic context as well as to analyze the new meanings produced via their recontextualization within certain Spanish films, each with its own specific historical and cultural circumstances.

Due to limitations of space, as well as to the focus of this volume, I will restrict my analyses to three "cases" chosen from among the list of films I cited earlier, one from the Francoist period and two from the group of films made since the death of the dictator and the return of Spanish democracy. The focal point of the first part of my study, Berlanga's *Bienvenido, Mr. Marshall,* shares with two of the other signal films from different ends of the Franco era, *Vida en sombras* and *El espíritu de la colmena,* a capacity for converting the escapist value of Hollywood genre pictures (the Western and film noir, the "woman's picture," and the horror film, for the three films respectively) into a form of strategic leverage that served to liberate both films and filmmakers from the constraints of Spanish commercial cinema's industrial and cultural apparatus.[4] Then, in the second half of the essay, I turn to two different but related examples of the use of Hollywood intertexts in the post-Franco cinema. I begin with an investigation of American intertexts in the films of Pedro Almodóvar, certainly the most celebrated "international" Spanish filmmaker of the period. Focusing on ¿Qué he hecho yo para merecer esto! I explore how the director's manipulation of multilayered cinematic sources works to expose the persistent legacy of Francoism despite the willed, postmodern break with the past otherwise evinced by his cinema. My study closes with a more extended analysis of the function of a single intertext, the mythic 1946 film noir Gilda, starring Rita Hayworth in the title role, in three Spanish films from the '80s and '90s. Here I demonstrate how Hayworth's extrafilmic and transnational "star image" is exploited to subvert stable notions of gender and national identity and to provide for a paradoxical reencounter with Spanish history.

Beyond the Dream Machine: *Bienvenido, Mr. Marshall*

According to Peter Besas, Berlanga's brilliant 1952 comedy *Bienvenido, Mr. Marshall* began as commission for an *españolada,* a folkloric comedy featuring primarily Andalusian dance and singing, typical of the government-supported products of the period.[5] While technically fulfilling the conditions of the film's producers—a setting in Andalusia and four musical numbers for newcomer Lolita Sevilla, sister of the established españolada star Carmen Sevilla—Berlanga and his co-scriptwriters, Juan Bardem and Miguel Mihura, concocted a double-edged paean to the illusionistic power of cinema that is at the same time a wicked critique of the Spanish film industry and the regime that supported it.

While the title makes reference to the Marshall Plan dollars Spain was never to receive (although its pariah status among Western democracies was soon to come to end with the 1953 Convenio granting the U.S. access to Spanish military bases), a more central theme of the film is the reach of Hollywood into the hearts and minds of even the most isolated inhabitants of a small Spanish town. The plot involves the town's preparations for the arrival of an American delegation, that, according to the delegado general and his band of Spanish bureaucrats announcing the visit, are sure to reward their Spanish hosts with cash and gifts. At the urging of the government officials, the mayor, don Pablo, and Manolo, the impresario and manager of the flamenco star

Bienvenido, Mr. Marshall
satirizes the dream of
Yankee dollars for Spain.

performing at the town's café, concoct a script to transform their Castilian village of Villar del Río into a movie-set version of Andalusia,
precisely the tourist poster image of Spain promoted by the españolada.

As in *El espíritu de la colmena* some twenty years later, the social
function of moviegoing and the preference for American genre films
over the homegrown product is documented in the townspeople's attendance at the weekly movie—usually a Hollywood Western, we are
told—in the town hall. Given the shape of Spanish film production in
the '40s and early '50s, this rejection was understandable. Dominated by
the tendentious didacticism of patriotic epics on one hand, and by the
nostalgic evocation of a harmonious rural existence of eternal Spain in
the españolada on the other, the regime-backed film industry left Spanish audiences easy prey for the clearly more alluring Hollywood imports.[6] Indeed this rejection of domestic cinema is thematized in the
film. Carmen Vargas (Lolita Sevilla), the visiting "songbird of Southern
Spain" hired by the mayor and café owner, performs in parallel scenes
that mirror the Spanish audience's attitude toward the genre. During

Vargas's first musical number, the café's clientele are quiet and her song's completion is met with attentive applause. But by the time of the second on-screen performance, several sequences later, the café-goers talk through her number and the applause is almost nonexistent.

A similar, interiorized representation of spectatorship within the text is the key to the film's most celebrated sequence, a series of four movie-like dreams within the film. Decades earlier the surrealists had explored the parallels between the dream experience and film viewing, and *Bienvenido* makes that connection comically explicit.[7] The activity of movie-going is characterized by the film's voice-over narrator as enabling or authorizing wishing and dreaming. Even the narrative chronology, in which the extended dream segment follows the townspeople's exit from Villar del Río's makeshift movie theater, confirms this linkage. Furthermore, at the conclusion of the last of the four dreams, the narrator comments on the dreamer's wish for a happy ending, noting that "all movies and dreams end like that." As this association makes clear, movies, like dreams, are not simply a form of escapism, but rather a means of indirect expression of thoughts censored by the conscious mind—or by a repressive government. Nevertheless, these filmic intertexts do provide a form of escape for Berlanga to move beyond the confines of an ahistorical formula film, the españolada, to project a critical vision of contemporary Spanish reality.

Although each of the dreams merits an extended analysis of the way it matches a distinct cinematic style to the expression of an individual character's wishes and fears (unlike Hollywood dream scenes from the period with their conventionalized representation of the dream state, the four dreams assume a clearly marked genre and even national identity, ranging from the Hollywood Western and film noir to the Spanish historical epic and the Soviet social [realist] romance of the agricultural hero), I will concentrate here on the dream of the village priest, surely the most provocative in its ironic juxtaposition of Spanish and U.S. intertexts. As the film's principal representative of Francoist *triunfalismo,* the priest from the outset expresses his suspicion of American materialist ideology. His words offer a prime example of what Carmen Martín Gaite has called the celebration of the *bendito atraso* (the "blessed backwardness" of Spain)[8] as he shuns the promised fruits of American beneficence: "They may have locomotives but we have peace of mind

In *Bienvenido, Mr. Marshall,* Mayor don Pablo dreams of cowboy heroics.

[*paz de espíritu*]. That will be our gift to them." Later, he interrupts the village schoolteacher's American geography lesson before the town to counter her recitation of U.S. industrial and agricultural production figures (10,000 tons of wheat or pig iron annually and so on) with some statistics of his own, noting the presence of millions of Protestants, Jews, Blacks, and Chinese among the American population. But this condemnation of American religious and racial pluralism will come back to haunt him. For despite his provincial horizons—we are told he has never traveled more than twelve miles from his home village—and rabid anti-Americanism, even his dream reveals the colonizing influence of American cinema.

Opening with a shot of Holy Week penitents marching in black-hooded robes to the cadence of a solemn funeral march, the dream scene lurches into nightmare as a blaring jazz score irrupts on the sound track and the hooded figures, who turn to reveal the initials KKK on their backs, carry off the frightened priest. The next frame places him squarely within the classic mise-en-scène of an American crime drama. In a dark room lit by the harsh glare of a single, swinging lightbulb, the priest, shot from a high angle, cowers under the interrogation of a

Crosscultural cold war paranoia: The priest from *Bienvenido, Mr. Marshall* has a dream in which he cowers before the Committee on Un-American Activities.

man identified as a hard-boiled police-detective type by the fat cigar clenched tightly in his teeth. Finally the dream cuts to a courtroom that evokes the German expressionist roots of film noir and where the camera reveals the priest as an even more diminished figure, dwarfed by a black-robed judge mounted on a tall tribunal that bears the inscription (in Spanish): Committee on Un-American Activities. A tape recorder re-plays his earlier disparaging references to the diversity of American ethnic and religious groups, and as each is mentioned, a black- or white-robed figure rises from the jury box to give him the thumbs down.

This use of film noir, beyond its simple representativeness as a recognizably American film genre, is clearly no accident. Given the form's cultural and historical context and its development in the closing years of World War II and the decade or so after, as the satisfaction over victory turned to insecurity, suspicion, and the anticommunist paranoia of the McCarthy years, it is a fitting irony that the priest's own xenophobic paranoia be expressed in such terms. Furthermore it is precisely the shared American and Spanish fear of communism that has brought the American "threat," in the form of the military base accord, to Spanish shores.

Postmodernism, Pastiche, and the Return of History:
¿Qué he hecho yo para merecer esto?

In contrast to the privileged intertextual role granted to Hollywood cinema in the films by Berlanga, Llobet Gràcia, or Erice, the eclectic jumble of sources—punk rock, comic book graphics, Latin American boleros, Spanish folklore, and TV advertising, in addition to Hollywood melodrama—characteristic of Almodóvar's films might stand as a defining example of postmodernist pastiche. And whether one grants a subversive or regressive value to such density of intertextual allusion, that crucial enabling role, of Hollywood cinema as the conduit of fantasy and wish-fulfillment inexpressable through more direct means, would appear to be superfluous, as Almodóvar's films, in their celebration of a newly liberated, post-Francoist Spain, flaunt the open expression of desire in all its vectors and forms. What, then, is the function or functions of the direct quotations from Hollywood films, the clips from *Splendor in the Grass, Duel in the Sun,* and *Johnny Guitar,* in *¿Qué he hecho yo para merecer esto!, Matador,* and *Mujeres al borde de un ataque de nervios*? As I suggested at the outset, I believe that American cinema continues to play a role in the construction of resistance to dominant discursive practices, both filmic and social. Almodóvar's use of Hollywood cinema allows him to articulate a position on the margins of Spanish social and cultural institutions, one that challenges the validity of master narratives, of whatever ideological stripe, in the representation of past and present realities and the relation between them.

Of the three films in which the director makes use of excerpts from American films, *¿Qué he hecho yo!* is perhaps the most politically pointed in its strategic use of cinematic references. Abandoning, at least temporarily, the campy contextuality of his first three features, the director turns initially to Italian and Spanish neorealism for the primary thematic and stylistic grounding of his film. From the musical theme of the opening/credit sequence, with its evocation of Nino Rota's scores for numerous Italian neorealist films, to a plot and mise-en-scène already familiar to viewers of the generally more satiric Spanish versions of the genre from the '50s and early '60s, the director situates his story of a working-class family's struggle for survival in present-day Madrid within a self-consciously filmic tradition. The echoes of much earlier films such as Marco Ferreri's *El pisito* (The Little Apartment, 1958), José

Gloria (Carmen Maura) and her son Toni (Juan Martínez) walk along the streets of working-class Madrid in ¿Qué he hecho yo para merecer esto? (Photo courtesy: Antonio DeBenito)

Antonio Nieves Conde's *El inquilino* (The Tenant, 1959), and Berlanga's *El verdugo* (The Executioner, 1962) lend a sharper edge to Almodóvar's social criticism, through which he reveals the lack of fundamental change despite the intervening years, years of the so-called economic miracle and the end of Francoism.

And yet while this general critique is grounded in the language of neorealism, the individual characters' personal discontent with their psychosocial reality is projected through an independent and often incompatible set of cinematic references, their mutual incomprehension represented through an allusive personal imaginary. Gloria, the harried housewife and mother whose struggle to provide for her family in both material and emotional terms constitutes the affective center of the film, is trapped—at least until the end of the picture—within the stifling libidinal (and literal) economy of the "woman's picture."[9] Her taxi driver husband, Antonio, on the other hand, is still obsessed with his experiences as a "guest worker" in Germany and his love affair with Ingrid Müller, an aging chanteuse for whom he forged a series of Hitler letters. The husband's narrative is characterized by its own film score, Antonio's repeated playing of his cherished cassette of "their song,"

"Nicht nur aus Liebe Weinen," sung by Zarah Leander, as his story plots the real historical drama of economic exile against a subversive version of the retro nostalgia film, reminiscent of Fassbinder's *Lili Marleen* (1980) or *Veronika Voss* (1981). The younger son, Miguel, though not tied to any specific film or genre, is portrayed as the "artistic" child of the family. The movie posters over his bed and the zoetrope he spins before turning out the light at night, as well as his precocious homosexuality, mark him as the director's playful stand-in.

Although each of these intertextual subplots merits more extended treatment, I will turn my attention to the only two characters who appear to share a common space of the imaginary: the grandmother and her older grandson. This alliance initially seems quite paradoxical, since the two would appear to be products of diametrically opposed social milieus, the small country pueblo in the case of the grandmother, urban Madrid in the case of Toni, the older son. Indeed both are endowed with a series of typical attributes that mark them as representative of their origins: the grandmother with her repertory of country sayings and religious superstitions, Toni with his successful drug trade.

This antagonistic axis—country versus city—is, of course, a classic theme of both Francoist and anti-Francoist cinema as indexes to a larger value system: tradition versus modernity, isolationism versus cosmopolitanism. But in Almodóvar's rewriting of cinema history, the opposition is more apparent than real. For grandmother and grandson share a dream of return to the pueblo, a longing for return to a natural paradise lost that receives ironic expression in two important moments in the film. Returning from a trip to the bank to deposit his drug earnings, Toni and the grandmother are shot in silhouette between a tree and telephone pole against the twilight sky, the claustrophobic urban landscape, for once, absent from view. In this unique scene of wide-open spaces the grandmother discovers a lizard huddled beneath a rock. Toni, the urban naturalist, proclaims him to be hibernating, but the grandmother takes pity upon a fellow creature, displaced, like her, from nature in a hostile urban environment. Scooping him up, she vows to take the reptile home, as the camera in a reverse angle reframes the characters and the now almost invisible tree against the backdrop of the family's high-rise building and a parking lot crowded with cars. As if the visual irony were not sufficient, the subsequent dialogue over an appropriate name for the animal further undercuts the pastoral moment. The grandmother

Grandmother (Chus Lampreave) holds her pet lizard, Dinero, in *¿Que he hecho yo para merecer esto?*

decides to name him after something she likes, dubbing him Dinero because he's green like money.

While the camera itself conspires to deny the viability of the characters' dreams in the scene just described, a later sequence portrays—once again—Hollywood cinema as the unlikely vehicle of a specifically Spanish social fantasy. Light streams from an unidentified source high up in the rear of a darkened room, evoking the dream scene of the psychoanalytic model of the spectator's experience of cinema. In the absence of any distinguishable images, an exchange of dialogue between an older and younger man expresses the latter's rejection of education as a path to success: "I'd like to work on that ranch you own outside of town." Finally the camera lowers its focus to the heads of the spectators, glowing in the flickering light of the movie theater, and grandson and grandmother come into view in the middle of the audience. Toni's identification with the rebellious son in the film is immediate: "Maybe I'll set up a ranch in the pueblo," he exclaims as the grandmother signals her enthusiastic assent. Their conversation continues after a brief ellipsis as they exit the theater, passing in front of a billboard for the film they have just seen, Elia Kazan's 1961 film version of the William Inge play *Splendor in the Grass,* starring Warren Beatty and Natalie Wood. The

irony for the (second degree) spectator in Bud Stamper's (Beatty) desire
to return to a simpler, American age of innocence in a small Kansas town
on the eve of the Stock Market crash underscores the untimeliness and
"unplacefulness" of Toni's dream as well. The small town is portrayed as
a stifling, sexually repressive place in the Inge/Kazan story, just as it is in
Spanish films of the period such as in Juan Antonio Bardem's *Calle mayor*
(Main Street, 1955).

Finally, in an ultimate irony, the character's flight from the city at the
end of *¿Qué he hecho yo?* though it marks the apparent fulfillment of their
shared dream, reenacts the conclusion of the founding film of Spanish
neorealism, José Antonio Nieves Conde's *Surcos* (Furrows, 1950). Hailed
as the "first glance at reality in a cinema of paper-maché,"[10] for its
treatment of the problem of the rural exodus to the cities, in the hands of
Falangist Nieves Conde, it also served as a cautionary tale regarding the
moral corruption and destruction of family structures that awaited new
immigrants to the city. The film's conclusion, tightened by the censors
to eliminate the undying lure of life in the city for the daughter Tonia,
projects the family's chastened return to the fields they never should
have left.

Far from an instance of the postmodern denial of history through
pastiche, as in Fredric Jameson's account of the mode,[11] through its
juxtaposition of filmic intertexts, the ironic American pastoral *Splendor*
with the Spanish cautionary tale *Surcos, ¿Qué he hecho yo?* casts suspicion
on the workings of the cinematic imaginary. The longing for return is
revealed as a return to the past of Francoism, a past Almodóvar's films
disavow even as they actively reevaluate its hold over the present.

Reen-Gendering the Past: *Gilda* and the
Spanish National Imaginary

In this final section, I wish to propose a slightly different take on the
phenomenon of transcultural intertextuality by pursuing the privileged
role granted to a single Hollywood film in a series of Spanish pictures
from the '80s and '90s: Aragón's *Demonios en el jardin,* Miró's *Beltenebros*
(1992, based on the eponymous novel by Antonio Muñoz Molina), and
Regueiro's *Madregilda.* Though products of the most recent post-Franco
era, each turns, paradoxically, to '40s Hollywood as the vehicle for a

reencounter with the Spanish past. The Hollywood film that mediates this encounter with history is the 1946 film noir *Gilda,* directed by Charles Vidor and starring Glenn Ford and George Macready, with Rita Hayworth in the title role.

To understand and evaluate the remarkable transatlantic impact of *Gilda* in these and other films, a brief look at its original American context and meanings is in order. Although hardly a smashing critical success—Bosley Crowther's *New York Times* review of *Gilda*'s Radio City Music Hall premiere deemed it "a slow, opaque, unexciting film"[12]—*Gilda* made its mark as the film that announced Rita Hayworth's consecration as an "American love goddess," as a *Life* magazine cover (November 10, 1947) proclaimed, largely on the strength of her sensual musical striptease to "Put the Blame on Mame." The plot, predictably opaque given the way classic noir often sacrifices logic and verisimilitude to atmospherics, via chiaroscuro lighting and extreme camera angles, grants the central role not to Gilda but to Johnny Farrel, played by Ford, a gambler on the skids down Argentine way who is literally rescued from the gutter by the mysterious Ballin Mundsen, a German casino owner who also controls a worldwide tungsten cartel. Also predictably, the woman provides the destabilizing element when Mundsen returns from a business trip with a wife, Gilda, who, it turns out, was once romantically involved with Johnny. As recent critical readings have shown, however, both despite and because of the film's faithfulness to requisite generic conventions, far from naturalizing the ideological underpinnings of contemporary American society, *Gilda* highlights and reveals the anxieties of the era. Richard Dyer demonstrates that the presence of a less-than-subtle homosexual subtext focusing on the Johnny-Ballin dyad subverts the traditional gender symmetries associated with classic Hollywood cinema.[13] Thus, although Hayworth is clearly coded through editing and mise-en-scène as the object of masculine desire for male protagonists and spectators alike, Johnny, the ostensible discursive subject of the film by virtue of his role as voice-over narrator, is repeatedly associated with the female position through verbal and visual cues. In addition to the film's subversion of gender identity, its "foreign" setting in a post–World War II Buenos Aires populated by American and German expatriates with shady pasts unsettles stable notions of national identity as it reflects the shuffling of

Gilda is a site of libidinal and economic investment in *Bicycle Thief.*

wartime alliances and anticipates the resurgence of xenophobic suspicion among a U.S. audience on the cusp of the cold war.

In Europe, in contrast, at least initially, the reception of *Gilda* responded to specifically national and hemispheric priorities. For European audiences struggling to rebuild their lives and countries after World War II, *Gilda* (both the film and the character) embodied all the escapist power of Hollywood glamour. The references to Gilda and Hayworth in the founding film of Italian neorealism, Vittorio De Sica's *Ladri di biciclette* (The Bicycle Thief, 1948) underscores this function, as the main character's precious bicycle, the bicycle that allowed him to get his job putting up movie posters, is stolen while he diligently smoothes out the folds of a life-size reproduction of Hayworth in evening dress and long gloves. This double-edged characterization of the Hollywood vamp as a site of libidinal and economic investment, with its concomitant danger and risk, would be played out subsequently upon its Spanish reception as well.

Gilda's arrival on Spanish screens in 1947 figures as an event that was to mark the collective memory of generations of Spaniards, although less perhaps for what was portrayed on screen than for the reaction it provoked among the regime's most influential factions. As historian Raymond Carr reports, the Falange took to the streets when the film opened on Madrid's Gran Vía, dousing the poster images of Rita Hayworth with ink, while priests threatened damnation from the pulpit for parishioners who dared to frequent theaters where it was shown.[14] The scandal surrounding *Gilda* in some sense both enlarged and reduced the potential response to the film itself, as the title alone came to serve as a kind of short-hand reference to the political and psychic repression and material deprivation of the most stringent years of the dictatorship, the '40s decade of the *años de hambre* (years of hunger). Beyond simple escapism, the appeal of Gilda the film and the world it evoked lay in the fact that they seemed to provide the exact denial and even refutation of the Spanish reality in which they appeared. *Gilda* thus became an almost obligatory reference for such films from the '70s and early '80s as Basilio Martín Patino's *Canciones para después de una guerra* (Songs for after a War, 1971; released 1976), Carlos Saura's *Dulces horas* (Sweet Hours, 1981), and Gutiérrez Aragón's *Demonios en el jardín,* which were concerned not merely with the mimetic recreation of the initial postwar years but with the formation and transmission of memories, both individual and collective, of the period.

In fact, no scenes from *Gilda* actually appear in Gutiérrez Aragon's *Demonios en el jardín.* As the director reports in an interview with Augusto Torres, he was unable to acquire the rights to a clip from the film at a price the producer could afford, so he had to settle for a roughly equivalent scene to Hayworth's "Put the Blame on Mame" number from Italian director Alberto Lattuada's *Anna* (1952).[15] According to Gutiérrez Aragón, for members of his generation during the postwar period, cinema attendance was hardly the passive consumption of a government-sponsored "culture of evasion" so characterized by mainstream historians. Rather, by virtue of the civil and ecclesiastical prohibitions provoked by a film like *Gilda,* film spectatorship became an act of political and psychic transgression against the repressive social and moral control exercised by the government and its sister institutions, the church and the family.

The plot of *Demonios* centers on Juanito, the illegitimate son of the *roja* ("red") Angela, and Juan, the second son of a well-to-do Santander family, who is taken in by his absent father's relatives. Thanks to his skillful manipulation of a childhood illness, Juanito becomes the temporary center of the dysfunctional family, where he reigns like a demanding and willful prince surrounded by his subjects. For Juanito, as for Gutiérrez Aragón, with whom he shares a number of autobiographical experiences, cinema is a key element in his coming of age. Forging a special relationship with his unhappily married aunt (a rival with Juanito's mother both for the maternal role and for the love of the boy's father, Juan), he convinces the cinephile Ana (played by Ana Belén) to take him to the forbidden nocturnal realm of the movie theater. In a later scene, lured by the strains of tropical music coming from the cinema, the boy returns alone to the projection booth, where he watches a scene from Lattuada's *Anna*. (The resonances of the three Anas—actress, character in *Demonios*, and the film-within-the-film Anna—also echo productively, contributing to the way cinema mediates Juanito's passage through the oedipal stage). After the projectionist informs the boy that "the movie has been excommunicated by the Pope," Juanito's eyes widen and then shut tightly as the camera cuts away from the images of a woman singing and dancing suggestively before an assembled audience. "This is my first mortal sin," he observes gravely.[16]

The association of a certain Hollywood cinema with transgression and the breaking of taboos is also behind the setting of *Gilda* in *Beltenebros*. In contrast to their appearance in *Demonios*, the references to *Gilda* come not through the intertextual reproduction of an actual film clip but through a multilayered reenactment of the "Put the Blame on Mame" striptease by the novel/film's principal female character that simultaneously emphasizes its faithfulness to and distance from the Hayworth original. At first glance, the borrowings from *Gilda* may appear motivated by a desire to authenticate a certain genre identity by invoking the films' affinities in that line: *Beltenebros*, novel and film, partakes of the recent boom in postmodern Spanish reworkings of fictional subgenres like the detective story and/or thriller. Performing "Mame" in the after-hours private Madrid nightclub, the Boite Tabu, Rebecca Osorio, singer, call girl, and chief romantic and sexual interest to three of the principal male characters, accrues to her role the attributes of the classic noir femme fatal, thus reinforcing her aura of unknowability, treacherousness, and heightened desirability. The danger in assuming the guise of such a mythically charged figure, however, is that the character may become reduced to a purely iconic function that may ultimately resist rather than attract local meanings. In the end the transposition of Gilda/Hayworth from movie-made 1946 Buenos

Aires to an even more unreal 1962 Madrid adds little to our understanding of this latter time and place. Thus in contrast to the workings of Hollywood intertexts in *Bienvenido, Mr. Marshall* and *¿Qué he hecho yo para merecer esto!* the national, historical residue of the American pre-text does not really illuminate its present filmic setting. In *Beltenebros,* the meaning and meaningfulness of this transtextual grafting lie elsewhere.

Beltenebros, or at least my reading of the film, mobilizes another aspect of *Gilda:* not so much the horizontal expression of Hayworth's on-screen performance within the film as the vertical backstory, external to the film itself, but equally available to audiences for her films, namely, the construction of her star image. The notion of a star image, theorized by critics such as Richard Dyer, John Ellis, and Rosemary Coombe,[17] is necessarily quite relevant for the type of readings I undertake here, since it also refocuses the analysis on the way spectators intervene in the construction and reception of individual films as well as bodies of work. Drawing upon extrafilmic texts, fan magazines, gossip columns, and promotional materials that circulated around and in some sense filtered the direct discourse of films themselves, studies of the star image have been particularly interesting in the way they apply a corrective to earlier psychoanalytic treatments that emphasized the circumscribed role of women in film (both characters portrayed on screen and the female spectator) and foreground the complex interactions between the largely female stars that most engaged the Hollywood publicity machines and their female audience. In the case of Rita Hayworth, what we and contemporary audiences know and knew of her construction as a glamorous "American love goddess" has particular significance for the study of the intertextual effects of her image and performance in *Gilda* in a series of *Spanish* films. For, as Adrienne McLean has emphasized in her studies on the actress, not only was Rita Hayworth of Spanish descent (her real name was Margarita Carmen Cansino and her start in show business came as a member of the "Dancing Cansino" family), but the knowledge of her ethnic background was a key factor in the off-screen characterization of the actress that helped to launch and then sustain her career.[18] McLean goes on to argue that far from suppressing knowledge of her ethnic origins or the literal makeover required to transform her Latin features and coloring into the red-haired all-American girl that beamed from four *Life* magazine covers in the decade of the forties, newspaper and magazine coverage stressed these facts. Thus audiences were treated to stories of how Hayworth changed her name (modifying her mother's Haworth), dyed her hair auburn red, and then endured two years of electrolysis treatments to reshape her hairline and enlarge her forehead.[19]

What, then, is the function of the Hayworth star image in *Beltenebros,* a film that tends, as in its treatment of historical and political referents, to blur the markers of ethnicity as well? Although the principal male characters are ostensibly all current or former members of the Community Party, engaged in the clandestine resistance against the Franco regime, they change names, citizenship, and country of residence with dizzying frequency, albeit by necessity. Furthermore, the film's international cast (the male lead is played by English actor Terrence Stamp and the Gilda figure, Rebecca, by another British performer, Patsy Kensit) and bilingual release (in both English and Spanish) tend to elide the meaningfulness of ethnic or national identities.

Instead, the most potent echoes of Gilda in *Beltenebros* come rather in relation to questions of gender and identity. In her performance of Gilda in the film, Rebecca Osorio mimes not only the "Put the Blame on Mame" striptease, updated to include full frontal nudity, but the constructedness of Hayworth's star image.[20] Her name, too, is a stage name, but a stage name provocatively borrowed from the pseudonym of a character in an earlier story line whose role she also inherits. (The complicated thriller/noir plot has Terence Stamp as the protagonist Darman returning to Madrid to kill a presumed traitor in a reprise of his similar role twenty years earlier. Then, as in 1962, the wrong man is killed despite the supplications of a woman also named Rebecca Osorio). The actress's doll-like appearance as well as the wig she dons for her off- and on-stage performances stress her role as the empty surface onto which men may project their desires. Unlike Gilda, however, her striptease fails to deliver what it implicitly promises: the naked truth of a real woman behind the guises she assumes. Dyer argues in his reading of the '46 film that the audience's knowledge of the "real" Hayworth, together with the destabilization of the traditionally dominant masculine position, construes Gilda as a source of resistance against the conventional passive, objectified position of women in cinema.[21] The Rebecca/Gilda of *Beltenebros* also embodies a kind of resistance, but of a more empty sort. The character of Rebecca would assume the star power of Hollywood, not to challenge conventional gender positioning but to proclaim

the interchangeability of women, the woman as icon, as floating signifier but one that resists the imposition of meaning.

In contrast, Regueiro's *Madregilda,* as its title suggests, is a film that
explicitly assumes its relation to *Gilda* as a key generator of meaning,
doing so in productively unexpected ways. As in *Dulces horas* or *Demonios,* the reference to *Gilda* functions initially as a cue to historical
setting; one of the opening sequences re-creates the infamous Falangist
demonstration against the film: a group of blue-shirted men singing the
"Cara al sol" (Face to the Sun) smash bottles of red ink or paint against a
twelve-foot-tall replica of the actress in her famous evening gown and
long black gloves, while the camera lingers over the violent image of red
liquid washing over her body. The film's focus is, in fact, the '40s años de
hambre, represented here in a treatment that owes less to the familiar
and ultimately sentimentalized realism of novels depicting the period,
such as Camilo José Cela's *La colmena* (The Beehive), and even less so
Mario Camus's cinematic version (1982), than to the Madrid, "absurdo,
brillante y hambriento" (absurd, brilliant, and hungry), of Ramón
María del Valle-Inclán's *Esperpento Luces de Bohemia* (Bohemian Lights,
1920).

The spatial center of the film, and, by implication, Spain itself,
appears in the form of an enormous garbage dump administered by
Longinos, an army colonel who is also Franco's aide-de-camp. Indeed,
the dump exercises a function similar to that of Doña Rosa's cafe in *La
colmena,* for it is here that the diverse and divergent strata of Spanish
society, personified in the soldiers who run it and the hungry citizens
who scavenge for sustenance, come together beneath the emblem of the
Spanish flag flying above the adjacent army barracks that rises and sets
with the sun. As the film script details: "Ahora comprobamos que la
mitad de los basureros, una cincuentena, son soldados rasos con el pelo al
cero, faenando entre las basuras, mendigos, mujeres, y niños astrosos, y
todos, ahora, en acatamiento total saludan a la bandera como presos de
una cárcel." (We now become aware that half of the garbage men, about
fifty, are in fact army privates with shaved heads, at work among the
heaps of trash, beggars, women, and shabbily dressed children, and
suddenly, all of them, with an attitude of total respect, salute the flag
like prisoners in a jail.)[22] That this garbage heap is indeed intended as a
metaphor for a Spanish society recently emerged from the Civil War is
clear from Longinos's exhortations to his troops:

¡La Patria no tiene despilfarros! ¡España tiene hambre, soldados! ¡El estiércol, a la izquierda, para hacer guano! ¡La madera, a la derecha, para pulpa! . . . ¡Los objetos de peso, al fondo! . . . ¡Los huesos mondados son calcio! ¡Energía para el esqueleto de la patria! Y España necesita mucha energía y mucho calcio y mucho esqueleto. . . . Y aquí hemos venido para servir los intereses de la Patria y a la Patria vamos a darle entre todos calcio! ¡Nada tiene desperdicio para la Patria! ¡Lo que la Patria caga, a la Patria vuelve!

(The Nation cannot afford wastefulness! Spain is hungry, soldiers! Dung to the left, for manure! Wood to the right, for pulp! Heavy objects, at the back! . . . Bare bones are calcium! Energy for the backbone of the Nation! And Spain needs a lot of energy and a lot of calcium and a lot of backbone. . . . We've come here to serve the Nation's interest and between us all we're going to give the Nation calcium! Nothing is wasted for the Nation! What the Nation shits, returns to the Nation!) (50, 53)

As for the specific role of Gilda in the closed, violent, and even cannibalistic Spain invoked in the words and images just described, the film itself explicitly engages in the sort of transcultural readings I have been pursuing here. For example, a number of characters comment knowingly on Hayworth's Spanish ethnicity. In an outburst that lucidly if unconsciously collapses the ironic circularity of centuries of political and cultural colonialism, a *sereno* (night watchman) witnessing the Falangist demonstration denounces the actress and film as worse than one of those "¡Putas extranjeras! ¡Esa Gilda que dicen que es una roja, una exiliada comunista, que ha renegado de la Patria! ¡Aquí lo que queremos es que nos devuelvan el oro de Moscú, que es nuestro, de los españoles: que para eso nos lo trajimos de America! ¡Oro y no putas, es lo que necesita España! ¡Viva Franco!" (Foreign whores! That Gilda who they say is a red, an exiled [Spanish] communist who renounced her country! What we want is for them to give us back the gold the Republicans sent to Moscow, our gold, our Spanish gold: that's why we brought it from America in the first place! Gold and not whores, that's what Spain needs! Long live Franco!) (30).

Later in the film, no less a fan of American movies than Francisco Franco himself remarks on her Spanishness: "¿Sabes cómo se llama en realidad esa señorita, Rita Hayworth? Margarita Cansino. Española de pura cepa. He ordenado que se inicien gestiones para traerla a hacer películas a la Patria. Lo que es nuestro, es nuestro y no estamos para despilfarros" (Do you know Rita Hayworth's real name? Margarita Cansino. Of pure Spanish stock. I've ordered that arrangements be made to bring her here to make movies for the Nation. What's ours is ours, we can't afford wastefulness) (108). Like the old chestnut about the *oro de Moscú,* or the historically documented attempts by the Spanish government during the '60s to seek the "return" of Picasso's *Guernica* to its rightful home, the dictator's imagined words reflect the mystifications of the regime's belief in transnational ties of blood or race. (Ironically, Hayworth's Spanish lineage included her father's first cousin, writer Rafael Cansinos Assens, a well-known analyst and proponent of the Judaic and Arabic origins of the Andalusian *copla,* the flamenco song that served as the basis for the folkloric españolada, which the regime would later promote as the essence of unproblematic Spanishness.)

But it is in the identification of Gilda with an equally mythified maternal role that the film achieves its most compelling reinscription of the multilayered textuality of the film/actress Gilda in a Spanish context. In a movie world where what transpires within the confines of the Cine Odeón is at least as real as the film's other principal settings—the garbage dump; the brothel run by Longinos's mother; the tavern La Bodeguilla, where Franco comes the first Friday of every month to play a few rounds of *mus* with his regular card partners, Longinos, Miguel, an old *legionario* who is the image of Millán Astray, the infamous founder of the Spanish Foreign Legion, and a lascivious soldier-priest who has just impregnated his "niece" with her thirteenth child—Longinos's pubescent son Manuel meets nightly with his dead mother, who appears to him in the guise of Gilda. As represented on-screen in a particularly effective special-effects montage, the son's encounter with his absent mother is literally embedded in the text and texture of Vidor's *Gilda.* Seated just behind the balcony railing, at a prudent distance from the other, adult spectators, Manuel is shown avidly watching the scene that heralds Gilda/Hayworth's first appearance in the film. Manuel's barely contained anticipation doubles that of the film-within-the-film's Johnny (Glenn Ford), found standing and waiting at the bottom of a long marble staircase in the mansion home of Ballin Mundsen. Summoned there by the recently returned Ballin, who has promised some important news of his trip, Ford ascends the stairs toward Ballin's bedroom with marked trepidation when he hears from within the voice of a woman,

Angeles, the Madregilda, embodies the mother/whore dichotomy.

humming, Ballin addresses the still-unseen woman, "Ready, Gilda?" Johnny stares directly at the camera, at the off-screen space presumed by editing conventions to be occupied by his former lover. But before the expected reverse shot can display the face of the woman, Manuel's own expectant gaze is sutured into the sequence. The reverse shot finally reveals the woman, her tousled hair hiding her features, as in the 1946 original, but in this transtextual appropriation, when the woman lifts her head to display her face behind the cascade of hair, it is not Rita Hayworth but Manuel's mother, who greets him from the screen: "Hola Manolito."

In the conversation between mother and son that follows, the contrast between the motherly sentiments expressed by the Madregilda's words and her eroticized, femme fatal appearance—she is wearing a strapless gown and puffing at intervals on a cigarette—emphasizes the scene's charged oedipal content. In one exchange, the prohibition attached to viewing the film is consequently transferred to Manuel's contact with his mother as she asks: "Sabe tu padre que vienes a verme?" The son answers, "No, si se entera saca el cinto. Es pecado para un niño ver esta película" (Does your father know you come to see me? No, if he finds out he'll take out his belt [to beat the child]. It's a sin for a child to see this movie) (41). Indeed, Manuel is beaten when his father finds out that he has been watching the film, but not, ostensibly, for his violation of oedipal taboos. Still unaware of his wife's miraculous cinematic resurrection, Longinos punishes his wayward son for his predilection for "foreign movies and bad women." However, as in other instances of the Spanish oedipal narrative recently explored by Marsha Kinder in *Blood Cinema,* the mother-son relationship has implications for larger psychic issues played out on a national scale.

As soon becomes clear, like the Gilda/Rebecca of *Beltenebros,* the Angeles/Gilda of *Madregilda* is also a kind of everywoman, but here of a specifically Spanish sort. Although, by her own testimony, Angeles's recollection of the details of her death is quite fuzzy, the spectator soon learns that she died giving birth to Manuel through a series of particularly gruesome and violent circumstances. On the night before the battle of Brunete, where she was serving among the Nationalist troops, the order went out from an officer on high that the entire company rape her as a way of relaxing the company and raising morale. Nine months later, upon seeing her for the first time since their wedding day on the eve of the Spanish Civil War, her husband finds her pregnant and seeking to avenge his honor, plunges a knife into her swollen belly. Taking his bastard son, he leaves her for dead. Years later, in the present tense of the film, he refuses to speak of his wife to his son but maintains his own worshipful relationship to her image. In a chapel within his quarters he keeps a statue he ordered made in the image of his wife that he dresses in the seasonal liturgical finery normally reserved for the Virgin Mary. Through this double imaging of the woman as both filmic and religious icon, the film champions the illusionistic power of cinema to create a new sacred, one that would challenge the hold of the Catholic Church as the principal institution responsible for constructing and controlling the representation of woman in Spanish society. In effect collapsing the destructive dualism of the mother/whore dichotomy into a single figure, the Madregilda, the film goes on to suggest and even demonstrate woman's almost supernatural power to shape the course of history.

Subsequent plot developments reveal the contours of this influence. Longinos discovers that his wife did not die on the battlefield. As Franco informs him, she lived and was responsible, although inadvertently, for

winning a battle unrecorded in the annals of history, one that turned the
tide of the war in the Nationalists' favor. By the Generalísimo's own
admission, then, Angeles, not he, was responsible for winning the Civil
War. And now, after a number of years absence, Angeles, like Gilda/
Hayworth, has returned to Spain, with the goal, according to Spanish
intelligence services, of assassinating Franco.

Taking a parodic page from the spy thriller, the film presents Angeles's clandestine arrival in Madrid, staged not as some symbolic descent from the terrestrial firmament of the Hollywood star, but as the
emergence of an equally mythic if incongruous Persephone in a red
dress; she proceeds from the subterranean depths, crawling out from
beneath the cover of a sewer drain. Although this goddess figure does
not bring spring but instead the snows of Christmas Eve, her transformative power over her family is immediately apparent. Angeles now
reunited with Manuel, mother and son re-create a pre-oedipal union
destroyed years earlier at the moment of his violent birth. When Longinos returns to his quarters, he finds the dismembered limbs of the
Virgin/Gilda on the floor of the chapel, her place now occupied by
Angeles, a guitar on her knee (in a reprise of the reprise of the "Put the
Blame on Mame" number from *Gilda*), her jagged abdominal scar visible under the folds of the Virgin's glittering cape. Her influence over
her husband subsequently manifests itself in a more public realm as
well. Exchanging his military uniform for a suit and tie, Longinos
addresses his assembled company of soldiers/garbage men. In a dramatic
metamorphosis, the previously illiterate Longinos signs his name to a
written report, renounces the corrupt kickbacks he had considered his
due, and denounces the cruel and violent society he once served as a
world of "pobreza, injusticia e ignominia" (poverty, injustice, and igno-
miny; 157). As a final gesture he sends his troops off to see the film he
once condemned as foreign trash, "esa Gilda de las películas . . . española
de pura raza . . . emblema de las virtudes de la mujer española" (that
Gilda from the movies . . . of pure Spanish race . . . emblem of the virtues
of Spanish womanhood; 158).

However, Angeles/Gilda's mission in Spain is not complete. In the
course of a Christmas dinner reunion of all three members of this unholy
family, Angeles makes her purpose known and secures her husband's
promise to kill Franco, who, as supreme military commander at Brunete, was the figure ultimately responsible for destroying Longinos's

family in the first place. Longinos carries out his charge, shooting Franco during the monthly card game. But the fulfillment of this ultimate revenge fantasy in a film steeped in dreamlike imagery does not bring about the collective liberation it seemingly promised.

Despite *Madregilda*'s repeated demonstrations of the mythoclastic and liberatory powers of cinema, the film's ambiguous conclusion acknowledges the inescapability of a certain historial reality, the superior power of a nightmare of history from which there is no awakening. Franco is dead, but his handlers quickly enlist the services of the dictator's double to assume his place, and nothing, it is implied, changes. The fate of Angeles, the film's Madregilda, is similarly ironic. Returning to the Cine Odeón, a clip from the Spanish newsreel, the NO-DO, portrays a glamorous Angeles in a red dress, accompanied by her son, being honored by Franco in a reception at the Pardo palace, where she is hailed as the "heroína impar de nuestra Cruzada y Agustina de Aragón de la Nueva España" (peerless heroine of our Crusade and Agustina de Aragón [a famous heroine of the nineteenth-century Spanish War of Independence against the French] of the New Spain; 183) and awarded the "Gran Orden de Isabel La Católica" (Great Order of Isabella, the Catholic Monarch; 183).

With all its pessimism and dark cynicism, I suggest that this ending is perhaps more open ended than it might seem. On the one hand, it would appear to corroborate the endless capacity of repressive systems, both political and industrial, to co-opt and contain the potentially subversive effects of the kind of intertextual and transcultural interventions I have been tracing here. On the other, such rearguard actions launched from the cinematic imaginary against the presumed reality of history urge us, along with Spanish audiences, toward the need to renegotiate our relation to our pasts from the vantage point of an ever-changing present.

Finally, the strategic, intertextual role of Hollywood films in Spanish cinema carries a challenge for spectators in both cultures. As we have seen, for Spanish viewers under Francoism, the forbidden fruits of Hollywood fantasies of dubious heroes and alluring, unknowable women offered more than mere escapism. In the hands of directors like Berlanga, these fictions served to take the true measure of the misery and mystifications passed off as truth by the powers-that-were. Since the dictator's death, the already ambiguous, fissured texts of films such as

Splendor in the Grass and *Gilda* have provided for an ironic reencounter with a Spanish history that some feared forgotten in the collective euphoria and willed amnesia of the immediate post-Franco years. For American spectators, on the other hand, the process of seeing the icons and images of our own cultural inheritance and history refracted through the lens of Spanish cinema gives evidence of a shift in the logic of cultural exchange that finds Hollywood cast in the role of vehicle to complex reconsiderations of Spanish identity rather than that of model—artistic or industrial—to be imitated. The effects of this displacement must continue to be cultivated for their capacity to generate new, defamiliarizing readings of ourselves and our stance in an increasingly decentered, globalized world culture.

Notes

1. As reported in *Variety,* the French fired the first salvos when Minister of Culture Jacques Toubon attacked United International Pictures, the joint distributor (in a collaboration between Paramount and Universal) of Steven Spielberg's blockbuster *Jurassic Park,* then poised for its French, Spanish, and Italian debut, for abusing its dominant position in Europe to prevent free competition. He went on to criticize the film itself in terms that generally emblematize long-time characterizations of the French film intellectual David versus the mechanized American Goliath, as "a film which carries Spielberg's name but which does not reflect his personality, because it is only an assembly of special effects." Adam Dawtrey, "GATT Gets France's Goat," *Variety,* September 27, 1993, 31. The Empire subsequently struck back when U.S. directors Spielberg and Martin Scorsese issued press releases denouncing some Europeans' efforts to exclude culture from GATT. Echoing the party line of Motion Picture Association of America (MPAA) boss Jack Valenti, Scorsese's statement rather piously defended the principle of cultural diversity, noting, however, that such a worthy end in no way justified protectionist means, and, besides, European audience just like our movies better: "Closing the borders would not guarantee a rise in creativity in the local countries or even a rise of interest on the part of local audiences. National voices and diversities must be encouraged but not at the expense of other filmmakers." Leonard Klady, "Scorsese, Spielberg in Euro GATT Spat," *Variety,* November 8, 1993, 7. In late October 1993 seven influential European directors and producers, including Pedro Almodóvar, Bernardo Bertolucci, David Puttnam, and Wim Wenders, addressed a letter to their U.S. counterparts, in the form of a full-page advertisement in *Daily Variety.* Raising the specter of the "complete annihilation" of

the European film industry should all barriers be removed, they pointed out that it is hardly a question of an attack on free trade when, even with the support of screen quotas and government subsidies, U.S. productions fill more than 80 percent of European screens whereas European films reach 1 percent of the American public.

2. Santiago Pozo, *La industria del cine en España* (Barcelona: Publicacions i Edicions de la Universitat de Barcelona, 1984); Manuel Vázquez Montalbán, *La penetración americana en España* (Madrid: Cuadernos para el Diálogo, 1964); Marsha Kinder, *Blood Cinema: The Reconstruction of National Identity in Spain* (Berkeley and Los Angeles: U of California P, 1993).

3. Maureen Turim, "Gentlemen Consume Blonds," in *Movies and Methods,* ed. Bill Nichols (Berkeley and Los Angeles: U of California P, 1985), 377.

4. Both Jesús González Requena's psychoanalytic reading and Marsha Kinder's more broadly conceptual and historical analysis of *Vida en sombras* stress the key role played by Hitchcock's *Rebecca* in shaping Llobet Gràcia's cinematically self-conscious treatment of one man's experience of the Civil War and its aftermath in Barcelona. Jesús González Requena, "Vida en sombras," *Revista de Occidente* 53 (October 1985): 76–91, and Marsha Kinder, *Blood Cinema,* 401–12. In her study of *Vida,* Kinder elaborates a theory of what she terms "politicized intertextuality" that clearly anticipates important elements of my own arguments here. For filmmakers as for spectators, notes Kinder, "foreign films can function as . . . an imaginary form of exile . . . a potent form of inner exile or resistance against the xenophobic Francoist culture" (410). Kinder also cites Almodóvar and Erice's *El espíritu de la colmena* as examples of this practice. See also her earlier analysis of the Frankenstein intertext in *El espíritu:* ("The Children of Franco in the New Spanish Cinema," *Quarterly Review of Film Studies* 8, no. 2 (1983), especially pp. 60–61. Erice's own account of the genesis of *El espíritu,* his feature debut, highlights the complex enabling role of the James Whale original, as he recounts to Peter Besas: "I had presented various projects to Elías Querejeta, until one day I suggested doing a film on Frankenstein, and he accepted it. I wrote a treatment which more or less followed the classical lines of the tale, perhaps with some influence from silent cinema, especially German expressionism. . . . But after several weeks, I changed my tack. I thought of doing a story about two sisters who see the Frankenstein film. I wrote a treatment of some 15 pages and then started on a script with Angel Fernández Santos." Peter Besas, *Behind the Spanish Lens: Spanish Cinema under Fascism and Democracy* (Denver: Arden, 1985), 130.

5. Besas, 35–36.

6. The story of the regime's tacit encouragement of this state of affairs, beginning with the 1942 law requiring obligatory dubbing of all foreign films and further promoted by the financing schemes of the forties and early fifties, which

granted subsidies to government-approved films in the form of import licenses, merits further discussion.

7. For Luis Buñuel, not only film viewing but filmmaking was comparable to the dream state, to "the work of the mind during sleep. A film is like an involuntary imitation of a dream . . . a voyage into the unconscious. . . . The cinema seems to have been invented to express the life of the subconscious." Cited in Ado Kyrou, *Luis Buñuel: An Introduction,* trans. Adrienne Foulke (New York: Simon and Schuster, 1963), 110–11. In the '70s, psychoanalytic film theory would build further on those insights. See, especially, Jean-Louis Baudry, "Ideological Effects of the Basic Cinema Apparatus," *Film Quarterly* 28, no. 2 (1974): 39–47, and Christian Metz, "The Fiction Film and Its Spectator," *New Literary History* 8, no. 1: 75–105.

8. Carmen Martín Gaite, *Usos amorosos de la postguerra española* (Barcelona: Anagrama, 1987). "Bendito atraso" is the title of the first chapter of her book, a brilliant social history of women's everyday life during the first two decades following the Civil War. The phrase is a quotation from a 1948 essay she cites as an example of the spiteful yet celebratory xenophobia that dominated the official rhetoric of the period.

9. For an extended analysis of the parallels between the woman's picture and *¿Qué he hecho yo?* see my essay "Melodrama Against Itself: Pedro Almodóvar's *What Have I Done to Deserve This?" Film Quarterly* 46, no. 3 (1993): 28–40.

10. José María García Escudero, *La historia en cien palabras del cine español* (Salamauca: Cine-Club del SEU de Salamauca, 1954) cited in John Hopewell, *Out of the Past: Spanish Cinema after Franco* (London: British Film Institute, 1986), 56.

11. Fredric Jameson, "Postmodernism and Consumer Society," in *The Anti-Aesthetic,* ed. Hal Foster (Port Townsend, Wash.: Bay Press, 1983), 111–25.

12. Bosley Crowther, Review of *Gilda, New York Times,* March 15, 1946, 27, col. 2.

13. Richard Dyer, "Resistance through Charisma: Rita Hayworth and *Gilda,"* in *Women and Film Noir,* ed. E. Ann Kaplan (London: British Film Institute, 1980), 91–99. Other important readings that also explore the gender ambiguities and narrative fissures of this "classic Hollywood text" include Mary Ann Doane, "*Gilda:* Epistemology as Striptease," *Camera Obscura* 11 (fall 1983), reprinted in her *Femme Fatales* (New York: Routledge, 1991), 99–118, and Linda Dittmar, "From Fascism to the Cold War: *Gilda's* 'Fantastic' Politics," *Wide Angle* 10, no. 3 (1988): 4–18. On the film's proto-cold-war setting, see Dittmar, 13–15.

14. Raymond Carr, *Modern Spain, 1875–1980* (New York: Oxford University Press, 1980), 164.

15. Augusto M. Torres, *Conversaciones con Manuel Gutiérrez Aragón* (Madrid: Editorial Fundamentos, 1985), 161–62.

16. In his *New Cinema in Spain* (London: British Film Institute, 1977), Vicente Molina-Foix summarizes the Catholic "ranking system" for films: "There were five moral categories accorded by the ecclesiastical board of censors, each symbolised by a colour on the chart placed prominently on the doors of churches and schools. Films in Category 1 were 'authorised for everyone, even children,' and were marked white. Those in Category 2—'authorized for the young'—were accompanied by a pale blue colour, while those in Category 3—'authorized for adults'—were violet. Films classified 3R were already in a doubtful category, designated 'for adults with reservations.' Finally entailing the danger of mortal sin (which had to be confessed) there were films in Category 4—'seriously dangerous'—appropriately represented by red. No Spaniard born between 1935 and 1955 will forget that rainbow of salvation which, for many years, was the nightmare of every adolescent with any interest in the cinema" (4–5).

17. Richard Dyer, ed. *Heavenly Bodies: Film Stars and Society* (New York: St. Martin's, 1986); John Ellis, "Stars as a Cinematic Phenomenon," in *Visible Fictions: Cinema, Television, Video* (London: Routledge, 1982), 91–108; and Rosemary Coombe, "Authorizing the Celebrity: Publicity Rights, Postmodern Politics, and Unauthorized Genders," *Cardozo Arts and Entertainment Review* 10, no. 2 (1992): 365–95.

18. Adrienne L. McLean, "'I'm a Cansino': Transformation, Ethnicity, and Authenticity in the Construction of Rita Hayworth, American Love Goddess," *Journal of Film and Video* 44, nos. 3–4 (1992): 8–26. In addition, see McLean's "'It's Only That I Do What I Love and Love What I Do': *Film Noir* and the Musical Woman," *Cinema Journal* 33, no. 1 (1993): 3–16.

19. McLean, "It's Only That I Do," 10.

20. With regard to this aspect I should make clear that I am speaking of the film exclusively. Although generally quite "faithful" to the novel by Antonio Muñoz Molina, *Beltenebros* (Barcelona: Seix Barral, 1989), the film never resolves the question of why the Rebecca Osorio of 1962 shares the name of a woman who played an important role in an earlier, parallel plot line from 1946. In the novel, Rebecca Osorio II turns out to be the daughter of Rebecca Osorio I.

21. Dyer, "Resistance through Charisma," 96–98.

22. Angel Fernández Santos and Francisco Regueiro, *Madregilda* (Madrid: Alma-Plot Ediciones, S.A., 1993), 47. Further citations of page numbers from the published screenplay will be included in the text.

MARSHA KINDER

Documenting the National and Its Subversion

in a Democratic Spain

The complete political process of transition from the dictatorship to democracy was recorded in . . . films that adopted the techniques of *cinéma vérité* and of reportage.—Román Gubern, "The Civil War: Inquest or Exorcism?"[1]

The documentary form seduces us with the promise of the constative, the promise of a plenitude of meaning embodied in a referent. . . . To speak of a cinematic moment as performative is to turn . . . on the spectator . . . in an act of aggression, . . . displacing the mastery of knowledge sought in the documentary image.—Susan Scheibler, "Constantly Performing the Documentary"[2]

As in most other cultural contexts, documentary film in Spain remains a marginal form confined to the shadows of fiction, one that receives relatively little critical attention. This essay on post-Franco documentary will explore not how this genre (in Gubern's terms) "recorded" the crucial transition from "dictatorship to democracy" but rather how it reflexively "performed" the subversive refiguration of the nation at three stages of that political process: (1) the transition between 1975, when Franco died, and 1977, when the first free elections were held and censorship was suspended, (2) the mid-1980s, after the Socialists were voted into power (1982) and were eager to demonstrate a sharp break with the Francoist past, and (3) the early 1990s, when a Socialist Spain celebrated the 500-year anniversary of 1492 and moved toward convergence with the European Union (EU). Adapting Scheibler's theory of documentary as performance, this essay will emphasize works that transgress the boundary with fiction (for, as she argues, "these performative moments which deconstruct documentary erupt when the fictional aspects and the nonfictional collide" [145]). It will examine a series of discursive strategies operative in fictional films of the same period, for I share Michael Renov's assumption that the poetics of documentary is driven by the same figurative forms of expressivity and desire as its fictional counterpart.[3] It will also address works that fit Bill Nichols's definition of "the performative mode," a form of documentary that features the filmmaker as subject.[4]

Selecting a few works from each of these three periods in Spain, I will examine how they negotiate the paradoxical relations between two contradictory desires: the desire to record history and the equally strong desire to expose the unreliability of such representations. More specifically, in each case I will trace how the film adapts three related discursive strategies to its own specific historical project: (1) the incorporation of historical documents or texts whose referents are destabilized and meanings reinscribed, (2) the assemblage of a new community unified through its rereading of public and private memories, and (3) the dramatization of this process of reinscription as performed by the filmmakers, subjects, and spectators.

Before beginning this analysis of the post-Franco documentary, it is important to note two factors that gave the earlier history of this genre a specific Spanish inflection and that help explain what was politically at stake in the process of negotiating these desires. As in other cultural contexts, the documentary or actualities was one of the first genres to emerge in Spain—one that could be used to assert the cultural distinctiveness of the nation or local region, particularly as it gained access to an advanced technology imported from the outside. The Spanish documentary genre quickly became associated with questions of local identity and the dialectics of insiders versus outsiders, issues that acquired new levels of political resonance in subsequent periods. It is hardly surprising, then, that documentaries featuring local customs, costumes, rituals, and landscapes were frequently emphasized in those film histories that were driven by a desire to prove the existence of an autonomous regional culture, such as Alberto López Echevarrieta's *Cine vasco: ¿realidad o ficción?* (Basque Cinema: Reality or Fiction?, 1982) and José María Unsain's *El cine y los vascos* (Cinema and the Basques, 1985). Even in Castile, two ironic documentaries about village life near Cuenca aroused dramatic response, in the 1930s and 1950s: Luis Buñuel's *Las Hurdes/Tierra sin pan* (Land without Bread, 1932) evoked the Republican government's condemnation, and Carlos Saura's *Cuenca* (1958), despite the displeasure of the government officials who commissioned it, served as an auspicious debut for this filmmaker who would lead the cinema of opposition in the 1960s.[5]

In the early post-Franco period the genre's legacy of localism acquired new militancy, particularly in Catalonia with Francesc Bellmunt's groundbreaking 1976 documentaries, *La nova cançó* (The New Song) and *Canet Rock,* and in the Basque country with Imanol Uribe's *El proceso de Burgos* (The Burgos Trial, 1979), for in these two regional cinemas the nationalist drive was strongest. But a decade into the Socialist era, that legacy turned toward tourism, particularly during the celebrations for 1992, when most of the autonomous regional governments commissioned documentaries to articulate their own cultural distinctiveness in the festivities.

A second culturally distinctive feature of Spanish documentary is the special subversive potential the genre acquired during the Francoist period. Although the documentary had been a viable form during the 1930s and a potent ideological vehicle for the various political factions that participated in the Civil War, in 1942 a government ban was imposed on the shooting, editing, and processing of any documentary footage other than that produced for the state-controlled Noticias Documentales. By means of these regulations the "NO-DO" newsreels gained the exclusive right to present the "official" version of the news in Spanish movie theaters. Gathered from both home and abroad, this "news" covered major historical events (such as World War II) as well as the banalities of everyday life, both naturalized through a mediating Francoist point of view. These dynamics are satirized in a wonderful sequence in Juan Antonio Bardem's *Muerte de un ciclista* (Death of a Cyclist, 1955), in which the protagonist sits in a movie theater watching a NO-DO newsreel that features a seemingly trivial charity event, which is attended by his mistress and sister and which provides the setting for his powerful brother-in-law (a Francoist technocrat) to deliver a fiery political speech about the glorious future of Spain's "national life." As if highlighting the ideological implications of NO-DO juxtapositions, the speech is followed by a report on a U.S. disaster that playfully evokes the "international relations" of the film's communist director—a fire in Tucson, Arizona, in stores owned by the Bardems.

According to Kathleen Vernon, "The concrete effects of these prohibitions on non-fiction film production in Spain must be reconstructed from scattered references in a number of sources; the standard Spanish and English-language histories of Spanish cinema are silent on the question of documentary as a genre."[6] Joining Vernon in breaking this silence, I would argue that this censorship policy had several significant effects on how Spanish spectators subsequently perceived not only the documentary genre in particular but also cinematic representation in general. First, this policy privileged documentary as a key site of struggle for control over popular memory. Although the regulations ensured that the government would win this struggle in the short run, they also imbued the genre with a new political potential that promised to surpass that of fiction, a potential first realized in the choice of Italian neorealism during the early 1950s as the documentary-like aesthetic that could counter the artificiality of the Francoist cinema and then in the recuperation of documentary itself during the post-Franco era.

Second, it made the issue of generic definition politically significant, for the "art documentary" did continue to flourish through this period, as Carlos Fernández Cuenca details in his annotated filmographic study of this subgenre, so long as it could be defined as a different genre.[7] Although Cuenca does not address the relation of this subgenre to the 1942 ban on documentary (perhaps because he was still writing within the Francoist era), he observes: "There have certainly been many *artistic* documentaries, but the *art* documentary is another thing" (8). The "art documentary" was established as a potential site of displacement during the Francoist era, when political issues could be addressed only indirectly (as frequently occurred in melodrama). Thus, even in one of the most powerful and celebrated documentaries of the immediate post-Franco period, Jaime Chávarri's *El desencanto* (Disenchantment, 1976; a film I have discussed at length elsewhere),[8] its devastating political analysis is framed and at first mystified by a monumental work of art, the draped statue of Franco's dead poet laureate, Leopoldo Panero, who died on August 28, 1962, and to whom this monument was now (in 1974) being dedicated at a public ceremony. The statue remains a structuring absence, never unveiled; instead the film turns to an old photograph of the family survivors, the widow and her three sons (all poets like their father), which this performative narrative activates and extends, creating an ironic portrait of a fascist family through which it is possible to

The widowed mother sits between two of her rivalrous sons in *El desencanto.*

tease out the broader social political climate of Spain at this crucial moment of transition.

Third, and perhaps most important, this policy tended to make Spaniards suspicious of any constative claims for documentary, for it was based on the assumption that all images carry ideological implications and could acquire new ones by being placed in a different context (such as the NO-DO newsreel). Thus, it is hardly surprising that after the death of Franco, instead of generating new images, the first group of documentaries were compilation films that reedited and recontextualized the meanings of existing footage. Avoiding the imposed meanings of "voice-of-God" narrations, these documentaries cultivated a pervasive ambiguity that required filmmakers and spectators to perform a more active reading of historical representations. The key question, then, for the Spanish spectator was not merely what was being documented (the *referent*) but from which political perspective and for what end. In other words, what ideological function it was *performing.*

These dynamics called attention to issues of representation, which helped cultivate a reflexive tradition in Spanish documentary as well as in other genres. Although Vernon claims this reflexive tradition is rare in documentary, it is crucial in the work of Dziga Vertov as well as in that of Luis Buñuel—not just in the latter's surrealist documentary *Tierra sin pan* but also in the documentary elements that are parodied in *L'Age d'or* (The Golden Age, 1938) and *Los olvidados* (The Dispossessed, 1950). This tradition actually controls Lorenzo Llobet Gràcia's early Catalan masterpiece *Vida en sombras* (Life in Shadows, 1947–48), a reflexive melodrama that puts a documentary filmmaker at its center (rather than a director of fiction, as in Federico Fellini's *8½* [1963] or in François Truffaut's *La nuit americaine* [Day for Night, 1973]). It also is pervasive in the "art documentary" subgenre, where there is frequently an implicit comparison between the documentary filmmaker and the artist being documented. This reflexive tradition helped to blur the boundary between documentary and fiction and to generate the kind of performative approach to the genre only now being theorized by scholars such as Scheibler, Renov, and Nichols. The rest of this essay will be devoted to concrete instances from Spanish documentaries, for "Performativity—as any reader of Austin will recognize—lives in the examples."[9]

Reconstructing Popular Memory during the Transition

The post-Franco documentaries that have thus far received the most critical attention are a cluster of revisionist compilation films that appeared during the transition. This cluster includes Basilio Martín Patino's *Canciones para después de una guerra* (Songs for after a War, 1971), a subversive collage of popular images and songs from the 1940s and 1950s, and his *Caudillo* (1975), an ironic biography of Franco comprised of found footage tinted in different colors to indicate the ideological bent of the source; Jaime Camino's *La vieja memoria* (Old Memory, 1977), more than two and one-half hours of conflicting testimony on the Civil War selected from twenty-five hours of interviews with participants from all ideological perspectives; and Gonzalo Herralde's *Raza, el espíritu de Franco* (Race, The Spirit of Franco, 1977), a witty deconstruction of *Raza,* the popular 1941 Civil War epic based on Franco's idealized portrait of his own family and written under a pseudonym. Taking a sophisticated "cultural studies" approach to popular memory, these documentaries appropriate and recontextualize images from old newsreels, popular movies, newspapers, magazines, advertisements, and family albums to challenge the monolithic "official history" of the Francoist regime. They also expose the "imaginary" nature of the community that had been forcibly unified by the consumption of those images during the Francoist era. Thus these documentaries not only provide an *archival record* of popular memory (a function that Thomas Elsaesser now ascribes to European television)[10] but they also *perform* a historical and ideological analysis of this material. Because these documentaries have received more critical attention than those from the two later periods, my discussion here will be relatively brief.

Canciones bombards us with a cascade of images, words, and songs whose mixed sources (from NO-DO newsreels, popular movies, newspaper articles, and so on) are rarely identified and whose rapid juxtapositions generate a plethora of subversive meanings that (partly because of the rapid pace of the editing, the detachment from the original context, and the reassembly within a postmodern pastiche) remain sufficiently ambiguous to avoid political accountability. The film implies this subversive form of mental editing was accessible to those so-called inner exiles living within Francoist Spain, who could use their own popular memories of quotidian life to challenge the official meanings imposed by the state—a process that requires the kind of active reading demanded by Vertov's *Man with a Movie Camera* (1928) and that is analogous to the task performed by Spain's most notorious exiled filmmaker, Luis Buñuel, at MOMA (New York's Museum of Modern Art), where between 1939 to 1945 he dubbed and reedited Spanish versions of documentaries, including fascist documentaries such as Leni Riefenstahl's *Triumph of the Will* (1934).

That the release of this innovative 1971 film was delayed by Francoist censors until 1976 weakened the political impact of Patino's performance. It failed to function as (what Elsaesser calls) the "collective guardian" of the everyday because it lacked the *immediacy* of television. Yet such immediacy tends to mask the "constructedness" of the archival record, and it was precisely this *constructedness* that these compilation films were designed to expose—a point noted by Román Gubern, who collaborated with Camino on the conceptualization of *La vieja memoria:* "With very elaborate editing and false linkages that paid tribute to the sophistry of Orson Welles's *Fake* (1974), Camino constructed an inter-

Archival footage from *La vieja memoria* shows a victory parade.

active montage of false dialogue, in which people seemed to be listening
to and contradicting each other as if seated around the same (and impossible) table. . . . Emphasizing their weaknesses, manipulations, and
contradictions, . . . *Old Memory* implicitly demanded a critique of the
neutrality of the archives, . . . the first of those archives being the
individual's own memory."[11]

There is a fascinating juxtaposition between personal memory and
archival footage in the moving sequence from *La vieja memoria* in which
José Luis de Vallalonga recounts his traumatic experience as a youth on a
Nationalist firing squad. Although his words now condemn the gruesome violence he was commanded to perform, the manner and tone of
his narration—with its ironic smiles—contradict what he says, particularly when his account is intercut with graphic documentary footage
of many executions. Yet—and this is what I want to stress—the presentation of the archival footage is just as mediated as his narrative. The use
of parodic music, slow motion, and transitional wipes all blatantly
reveal the constructedness of the sequence, and clearly these devices
heighten rather than diminish its emotional power. The movements
inward for successively tighter close-ups of the elegant narrator (after
each cutaway to the firing squad in action) reveal the inflated self-

importance of this survivor, especially in comparison with the anonymous victims. These movements also encourage us to scrutinize his face
and gestures for signs of deception. We notice how his right hand
confidently holds a cigar while his left hand nervously plays with his ear,
his neck, and his hair. The "virtual space" of the discourse *evokes* rather
than documents the virtual space of history, and in both spaces we must
scrutinize a series of contradictory performances.

Le vieja memoria must also be contextualized within the Catalan cinema. Born in Barcelona in 1936, Camino had been an important force
in this regional movement, founding his own production company
(Tibidabo) and the Institut de Cinema Català and emerging in the
mid-1960s as one of the key filmmakers of the Barcelona School. In a
perceptive essay on Catalan cinema, Marvin D'Lugo argues that Camino
manages to introduce this regional discourse on Catalan identity into *La
vieja memoria* by emphasizing interviews and periods of the war that
relate directly to Catalonia in general and Barcelona in particular.[12]
Instead of ending with the authorized images of fascist victory in
Madrid, as in *Raza,* Camino emphasizes the repressed footage of destruction, defeat, and exile and of Catalonia's marginalization. Although
Gubern may be correct in saying that *La vieja memoria* presents "the
most complete eye-witness account and the most complex exploration
of the politics of both sides of the Civil War in Spanish film history,"[13]
Camino still enables us to see that its synthesis is filtered through a
distinctively Catalan perspective.

Remapping Madrid in the 1980s

Whereas the documentaries from the transition were refiguring Spanish
history primarily for home consumption, those made during the Socialist era took foreign perspectives into account (even though they did not
succeed in the global market). This shift can be partly explained by the
increased share of Spain's domestic market dominated by foreign films
(92 percent in 1989 as opposed to only 70 percent in 1970). Because
these films were more interested in showing the process of change in the
present, the privileged subject for the documentary portrait became the
capital city of Madrid, a spatial trope that facilitated a remapping of
the Spanish imagined community. After noting "the Francoist ani-

mosity toward urban culture," Marvin D'Lugo describes how this trope functioned not only in Pedro Almodóvar's popular comic melodramas set in Madrid but in many fictional films of the early 1980s, including Manuel Gutiérrez Aragón's *Maravillas,* Carlos Saura's *Deprisa, deprisa* (Fast, Fast), and Fernando Trueba's *Opera prima,* all made in 1980.[14]

This capital model can be illustrated in Antonio Giménez Rico's *Vestida de azul* (Dressed in Blue, 1983), a documentary portrait of six transvestites (Tvs) who have migrated from various regional communities to Madrid in order to change their gender and live a "modern life," and in Patino's *Madrid* (1986), a fictional film about a German filmmaker who comes to Madrid to make a documentary about the fiftieth anniversary of the Spanish Civil War for West German television. In both films the privileged perspective of defiance belongs to outsiders, who are not merely Spaniards with a different ideological viewpoint (representing the documentary filmmaker and his collaborators, as in the compilation films from the transition) but recent émigrés whose Otherness is represented on screen in terms of nationality or gender. An analogous slippage occurs on the level of genre, as if suggesting that a documentary project can be "authentic" only when dialogized with its fictional shadow. This use of the Other to reinterpret Spanish history facilitated the refiguring of national identity and its stereotypes. Not only was this configuration compatible with the Lacanian theory of subject formation (in which a subject enters the symbolic order by becoming a signifier in the field of the Other) but it also served the pragmatic function of helping to make Spain's capital and culture more accessible and appealing to foreign spectators in the global market.

In *Vestida de azul* all six subjects are gay men who successfully cross-dress as women. The film does not clearly distinguish among transvestism, transsexuality, homosexuality, and bisexuality for most of these "queens" use cross-dressing as an important step in a long, complex process of sexual inversion that ultimately leads back to heterosexuality. The key issue is not whether they can pass as "real" women but how far along they are in the process—e.g., whether they have told their families, obtained an ID card, started hormonal therapy, acquired "real" breasts, or snipped off their penis and testicles. This dynamic is dramatized in the story of the glamorous performer Eva, whose anatomy is carefully scrutinized by an "ugly old" woman backstage, who bluntly asks, "Where's his cock?" When Eva's friend tells her, "He chopped it off," we spectators (who may have been asking ourselves the same question) are not sure whether he is lying, that is, until the dramatic moment when Eva displays her penis on stage as the climax of her performance.

Significantly the six TV subjects all still have a penis because they realize it is the primary signifier of power within the phallocentric homophobic culture they abhor. One says: "If you're a man, it's easier—even if you're a queer." The film focuses not on the loss of the penis but on the acquisition of breasts, which are reempowered within this subculture through painful implant surgery shown in graphic, agonizing detail.

The film presents a sophisticated conception of gender and sexuality as social constructs with a wide range of possibilities rather than as clear-cut binary oppositions. This complexity is also apparent in some of the johns, such as an older rich man who pays Eva handsomely to help him put on female drag for their sexual encounter as lesbians. Not only do the queens identify with both genders (one describes herself as "a woman's body guided by a man's brain—that's a money-making machine!") but they value the queerness of transvestism and homosexuality precisely because it undermines that binary opposition on which all patriarchal order is propped ("Homos are perfect . . . they're neither this nor that!"). Apparently they share Judith Butler and Eve Sedgwick's assumption that both sexuality and gender are performative.

This rejection of binary opposition is also extended to genre. In the opening we see streetwalkers approaching prospective johns in what looks like a fictional film. But the hookers turn out to be transvestites, the johns the cops who bust them, and the film a documentary. Printed titles inform us: "All the characters in this film are real. What we are going to see really happens to them." Yet we still do not know whether events are staged or reconstructed. When the opening credits present the names of the transvestites as if they were stars (fulfilling their dreams of fame), we know the film is still masquerading as fiction. Like the cross-dressing of the queens and the plainclothes of the cops, the visual packaging of this documentary is designed to raise false expectations and to transgress the borderlines between genres.

The six portraits are unified in a series of scenes that show the transvestites meeting in an elegant Madrid setting to discuss their common experience as prostitutes and their shared dreams of normalcy, love, and consumerism. Their conversation constantly returns to issues of class and to their perpetual competition over who earns the most money and spends it most wisely. We have no way of knowing whether these Tvs knew each other prior to the film or whether this imagined community and its rivalries have been constructed by the filmmakers.

After the opening, the first interview is with the eldest Tv, who came out during the repressive Francoist era and who is repeatedly associated with resistance against repression. Her interview begins with a description of her time spent in prison, where she claims she had to fuck only those she desired. As if complicating any simple notion of linear progress, she seems the most spirited of the group, proudly sporting her voluptuous "Sophia Loren breasts" and her comic stories about servitude—being a *maricón* in the military (with painted eyebrows and limp wrists) and being a butler in the home of a count (where she heard juicy gossip about the sexual exploits of decadent aristocrats, whose names are discreetly censored with comical beeps).

As in *La vieja memoria* there are many old photographs of the subjects in their youth, which are closely scrutinized as if searching for some essentialist sign of the sexual inversion to come. There are also candid interviews not only with the transvestites themselves but also with their relatives (parents, brothers, ex-wives) and with straight officials (doctors, priests, bureaucrats) who are trying to regulate them within a broader unifying discourse of "cultural transformation"—a project the film itself alternately performs and parodies. At one point the priest (whose clothes and policies have also undergone a dramatic liberalization) compares the Tvs with witches and advises them to improve "their image" so that they can become more acceptable to the general public. For David Garland the film "seems finally to posit contemporary Spanish transsexualism as an ideologically unstable and ambiguous lightning-rod for shifting boundaries between and within religion on the one hand and class on the other."[15] While the film celebrates these Tvs for their courage, it also reveals that their consumerist dreams of normalcy and sexual inversion are blatantly mainstream. Thus, they can only expose rather than seriously challenge the homophobic oppression that still exists in a democratic hyperliberated Spain.

Ironically, this subculture (whose excesses were first screened in Aranda's *Cambio de sexo* (1977) and popularized worldwide by Almodóvar) has now become the new cultural stereotype of a liberated post-Franco Spain, one that replaced the old regional Andalusian stereotypes

I've sung her songs, I've
danced like her...

The gypsy transvestite Juan Muñoz impersonates Isabel Pontoja in *Vestida de azul*.

of gypsies, flamenco, and bullfighting promoted in the *españolada* during the Francoist regime. In *Vestida de azul* this substitution is most powerfully dramatized in the gypsy transvestite Juan Muñoz (Tamara), who literally combines both stereotypes, particularly when imitating great flamenco stars like Isabel Pantoja and Lola Sevilla. She also evokes the "black legend" of Spain with poignant stories about being abused as a child and with images of her family's poverty. By seeing that she is cross-dressing in terms of class as well as gender, we realize it is no coincidence that the gypsy subculture is both the most impoverished and most macho in Spain.

Although this film was not widely seen outside of Spain, it belongs to an international subgenre of documentaries on transvestites, which use these transgressive figures to explore the cultural and historical specificity of the nation in which they are struggling to survive. This subgenre includes not only a later American box-office success like Jenny Livingston's *Paris Is Burning* (1991) but also a pair of fascinating films from Spain's former colony, the Philippines—Nick Deocampo's *Oliver* (1983) and *The Sex Warriors and the Samurai* (1995), in which Filipino transvestites use their gender-bending performance as dancers and prostitutes to support large impoverished families and thereby become the exportable maternal breadwinners who epitomize the role of this Third World nation in the global economy. By positioning *Vestida de azul* in this global context, we can better appreciate the cultural specificity of its depiction of Spanish transvestism.[16] For example, a great deal of attention is paid to family visits so that the camera can show the roots and class origins of these prodigal sons. Being accepted by the family is obviously crucial for these Spanish Tvs, particularly for the redhead, who is seen at the end of the film writing her mother about her sex change as we hear the pop song "No te quiero" (I don't love you). This pattern is in marked contrast to *Paris Is Burning,* where the Tvs belong to "houses" that substitute for the biological families that rejected them, and to Deocampo's films, in which the Filipino Tvs, because of the extreme poverty, still live with and support their large families.

In *Vestida de azul* such cross-cultural comparisons are appropriated and commodified by the Spanish Tvs, who want to participate in Spain's growing empowerment within the global economy. When one of them uses the terms "Thai job" (for bathtub sex), "Greek job" (for anal sex), "French job" (for oral sex), and "British job" (for S & M), she claims that the choice of these terms is "a matter of class," but this multinational discourse on desire also demonstrates that Spain's body politic is no longer xenophobic. The film's structure encourages us (like the straight officials) to read these six portraits as part of a national discourse on Spain's "cultural transformation" from fascism to democracy. Yet we are also led to see that by being posed in terms of a transgressive subculture that has been marginalized and oppressed worldwide, this political conversion gains even greater global appeal, particularly in a postcolonial era in which notions of periphery and center are reversible.

It is precisely this assumption of radical conversion that is seriously questioned in Patino's film *Madrid,* in which a visiting German filmmaker insists on moving between archival footage of the Spanish Civil War and current political unrest in a Socialist Spain. This juxtaposition begins in the opening sequence with his running to the window to shoot a street demonstration being conducted against NATO and the U.S. military bases in Spain, and it ends with his being fired off the film for complicating it with such comparisons. In the very opening shots, the film documents people looking at a contemporary exhibit of artifacts from the Civil War. This scene evokes the opening of the favorite French new wave film of many left-wing Spanish filmmakers such as Patino: Alain Resnais's 1959 debut feature, *Hiroshima, mon amour,* another fictional film whose protagonist is a foreigner working on an inset documentary about a past war. In *Madrid* we spectators are immediately positioned by Patino to perform this same action, that is, to examine historical documents from the past that enable us to see contemporary events in a new light. The filmmaker's movement into the streets is merely an extension of the same process. Thus this opening encourages us to think about the historical mediation of filmic representation as well as the relationship between past and present: not only how the present shapes the meaning of the past but also how the past affects our understanding of the present.

It is easy to see the line of continuity with Patino's earlier compilation films. In the best article published thus far on *Madrid,* Kathleen Vernon puts Patino's work "at the forefront" of the post-Franco "renaissance in documentary filmmaking," particularly for "its insistent interrogations of the conventions of the genre," and specifically reads *Madrid* as "a retrospective reflection on that documentary tradition as well as [on] Patino's own documentary practice in *Canciones* and *Caudillo.*"[17]

Madrid is a multilingual film (in Spanish, German, and English) that shows the complex interweaving of European influence: the subject excessively Spanish, the treatment blatantly Godardian, the ponderous protagonist and his pronouncements decidedly German. Like Vertov's *Man with a Movie Camera* and Jean-Luc Godard's *Deux ou trois choses que je sais d'elle* (Two or Three Things I Know about Her, 1966), it combines the modernist "city symphony" genre with a reflexive filmic essay on representation. Yet, as Vernon observes, "while the film . . . celebrate[s] the Spanish capital as being in the same league as other cities memorialized on film (Berlin, Paris, New York), the viewer is reminded that the potentially nostalgic recovery of the city's folkloric charm is shadowed by the legacy of Madrid's violence."[18] This view requires a constant interplay between past and present in order to ascertain not merely what still survives but what is still relevant and interesting.

Unlike Vertov's and Godard's city symphonies, Patino's film includes a romantic subplot, perhaps to help hold our interest. The German filmmaker Hans is played by Rudiger Vogler, who consistently performs the reflexive role of artist/filmmaker in the movies of Wim Wenders and who continues to do so in postmodernist variations like

Until the End of the World (1991), where he is a high-tech private eye, and *The Lisbon Story* (1995), where he is a cinema soundman arguing in favor of European reflexive "city" documentaries in the tradition of Vertov's *Man with a Movie Camera* and Fellini's *Roma* (1972) (and, we might add, Patino's *Madrid*). Patino's choice of a lead actor linked to the New German Cinema, the movement that helped refigure German national identity in the postwar period, resonates in the Spanish context, where this goal appealed both to Franco's regime and to the leftist opposition in which Patino was a crucial figure. Hans becomes romantically involved with his Spanish editor (Verónica Forqué), who becomes emblematic of Spain—full of life, humor, and contradictions, especially in contrast to the "Teutonic" Hans. As part of his crew, she is clearly subordinate to her director/lover, a dynamic that figures powerfully on the national register. She fears that once their affair is over, he will return to Germany to make more films while she will remain in Madrid, forced to work on advertisements and other crappy projects. He treats her as part of his subject, finding her complicated life almost as intriguing as the Civil War footage. As in the españoladas, even on their home ground Spaniards are cast as the exotic Other, who must be investigated and interpreted by the foreigner.

Like Hans, Patino creates a collage that combines a heteroglossia of representational forms: black and white and color footage, fiction and documentary, silent cinema and talkies, visual spectacle and verbal pyrotechnics (presented both through poetic voice-overs and printed graphics), and (like Patino's earlier compilation film *Canciones*) a melange of popular media, including television, photography, painting, music, poems, magazines, newspapers, political posters, and advertising. The list also includes the Spanish zarzuela, a distinctive form of light musical comedy variously described in the film as "a popular rite of self-affirmation" and "a symbol of the freedom and progress of the working class." According to Vernon, the film uses the zarzuela as the "central agent in the reconstruction and re-presentation of this authentic Madrid."[19]

As in Resnais's masterful documentary on the holocaust, *Nuit et brouillard* (Night and Fog, 1955), Hans and Patino, despite their heavy reliance on archival footage, expose the subjective processes of mediation, which are always operative in documentary, and stress the impossibility of ever capturing objective truth on celluloid. At one point, Hans says of the archival footage: "Camera lenses never transmit the whole truth. Their essence is not truth or lies but fascination." Yet we see that cultural specificity helps determine what fascinates a spectator. In one scene a group of middle-aged Spaniards ask to watch the footage of Franco taking communion and are obviously fascinated by the difficulty he has in holding the wafer on his tongue and by the possibility that he may swallow it.

Part of what makes footage fascinating is "the poetic force of ellipsis," which avoids the boredom of repeating what is already known and allows the spectator's imagination to fill in the gaps. Avoiding a monolithic interpretation of history, which they consider fascistic, Hans and Patino use a disjunctive style of editing that makes this film complicated and poetic and that encourages spectators to construct their own meanings—the same strategy used in *Canciones*. In both films editing is the key, yet ironically here it is performed by the subordinate Spanish female editor rather than by the German male director. This paradox eroticizes the editing process and helps initiate the affair between them. It begins in a fascinating scene in which she edits a sequence to a fox-trot (whose lyrics are about seduction at the Ritz), rhythmically cutting the sensuous images to the cadence of the dance. When he watches her footage, she dances to the music, and it is his perception of the *relation* between her performative moves both on the Moviola and the dance floor that turns him on.

At the end of the film, when Hans is forced to leave the documentary project because he refuses to deliver what is expected, he tells his crew that he might turn to fiction and he begins describing the Patino film we have just seen. This reflexive move is reminiscent not only of Fellini's *8½* but also of Llobet Gràcia's *Vida en sombras* (1947–48), a lost Catalan film revived in 1984, which tells the story of another documentary filmmaker who turns from shooting dangerous documentary footage of the Spanish Civil War to making a boldly original, reflexive melodrama about cinematic representation.

Although the conceptual power of *Madrid* and *Vestida de azul* puts them at the cutting edge of Spanish cinema, they were still looking backward—reinscribing old stereotypes of the españolada, zarzuelas, machismo, and Civil War with new meanings for a Socialist era under-

going change. Yet both not only addressed a new generation of Spaniards but also recognized new global circumstances, the effects of which
were now becoming more accessible to Spain.

Decentering Spain in the 1990s

In 1992 Spain was celebrating the 500-year anniversary of the 1492
discovery of America. The González government was also looking forward to being included among those elite members of the EU who could
meet the strict economic criteria established in Maastricht in 1991.
These "looks" backward and forward seemed at odds, especially because
the lavish expenditures for 1992 put a strain on Spain's efforts to satisfy
the Maastricht criteria (a strain that included two devaluations of the
Spanish peseta in fall of 1992 and that helped lay the groundwork for
the defeat of the Socialists in the general elections of 1996).

I am more interested here in the issue of cultural specificity. Whereas
the look backward highlighted Spain's *unique* history, the look forward
redefined it as one of several modern nations that would merge in a
new "Europe without borders." These contradictions were cosmetically
resolved in Spain's self-promotion as "the new cultural capital of Europe"—a position for which Madrid and Barcelona fiercely competed.
Although the founding of the Spanish nation was linked historically
with the expulsion of the Moors and Jews and although its borders had
been closed to foreigners ever since, Spain was now not only drawing
thousands of new immigrants but also actively recuperating its unique
multicultural heritage of the three cultures (Jewish, Islamic, and Christian), a theme prominently emphasized in the Spanish pavilions at the
Expo '92 (World's Fair) in Seville. In October 1991 Madrid was symbolically chosen as the opening site for the important international
peace talks between Mideastern Arabs and Jews (with Bush and Gor-
bachev in attendance). What better site could there be (so the logic
went) for inspiring peace between those longtime enemies that had both
been expelled from Spain? If this xenophobic "holy land" could be
miraculously transformed into a reasonable member of the global community, then there was also hope for peace in the Middle East.

I dwell on this example because it demonstrates that Spain is widely
perceived in the 1990s as a model of post-cold-war reconfiguration—

particularly in the way it peacefully handled the nationalist drive toward independence by several of its regions. In 1978 Spain's parliamentary democracy deftly restructured the nation into seventeen *comunidades
autonómicas* (autonomous communities), with new powers to administer
their regions and to promote their own distinctive language and culture,
particularly through new regional television stations. Although this act
was widely perceived at home and abroad as a liberal step toward dis-
mantling Franco's monolithic centralized nation-state, the more radical
nationalists in the Basque country and Catalonia tended to perceive it as
a strategic move to co-opt and thereby defuse their own drive toward
independence. By being lumped together with fifteen other regions,
they could hardly make as strong a case for the unique nature of their
own historic claims to nationhood. The situation was exacerbated by the
fact that Madrid was redefined as one of these autonomous communities,
implying it has always been a microregion masquerading as the nation,
which is another reason why it became a privileged subject for documentary portraits in the 1980s. In the sphere of international media,
Madrid's masquerade evoked an analogy with Hollywood, a national
cinema functioning as a global standard and thereby colonizing the
world.

Two remarkable documentaries in the early 1990s addressed these
dynamics of decentering in subtle ways: *Innisfree* (1990), by Catalan
filmmaker José Luis Guerin, and *El sol del membrillo* (The Quince Tree
Sun, 1991, screened in the United States under the title *The Dream of
Light*), by Basque-born director Víctor Erice. Both were made by filmmakers from regions seeking autonomy and were co-financed by government agencies both at the regional and national levels (as well as by
TVE, Spanish public television, in the case of *Innisfree*). But instead of
addressing microregional issues the two movies feature foreign characters from outside Spain. Both films focus on a specific place (a small
village in Ireland and a backyard in Madrid) much narrower than the
urban cityscape, yet they concretely dramatize the local/global nexus.
Both are reflexive films that extend the exploration of representational
issues to media other than cinema—to poetry, music, painting, video,
and tourism. It is not only nationality and genre that are being decentered in these works but also the cinematic medium and its ability to
document cultural specificity and historical change.

The Irish community documented in Guerin's *Innisfree* is literally reimagined not only through the W. B. Yeats poem "The Lake Isle of Innisfree" but also through John Ford's 1952 Hollywood classic, *The Quiet Man,* which allegedly was his favorite among his own movies. Starring John Wayne as an Irish American returning to his homeland to take a bride, played by Maureen O'Hara, this vehicle enabled Ford to explore his own ethnic roots and (as the film documents) the small Irish village where his family, the O'Feeneys, are still well remembered. Rather than positioning Ford as his protagonist, Guerin's film focuses on the imagined community of Innisfree. Using English and Gaelic, it shows how the present inhabitants of Cunga St. Feichin are still affected by the movie made there thirty-seven years ago: the old veterans reliving their experiences through stories and songs in the local pub, the young-sters perpetuating the myths passed down by their elders, the local businessmen exploiting the film legend for a thriving tourist trade, and Guerin recycling all of this material for a fascinating postmodernist documentary. Guerin uses many excerpts from *The Quiet Man,* at first merely poaching parts of the sound track to juxtapose with his own images of landscapes and people in the present but eventually importing full clips freely intercut with his own footage to create an enlarged intertextual narrative.

Throughout this ethnographic film we are never certain whether Guerin is merely documenting these Innisfree exercises in popular memory or whether he is actually staging them. All we are told is that the film records "things seen and heard in and around Innisfree from September to October 1988." This dynamic of uncertainty is particu-larly strong with regard to the beautiful young redhead, who, after returning from a brief period of exile in Pittsburgh (the same city from which the John Wayne character derives), is now working as a sim-ulacrum of Maureen O'Hara in the local tourist trade. We do not know whether Guerin found her in this job or actually cast her in this role. At times he flagrantly uses fake images, such as the obvious process shot in the horse race sequence, or several scenes in which locals are self-consciously posed in front of quaint backdrops for their filmic portraits, replicating familiar images from history, movies, or other forms of pop culture. The strongest instance is a fascinating sequence involving the village children looking directly into the camera as they take turns reciting from memory the story of *The Quiet Man,* a film made long

An *Innisfree* character acts as a Maureen O'Hara simulacrum.

before any of them was born but which still defines the imagined community they now inhabit.

Even if their performance is an authentic local ritual (as opposed to being staged for the documentary), Guerin reinscribes it as a parable for how all mass media redefine our world. He himself is as removed from the original story of *The Quiet Man* as the children, not by time but by geography, ethnicity, language, and national identity, yet he performs his own reinscription by generating another narrative cycle that re-imagines (and enlarges) the community, demonstrating that the concept of the nation has been displaced by the local/global nexus, which depends on the touristic potential of mass media such as television and cinema.

On the surface, this does not seem to be a likely topic for a Spanish or Catalan documentary—in fact, the press kit contains a statement defending a Spaniard's right to make films about other cultures. *Innisfree* reverses the premise of Patino's *Madrid,* making the foreign documentary filmmaker Catalan rather than German but still privileging his foreign perspective in this ethnographic investigation of the community's mythologized past—one in which stories of the Hollywood movie are blended with local legends about Cromwell and the Black and Tans, and myths about the waves of Celtics, Vikings, Normans, and British who also conquered the Irish. The film creates an archaeological layering of cultures, "ruins built on ruins, one alphabet . . . [replacing] another." Despite having their own unique histories, languages, and cultures, Ireland and Catalonia have undergone similar hardships: both survived a bloody civil war, and have been colonized by other nations with a long colonial history (England and Spain), nations that have appropriated the rich cultural contributions of the colonized lands as their own. Most important, even within this so-called postcolonial era, Ireland and Catalonia not only remain stuck in this colonized position but also are increasingly subjected to another layer of colonization by global mass media.

Although *Innisfree* focuses on how global media have led these Irish villagers to dwell within a fictionalized version of their past, in one fascinating sequence near the end of the film we also glimpse a possibility of change, one that is equally disheartening. Evoking those communal dance sequences that lie at the heart of most John Ford movies, it begins as a humble community gathering—a nationalist discourse on the Irish jig that shows how this folkloric ritual unifies the many generations of dancers, whose legs and feet are seen in interchangeable close-ups; but as soon as hard rock displaces the folk music on the sound track, it suddenly transforms into a generational discourse, which reduces the old-timers merely to passive spectators as the teens snap their heads and lash their long hair spasmodically to the beat in gestures of a global teen culture recognized worldwide.

As a Catalan filmmaker, Guerin is linked to his Irish and Irish American subjects by an investment in global media culture and by common preoccupations with marginality and exile—issues that became more compelling in the media wars during the recent GATT negotiations in which Europeans were trying to protect their own culture industries from this second level of colonization. *Innisfree* shows how a man from a marginal location who emigrates to another region can still draw on his cultural roots—a story with relevance not only to Guerin and to "O'Feeney's boy" (as John Ford is called in the village) but to filmmakers from any nation or region colonized by Hollywood. In one scene a woman villager watches Maureen O'Hara accepting an award on Irish

Víctor Erice (left) and Antonio López (right) on the set of *El sol del membrillo.*

television. When the actress declares that she has been all over the world and has won many awards from Spain, Mexico, and other nations but never before from the land where she was born, the viewer angrily responds, "Nonsense!" for in her Irish village O'Hara is constantly being honored.

The film demonstrates how myths about one's own community can be constructed by others and reified in mass media but then reappropriated and recommodified by the indigenous population, a dynamic that occurred with the Andalusian stereotypes of the españolada and with Almodóvar's reconstruction of a superliberated Madrid. Above all, *Innisfree* reveals that all moviegoing is a form of tourism that fosters nomadic subjectivity.

Erice's *El sol del membrillo* seems to depict precisely the opposite—the firmly grounded subjectivity of a well-known Spanish realist painter, Antonio López García, who daily occupies precisely the same carefully marked position in his own backyard as he attempts to paint a specific quince tree.[20] Yet both he and his collaborator, Erice, capture their own interaction with history and culture and Spain's growing involvement with the rest of the world. The film gives new concrete meaning to the old dictum by Renoir that the deeper you plunge into your own cultural specificity, the greater the international appeal of your work. Erice's film succeeds in capturing not some kind of idealist Bazinian universal but rather the local/global nexus of a postcolonial subjectivity.

Although one could call *El sol del membrillo* an "art documentary," as in the case of *Vestida de azul,* I think it is more productive to discuss it in the context of an international subgenre of documentary that transgresses the borders with fiction—in this case, meditative films on representation that renegotiate the blurred boundaries between art and popular culture, modernism and the postmodernist condition. Prefigured by Orson Welles's *F for Fake* (1973), this subgenre also includes more recent works such as Godard's *JLG/JLG: Autoportrait de Decembre* (JLG by JLG: December Self-Portrait, 1994), Michelangelo Antonioni's *Par-dela les nuages* (Beyond the Clouds, 1995), and to a lesser extent, Wim Wenders's *The Lisbon Story* (1995). All of these films are by international auteurs whose works now (at the time of this production) seem more peripheral in a world cinema dominated by Hollywood action films and megamarketing. As Godard says in *JLG by JLG,* "Europe has memories, America has T-shirts!" These auteurs all refer reflexively to their own earlier films, either through direct allusions or allusive intertextual imagery. In reaffirming the exceptional value of art, they all make prominent reference to painting (López and Michelangelo in the case of Erice, Cézanne in the case of Antonioni, Rubens in the case of Godard), developing an analogy between the visual art forms of film and painting, which are contrasted with television and video. They all focus on the specificity of their own familiar landscapes (Erice's Madrid, Antonioni's Ferrara, and Godard's native Switzerland), presenting them as a means of reasserting the unique value of their own localized identity, particularly against the onslaught of a postmodern global culture dominated by American mass media.

In the press kit Erice describes the film as follows: "It consists, in essence, of capturing a real event: the drawing and painting of a tree . . . in front of a film-crew equipped with a camera and a sound-recorder, which tries to capture the images and sounds of the event."[21] Thus the film is about representation, or (in Erice's terms) the "secret relationship between painting and cinema" and their shared dream of "the perfect capturing of light . . . [which] obeys—as André Bazin so rightly pointed out—the same mythical impulse: the ingrained need to conquer time through the perpetuity of forms; the desire to replace the external world with its double." Erice's statement is reminiscent of what Scheibler describes as the constative promise of documentary: "The document promises that the limitless text of existence will take on a manageable form and substance, providing the spectator with a position of mastery over a potentially threatening world."[22] Yet within Erice's film that mastery is denied to the community of artists performing on screen, who are never seen completing their work: not only López who fails to finish the painting of the quince tree but also to the other inhabitants of his house who are painters. Although Erice's film *is* presumably finished, he and his crew are never visible on screen; we see only still lifes of his photographic equipment, hardly an image of mastery.

In Erice's written statement about the film, the threatening world of postmodernism is explicitly identified with television and video, which "have now taken over, amplifying to an extraordinary degree the reach of this revolution in the status of the image, generating in the process a crisis in the cinema and a concomitant sense of self-demise." Yet Erice uses video in the film to document López's work, making it analogous to the painter's use of drawing. Video is merely one of several media that capture the image of López, whose subjectivity is performed within a series of textual representations by himself and others, including his wife, María Moreno, who is the producer of the film and who works on an unfinished painting of him sleeping and gradually moving toward death. At one point his old friend Enrique Gran describes an old photograph taken of him and López when they were young painters in art school, an image we do not actually see but that remains a potent imaginary signifier that apparently still helps to drive Gran's painting. The self-portrait that we *are* permitted to scrutinize is Michelangelo's self-representation on the flayed skin of St. Bartholomew in his *Last Judgment,* which López and Gran discuss in great detail.

Erice's film is preoccupied with the serial performance of self-representation, which (no matter how narcissistic) must inevitably be historicized. The film demonstrates that no matter what subject you are documenting (on canvas or on celluloid, on paper or video), you are still representing yourself and your medium and bearing witness to the historical and cultural moment that shaped your subjectivity. Like *Innisfree,* both López's painting and Erice's filmmaking capture the traces of what is perceived and remembered: the street noise, aromas, and visitors that enter the painter's garden; words and music that run through his mind; world events and media culture transmitted on radios and television screens; memories and dreams that color the present moment; intense conversations with family and friends. It is the emotional power of these quotidian words and images that helps make the film so extraordinary. Even Almodóvar (whom many consider Erice's antithesis) claims it "made me feel again the need to get together with my mother and make a movie with her words. I suppose it was the [film's] exciting sharpness, the basic emotion . . . which inspired and motivated me. If I were to make a film about 'my mother's words,' Erice's . . . style would be the ideal one. But . . . instead I shot *The Flower of My Secret*."[23]

Although Erice's subject seems very narrow, his treatment is rich and comprehensive and demonstrates what one of López's art teachers called "fullness," a concept he and Gran did not understand when they were students but which has now become the primary goal of their art. This concept of fullness is embodied not only in the maturation of the fruit and the growing heaviness of the tree, but also in the image of the painter working on the outer edge of his prime at full strength. It is also narrativized in López's dream of dwelling in Paradise with his parents, realizing their mortality and acknowledging his own fear of death—a dream that develops the biblical resonance of the quince tree.

As in his earlier fiction film *El espíritu de la colmena* (The Spirit of the Beehive, 1973), Erice uses an elliptical, repetitive style to create the iterative mode, representing time as habitual daily (or annual) actions and exploring subjectivity within the quotidian flux of historical change. Erice's jump dissolves and time-lapse shots not only mask and mark the temporal gaps, but also evoke López's strategy of starting again the following year with the new fruit of the tree.

Though the film is positioned precisely in the present (starting on Sunday, September 30, 1990), it looks back to earlier personal experiences of López and Gran in Francoist Spain and to earlier influences on their work. The film is located in Madrid and grounded in Spanish specificity (with a song celebrating the Andalusian city of Seville), but it documents the nation's involvement in the changing world: through images of a postcolonial film like *Sammy and Rosie Get Laid* (1988) flickering on television screens through the windows of high-rise apartment buildings; through radio allusions to the Gulf War, the Eastern European revolutions, and the post-cold-war era; through the inclusion of Polish workers remodeling López's house and Chinese artists coming to look at his paintings. Like Spain's three exhibits at Expo '92 in Seville, Erice's film combines an acknowledgment of Spain's great cultural heritage in painting (at one point using a mirror shot that alludes to *Las Meninas,* the Velázquez painting Michel Foucault helped establish as Western culture's privileged instance of modernist representation)[24] with a demonstration of its current mastery of contemporary media, its openness to other cultures and languages, and its engagement with international issues. The fact that a brilliant, demanding documentary like *El sol del membrillo* can win two major prizes at Cannes (the International Critics Prize and the Jury Prize) is a heartening sign that in a democratic Spain it is possible for Spaniards to retain the cultural specificity of their own backyard while still making contact with the world.

But not all Spanish documentaries of the 1990s turn outward. Two of the most fascinating works from the mid-1990s turn inward to earlier historic Spanish films and their stereotypes to see whether it is possible to recast them in a new light: Ricardo Franco's *Después de tantos años* (After So Many Years, 1994) is a sequel to Chávarri's *El desencanto* (1976); and Saura's *Flamenco* (1995) reinscribes the art form he dramatized in his dance trilogy from the 1980s: *Bodas de Sangre* (Blood Wedding, 1980), *Carmen* (1983), and *El amor brujo* (Love, the Magician, 1986).

Saura's *Flamenco* has many similarities with Erice's *El sol del membrillo.* Both are art documentaries that record a series of performances by the artistic subjects as well as by the filmmakers. Both rely on intertextual relations with the rest of the directors' canon, which produces a coda to a long career. Both cultivate a paradoxical combination of purity and diversity, minimalism and fullness—a combination that works on several levels and that provides aesthetic variations on the slogan of European convergence, "Unity in Diversity."

Carlos Saura's stunning documentary recuperates the art of flamenco as an icon of Spain but with a different meaning for the 1990s. It is presented not, as in the 1950s, as a unique regional form from Andalusia falsely imposed on the whole Spanish nation to bolster its cultural unity, nor as an internationally recognized export from Spain that could launch Saura's global comeback in the 1980s. Rather, as we are explicitly informed in one of the film's few lines of dialogue, flamenco is presented as a foreign import brought by nomadic gypsies from India to the Iberian peninsula, where it matured into a highly diversified, sophisticated form that can now be fully appreciated in the postcolonial 1990s.

Documenting two hours of performances, the film rigorously pursues a paradox: on the one hand, it strives for aesthetic purity, stripping flamenco of its touristic trappings, yet at the same time it emphasizes the great diversity of performers and styles that fall within its domain, ranging from classical flamenco to avant-garde and pop variations and including a variety of flamenco subgenres: *la bulería, la alegría, el martinete, la soleá, el tango, el fandango, la siguiriya, la taranta, la farruca,* and *la rumba.* This duality of purity and diversity is expressed in the selection of the hundreds of performers included in the film, who vary greatly in age, shape, costuming, and style: from old men and women with lined, weathered faces, gold teeth, and aging bodies, who give some of the best performances as singers, to ravishingly beautiful slender young men and women who snap their lithe bodies with matchless grace, to a virtuoso solo performance by a precocious young boy trained by his elders.

This duality of purity and diversity is also emphasized in the brilliant lighting and camerawork by Saura's internationally renown Italian director of photography, Vittorio Storaro, one of the best cinematographers in the world. The film opens with the camera panning across angular mirrors artfully arranged into striking abstract architectural designs within a large open space—an empty train station somewhere near Andalusia. The camera draws our attention to the leaded windows decorated with the Star of David, evoking the analogy between gypsies and Jews, the two nomadic groups of persecuted people who have long been a part of Spanish history and who have helped to diversify its culture. The camera also studies a simple line of empty chairs, which (like the open space) await the performers and heighten our anticipation of what is to come.

Throughout the film the performers are positioned against sculpted blocks of light that change color and shape to enhance the instruments, costumes, and skin tones of the artists, demonstrating the rich variations and dramatic effects that can be achieved with the simplest materials—shapes, colors, light, movement, and sound. At times the camera encircles the performers, participating in the dance. There is frequently a movement between long shots of dancers in silhouette and

Throughout Saura's *Flamenco,* performers are positioned against sculpted blocks of light that change color and shape, emphasizing both purity and diversity.

extreme close-ups of the mouths, faces, and fingers of famed singers and musicians such as well-known guitarist Paco de Lucía. One performance begins with the silhouetted detail of fingers snapping against a yellow circle of light, creating animal shadows. When the camera reveals another orange circle below, against which we see the dancing legs of the seated performer, the two circles create a figure eight dramatically lit against a rich black background. In another performance, we see the black silhouette of a slender female dancer against a panel of white light, bordered on both sides with black. When she moves to her left, into the light and against the black background now bordered with white, we see the color of her silver-grey gown, which unifies the contrasting black and white blocks of light. The lighting repeatedly demonstrates the rich variations that can be achieved within narrow limits—the same dynamic demonstrated by the flamenco performers with their music and moves.

This minimalist aesthetic convinces us that less is more. Yet in the final number, a flamenco rock variation, a mass of beautiful young dancers dressed in ordinary street clothes stream into the space, their numbers multiplied by mirrored reflections, as the camera rises to an overhead shot of the whole ensemble and then moves up to the ornate ceiling of the station, ready to move outside into the city. As the end credits roll, we hear the banal sounds of urban traffic, reminding us that we have been released from two hours of total immersion in this intensely vibrant world of pure flamenco—this art form that is the most significant import and export in Spain, one that has flourished, proliferated, and diversified over many decades and throughout its many regions.

Después de tantos años returns to the early years of the transition, where the post-Franco era and this essay began. This reflexive sequel also returns to the three Panero brothers (of *Desencanto*) twenty years later (and ten years after the death of their mother) to assess how these subjects formed under Francoism are now performing at the close of the Socialist era. Although the project was originally proposed (first to Jaime Chávarri and then to Ricardo Franco) by the youngest brother Michi (who is a friend of *both* filmmakers), the three Paneros agreed to do the sequel only on the condition that they *not* be filmed together. Partly for this reason, Franco claims, "It is not a film on the Panero family, which no longer exists, but the story of three men of my generation, the story of *my* generation."[25] At the American Cinematheque screening of

the film in Los Angeles (February 25, 1995), at which this comment was made, Franco also acknowledged the subjectivity of his own mediating directorial performance as well as his awareness that all three Panero brothers are consummate actors who have created fictional personae in the film—personae based on a tissue of extravagant lies. Thus Franco claims that *Después de tantos años* is really a fiction film rather than a documentary, but no less powerful or valid in telling the story of his generation and its subjectivity. Yet what the sequel reveals is not new insights about the brothers and their complex relations but rather the powerful impact the first film had on the Panero family and its culture. Freely poaching and reinscribing footage from *El desencanto* (the way Guerin did with *The Quiet Man* in *Innisfree*), this reflexive sequel destabilizes the constative meaning of the original and any lingering promise of plenitude, transforming the documentary referent into a series of performative moments.

Like Michael Apted's British documentary series *28 Up* (1984), Franco's sequel extends its case study into a serial diagnosis of Spanish culture that is able to broaden and deepen the historical context against which it reads its subjects and their deterioration, particularly that of the middle brother, Leopoldo María, a brilliant deranged poet now institutionalized in a sanitarium. Although all three brothers are depicted as desolate and alienated, a scene in which Leopoldo and Michi are shown walking together in a graveyard reveals that the dark humor of their sarcasm makes their misery more bearable for themselves and their audience. It is the eldest brother, Juan Luis, whose isolation is unrelieved, and whose disavowal of his misery seems most severe. This disavowal is expressed in the film through a series of beautiful landscapes that at first appear ironic, perhaps even evoking El Caudillo's notorious false vision of Francoist Spain as a peaceful forest. Yet as the film progresses, the beautiful images of nature (particularly when contrasted with the grating musical track) begin to provide relief for the spectator as well, or at least some consolation that the Panero miseries may be man made and therefore possibly avoidable or at least not necessarily repeatable—an assurance that makes the historical predicament of their generation all the more absurd.

All these Spanish documentaries exploit the subversive potential of the genre that was intensified under Francoism. They all challenge earlier representations of their subjects—a tendency that was strongest in the mid-1970s and mid-1990s as Spain headed either out of or into a major political transition. Their reflexive meditations on artistic representation and cultural transformation became more expansive in the first decade of the Socialist era, whether focusing on specific tropes (such as transsexualism and exile) or on abstractions (such as history and light). Instead of providing a mastery of knowledge, they demand active participation from their spectators to fill in the gaps and assess the film's relationship to history. By adopting a performative approach to documentary, these works acknowledge the "fictional" nature of their representations and thereby imply there are various versions of the past, which frees their subjects from being doomed to repeat any one of them. Rather, these films imply that subjects can choose to refigure themselves and their nation by performing an action as simple and regenerative as the singing of a *canción,* the dancing of a jig or fandango, or the painting of a quince tree.

Notes

1. Román Gubern, "he Civil War: Inquest or Exorcism?" in special issue, "Remapping the Post-Franco Cinema," ed. Marsha Kinder, *Quarterly Review of Film and Video* 13, no. 4 (1991): 111.

2. Susan Scheibler, "Constantly Performing the Documentary: The Seductive Promise of *Lightning over Water,*" in *Theorizing Documentary,* ed. Michael Renov (New York and London: Routledge, 1993), 146, 149.

3. Michael Renov, "Introduction: The Truth about Non-Fiction," in his *Theorizing Documentary,* 3.

4. Bill Nichols, *Blurred Boundaries: Questions of Meaning in Contemporary Culture* (Bloomington and Indianapolis: Indiana UP, 1994). As if in response to Renov's work, Nichols added "the performative mode" to the four historical categories of documentary he had earlier theorized in *Representing Reality.*

5. For a perceptive reading of this film and its political implications, see Marvin D'Lugo, *The Films of Carlos Saura: The Practice of Seeing* (Princeton: Princeton UP, 1991), 23–28.

6. Kathleen M. Vernon, "Crossing City Limits: Fiction, Documentary, History in Basilio Martín Patino's *Madrid,*" in *Cine-Lit II: Essays on Peninsular Film and Fiction,* ed. George Cabello-Castellet, Jaume Martí-Olivella, and Guy H. Wood (Portland, Oreg.: Portland State UP, 1995), 183.

7. Carlos Fernández Cuenca, *30 años de documental de arte en España* (Madrid: Escuela Oficial de Cinematografía, 1967).

8. See my *Blood Cinema: The Reconstruction of National Identity in Spain* (Berkeley and Los Angeles: U of California P, 1993), 200–204.

9. Andrew Parker and Eve Kosofsky Sedgwick, "Introduction: Performativity and Performance," in *Performativity and Performance,* ed. Andrew Parker and Even Kosofsky Sedgwick (New York and London: Routledge, 1995), 5.

10. Thomas Elsaesser, "European Television and National Identity: or 'What's There to Touch When the Dust Has Settled?'" (unpublished paper presented at "Turbulent Europe: Conflict Identity and Culture," a conference held in London, July 1994).

11. Gubern, 112.

12. Marvin D'Lugo, "Catalán Cinema: Historical Experience and Cinematic Practice," *Quarterly Review of Film and Video* 13, nos. 1–3 (1991): 131–47.

13. Gubern, 112.

14. Marvin D'Lugo, "Almodóvar's City of Desire," in Kinder, ed., "Remapping the Post-Franco Cinema," 48.

15. David Garland, "A Ms-take in the Making? Transsexualism Post-Franco, Post-Modern, Post-Haste," in Kinder, ed., "Remapping the Post-Franco Cinema," 96.

16. It would be possible to take a similar approach with *El desencanto,* that is, using well-known American documentaries like *Grey Gardens* (1975) and *Crumb* (1994) to reposition the Spanish film in a global context and to thereby better appreciate the cultural specificity of its depiction of the Spanish family.

17. Vernon, 175.

18. Ibid., 180.

19. Ibid., 178.

20. This discussion of Erice's film builds on my earlier analysis included in the epilogue to *Blood Cinema,* 444–47.

21. Press kit for *El sol del membrilla* (Lerner and Lerner, 1991).

22. Scheibler, 138.

23. Press kit for *The Flower of My Secret* (Sony Pictures Classics, 1996), 12.

24. Michel Foucault, *The Order of Things: An Archaeology of the Human Sciences,* trans. Les Mots et les Choses (New York: Random House, 1970), ch. 1.

25. Comments made by Ricardo Franco at the American Cinematheque screening of *Después de tantos años* in Los Angeles, February 25, 1995.

DONA M. KERCHER

The Marketing of Cervantine Magic for

a New Global Image of Spain

This essay, primarily on Manuel Gutiérrez Aragón, maps out what at first glance are two contradictory cultural moments of that most symbolic year, 1992: whereas the Spanish Ministry of Culture was releasing a montage of Orson Welles's *Don Quixote,* Spanish national television (RTVE, or TVE) was broadcasting Gutiérrez Aragón's adaptation of Cervantes's masterpiece. While Welles modernized the *Quixote,* Gutiérrez Aragón paradoxically remained faithful to the original. I say paradoxically for Gutiérrez Aragón had made other more daring adaptations of Cervantes's work previously, namely *Maravillas* (1980) and *La noche más hermosa* (The Most Beautiful Night, 1984). Furthermore, the latter can be read as an indictment of the very kind of project Gutiérrez Aragón was now directing. As I will argue in this essay, his two earlier films require an intertextual reading that is more faithful to the original texts than is his later TV adaptation. In the process of tracing Gutiérrez Aragón's use of Cervantes' texts, I will explore the new role that "Cervantes" has played in the reorganization of power since the death of Franco. By no means am I suggesting that a single individual's discourse can shape and order the cultural terrain; instead, I am proposing the Gutiérrez Aragón's films can be seen as an event through which we can gain access to the enormous changes that have taken place in the political, economic, and cultural life of Spain during the past two decades. I propose that these two films in their gaps and discontinuities are representative of an emergent discourse on hybridity whose potential dissonance is absorbed and repackaged by the dominant cultural hegemony as the crowning achievement of the Spanish Socialist government.

The Persistence of Cervantes in Cultural History

Throughout the twentieth century, Cervantes—understood as texts, cultural sign, and commodity—has played a salient role in the articulation of Spanish national identity. In his 1991 study *Cien años de urbanidad* (One Hundred Years of Urbanity)—whose very title evokes Gabriel García Márquez's masterpiece and thus slyly differentiates Spanish "urbanity" from Latin American "solitude," the sociologist Amando de Miguel codifies descriptively and prescriptively current social mores through allusions to *Don Quixote.* De Miguel uses the novel to show that class distinctions endure in contemporary Spain, that the nation aspires intellectually only to TV literacy, and that it now readily accepts the public display of wealth. Like the books of etiquette that he studies, de Miguel's social history is a manual for the new ruling class. He circumscribes his intended audience when he praises José María Aznar, then the up-and-coming opposition leader, now the prime minister, for his clever and properly handwritten acknowledgment of de Miguel's book *Fantasía fiscal* (Fiscal Fantasy).[1]

Although de Miguel's work is confined to the world of Spanish book-readers, the extent of the identification of the new Spanish ruling class and of the Spanish government itself with Cervantes is greater.[2] On March 21, 1991, the Spanish Cortes institutionalized this identification by passing a law establishing the Instituto Cervantes (IC), an international network of Spanish cultural centers. Although the Instituto Cervantes was intended to work in conjunction with the Ministries of Education and Culture, it was organized autonomously under the direction of Asuntos Exteriores, the Spanish equivalent of the State Department. With a head office in Madrid, the Instituto Cervantes created or reaffiliated forty branches in international capitals and other major cities in Europe, Asia, Africa, and America.[3] Each Instituto Cervantes branch organizes its own cultural events, serving as a forum for visiting Spanish and Hispanic authors, filmmakers, and artists. From its inception, film was envisioned as a significant part of the project. The larger institutes, such as those in New York, Paris, and Rome set up *videotecas,* free lending libraries of Spanish feature films and documentaries on video for educational use. Román Gubern, a prominent Spanish film critic and occasional filmmaker, was named head of the Instituto Cervantes in Rome. Although the PP government has frozen the IC budget and forced it to look to private funding to underwrite any new sites, such as the one in Chicago, film and video continue to figure strongly in the current marketing strategy. The new IC director, Santiago de Mora-Figueroa, Marqués de Tamarón, has moved to expand the IC Web site (www.cervantes.es) by the end of 1996. According to *El País* (October 30, 1996, 39), Tamarón is counting on the IC to earn auxiliary funds off the Web from the sale of videos, CD-ROMS, films, and music. The IC marks a moment of cultural ascendancy and the concomitant desire to promote diverse cultural practices abroad that can be taken as signs of a new Spain.[4]

Given that the Spanish government decided to market its cultural hegemony under the sign of Cervantes, it should not surprise us that as part of its participation in the quincentenary celebration of Columbus, the Spanish Ministry of Culture should acquire the rights to Orson Welles's unfinished movie *Don Quixote.* In the commemorative project "Don Quijote y Don Juan: la seducción de la utopía" (Don Quixote and Don Juan: The Seduction of Utopia), for Expo '92 (the world's fair in Seville), they projected a montage of Welles's "lost" footage. In connection with this event, the Asociación de Directores de Escena de España (Association of Spanish Stage Directors) crossed artistic boundaries and published a special critical volume on film, *Don Quijote,* which includes a Spanish translation of sequences from Welles's script and articles by film critics Juan Cobos and Esteve Riambau.[5] There is a beckoning subliminal logic here—that if the great Welles was obsessed with Spain, then the rest of the world should buy into its images, too.

Welles's "lost" footage is itself a "modern" *Quixote.* The film transposes the action to a city full of cars and motorcycles, drugstores and junkyards, radios, televisions, and movie cameras. As cited in Cobos's copy of the script, the initial sequence opens with Rocinante tied to a lamppost and Don Quixote a first-time spectator at a movie. The enchantment here is a period movie, and predictably Don Quixote attacks the bad guy, whom he confuses with the movie screen itself, the enchanter seen as the technological mode of production. Assailing the screen is not enough for Don Quixote. He futilely searches for the "voice," the speaker(s), as Welles writes: "We see the speakers. Don Quixote's sword, impotent against the soundtrack, continues to attack savagely, while fragments of the movie's violent action are projected on the face of the knight."[6] Although this opening scene from the script was apparently never filmed, many others that were show the disruption of modern technology, especially cinema.[7] This passage from the script, however, highlights the archival dilemma and critical problematic surrounding Welles's unfinished *Don Quixote*—Welles's own dramatic voice. He intended both to appear on screen as a director and to dialogue in voice-overs with the characters. Dubbed in Spanish, the Expo '92 montage could not authentically reconstruct the latter.[8]

Given the fragmentary nature of the Welles artifact and the self-reflexive attack of its modes of production in the opening and other scenes,[9] it is surprising that in 1994 Gutiérrez Aragón used a dismissive tone when recounting that he had seen the montage at Expo '92.[10] In his opinion Welles's montage resembled a "home movie" and must be understood as a prospectus, or film pilot, in the context of Welles's never-ending search for funds to complete the ambitious *Quixote* feature-film he envisioned. These remarks might well reflect and/or deflect an anxiety of influence inasmuch as Gutiérrez Aragón's directorial style, or more broadly, authorship, is heavily invested in exploring the nature of representation itself.[11] They also signal the shifting status of Cervantes in refashioning Spain, a theme that has a prominent position within the corpus of Gutiérrez Aragón's production.

The Reception of Gutiérrez Aragón Prior to *Maravillas*

Of the ten feature films Gutiérrez Aragón has directed since 1965, *Maravillas* (1980) marks a critical and technical break. The three movies that preceded it—*Camada negra* (Black Brood, 1977), *Sonámbulos* (Sleep-walkers, 1978), and *El corazón del bosque* (The Heart of the Forest, 1978)—were dark and difficult dramas. They are rooted in the historical specificity of the Franco era. Each was inspired initially by remembered actions of political protest. The viewer feels cornered with the threatening knowledge respectively, of fascist perversions, family betrayal of political allegiance, and the sadness of ineffective militancy. Although the violence and explicit sexuality in these movies mark them as post-Franco films, they are constrained by a certain view of what constitutes politics. All three movies question the implicit assumption that the seizure of power is a first step to bring about social change. It was becoming apparent that after Franco's death the catalyst for social change could be cultural transformation. Gutiérrez Aragón's explanation to the interviewer Augusto M. Torres of why he left the Communist Party in 1977 just when it was legalized illuminates this shift and helps us see his career in a larger context of the role of the intellectual in democratic Spain: "The Communist Party demands, or at least demanded, a great discipline of militancy, and a certain ideological discipline. Both things were desired by the militants just as the man who professes in a religious order wants strict norms. That seems necessary to me in the same way that it disturbs me fundamentally and intellectually. Besides I do not really understand a Communist Party that is not revolutionary and somehow not insurrectional or something like that. To be a social-democratic party, the P.S.O.E. is already in place."[12] These three "ideological escape" movies of the late 1970s refract Gutiérrez Aragón's search for a new pluralistic role for the intellectual in the Socialist era. It is against this background that we must start to understand the absence of overt political actions in both *Maravillas* (1980) and *La noche más hermosa* (1984).

Upon the release of *Corazón del bosque,* which immediately preceded *Maravillas,* a debate ensued around the question of adaptation. The title's allusion to Conrad's *Heart of Darkness* fueled the debate. In interviews, Gutiérrez Aragón denied he had adapted Conrad's novel and emphasized the historical specificity of the maquis.[13] Nonetheless, the allusion to Conrad opened previously closed doors. *Corazón del bosque* was the first Gutiérrez Aragón movie to play at the Alphaville theater in Madrid. This movie house is known for showing international movies in their original, subtitled versions; few Spanish movies ever play there. The prestige of playing there launched the movie critically, giving it an international patina, if not an international market. Whatever lessons Gutiérrez Aragón learned from this debate, he certainly divested them in *Maravillas.*

Maravillas's Restaging of a Culturally Diverse Spain

Maravillas's tenuous narrative thread overtly follows a jewel robbery and subsequent fencing of the goods by a juvenile gang. The female protagonist, a young girl named Maravillas, becomes involved with the robbery. The movie opens onto a traveling shot of a Madrid street populated with young people loitering, smoking, and moving to a reggae beat. The movie ends with a sustained medium shot of Maravillas and her father on the rooftop terrace of their building. The statue of Don Quixote and Sancho on the Plaza de España is clearly visible behind and between the two of them.[14] Structured by this trajectory of images, *Maravillas* progresses from the realistic portrayal of a contemporary issue to the symbolic reworking of cultural icons. In the early 1980s juvenile delinquency was a "hot topic" in Spain, which could be found not only in *Maravillas,* but also in Carlos Saura's *Deprisa deprisa* (Fast, Fast, 1980). Both filmed masterfully by Teo Escamilla, they responded not only to social but also to economic pressures. In 1981, Luis Megino, *Maravillas*'s producer, remarked in interviews on the need for Spanish cinema to reach the true moviegoing public, the fifteen- to twenty-five-year-olds, who filled the houses for American movies. Presumably this segment would be attracted to Spanish movies that have protagonists of their own age. Whereas Saura relied on elements from gangster movies and on the style of popular American adventure pictures to "sell" his delinquents, Gutiérrez Aragón paradoxically turned to *Don Quixote.* While Saura "humanized" the delinquents,[15] Gutiérrez Aragón transformed the world of delinquents into "a magical universe, but at the same time very realistic, a world deep down very Cervantine," for like La Mancha, it is "an actual place where magical episodes take place . . . something typical of Spanish culture."[16]

The initial and closing images of *Maravillas* delineate this transformation, which produces a hybrid text. It is not an adaptation of Cervantes's novel, but the intertextual play between novel and film constructs a symbolic realm that defines both works as versions. In this process *Maravillas* constructs an image of a culturally diverse and newly culturally tolerant Spain.

A New *Convivencia*

Maravillas broke new cultural ground in Spanish cinema by portraying the Jewish community of contemporary Madrid, literally entering a Madrid synagogue. Conversely, Jewish uncles of Maravillas's come to an important family gathering: Maravillas's First Communion party. The situation is highly original in its evocation of a medieval *convivencia* of religions, of Jews and Christians living more or less peacefully together. Maravillas is an only child being raised by her father, Fernando. Her mother is dead. Her Sephardic "uncles" (the film does not make clear whether they are blood relatives or family friends), a formidable trio, maintain a close watch over her, by overwhelming and excluding the bumbling father. One early stunning sequence opens on the roof of Maravillas's urban apartment building, where the party is in progress. A makeshift canopy covers chairs and food in the center of the terrace. A number of shots show latticework dividers, which visually prefigure the dividers that segregate the congregation in the later synagogue sequences. The music, whose theme reappears throughout the film, is a haunting, majestic Middle Eastern melody from Hipolyto Ivanov's "Procession of the Sardow." When Maravillas appears in her white Communion dress, the "uncles" fuss over her and then walk, almost in processional, with her around the perimeter of the roof terrace. The music, decor, and movements add a different cultural layer to the Communion party, so clearly identified visually in Maravillas's dress, with the Bat Mitzvah, the Jewish rite of passage of girls into womanhood. The movements of the "uncles" are like the rabbi's and elders' encircling of the temple toward the end of the ceremony.

Quixotic Motifs

Through the personages of the father, Fernando, and the *padrino* (godfather) Salomón, the favorite Jewish "uncle," *Maravillas* sets in play two principal networks of quixotic motifs or stories. It juxtaposes old and new modes of representation. Besides the finalized ideal vantage point of two focal planes in *Maravillas*'s ending, where Maravillas's father foregrounds the Quixote statue of the Plaza de España, there are numerous other sequences in which the father Fernando reminds us of Don Quixote.

To begin with, Fernando is played by Fernando Fernán Gómez, who starred as the knight in Roberto Gabaldón's *Don Quijote cabalga de nuevo* (Don Quixote Rides Again, 1972). The enmeshing of Fernán Gómez's real-life career as actor and director of twenty-three movies is pronounced,[17] for *Maravillas* places the character Fernando behind the camera as a minimally successful portrait photographer. In one sequence

Say "Yes." Maravillas (Cristina Marcos) stands next to Fernando (Fernando Fernán Gómez) as he takes a publicity photo of the actor who plays Chessman.

he stands behind the camera in his home studio taking a publicity photo of a truly homely actor, a job sent his way by a relative. In a series of shot/reverse shots between subject and photographer, we see Fernando's sole, repeated direction to say "yes" in English and the resultant frozen smiles of the portraits. It is not too far-fetched to extrapolate that portrait photography, as represented by Fernando, is no longer at the center of Spanish culture or consumer desires, having been usurped by other media, such as television and the movies, controlled mono-syllabically by Americans. Just as Don Quixote was ridiculed for his books of chivalry, Fernando is cast in a farcical role.

Fernando is obsessed with the ideal women of girlie magazines, which his friends, "priest," and family burn in a final *escrutiño* (scrutiny of the library). This Quixote allusion is established in an early time-lapse sequence of the father reading one of his magazines, napping, and awakening on a fainting sofa. The sequence of incipient madness through reading stands out for its staged quality; the background is black, unlit, and the action is centered on Fernando. An analogous, and more extensive use of time-lapse shots and the same couch prop centers on the daughter Maravillas.[18]

Whereas these early time-lapse sequences taken in isolation are conventional techniques for narrative characterization, perhaps inviting later psychoanalysis, the stilling of the gaze that occurs in the time-lapse dissolve and the freeze-frame in the movie's ending are connected to the narrative code in yet another way, and as such comments on modes of production. Just as Don Quixote visits a print shop in Barcelona and comments on the nature of reality as representation,[19] Fernando is caught up in the production of his own anachronistic story. Like Quixote defending the novels of chivalry, Fernando is marginalized in contemporary society as a portrait photographer and as a defender of an old *tertulia* (round-table) society of intellectuals who used to meet in his home. The marginalization is conveyed through the set decor and by the action. He reveals his dependence on his daughter by constantly trying to steal money from her purse. The neon lights advertising his studio face inward; they hang over and within the building's interior staircase and are seen from the point of view of the father standing inside the apartment saying good-bye to his daughter as she leaves the house for the day.

The print media responded to *Maravillas* in ways that recall the history of Cervantine criticism, particularly the "*Quixote* is a funny book" controversy. Matías Antolín was particularly incensed that his fellow movie critics were becoming excessively intellectual, too focused on metacriticism: "*Maravillas* possesses, according to its director, great doses of humor and irony, and we hope that the cryptic critics (in my opinion more than his films) succeed with greater ease in going beyond that shell of ferrous intellectualism that protects and hardens the work of Manuel Gutiérrez Aragón."[20] As an antidote Antolín invoked *Maravillas*'s food scenes, in which the father is manipulated by his daughter, and hence returned to the opening of *Don Quixote.* Cervantes characterized Don Quixote in part 1, chapter 1 by his diet: "A stew of rather more beef than mutton, hash on most nights, bacon and eggs on Saturdays, lentils on Fridays, and a pigeon or so extra on Sundays consumed three quarters of his income."[21] Likewise, Fernando's daily fare characterizes and limits him. One of his *desgracias* (misfortunes) is that his diet is controlled, manipulated by his daughter, not so much for more modern, weight-loss reasons as for economic ones, as was the case in the innkeeper's control over Don Quixote's diet. The daughter gives her father a solitary, little fried fish and then gobbles the baked ham herself. This control game climaxes symbolically in a much noted scene in which Fernando and Maravillas's former boyfriend are left to share a single fried egg, to eat their *huevo,* Spanish slang for "one testicle."

The other network is embodied in the *padrino,* who restages the "Retablo de maravillas." For readers of the *Quixote* the word *maravillas* evokes the chapters of the theater of Master Pedro, part 2, chapters 25–27. The traveling theater is announced by his page, "declarador de sus maravillas," "the boy who was to explain its wonders."[22] In this context "maravillas" refers to the illusions, the suspension of disbelief that occurs in theater. One traditional interpretation of the episodes of the intercalated theater of Master Pedro is to view it as a reprise of the windmills of part 1. Don Quixote attacks the puppets to save Melisendra because he cannot distinguish between reality and the theatrical illusion. More specifically, as Ruth El Saffar observes in *Beyond Fiction,* "This incident, for which Don Quixote's greater sensitivity, intelligence, and patience in Part II leave the reader ill-prepared, perfectly demonstrates the hidden control the dream of knight-errantry continues to exercise over him."[23]

The movie *Maravillas* has its own professional master of illusion with his traveling theater in the person of Salomón Toledo, according to the script, Maravillas's *padrino,* who is a wise, compassionate presence for her. We can read Gutiérrez Aragón's concept of "magical episodes" through the mise-en-scène of Salomón's theater, which is presented in three key locations: on the cornice of the rooftop theater, inside a theater, and in a vacant lot in Madrid.

But first it is necessary to contextualize Salomón's episodes. Salomón arrives at Maravillas's First Communion party with a gift, a ring. He makes her walk along the cornice of the rooftop terrace to get it, promising her that passing this test means she will never be afraid. Salomón's test leads to his being banished from the family circle. Years later he returns to Madrid and presents a show, the true story of the execution of the American bandit Caryl Chessman. As a member of the audience, Maravillas falls in love with the actor who plays Chessman. After the show, she becomes casually involved with the jewel robbery. When the pawnbroker (whom the delinquents were using as a fence) turns up strangled, everyone is suspected of the crime. Salomón returns to solve the mystery. With Maravillas and her father in the audience, he makes

Rite of passage: with Madrid as backdrop, Maravillas at her First Communion party walks along the edge of the roof toward her uncle Salomón.

the Chessman actor confess in a balancing-beam stunt that resembles Maravillas's earlier rooftop test.

Recalling the traveling theater of Master Pedro, which would have been a familiar event for the readers of Cervantes's time, Gutiérrez Aragón has commented in an interview how he witnessed the story of Chessman staged at the Torrelavega Fair.[24] In *Maravillas,* Gutiérrez Aragón stages both Chessman scenes in darkness. Salomón tells Chessman's tale on camera to the audience. In this telling he resembles both Master Pedro and the latter's page, who also narrates the anachronic balladic rescue of Melisendra from the Moors by her husband Gaiferos. When Don Quixote becomes aroused (because he sees Gaiferos outnumbered by Moors), he hacks all the puppets to pieces, which also abruptly ends the evening show. A long exchange between Master Pedro and Don Quixote follows in which they set the amount of restitution for each of the damaged puppets, "in good Castilian currency."[25] It is a multiple-version story about loss, restitution, and reconciliation—Gaiferos rescuing his wife and Master Pedro (who compares himself to Rodrigo lamenting the loss of Spain) being paid for his broken puppets. The

Salomón Toledo and Maravillas walk in the vacant lot/theater of Madrid.

climax of Don Quixote's exchange after the rumpus is a legalistic restitution in which he does not admit ultimate guilt but nonetheless
declares a perceived personal liability: "The fault is not mine, but that of
the wicked beings who persecute me" (575). Don Quixote maintains,
"Nevertheless, I am willing to shoulder the expenses of this error of
mine, though no ill will lay behind it" (575). I would suggest that
Quixote's spirit of liberality allegorically suggests a Christian reconciliation with Moorish heritage at the contemporary moment of Cervantes's age.

Comparing the sequences in which Salomón appears, we see in all of
them the image of staging. The most obvious are the interior theater
segments, but the most revealing is the second encounter of Maravillas
with her uncle in a vacant lot in Madrid. Unlike the junkyard locale that
is associated with the youth gang and where the pawnbroker is mur-
dered, this setting looks like a construction site, where urbanization
projects continue. It has a barrenness to it, but one pregnant with
potential development and economic progress. The parking garage behind the actors simulates the horizontal plane of the stage platform,
making the viewer aware of the composition of the scene. It is a bizarre
sequence in the movie because it is virtually unmotivated. After the

Salomón narrates his show, the execution of the bandit Caryl Chessman.

theatrical execution, Maravillas and Salomón appear to be walking in a vacant lot. The most sustained shot of the sequence is the light inverse of the gas chamber theater tableau with Chessman. The buildings, which tower behind Maravillas and Salomón, rise around them like the verticals of the isolation booth or stage set. In his review of *Maravillas,* Jesús Fernández Santos remarked on the lack of fusion between old and new Spain in Gutiérrez Aragón's version of the "Retablo de Maese Pedro": "So appears this new puppet theater (*retablo*), titled very appropriately *Maravillas,* modern in its form and at once so Spanish in its double watershed referring to present day Spain and to that which looks toward the other Jewish Spain. They extend a hand to one and other, more juxtaposed than fused, by means of a few characters who revolve around the pair of protagonists."[26]

It is important to recognize that the placing of these elements on the same "magical" stage, whether Madrid or the theater, makes the spectator look at them anew. Repeatedly the reviewers commented how very different, and artistic, their Madrid looked in *Maravillas.* For instance, Pedro Crespo wrote in the newspaper *ABC:* "Maravillas has a threshold of accessibility. Once crossed over, the movie entices and fascinates with the unusualness of its images of a new and almost esoteric Madrid, within its precise formation."[27]

"Maravillas" and Prophecy

This emphasis on intertextual reading and attention to mise-en-scène makes one return to *Don Quixote* to look at the details of the *retablo* episode in a more cinematic sense. For example, the celebration of special lighting in the inn—"Don Quixote and Sancho obeyed him and went to where the puppet theater was already set up and uncovered, surrounded with small candles that made it look bright and attractive"[28]—reminds us of our entering a theater or cinema, which is what we do in *Maravillas*. In these preparatory sequences to the "retablo de maravillas" one is also more aware of segmentation. By "reading" the two versions together, the reader of *Don Quixote* is struck by the passages where "maravillas" are discussed. These are not the spectacle of theater itself, but the critical framing of it in the segments of the *mono adivino* (divining ape). In this episode, Master Pedro prepares his visits to towns to present his plays in several stages: he first sends someone ahead to learn about his audience and what has happened in the town; then he arrives with his monkey who reveals these facts to the townspeople and spectators. The monkey show precedes the plays, foregrounding the intertextual theatrical illusion. When Don Quixote and Sancho confront Master Pedro's monkey, Master Pedro clearly tells them his limits: "Señor," he said, "this animal gives no answer or information about things that are to come. Of things past he knows something, and more or less of things present" (566). Sancho is humorously content with this answer, for he wants to check on what his wife is up to in his absence. Don Quixote wants to know about the veracity of his experience at Montesinos. The basis of the knight's distrust is much more philosophical, theological:

I am led to believe this by observing that the ape only answers about things past or present, and the devil's knowledge extends no further. He knows the future only by guesswork, and that not always, for it is reserved for God alone to know the times and the seasons. For him there is neither past nor future, all is present.

This being true, as it is, it is clear that this ape speaks in the devil's style. I am astonished that they have not denounced him to the Holy Office. (568)

Don Quixote denounces the heresy of false prophecy, not just of card readers and Master Pedro's monkey. In the seventeenth century a discussion of an unconventional prophecy implied suspicion of Jewish heritage. In satirical texts, such as Quevedo's *Sueños* (Visions), Jews were described as those still waiting for the Messiah. I do not mean to suggest that we all return to the Américo Castro controversies, to a search for *conversos* (converts). What I do want to propose is that we read the questioning of heritage, the problematic of what prophecy is, as the crux of a metacritical discussion of the nature of art and illusion in both Cervantine "maravillas."

As in *Don Quixote,* three separate, but analogous sequences with the illusionist Salomón invite the spectator to consider the role of prophecy in *Maravillas.* At the First Communion party Salomón puts Maravillas through a test, walking on the roof's edge, and predicts that its successful completion means she will not know fear. This instance resembles the conventional ideal of prophecy—a prediction of the future. However, when in a later sequence Salomón forces a blindfolded Chessman into a similar edge game, that is, to walk a balance beam on stage, Chessman confesses his role in the murder of the pawnbroker to the audience of Salomón, Maravillas, and Fernando. What was a predictive test is now modified and used to reveal the *past* of the assassin Chessman. Not surprisingly, the prophetic protection of the uncle's test fails Maravillas. She is moody, she cries, and Salomón now repeats his edge game a third time with Chessman's little daughter. In a sense, Maravillas is led to focus on and try to understand "the things past and present."

Marginalization

Although I have just retold the tripartite story of life on the edge in a straightforward Hollywood style of situation, complication, and resolution, *Maravillas*'s narrative unity is far from this Hollywood model. Gutiérrez Aragón himself described *Maravillas*'s compositional unity in the following terms: "It seems that it is composed of elements that are very distinct from one another, but which are deep down a type of tonal variation on the consciousness of marginalization, since it does not always deal with the marginalized, but with people who consider themselves marginalized. . . . The reason is that today everyone considers himself a little marginalized. Even people who have a good social position also have a certain consciousness of marginalization as if the centers of power, the centers of decisions, were always far from us."[29]

Their marginalization, then, is an ontological category, as much as a sociological or political alienation. The juxtaposition of movie and novel encourages us to read the symbolic register of both. It reemphasizes the discussion of prophecy and posits structures of religious and ethnic tolerance in both texts. Our reading underscores the recuperation of lost heritage—Moorish and perhaps converso in the *Quixote,* and Jewish in *Maravillas,* in which the First Communion sequences stress the convivencia of Jews and Christians, the cultural diversity of the new Spain. The movie participates in a social process of constituting a new image of Spain.

La noche más hermosa: Reimagining Sexuality as a Cultural Process

Like *Maravillas* (in which Fernando is reflexively depicted as an image maker), Gutiérrez Aragón's 1984 film *La noche más hermosa* also depicts directing, in this case a comic theatrical adaptation for Spanish television of a fictitious literary classic. While the TV movie is ostensibly staging Molière, in the feature movie the characters engage in actions that parallel the plot motifs of "El curioso impertinente," (The Story of Ill-Advised Curiosity), an intercalated novel in *Don Quixote* (pt. 1; chaps. 33–35), and *El celoso extremeño* (The Jealous Hidalgo), one of Cervantes's *Novelas ejemplares* (Exemplary Novels).[30] Whereas *Maravillas* foregrounds the questions of convivencia and marginalization, *La noche más hermosa* reimagines sexuality as a cultural process, for here intertextual shifts in simulation produce the effect of stimulation.[31]

As the movie unfolds, *La noche más hermosa* does not explore the antithetical positions of film and television. Instead, it describes their compatibility, their simultaneity, and ultimately the capital efficacy of their coexistence. In short, it reframes the tension between film and TV not in terms of screens, but in terms of pleasure. The movie fuses the issue of how desire is formed, charged, and inflected within the social

In *La noche más hermosa,* transsexual actress Bibi Andersen is cast as Doña Inés.

body around the image of Bibi Andersen, a well-known transsexual, who at a certain moment was synonymous with the art of Almodóvar and the gay world of the *Movida,* the youth culture movement that emerged in Madrid after the death of Franco. Bibi's involvement in *La noche de Don Juan* (later renamed *La noche más hermosa*) is due to the persistence of the top television executives. They are enamored of Bibi's screen presence and insist on casting her. Since she/he must star, they settle on the role of Doña Inés; but the production falters because the love scenes are a disaster and no actor will risk playing Don Juan opposite Bibi.

Off the television set, Bibi Andersen plays the mistress of *La noche*'s producer Federico. He visits her apartment early in the movie and they make love, in the daylight, under white satin sheets. She emerges from bed wearing plain black underpants. What appears as an implausible act of modesty or visual censorship signals the overdetermination of Bibi's role. Both instances play with the idea that what you see is not all there is to see. Furthermore, they speak to changes in the modes of consuming an image. The spectator's response to Bibi's sexuality can point to an individualizing mode of viewing her as the desire to be different, or an identificatory one, identity in mass production. Rather than one superseding the other, these two modes coexist in Bibi Andersen's own experiential ambiguity, for in the movie she plays herself. This self doubles another actress, Bibi Andersson of Ingmar Bergman's films, among them *The Devil's Eye* (1960) in which Don Juan returns to tempt a virgin bride-to-be played by the Swedish Bibi. This doubling creates a nostalgia for fullness that in this particular case is already there in the question of who is Bibi Andersen.

Within the framework of film studies, various feminist theorists (such as Kaja Silverman, Laura Mulvey, and Teresa de Lauretis) have analyzed the gaze in its relation to and recuperation of visual pleasure as it is threatened by the image of woman on film. This form of visual pleasure is not exclusively male, but is predicated on a masculine subject position available to both male and female viewers. Thus, we may conceive the gaze directed toward Bibi Andersen not as the representation of sexuality, but of the empty space of that which threatens the gaze: nothing. Whether it is lack or excess does not really matter. The movie makes room for all kinds of identifications and shifting alliances. Just like the characters inside the movie, the viewing subject is caught in the dynamics of voyeurism versus erotic fetishism. The movie links voyeuristic pleasure with a transgressive narrative of cuckoldry, or unfaithfulness and woman's guilt. It is at this crossroads that *La noche más hermosa* shifts from the filming of *Don Juan* to Cervantes. The movie gives credence to this linkage.

La noche's producer, who is having an affair with Bibi, is in the midst of a midlife crisis. While discussing his performance with Bibi, he imagines his young wife Elena unfaithful. To test Elena's fidelity, the producer actually bribes his best friend Oscar, also *La noche*'s first-time director, to play footsies with her at an evening dinner party at their house. The setting, particularly how the patio lights resemble photographic illumination, alerts the viewer to the artificiality or theatricality of the event. This test is simultaneously a tryout for a romantic part in the production. Thus Federico enacts the roles both of Cervantes's Carrizales, the excessively jealous and aging husband of *El celoso extremeño,* who imagines and simulates his wife's infidelity; and of Cervantes's Anselmo, the "impertinent" husband who stages his wife's adultery with his best friend. Before this tryout, it is Bibi who has defined the signs of a woman in love when she talks with Federico about his wife's possible infidelity. According to Bibi, telltale signs of a woman in love are when the woman sighs, when she jumps to answer the phone first, and when "she lingers contemplating the heavens" (se queda contemplando el cielo).

Federico's fears come to pass when his wife's gaze is elsewhere—that is, fixed on the TV set. Absorbed by the television, Elena sighs. When the husband hears her sigh, he imagines her infidelity and doubts her attachment to him. As Federico imagines her infidelity, the camera swings around to Federico's sighting of Elena. The camera places Elena in Federico's line of sight to the television and thereby connects her to his simulated reality. This shot recalls the ending of *Maravillas* discussed earlier. In *La noche más hermosa* the television now occupies the deep-shot position of the statue of Don Quixote and Sancho.

It is only fitting that the modern house containing this scene of infidelity between the middle-aged husband and the young wife be itself enveloped by the blue light of the television tube, which colors virtually the entire movie.[32] Although much of the movie's action occurs on a sound stage, Estudios Bronston, the lighting obviates the difference between interior and exterior shots. The night sky "outside," for example, is always the same blue color as the fake night sky on the sound stage; the light in their dining room is the same as in their bedroom. Due to the married couple's attachment to the television in all of its manifestations—as site of production, viewing apparatus, and product—there is no difference between public and private spaces, or between state television narratives and home bedroom scenarios. This collapse is a symbolic intensification of the photo studio sign in *Maravillas* hung over an interior staircase, advertising inward. Everything is simulation.

Not only does Federico incorporate Cervantes's husbands' identities, but also as a product of TV and its codes of behavior, he is his own double. Whereas in Cervantes's novela ejemplar the lover Loaysa has to breach the splendid house/fortress in which the husband guards his wife, "television" has already done in Federico. In a world defined as simulation, there is nothing else to do but further simulation. Federico proposes to Elena, played by Victoria Abril, that she pretend she is sexually attracted to Luis, the chief executive of TVE, who is played by Fernando Fernán Gómez. Like a ruler in a Golden Age drama, Luis is also an amateur astronomer, waiting for the appearance of a comet, his "noche más hermosa."

Eager to be the star, Elena approaches Luis on a hilltop as a crowd awaits the comet. Instead of seducing Luis, she confesses Federico's scheme. Compassionately, he tells her of Federico's affair with Bibi, commenting, "What a queer!" (¡Qué maricón!). She, nonplussed, replies she has known for a long time, a response that echoes Cervantes's text's stressing the excessive and hence questionable sexuality of both the husband Carrizales and the young lover Loaysa. The chief executive then reveals, "I who have always been a man without any sexual perversions, but who I really like . . ."[33] "Is Bibi," answers Elena for him, and subsequently makes a deal to help Luis obtain Bibi's favors in exchange for Bibi's part of Doña Inés. Whereas the widow Leonora's decision to shun her lover reinscribes and affirms the traditional view of marriage and sexuality in *El celoso extremeño,* Elena's acts foreground the erotic and technical effects that are embodied by Bibi Andersen as simulation.

After this exchange, Elena is cast as Doña Inés. She appears to be in control when she defines who should play Don Juan—"the one who best simulates love"—and then adds, "someone who has to simulate as a profession."[34] Although the solution to this casting dilemma has not been determined, the answer is all too obvious: Bibi. Unaware of the various roles in which she has been scripted and has scripted, Elena must undergo more tryouts, now with the actors to play opposite her. More than an acting job is at stake when the husband behind the camera agonizingly coaches his wife to show she passionately loves Don Juan. Federico continues to be entrapped as Carrizales and Anselmo. Unshaven and wearing pajamas under a raincoat, Federico is at the peak of his distress in this scene. His attire alerts us to the underlying bedroom scene. The transgressive implication, seen on Federico's face, echoing the fatal distress of Carrizales in *El celoso extremeño,* is that simulation of adultery substitutes for reality; his perspective suggests Golden Age morality. The viewer, however, whirls with the camera following it around Elena/Doña Inés's bed, as the actress/wife obediently responds to direction. While this camera movement is most conventionally associated with the depiction of madness, the encircling is likewise a totalizing gesture, a moment like the intervention of a narrative "I" in Cervantes. The circularity makes it obvious that obedience and transgression are equivalent in parody and that the only crime, if there is one, is in cancelling the difference, to paraphrase Jean Baudrillard. Cervantes closes *El celoso extremeño* with the intervention of a narrative "I" preoccupied with the silence of Leonora in not protesting her innocence, that is, in not asserting the difference between simulation and reality: "The one thing I do not know is why Leonora did not make more of an effort to excuse herself and convince her jealous husband how guiltless she had been in that whole affair. But confusion tied her tongue, and the rapidity of her husband's death gave her no opportunity to exonerate herself."[35]

While chastising women for not speaking up, Cervantes reaffirms a hierarchy: men have voices; women, none. In *La noche más hermosa,* on the other hand, Bibi can speak up because gender has been displaced: she can occupy both masculine and feminine positions simultaneously.

At the end of *La noche más hermosa,* Bibi emerges triumphantly. She plots with the dissident union members to lock the bosses in the TV studio, moments before the comet's arrival. Her lock-in, unlike Carrizales's incarceration of his wife, is successful. Ironically, Federico exalts, "Television is one big family. The country works!"[36] Bibi is able to undertake the "masculine" strategy of Carrizales's lock-in and the "feminine" strategy of embracing the top executive Luis in "la noche más hermosa," in the movie's final scenes.

Bibi's embrace rationalizes the two conflicting quests that have driven the movie: on the one hand, the attempt to disavow the cleavage of its star and hence restore a disembodied gender to the visual; and on the other, the desire to complete the break absolutely and to naturalize the gender/identity split. It is the cultivation of lack itself and the congruent fetishization of technology that produces the lack. While this final embrace ensures the cancellation and conclusion of *La noche más hermosa,* it simultaneously allows the film to distance itself from commercial television as an inferior technology that is not willing to mine any simulation of wholeness.

As a movie about television, *La noche más hermosa* also engaged the conflictive history of *Maravillas,* which had elicited a torrent of protest letters to *TeleRadio,* a Spanish equivalent of *TV Guide,* when it first aired on Spanish television in 1983, the year before *La noche*'s release. While Gutiérrez Aragón received plenty of commentary, pro and con, about his depiction of the Jewish community in *Maravillas* from the popular press as they re-reviewed *Maravillas* for its TV release, the primary protest was not against the depiction of Jews. Instead, it was the reversal of power relations between generations (father and daughter) and genders (Maravillas was on top of her boyfriend in the sex act) that caused the

Confederación de Padres de Familia (Parents' Confederation) to condemn the movie for family viewing. In an editorial in *TeleRadio* entitled
"Censorship in Wonderland," José Carlos Arévalo came to the defense of
Maravillas and the medium: "A careful reading of the objecting letters
has convinced us that it wasn't the accusations of pornography, argued
on the first basis, but the spiritual sting that art always provokes when it
raises its head as mirror to society, which has moved pens and ball-
points. But in these times of crisis and transformation it is not going to
be RTVE who sweetens reality, and on its screen discriminates against
testimony to what is happening and against the art of our time."[37]

La noche más hermosa comments on *Maravillas*'s reception in an early
sequence in which Federico returns home from jogging. He saunters
into the living room, where his daughter is doing her homework. The
movie has cast her as a version of Maravillas, for she indirectly controls
his diet through her comments. She asserts her autonomy above all by
refusing to watch TV or to acknowledge her father's job. He asks her
about her homework and then turns the TV on with the remote. To his
query she blurts, "Fuck television!" Her straightforward, ethically correct rebellion inverts the desired paradigm of the Confederación de
Padres de Familia in a TV nation.

Through the use of various paradigms of simulation *La noche* re-
imagines and represents a sexuality entirely appropriate for a society
with new pluralistic ambitions. To accomplish this task, Gutiérrez
Aragón mines major as well as minor Cervantine texts. This approach
allows Cervantes to still function as a cultural icon through which
Spanish identity can be articulated. Although *La noche* is a superb
critique of TVE, it also indicates how Spanish public television responds
to transnational market pressures. Anxious for a homegrown media
industry with which to counteract and resist Hollywood's perennial
presence in the Spanish home, TVE bought the rights for television
broadcast two years before the movie opened, thus underwriting its own
critique. TVE can discount the ethical dimensions within such national
films as *La noche más hermosa* as long as the film maintains the affective
power of TVE and by extension Spain itself. In this heightened cultural
atmosphere traditional questions, including those of adaptation, give
way to market considerations, indicating perhaps that power in contemporary Spain is more than ever positional. Contrary to Gutiérrez Ara-

gón's sarcastic comments in an interview on his effect on TVE ("Certainly, some have begun to get mad already," and further, "Yes, and it was about time! I was hurt that they hadn't gotten mad.")[38] *La noche* did not prevent its director from being chosen to participate in one of TVE's major subventions for the quincentenary: the filming of *Don Quixote*.

TVE's *Don Quixote:* Conclusions

Unlike the U.S. and major European film industries that celebrated the Columbus quincentenary by releasing new films on the life and deeds of the explorer, Spanish TV judiciously distanced itself from the Genovese and followed the lead of the Spanish government, which recast the discovery and conquest of the Americas as "an encounter." In conjunction with the Cuban and Mexican Film Institutes, TVE subsidized Paul Le Duc's film *Barroco*. Inspired by Alejo Carpentier's novel *Concierto barroco,* but structured like a concerto in four movements, Le Duc's film begins by showing how music can serve as a cultural divide but ends by celebrating how it ultimately unites natives, conquerors, and slaves. In short, the film projects the discovery and conquest as an encounter that produces a hybrid culture in which differences are highlighted rather than erased. TVE's other major subvention for that most symbolic year was for the adaptation of Cervantes's masterpiece *Don Quixote*.

Because so many political and cultural trajectories we have been discussing converge in it—particularly the role of Cervantes in selling Spain and the way market forces affect the problematic of adaptation—it is instructive to review the combative history of this prestigious TV project. Its producer Emiliano Piedra (who had worked on Welles's *Don Quixote*) was given a financial go-ahead in 1988 in the final months of Pilar Miró's tenure (1986–89) as directora general de Radiotelevisión Española.[39] The ambitious *Quixote* project is strongly associated with Miró's artistic tenure and rightly or wrongly with what were perceived as excesses of that era. Conceived of as a two-part series, and as a "quality" program[40] that symbolized the high, even elitist cultural aspirations of the new Spain, Miró and Piedra contracted Camilo José Cela, the Nobel Prize–winning Spanish novelist (and an outrageous TV talk show personality), to write the script for a hefty fee. From the inception of this period piece, the producers had an international market in mind. Miró initially selected Manuel Gutiérrez Aragón to direct the first part and Mario Camus, the second.

Although Gutiérrez Aragón had won the commission for part 1 of the series, the battle for artistic control and public recognition was only beginning. When Gutiérrez Aragón saw Cela's script, he pronounced it unfilmable and threatened to leave the project. The conflict received a great deal of attention in the press. Eventually Gutiérrez Aragón was given free reign to rewrite it as he pleased albeit Cela continues to receive on-screen credit for the script.

It is important, moreover, to see the casting of this TV series and the images of Don Quixote and Sancho that consequently came to the screen in the context of Spanish film history, as much as in the context of Gustav Doré's engravings, Picasso's drawings, or the Lladró company's international line of Quixote figurines. Very early in the script development the role of Sancho was given to comic actor Alfredo Landa, who is best known recently for the box-office hit *La vaquilla* (The Heifer, 1985), which led to another typecast role in a 1992 comedy *La marrana* (The Sow, 1992). The casting of Fernando Rey, who has been celebrated internationally for his work in Luis Buñuel's films, as Don Quixote came much later. By casting major actors with international reputations who were now in the latter stages of their careers, the producers assured that Spanish viewers of the series would draw on a cinematographically defined "cumulative iconography."[41]

Part 1 of the *Quixote* TV series, first aired in the early months of 1992, received a large audience and favorable criticism in Spain. At a Cannes television festival the series also won prizes. These positive signs pushed the project forward despite major bureaucratic and economic upheavals, namely the demise of the TVE monopoly in the interim. Gutiérrez Aragón was contracted both to write and direct the second part (instead of Mario Camus as originally planned). Building on the TV success, each group of episodes of the two parts of the project were spliced together into a separate full-length feature film. These movies were exhibited in Spain and exported to film festivals in New York and Los Angeles, among other places. Since then, the series has been released on video as well. It might be argued that the episodic structure of Cervantes's work made it possible to recombine with commercial success the installments of the TV series into a full-length feature film.

As expected, many thousands of Spaniards, as well as foreigners with access to subtitled versions, happily bought the two-cassette video package of *Don Quixote,* put out by TVE, for their home video libraries. It is now a video classic that will perpetuate the story of Don Quixote, quite sophisticatedly, for more millions who will never read the book. For anyone with slightly more intimate knowledge of Cervantes's works, however, the video twosome is a disappointment because this viewer expects video 1 and video 2 to correspond to part 1 and part 2 of *Don Quixote.* They don't. The package adapts only material from part 1. Gutiérrez Aragón has said he will never film the novel's 1615 second book. Moreover, with the death of Fernando Rey in 1994, the Quixote of the TV series, it is unlikely, though not impossible, that anyone else will continue the TV project. Obviously what is lost in the representation of *Don Quixote* only as book 1 is the considerable intertextual play between the two books.

I do not intend in this essay to critique the TV series as a reading or version of *Don Quixote* beyond praising its high production values and situating it in a general context of an iterative use of Cervantes's text in recasting a national identity at a particular historical moment. The TV series presented itself overtly as literary adaptation, and most reviewers praised its "faithfulness" to the novel. One of the more interesting sequences for further study on literary adaptation is the beautiful sequence in part 2 of the series in which Cervantes the author appears as a character walking through a bazaar and picks up a page—the Arabic version of *Don Quixote*—stuck to the bottom of his boot. It is especially here, in the section dealing with chapters 8 and 9 of the novel, the first internal break in the first book (1605), that one can compare how filmic and literary languages handle transitions.

The novel *Don Quixote* presents itself as a copy, a translation from the Arabic, thereby marking its faithfulness for source material. But since these citations are fictitious, as problematized by the interventions of Cide Hamete Benengeli in the novel, and since, Cervantes's second part of the novel responds to Avellaneda's apocryphal Quixote continuation (as well as to Cervantes's own first part), we can call *Quixote* a modern hybrid. Gutiérrez Aragón makes a gesture to this hybridity in the TV series in the bazaar sequence just cited. However, as we have shown in our close readings, he went much further in this direction in both *Maravillas* (with its quixotic motifs) and *La noche más hermosa* (with its

The ivory tower office of Gutiérrez Aragón, first filmmaker to be chosen president of SGAE, exudes "a touch of nobility."

movie parodied within a movie), for the commodification of the filmic image is consistently mined in these films through the questioning of modes of representation. Unlike the TV series, they are postmodern hybrids, an emergent form of the new democratic Spain, which in some small way constituted the social reality, and which used Cervantes's texts as a filter to access a contemporary critique.

In sum, the contradictions of Gutiérrez Aragón directing a "faithful" *Quixote* TV series, after having parodied TVE's literary adaptations and the new corporate Spain and having sworn publicly for years that he would never do a television series, confirm Raymond Williams's observation about the cultural terrain as a dynamic field that is constantly being renegotiated.

We are left asking why Gutiérrez Aragón shifted his approach to Cervantes. One answer may lie in the two films that alternated with the Cervantine versions: *Demonios en el jardín* (Demons in the Garden, 1982) and *La mitad del cielo* (Half of Heaven, 1986). These films were his greatest box-office successes and continue to be the most available of his

Manuel Gutiérrez Aragón poses
in his SGAE office, May 1994.

films in subtitled versions in the United States. Their successes abroad
were partially due to accessible, more classical narrative structures.
While viewed within Spain as chronicles of specific decades of the
Franco era (*Demonios* of the '50s and *La mitad del cielo* of the '60s),
internationally each of these films accessed contemporary cinematic
subgenres—*Demonios* the cinematographer's "autobiographical" tale of
childhood, and *La mitad del cielo,* the feminist generational stories—
genres that had strong markets abroad. These economic triumphs may
have dampened his drive to explore Cervantes and the contemporary
national terrain through a more postmodern focus, and the favorable
reception of chronicles may have led to the less ambitious, yet historically "faithful" TV adaptation.

After his success with the *Quixote* TV series, Gutiérrez Aragón was
granted, in his own words, *un rasgo de nobleza* (a touch of nobility) by
being elected president of the Sociedad General de Autores de España
(General Society of Spanish Authors, SGAE). Until his term ended in
1995, he was literally ensconced in an ivory tower office of the SGAE's
palatial building in Madrid.[42] His election to the presidency of SGAE

was extremely symbolic. He was the first cinematographer to hold the position, which represents the legal rights of all Spanish authors internationally. As he explained it, Spain (like the rest of Europe) differs from the United States in that artistic rights rest ultimately with the author rather than with the producer. Although most current work of SGAE deals with music royalties and not directly with film, the election of Gutiérrez Aragón as titular head of SGAE signifies that the artistic rights of filmmakers have been officially recognized under the legal code. This institutionalization represents an economically based notion of directorial authorship and of the filmic image. From an economic legal angle, there are clear boundaries to artistic production and definable iterativeness to the filmic image. Whereas a movie such as *Maravillas* or *La noche más hermosa* crosses media boundaries between literature and film, this hybridization is rarely celebrated in official discourse. It is thus no surprise that as director of a Cervantes text Gutiérrez Aragón has come to the realization that not only did he perceive similar patterns of his previous work in Cervantes, but that there is a unity to the body of work of a director. Or does he realize that this unity is an artistic legal right to be defended?

When I was filming I came across many things that to me seemed from a movie invented by me. Which reaffirms for me the idea that the authorship of a film director does not come only from inventing a text. The unity that there is in the work of, for example, John Ford, comes from his director's side. It's a discovery that I've made after ten movies and a series, it was about time that I made it![43]

What is interesting about the trajectory of the career of Gutiérrez Aragón is not necessarily that he has now espoused a conservative auteurist position in film theory, but how his films raise interlinked questions of representation, cultural history, and hegemony.

Notes

1. Aznar, who was satirized in *Fantasía fiscal,* is lauded both for his business etiquette and for still being counted as a reader like Don Quixote. *Cien años de urbanidad: Crítica de costumbres de la vida española* (100 Years of Urbanity: Critique of Customs in Spanish Life) (Barcelona: Planeta, 1991), 111.
2. As I was finishing this essay, the *New York Times* published a front-page

article on Felipe González entitled "Spain's Modern Quixote Awaits a Final Tilt" (April 12, 1995). The article discloses that the prime minister keeps a copy of *Don Quixote* on his bedside table.

3. Although there were expanded directives and new funding associated with this parliamentary decree, in many cases the branch Instituto Cervantes assumed the functions and personnel of existing institutions. In New York City, for example, the Casa de España became the Instituto Cervantes in 1992 and Enrique Camacho continued as head of the newly named body.

4. The first director of the Instituto Cervantes, Nicolás Sánchez-Albornoz y Alboín, demonstrates his sensitivity to vestigial charges of postcolonial, cultural imperialism in the founding report: "Throughout the parliamentary debate that preceded its approval it became manifest that the objective of the Instituto and the reason for its creation is to promote and disseminate Spanish as a language belonging to the Spanish-speaking community and not only as the official language of Spain." (A lo largo del debate parlamentario que precedió a su aprobación quedó de manifiesto que el objetivo del Instituto y motivo de su creación es promover y difundir el español como lengua propia de la communidad hispanohablante no sólo como lengua oficial de España.) *Instituto Cervantes* 1992, publicity material, p. 9.

5. These critics subsequently wrote books—Cobos, *Orson Welles: España como obsesión,* and Riambau, *Orson Welles: Una España immortal*—for a two-volume luxury set published in 1993 jointly by four government cultural bodies, two national—Filmoteca Española and Ministry of Culture—and two from the Valencian autonomous region—ICAA and IVAWCM. This was Riambau's second book on Welles. The first was *Orson Welles: El espectáculo sin límites* (Barcelona: Fabregat, 1985).

6. "Vemos los altavoces. La espada de Don Quijote, impotente contra la banda sonora, continúa atacando encarnizadamente, mientras fragmentos de la violenta acción de la película se proyectan en el rostro del caballero." Orson Welles, "Secuencias de Don Quijote," in *Don Quijote,* trans. Juan Cobos, Publicaciones de la Asociación de Directores de Escena de España, Literatura Dramática series, no. 24 (Madrid: Álvaro Campos, 1992), 91.

7. The montage of Welles's film shown at the MOMA in New York in October 1994 opens with a sequence of windmills dissolving in light, which gives the impression that the film itself is self-destructing. The movie then cuts to images of the statues of Don Quixote and Sancho Panza in the Plaza de España in Madrid.

8. According to the employees of the Filmoteca Española in Madrid, the heirs to Welles's estate obtained a court injunction blocking any viewing of the Spanish montage of the film after Expo '92. Due to these legal barriers, I have repeatedly been denied access to the Filmoteca's copy. My remarks are based on the English-language montage, which incorporates soundtracks of Welles's

own voice and which was screened at the MOMA in October 1994 and introduced by Welles's friend Oja Kadar. See also William E. Schmidt, "New from
Orson Welles: Updated 'Quixote,'" *New York Times,* August 25, 1994, C15, a
review of this same English montage shown at the Edinburgh Film Festival.

In 1996 the Expo '92 Spanish-language montage was finally released for
commercial exhibition in Barcelona. In a review in *Dirigido* 242 (January
1996), entitled "*Don Quijote,* el film que nunca existió" (*Don Quixote,* the film
that never existed), Tomás Fernández Valentí criticizes Jesús Franco, who
supervised the project, for the film's consistently bad dubbing, which he finds
"especially abject in the interminable San Fermín scenes, with people from
Pamplona shouting in Andalusian accents," and the "horrible, computer digi-
talized manipulations of the frames of the windmill sequence" (95).

9. Many Cervantine critics have noted and studied the self-reflexivity of *Don
Quixote.* One of the better studies of the nature of representation in Cervantes's
masterpiece is Robert B. Alter, *Partial Magic: The Novel as a Self-Conscious Genre*
(Berkeley: U of California P, 1975). In the first chapter, "Mirror of Knighthood,
World of Mirrors," Alter makes the following cinematic comparison: "There is
a perfect appropriateness in the fact that, toward the end of Don Quixote's
adventures, when he comes to Barcelona, he should stumble into a printing
shop where he witnesses the processes of proof-drawing, type-setting, revision,
and is treated to a disquisition on the economics of publishing and book-selling
(2:62). The effect is not very different from the cinematic device that has
recently been put to such abundant and various use in which cameras, klieg
lights, costumes, and props obtrude into the filmed scene. At such a moment
we can hardly forget that Don Quixote himself is no more than the product of
the very processes he observes, a congeries of words set up in type, run off as
proof, corrected and rerun, bound in pages, and sold at so many reales a copy.
Cervantes, moreover, repeatedly reminds us that without the rapid activity of
presses like these churning out the first part of his hero's adventures, most of
the adventures of the second part could never have taken place" (3).

10. Gutiérrez Aragón, interview by author, Madrid, May 23, 1994.

11. Likewise, current academic criticism on the nature of representation continues to be renewed through its attention to Cervantes. See, for example,
Stephen Hutchinson, *Cervantine Journeys* (Madison: U of Wisconsin P, 1992),
which studies Cervantes's language of movement within the context of the
discursive practices of world literature.

12. "El Partido Comunista exige, o menos exigía, una gran disciplina de mili-
tancia y también una cierta disciplina, ideológica. Ambas cosas eran queridas
por los militantes como el señor que profesa en una orden religiosa quiere unas
normas estrictas. Eso me parece necesario en la misma medida que vital e
intelectualmente me estorba. Además no entiendo mucho un Partido Comunista que no sea revolucionario y de alguna manera no sea insurrecional o algo

así. Para ser un partido social demócrata ya está el P.S.O.E." Augusto M. Torres, *Conversaciones con Manuel Gutiérrez Aragón,* 2d ed. (Madrid: Fundamentos, 1992), 84. In the European style of personal interview criticism, this is the best, most comprehensive study to date on Gutiérrez Aragón.

13. See Torres, 101.

14. Technically, in terms of its depth of field this shot recalls some of the deep-space views for which Orson Welles was admired. See Kristin Thompson and David Bordwell on Welles's *Chimes at Midnight,* in *Film History: An Introduction* (New York: McGraw Hill, 1994), 400, fig. 15.44.

15. When Diego Galán makes this observation in his interview of Saura in *El País,* March 28, 1981, Saura replies, "I have received some indignant comments because the characters of the movie are seen with affection, they are not presented as monstrous and horrible beings. They not only want them to die at the end, but also to receive moral punishment." (He recibido algunos comentarios indignados porque los personajes de la película estén vistos con cariño, no se presenten como seres monstruosos y horribles. No sólo quieren que mueran al final, sino que reciban también castigos morales.)

16. "Un universo muy mágico, pero al mismo tiempo muy realista, un mundo en el fondo muy cervantino" porque como La Mancha es un "lugar concreto donde suceden episodios mágicos . . . algo propio de la cultura española." Torres, 135.

17. That the recent book on Fernán Gómez, *Fernando Fernán Gómez: El hombre que quiso ser Jackie Cooper,* ed. Jesús Angulo and Francisco Llinás (San Sebastián: Patronato Municipal de Cultura, 1993) is being subventioned by national and autonomous cultural institutions shows Fernán Gómez's stature as a national artistic icon.

18. When her father lays her down on the couch as a young child, after a traumatic incident at her First Communion party, the movie cuts to an adolescent Maravillas asleep on the same couch surrounded by her Sephardic "uncles," who comment admiringly on how she has fallen asleep reading mathematics texts. Time-lapse shots, close-ups of Maravillas, are used several other times in the movie to denote introspective moments, as she concentrates on an intricate, Escher-like drawing or simply covers her face with her hands, trying unsuccessfully to cry. These time-lapse close-ups suggest not a Cervantine archetype, but a more generic literary one of a little girl in a fable who is put to a test, an *Alicia en las tierras de maravillas* (Alice in Wonderland).

19. In a recent article, "Don Quijote's Encounter with Technology," *Cervantes* 14 (1994), 74–95, Iván Jaksic argues that the continued attraction of the *Quixote* may be due to the theme of technological challenge: "Until shortly before his death, he fails to see that the very pastoral-medieval identity that he has so passionately embraced has been the product of a modern innovation, the printing press. But is this not a recurring theme of modernity, as individuals

struggle to comprehend a rapidly changing technological environment? Perhaps our fascination with *Don Quijote,* and its continued currency, has much to do with the way our concepts and ideals are constantly challenged by technological change" (95).

20. "*Maravillas* posee, según su director, grandes dosis de humor e ironía, y esperemos que la críptica crítica (en mi opinión más que sus películas) logre traspasar con más facilidad esa coraza de férreo intelectualismo que protege/ endurece la obra de Manuel Gutiérrez Aragón." From a newspaper article entitled "Un cineasta abre fronteras," February 1981.

21. Miguel de Cervantes, *Don Quixote: The Ormsby Translation, Revised* (New York: Norton, 1981), 25.

22. Miguel de Cervantes, *El ingenioso hidalgo Don Quijote de la Mancha,* ed. Luis Andrés Murillo (Madrid: Castalia, 1978), 240, 570.

23. Ruth El Saffar, *Beyond Fiction* (Berkeley and Los Angeles: U of California P, 1984), 117.

24. "They told it in a very realistic manner, but at the end it became very irreal and some devils came out who tormented Chessman. It was just as it appears in the movie with the exception that Chessman disappeared and in his place there appeared some skeletons that terrorized the staff." (La contaban de una forma muy realista, pero al final se hacía muy irreal y salían unos demonios que atormentaban a Chessman. Era tal como aparece en la película con la salvedad de que Chessman desaparecía y aparecían unos esqueletos que aterrorizaban al personal.) Torres, 143.

25. Cervantes, *Don Quixote: The Ormsby Translation,* 575.

26. "Tal aparece este retablo nuevo, titulado muy justamente *Maravillas,* moderno en su forma y a un tiempo tan español en su doble vertiente referida a la España actual y a la otra España judía. Una y otra se dan en él la mano, más yuxtapuestas que fundidas, a través de unos cuantos personajes que giran en torno de la pareja protagonista." *El País,* February 18, 1981.

27. "*Maravillas* tiene un umbral de accesibilidad. Una vez traspasado, la película interesa, fascina lo insólito de sus imagenes con un Madrid nuevo y casi esotérico, dentro de su puntual formulación."

28. Cervantes, *Don Quixote: The Ormsby Translation,* 569.

29. "Parece que la integran elementos muy distintos unos de otros, pero en el fondo son una especie de variaciones tonales sobre la conciencia de la marginación, puesto que no siempre se trata de marginados, sino de gente que se considera marginada. . . . El motivo es que hoy todo el mundo se considera un poco marginado. Incluso gente que tiene un buen puesto social también tiene una cierta conciencia de marginación como si los centros de poder, los centros de decisión, siempre estuvieran lejos de nosotros." Torres, 138–139.

30. Of the two Cervantes texts, *El celoso extremeño* is by far the less well-known and most problematic. The endings are different in the Porras manuscript and

in the 1613 published edition. Cervantes rewrote its ending and changed the characters' fates. Most readers are troubled by the manuscript ending, considered more severe. The old man Carrizales dies of his own obsession, leaving final wishes in his will that his unfaithful wife marry her lover. However, his wife goes against his desires and chooses instead to enter the convent. Although most Cervantine scholars now consider the Porras manuscript spurious, it has been the subject of substantial debate in modern criticism. The dissonance between the two versions highlights the importance of gender markings in *El celoso extremeño.* See also Myriam Y. Jehenson, "Quixotic Desires or Stark Reality?" *Cervantes* 15, no. 2 (1995): 26–42.

31. Parts of this section on the question of simulation in *La noche más hermosa* were published previously in a volume of selected conference papers under the title "Cervantes on Film: Exemplary Tales and *La noche más hermosa,*" in *Cine-Lit: Essays on Peninsular Film and Fiction,* ed. George Cabello-Castellet, Jaume Martí-Olivella, and Guy H. Wood (Portland, Oreg.: Portland State UP, Oregon State U, and Reed C, 1992), 25–30.

32. In order to achieve this blue tone technically, Gutiérrez Aragón sought a different cinematographer, Carlos Suárez, with whom he had not worked before.

33. "Yo que siempre he sido un hombre sin sospecha de desviaciones sexuales, pero la que realmente me gusta . . . "

34. "La que mejor finja el amor." "Alguien que tiene que fingir por profesión."

35. Miguel de Cervantes, *Six Exemplary Novels,* trans. Harriet de Onís (Woodbury, New York: Barron's, 1961), 239.

36. "La televisión es una gran familia. ¡El país funciona!"

37. "Una lectura atenta de las cartas discrepantes nos ha convencido que no eran las acusaciones de pornografía, argumentadas en primer término, sino el escozor espiritual que siempre provoca el arte cuando se yergue en espejo de la sociedad, lo que ha movido plumas y bolígrafos. Pero en estos tiempos de crisis y transformación no va a ser RTVE quien edulcore la realidad, y discrimine de su pantalla el testimonio de lo que pasa y el arte de nuestro tiempo." "La censura en el país de las maravillas," *TeleRadio,* February 18–24, 1983, 9.

38. "Por cierto, ya han empezado a enfadarse algunos." "Sí, y ya era hora. Estaba dolido de que no se enfadaran." Torres, 187.

39. Not only was Miró the first woman to head RTVE, but she was forced out in a financial scandal, regarding which she was found legally innocent in 1992 and which now truly pales in comparison to more recent political scandals in the Socialist government. The discussions in the chain of command regarding Bibi's wardrobe costs, depicted in the opening sequence of *La noche más hermosa,* allude to the "extravagant" budget line for Miró's clothes.

40. An English language summary, "The State of the Communications Media," of Telefónica's Foundation for the Development of Communications

(Fundesco) 1993 annual report states, "Television has maintained a stable trend with similar levels of advertising revenue. However, the Fundesco report points to a certain devaluation in the credibility and effectiveness of this medium and a substantial deterioration in the quality of programmes." *España 94* (Information Bulletin of the Diplomatic Information Office), no. 240, February 1994, 8–9.

41. Manuel Torres uses this same phrase (Iconografía acumulativa) as a section title in *Conversaciones con Manuel Gutiérrez Aragón,* 218–19.

42. Gutiérrez Aragón considered the profile of power in Spain before returning full-time to his life as director. His latest feature-length film *El rey del río* (The King of the River, 1995) deals with the genesis of a leader. The film traces the youth of two brothers growing up in trout-fishing northern Spain until one of them, César, decides to leave the region to succeed in politics. Ever the literate intellectual, Gutiérrez Aragón in a recent interview with Antonio Castro recalls Sartre's *L'enfant d'un chef* (La infancia de un jefe, The Childhood of a Leader, from the collection of stories *Le Mur*) and emphasizes how meaningful the title is for the story and his own film.

43. "Cuando estaba rodando me encontraba con muchas cosas que me parecían de una película inventada por mí. Lo cual me reafirma en mi idea de que la autoría de un director de cine no sólo viene de inventarse un texto. La unidad que hay en la obra de, por ejemplo, John Ford, viene de su lado de director. Es un descubrimiento que he hecho después de diez películas y una serie, ¡ya era hora de que lo hiciera!" Torres, 220.

ROLAND B. TOLENTINO

Nations, Nationalisms, and *Los últimos de*

Filipinas: An Imperialist Desire for

Colonialist Nostalgia

Antonio Román's 1945 film *Los últimos de Filipinas* (translated both as The Last from the Philippines and Last Stand in the Philippines) is part a body of cinematic works that marks "Spain's first phase of defascistization."[1] As an "authorized" film in General Francisco Franco's postwar nation-building project, the film seeks to valorize Spain's glorious past for the dual purpose of instilling national pride and stirring international interest in Spain's readiness for integration into the new world economic order. Set in its former colony the Philippines, Spain's last days of colonial involvement are renarrativized with the tropes of imperial heroism. Such heroism, however, is imbued with a colonialist nostalgia, since this attempt to reconstitute the nation's glorious colonial history was made during an era when Spain sorely lacked the industrialization and hegemony possessed by newer postwar imperial powers—the United States and most Western European nations. The film's turn-of-the-century setting marks the historical end of Spain's colonial adventure. But as Spain cedes the Philippines to the United States, the time is nevertheless transformed into the privileged moment of postwar memorialization of its colonial heritage: one characterized by valor and dignity, even in loss and defeat.[2] In the process, the film presents a way of erasing Spain's violent imperial history, especially experienced abroad; this erasure, in turn, is also a way of refurbishing its national ethos in the first phase of defascistization. Thus, the film narrative and context conflate time and space in ways that are geared toward the constitution of a postwar national valor and international acceptance.

Two operations work in the film's conflation of time and space: an

imperialist desire for the reconstitution of the lost empire, and a colonialist nostalgia for the utopian order in the colony.[3] Though concepts
such as imperialism and colonialism have come to be understood as the
discursive institutionalization of effects and affects of lasting hierarchies
of subjectivities, powers, and knowledges, in this essay the term "imperialism" will refer to a nation's global expansion through empire-
building, while "colonialism" will refer to the enforcement of the empire within the localized space of the colony.[4] In this sense, imperialism
is the language of empire, and colonialism the vernacular of the colony.

The psychoanalytic notions of desire and nostalgia further complicate
the working of empire and colony. Desire is characterized by its impossibility and failure; the manifestations of ideal representation become
unreachable for and unsatisfiable to the subject. As desire is a permanent
state, so too is the consequent alienation from the object of desire.
Spain's imperialist desire becomes a continuing state of aspiration, frustration, and alienation from its empire-building and the subsequent fall
of the empire. Nostalgia is similarly imbued in a paradox: not only does
destruction of the object lead to the mourning of what has been destroyed, but innocence is claimed in the aftermath. Spain's colonial
nostalgia, therefore, refers to the loss of its colonies and the innocence
assumed thereafter. Constructed around the masculine ideals of valor
and pride, such innocence effaces the literal and epistemic violence
unleashed and experienced in the colony; moreover, the movement
reverts not to the colonized but to the construction of ethos and subjectivity of the colonizer. What lingers is a lost vision of a utopian colony
where hierarchical spaces of knowledge and power lie within the realm
of the colonizers' prerogatives. What is mourned are the death, passage,
and memory of a "traditional" colony. Thus, a colonialist nostalgia refers
to the destruction and the memorialization of both the colonial violence
and innocence, a dual mode of remembrance and forgetting in the
narratives of nations and nationalisms.

In examining the rewriting of Spain's history in *Los últimos de Filipinas* for the national objective of "glorifying the national culture and its
unification under the Francoist regime," this essay will argue that both
imperialist desire and colonialist nostalgia are embedded within Spain's
nation-space.[5] It will also explore the implications of that rewriting for
the postcolonial relations between Spain and the Philippines, particularly since there is a dearth of materials on this topic. Specifically, I am

interested in the way the Philippine nation, nationalism, and culture have been utilized for Spain's own national project. This paper foregrounds the issue of identity construction through othering, one that deliberately misrecognizes the Philippines's own nationalist project. The film's setting (1898) is significant for the Philippines, as political scientists and nationalist historians mark the moment as the founding of "Asia's first republic."[6] The anticolonial struggle waged against Spain becomes the unifying nationalist cause that paves the way for a macrowide consolidation of diverse ethnic groups, classes, and regions. The founding moment, however, is dually marked—as the nation's birth, and as the onset of its consequent tutelage under the United States. This further complicates the analysis of Philippine society and culture, succinctly described as "400 years of the convent and 50 years of Hollywood."

This essay begins with a discussion of nation formation and the limits by which such construction and imagination are possible. The interrelations between the film narrative and context, and the various times and spaces alluded to are illustrative of the problematics in which the nation has been constituted in cinema. I will outline these issues by using conjectural motifs in the film to show how the narrative produces Spain's national project while suppressing that of the Philippines's.

Nations, Nationalisms, and Cinema

Although there is a general agreement with Benedict Anderson's theory of the nation as an imagined community, what has been widely adapted in cinema studies is film's taking over of print media as the technology by which to imagine the nation.[7] Two issues of content are elided in the process of emphasizing the "form" of imagination: the usage of vernacular and the historical context (Protestant Reformation). The vernacularization of print allowed not only the media to be widely disseminated to the people but also the shifting historical religious configuration to be understood by these readers. Technology, by itself, does not produce the mechanism for imagination; the content of what is being "technologized" invariably matters too. The underlying premise of content is a political consciousness. In Anderson's analysis, it is a resultant shift in linguistic and religious affinities that eventually produces the grid for the imagination of community in the poststructuralist sense, or the birth of nation-states in the sociopolitical sense. What I am emphasizing here is the absence of a discussion linking technology (film) to what is being "technologized" (political consciousness); in short, a linking of film's form with the content of nationalism.

Political consciousness relates to the nationalist project of identity formation through differentiation. This means that subaltern identity is constructed in relation both to the hegemonic identity and to other subaltern identities. Nationalism is a conscious political project because it seeks to actualize the transformation of structures. However, nationalism also comprises a political unconscious component because it is emotive and constituted on the individual level. The nationalist unconscious may be thought of as the individual's everyday practice of nationalism, a parole in the langue of nationalism. Such utterances of the conscious and unconscious kinds underscore the constitution of the nation; as Ernest Renan says, "a nation's existence is a daily plebiscite, just as an individual's existence is a perpetual affirmation of life."[8] Individuals, as Anderson similarly mentions of communities, therefore, "are to be distinguished by the style in which they are imagined."[9]

The various "styles" are linked to the various ways nations, nationalisms, and cinemas are configured in culturally and historically specific contexts. An assessment of theories of nation is necessary to call attention to other theories of nationalism and the ways these have been inscribed in cinema, a process that opens new possibilities for figuring nationalism's dialectics of inside/outside, and time and space. Within nationalist consciousness, for example, it is possible to further schematize inner and outer "nation" (community versus nation). This allows for the analysis of multiple mechanisms, one of which includes the constitution of the various embodiments of "nations" in cinema. Spectators who are able to *read* how filmic codes interface with national symbols are also capable of constructing deeper "structures of feeling" than those who are unfamiliar with these codes and symbols. The nation is imagined not as a monolithic entity but as a multiple embodiment of individual or people's nationalism(s). The nation is constituted in relation to other political, economic, and cultural categories of class, gender, and sexuality, and race and ethnicity, among others. A film of national allegory is read through the interfacing of these categories with the local, regional, and global conditions.

Another way the nation has been mapped is through nationalism's invocation of women. The female figure is posited as the personification of the nationalist discourse, simultaneously representing the condition of oppression and confirming the ideal of racial purity. Family melodrama or social drama films are read as national allegory through the engendering of women as index of the relentless struggle toward an ideal nation.[10] This engendering of women also functions in allegorical readings of historical drama films or films based on folktales and epics. By reworking the nationalist discourse along the dialectics of the inside/outside and its figuration in the female subject, I will link concepts of nation and nationalism with cinematic technology, as a way of generating specificities in which a nation identifies with the larger regional, international, or "Third World" collective.[11]

"Whose imagined community?" asks Indian subaltern historian Partha Chatterjee, a question that resonates as a critique of Anderson's proposition. While bringing a critical perspective to a traditional sociopolitical conceptualization of the nation entity, Anderson "treat[s] the phenomenon as part of the universal history of the modern world," obscuring other nationalisms and ways of constructing community.[12] Furthermore, in contextualizing Europe's construction of nation (largely focused on the development of print-as-commodity), Anderson's references to Asian experiences and literatures are reduced to the backdrop. The nation's grid is still integrated in the European history of national imaginary, reducing the Asian "moments" to nodes by which to reiterate such constructedness of nation.

Skepticism exists regarding the way "imagination" prefigures the nation. What is perceived to be a political stake is transformed into an individualized act, and Anderson's practice neglects issues of historical and cultural specificities. His notion of imagination as a "steady, anonymous, simultaneous activity" (as in the now classic example of an individual privately performing a mass ceremony by reading a newspaper while *meanwhile* imagining that other fellow nationals are doing the same) opens a poststructuralist ballpark that incorporates and universalizes all other imaginations within its own trajectory.[13] This conceptual frame flattens intertextual historical and cultural connections. As Chatterjee intervenes, the nation's grid becomes the sole mode by which other imaginations are measured: "if nationalisms in the rest of the world have chosen their imagined community from certain 'modular forms' already available to them by Europe and the Americas, what do they have left to imagine?"[14]

Similarly, Ernest Gellner, Eric Hobsbawm, and Ernest Renan (to a lesser extent) also privilege the industrial revolution as the fundamental moment of the emergence of nations.[15] Renan debunks the equivalence of race with nation, and sovereignty with ethnography and linguistics. In doing so, he makes the nation a metaphysical configuration, "a soul, a spiritual principle," the direction in which social formations are in some ways destined to evolve.[16] For Gellner, "nationalism is not the awakening of nations to self-consciousness: it invents nations where they do not exist."[17] As Anderson has pointed out, Gellner's proposition of "invention" is vested in the notion of falsity and fabrication rather than creation and imagination. This approach privileges the notion that there is a logical progression of human civilization that finds its highest embodiment in "nation." In Gellner's mind, high culture needs to be the hegemonic form in relation to the various folk cultures in the constitution of a nation. However, for Hobsbawm, the nation is a novelty in liberal bourgeois thought, signifying a shift from the traditional thinking of "nation" as a bonding of people based on certain commonalities—ethnicity, language, or history.

Simply put, what print capitalism is to Anderson's grid, the industrial society is to the rest of these theorists. A form of sociological determinism is posited from which the emergence of nations is always already determined as a Western sociopolitical and historical phenomenon. The underlying ideology of such an imposition is the Enlightenment project, whose objective is "to participate in the common work of civilization."[18] As Chatterjee observes of Anderson and Gellner's works (to which I add Hobsbawm's), "[they] see third-world nationalisms as profoundly 'modular' in character. They are invariably shaped according to the contours outlined by given historical models: 'objective, inescapable imperative,' 'too-marked deviations . . . impossible.' "[19] Renan, on the other hand, is for the most part silent on non-European societies.

What can be filtered from these theories of nation is the inverse move that constructs a metatheory by which other non-Western formations are to be "subjectivized." This means that the circuits of nationhood have already been entrenched for non-Western societies, and these are the sites from which their own narratives of nation are to be derived. Or to state it in another way, because the langue of nation has already been encoded, only a "Third World" parole is possible, not a "Third World" langue. Though it supposedly allows for a multiplicity of imagined nations, even Anderson's theory has already set the parameters that limit the imaginations.

Los últimos de Filipinas, Imperialist Desire, and Colonialist Nostalgia

Like Western theories of nation, *Los últimos de Filipinas* stakes out universalist claims that emanate from the scope of its own project: the construction of a national subjectivity/identity through a Manichaean dialectics of selfhood and othering. The film, after all, is designed to augment Franco's project of nation-building: to doubly forge national pride and international recognition, both drives politically motivated. International efforts to isolate Spain for supporting the Axis powers until 1943 should be recalled here. Franco's staunch postwar anticommunist policy furthered the national agenda for international recognition and announced its readiness to be integrated in the cold-war era. Spain needed to pull itself out of the economic recession that was largely caused by the Civil War, and cinema provided one possible source of income. "With more cinema seats per capita than any other European country, the Spain of the '40s and '50s was a nation of cinema addicts."[20] Thus cinema could serve both as a lucrative ideological state apparatus in disseminating the official Francoist ideology while catering to popular needs. So recognized was the propaganda content of *Los últimos de Filipinas* that the film went on to win first prize from Franco's movie business union. Critic Emilio Sanz de Soto would go to the extent of calling *Los últimos de Filipinas* "without a doubt our best historic film and our best patriotic film."[21] Drawing, "29,966 spectators, with 452,6211 pesetas" in 1945, the film was considered a commercial success.[22]

The film dramatizes the resistance put up by fifty Spanish soldiers under the command of Captain de las Morenas, and later by Lieutenant Martín Cerezo, against the attack of Tagalog revolutionaries in Baler after U.S. troops had conquered the Philippines. It is an account of the troop's 349-day defense amidst "isolation, sun, fatigue, struggle, loneliness and nostalgia."[23] A. Rigol and J. Sebastian correctly note the

Los últimos de Filipinas dramatizes the resistance waged by Spanish soldiers against an attack by Tagalog revolutionaries after U.S. troops had conquered the Philippines.

"double point of view" through which Antonio Román (a pseudonym for Antonio Fernández García de Quevedo) frames this historical film: first, the film narrative is set in 1898, which makes possible the reference to "an authentic episode" from Spanish history (specifically, Spain's "loss of [its] last colonies towards the end of the 20th century"); second, the film was produced in 1945, a fact that evokes "the political, economic, and social peculiarities of Spain in the first years of Franco."[24] The tension of the film derives from the oscillation between these temporal and spatial zones—movement that calls attention to Spain's national identity while it simultaneously obscures that of the Philippines.

Los últimos de Filipinas is an elegy to the passing colonial heritage. Even Román's career declined after the film project. As if considering Román emblematic of Spain, de Soto says of the filmmaker, "If he had continued in the line so personal and so brilliant at its start, today Román would be one of the decisive names in the history of our [Spanish] cinema. But that delicate line changed; in spite of the most laudable attempts to renew it, he would never again regain the inspiration of his youth."[25] The loss of colonialism would continue to haunt Spain in the postwar years of the Francoist era, becoming a source of national angst that helped prevent the nation from fully industrializing and modernizing.

The troop's isolation in the Philippines is analogous to the isolation of the Francoist regime from other nations. The value of defending the empire to death is the latent hegemonic nationalist call. In the construction of a national ego ideal, the film narrative glorifies the "conversion of the historical massacre into a religious sacrifice," one that is focused on "the fetishization of virility and sacrifice."[26] Catholic orthodoxy is entwined with militaristic adventurism. Ironically, in the move toward defascistization, the reaestheticization of politics invariably directs us to the fascistic nature of the film narrative, and consequently, its ideological imperative—the national project.

Nowhere do the flag and belfry so readily symbolize the nation's materiality and spirituality than in *Los últimos de Filipinas*.[27] While the flag constitutes the material basis of nation, one of masculine struggle in the defense of the nation, the belfry constitutes its spiritual basis, one that connotes racial purity and righteousness. Together with other patriotic symbols like the saber and cross, the flag and belfry reconstitute a religious-civil alliance that brought about Spain's colonialism in the first place. Conversion and coercion were potent processes that sought to instill Spanish hegemony in the colonies. Such fetishization of national colonialist symbols calls to our attention the constructedness of symbols, especially those that have become reliable icons of national heritage.[28] In constant usage and without parody, the symbols would nonetheless evoke a transhistoricity of filmic and historical times. Against worsening odds, the triumphs of both the troop and the Francoist regime then become more meaningful for the nation. With the disappearance in the film of a *barca* (boat) that provided the only means of contact with the outside space, the troops realize their total isolation. They move into the church compound, fortifying its defense against the Tagalog revolutionaries. A Spanish flag is hoisted in the church belfry. At one point in the film, Captain de las Morenas in the film states that the flag "is not a challenge, it is simply to give testimony that we are here." Lieutenant Martín would complement this statement: "that we are here and that we are not planning to leave." So central is the flag that historical accounts would further report, "when the wind and the elements tore [the flag] to pieces they patched it up with sacristans' red surplices and with yellow mosquito netting."[29] Like a phantasmagorical figure, the flag on the belfry provides a haunting presence particularly in the absence of a context to give it meaning: with the U.S. victory over the Spanish armada in Manila Bay, signaling the end of Spanish colonialism, a Spanish flag in a far-flung area becomes a signifier without a signified. The flag is now a relic of the past that is Spanish colonialism.

However, just as the flag haunts the Tagalog revolutionaries, so is the flag also haunted in the contested space and location from which it is poised. The flag haunts the troops, constantly calling attention to their willingness to die in defense of the nationalist cause. Lieutenant Martín wrote, "to see that glorious flag flying against the blue of the sky made it seem that all Spain was watching us and encouraging us, making us hope for its gratitude and remembrance if we did our duty well."[30] Suffering and death become options in the struggle to defend the territorial space. The friar brims with spiritual assurance to the doubtful: "God will provide. He orders and resolves our lives, he enlightens us while we are here and he can call us when He wants." "One has to look higher than heaven, where the heaven of the astrologer ends, the heaven of God begins." Thus, a kind of "national Catholicism" is called upon in the defense of the colonial territory; later in the film, such piety and heroism are rewarded with state honors and pensions for the endurance of their struggle.

Franco's own regime had a strong relationship with the church; "the architects of the new economic policy [of the mid-1950s period] which was to reconcile rapid industrial growth with its 'conditions' were technocrats associated with the Catholic lay order, Opus Dei."[31] Much earlier, there were two interpretations of Spain's reunion with Catholicism during the Civil War (1936–39), both of which are anchored on the premise of the " 'state of progressive despair' at the disappointing performance of Spain, once the greatest imperial power in Europe. . . . The Republican sought to raise Spain [. . .] by imitating the 'progressive' nations. For the more vocal Nationalist ideologists of 1936 only a return to the vision of a universal empire and the inward-looking values of Philip II could save Spain from the continuing ravages of a decadent materialism."[32] The film seeks to have it both ways, enshrining Spain's colonial legacy even as it anticipates acceptance within the international community.

The investment in symbols and significations was attuned with the Francoist hegemonic project in Spanish cinema. *Los últimos de Filipinas* invokes the righteousness of the struggle to continue defending the nation, through numerous montage sequences that show men heroically battling against the odds, under the shadow of icons (flag and belfry) that underscore both the political and religious dimensions of the scenes. The film encourages spectators to sympathize with Franco's isolation as the people's own isolation. A nationalist cause is founded on the people's affinity with national figures and conditions. Thus, "nation" acquires resonance in the film through its ability to be imagined and constituted differently and heterogeneously in and against the national project. A familiarity with the transhistorical usage of national symbols constitutes a deeper structure of national being. Spectators become aware of themselves as citizens of the nation.

Resistance to and nonrecognition of signs and significations, however, present a divergent dynamics of nation-building that can be antithetical to the "official" nation, or it finds affinity in "community" in the more "localized" variations of the hegemonic nation. The usage of Castilian ("the language of empire") in the film attempts to homogenize the vocabulary of nation. Speakers of Catalan language or advocates of Basque nationalism, for example, would register various gradations of acceptance and/or resistance to the film. Franco's nationalism, like state nationalism according to Eric Hobsbawm, is a "double-edged strategy": "as it mobilized some inhabitants, it alienated others . . . it helped to define the nationalities excluded from the official nationality by separating out those communities which, for whatever reason, resisted the official public language and ideology."[33] The refusal to belong or to assimilate becomes a choice since "not all are allowed to become full members of the official nation."[34] In other words, unlike the experience for the newspaper reader in Anderson's imagined community, the nation is a heterogeneous construction of recognition and acceptance (misrecognition and resistance) to collective bodies and geographies of nationhood. The narratives of nation are analogous to the modes of experiencing the "nation thing."

The national project of identity formation and international respectability was not to take effect until 1953, "with the Concordat and the rapprochement with the U.S., when the greatest democratic state accepted Franco as the 'sentinel of the West,' the most reliable anti-

Communist during the Cold War."[35] It was only in the further isolation of the Communist Eastern Europe bloc that Spain was relieved of its own isolation. However, even in 1962, as historian Raymond Carr points out, "the acceptance was never complete . . . the EEC (European Economic Community) refused to consider Francoist Spain as a potential member of the Community."[36] It was only later that Spain was finally accepted as a member of the EEC. Spain's nationalist project was an effort to become integrated within the new league and political nation-states that dominated the post–World War II global restructuring. However, the libidinal economy that fuels this effort to establish Spain's position in the global division of power remained vested in its colonial heritage. The renarrativization of this heritage, Anderson contends, involves a process of selective amnesia (of its history of literal and epistemic violence) and remembrance (a rememorialization of colonial heroism). To privilege a colonial history that is gasping its last breath implies a nostalgia for an imperial history (modeled on U.S. imperialism) that never existed in the first place. Yet Spain uses this same history to position itself within the new world order.

Spain's ceding of the Philippines to the United States signaled the end of most European colonialism and the beginning of the neocolonialist era, with the United States leading the new world order. Spain's early involvement with twentieth-century imperialism was minimal; it focused instead on managing the internal tensions among regional nationalisms and national political conflicts that would culminate in the Civil War. Thus, Spain's investment in its colonial heritage during an era of modern imperialism was symptomatic of its ineptness in grappling with the various informational and technological changes of the postwar period. However, Spain's desire for global integration followed the narrative of the modern nation that privileged industrialization as its modernizing feature. Its slow industrialization and its struggle for acceptance into the international community, therefore, stretched its historical narrative of colonial glory to the limits.

The film emphasizes two issues within its imagined imperial history: first, the centrality of the church in the colonial space; and second, the reactivation of the imperial family narrative in the exchange of the Philippines (from an aging colonialist to an emerging imperialist power). These two issues expose the contradictions in Spain's subsequent failure to grapple with newer operations of neocolonialism and late capitalism, an order that was mastered by the United States, the nation that was to possess the Philippines at the turn of the century.

The geopolitical spacing of the church and municipal building indicates the relinquishing of most of the Spanish civilian government's political and cultural functions to the church and its friars.[37] The friars' proselytizing endeavors brought to their reach more people and geographies. They had longer terms in the areas than civilian officials; they also managed the education of the children of the town elites, knew the vernacular languages, and owned huge tracts of land. Thus, the pueblo system—the construction of towns with the church as center; the municipio, plaza, and marketplace beside it; the residences of the town's elites around it; and the cemetery and school within its compound— proved to be effective in the administration of local feudal space, yet ineffective in the ensuing development of transnational capitalism involving new modes of neocolonial administration (overseas banking, postal and telecommunication systems, public school education, minimum social services, sanitation and public health management, and so on). In the film, disappearance of the barca as the sole connection to the outside space characterized the crucial lack of technological empowerment in the wars against both the Tagalog revolutionaries and United States. The quick defeat of the Spanish armada by Admiral George Dewey's naval fleet signaled a change of power, one in which a fleet with a better technological advantage triumphs and paves the way for a new imperial master.[38] Furthermore, Spanish heroism in Baler was based on the belated realization of U.S. triumph: the recognition of endurance and bravery is also a recognition of the time it had taken for the news of Spanish defeat to the United States to be realized.

Spain was prepared to engage neither in an imperial war nor in wars of independence. As the film is produced in the period of defascistization, the history of colonial state violence is omitted from the film narrative. As the film is produced in the period when Spain is renewing its efforts to join the global community, the reconstitution of Spanish heroism becomes the spiritual drive, so to speak, in the project of (inter)national image-building (invoked in the value of aristocratic dignity and heroism even in the face of defeat). However, even within the Catholic Church, Spain's "national Catholicism" would prove to be too limiting, with events like the Second Vatican Council providing greater openness and dialogue with the lay people. In choosing to align with the church, Spanish hegemony did not realize that the nation was fast becoming the new secular religion.

On another level, Spain's ceding of the Philippines to the United States involved a renarrativization of the imperial family mythology, one imbued with a discourse of sexualization. Spain's relinquishing of its colony involved a feminization of nationalist pride, as an older generation relinquished control to a younger, more modern imperial power. The 1898 defeat would continue to determine the prerogatives of Franco and his regime: "To the end of his life Franco regarded political parties as responsible for the disaster of 1898 (which had robbed him of a career in the navy) and the decline into the 'chaos' and 'communism' of the Republic."[39] However, in the film, Spanish national masculinity is recuperated for 1945 audiences through the valorization of the heroism of its colonial past.

In this sense, the exchange of the Philippines between an old colonial and a new imperialist order involved the constant positioning of the Philippines in the feminine space as virgin and resistant woman vulnerable to rape. Senator Alfred J. Beveridge's real estate pitch for U.S. conquest of the Philippines positioned the nation as a child-virgin territory waiting to be put to good use: "This island empire is the last land left in all the oceans. If it should prove a mistake to abandon it, the blunder once made would be irretrievable"; "No land in America surpasses in fertility the plains and valleys of Luzon"; "The Filipino . . . [has been] put through a process of three hundred years of superstition in religion, dishonesty in dealing, disorder in habits of industry, and cruelty, caprice, and corruption in government"; "The archipelago is a base for the commerce of the East."[40] Though there is no reference to Spain's faulty colonialism and its failure to bring the promises of Enlightenment ideals to the colony, the speech covertly blamed Spain for its failure to maximize the resources of the terrain—a failure that justified United States's takeover of the passive territory. When native resistance ensued, conquest became the recourse. The colonized nation is figured as an unruly woman, a trope that justifies the use of rape and violence in the pursuit of "manifest destiny," "benevolent assimilation," and the "white man's burden." Pacification of the female nation-space instigated the very same processes of nostalgia, destruction, then mourning.

With the exception of a Filipina character in love with a Spanish official, the film involves an all-male Spanish cast. Portrayed by a Spanish actress, the Filipina character Tala (guiding light) is made to represent the unattainable union of Spain and the Philippines; though the male officer realizes the impossibility of such a union, she mistakenly believes it is possible until the very end. The Filipina is despised by her own countrymen because of her xenophilia; hence, her impurity prohibits her from functioning as mother of the nation. In the 1945 context of the film, Spain once again negotiated between a masculine position (privileging heroism/bravery) and a feminine role (immersed in nostalgia for an aristocratic colonial past). During the same postwar period, the Philippines continued to be relegated to a feminized position— liberated by U.S. forces from Japanese rule and later forced by the United States to accept Japanese war reparations. At that point, Spain's effort to rejoin the international community was heavily focused on getting U.S. attention. The film's opening credits immediately acknowledge the U.S. Embassy's assistance in the making of the film. The reversal in the United States's role from enemy to ally both in filmic and historical times suggests a homosocial comradeship among imperialists.

The conspicuous absence of women in representations of both Spain's and the Philippines's nationalist struggles reifies the patriarchal imperatives of the nation project itself. "The fetishization of virility and sacrifice" in the film can be read as the drive that fuels the material struggle for nationhood.[41] Interestingly, even the spiritual aspect of the struggle, a traditional domain of women, is further aligned with men avowing chastity. The soldier's affinity with the friar's religious convictions provides the ideal to die for in the struggle for nation. However, no spiritual dimension is attributed to the Philippine nationalist struggle except its association with the sexuality of the sole female character, who is deemed impure. Thus, woman's sexuality is the abject object in the film narrative, marking the impossibility of signifying either union or independence of nations.

In instilling *amor propio* (dignity and love for the self), *Los últimos de Filipinas* became torn between self-love and self-hate, a conflict that further shifted configurations of time and space. The colonial past was made to haunt and glorify the present; Francoist Spain sought out the United States as partner; and the Philippines was exchanged between imperialists. The film foregrounded the usage of Philippine national and bodily spaces, as well as its nationalism, but only as the liminal terrain on which Spain inscribed its own (inter)national project. Thus,

Philippine identity and nationality were significant only as part of a peripheral vision whose sole function was to narrativize or mobilize a "coherent" image and subjectivity of the center.

This critique of the discursive rewriting of Spanish history (involving the double gesture of inscription and erasure) foregrounds some issues in Philippine colonial and postcolonial relations, and provides some contemporary intertextual (cultural and historical) references. Filipina critic Neferti Xina M. Tadiar has reconceptualized the constructedness of the Philippines in the Asian Pacific Rim as one involving a sexualization of transnational operations ("the marriage of the Philippines to the United States and Japan with Australia as the midwife").[42] These dynamics continue to expand as Filipino and Filipina workers are circulated overseas; among the 2 million migrant workers, some 60,000 Filipinas are working in Spain as housemaids. The Spanish colonial residue in the transnational era is manifested in other areas of Philippine popular culture. In the postwar films, the family narrative is reworked by using Spanish mestizos and mestizas as villains, who threaten to destabilize the social cohesion of the family and community. (Later in the foregrounding of U.S. and Philippine popular imaginations and the marginalization of Spanish heritage, the villainous Spanish mestizos would be replaced by Filipino mestizos and Americans.) The colonial privileging of whiteness as ideal still pervades the "colonial mentality" in the Philippines: saints and religious icons all have Anglo European features; movie stars are usually fair skinned and have "Western" features; the United States is readily preferred by Filipinos when given a choice among Western and Asian countries, including the Philippines.[43] However, cultural politics continues to shift with economics, as more investments and assistance pour in from Japan and Taiwan rather than from the United States; investments also continue to rise from the Philippines's Southeast Asian neighbors. Hence, the seemingly declining Spanish influence on contemporary Philippine culture needs to be reexamined especially if we are to understand why its legacy remains significant today in the areas of religiosity, folk cultures, and "colonial mentality." It is no overstatement to say that such a legacy continues to overdetermine Philippine political culture through the perpetuation of patronage politics, or "cacique democracy," in elections, family dynasties, and nation-building.[44]

This essay presents some conjectural linkages at stake in Spain's construction of nationalism, one that marginalized another culture's efforts at nation formation and nation-building. It may prove useful in connecting an anti-imperialist critique (in the turnover of imperial powers, from Spanish colonialism to U.S. neocolonialism) with postcolonial criticism (the disjunctures in the Philippines's nation-building project). This liminality foregrounds the more recent national drives to refigure the Philippine nation-state: from President Ferdinand Marcos's megalomaniac enforcement of modernization to Corazon Aquino's period of static foundational development, to Fidel Ramos's vision of the Philippines as the new Asian economic tiger with infrastructures in place by the year 2000. As multinationalism becomes the dominant economic mode of production, its cultural translation involves a complex negotiation between its enforcement from the outside and its indigenization (through assimilation and resistance) within the national setting. The proliferation of giant malls in metro Manila, for example, can be read along the matrix of cultural and historical grids. The practice of a "mall culture" in Philippine urban centers represents the multinational enforcement and reception in the national space, involving, among others, the transmutation of promenade space of the plaza in the Spanish colonial era into the present-day air-conditioned "Lunetas," after the most popular park; the construction of an ideal transnational space housing everything within one roof; the franchisement of middle-class entertainment and culture; the problematics derived from the more complicated task of organizing labor and people; the dream materialized of "First Worldization" in a "Third World" (Ramos's Philippines 2000); and a trope for discussing gentrification in a social formation where 70 percent of the people live below the poverty level. These connections provide a context for understanding the ways in which a "people without a history" have been positioned in the margins—a context that moves the Philippines to the foreground or at least into some relational space.

Notes

For their comments and suggestions, I am thankful to Marsha Kinder, Maria Luisa Aguilar Cariño, Bienvenido Lumbera, Rosario Cruz Lucero, Patrick Flores, and Peter Britos. I am also grateful to Professor Nena Barranco who provided a translation of the article by A. Rigol and J. Sebastian.

1. Marsha Kinder, *Blood Cinema: The Reconstruction of National Identity in Spain* (Berkeley and Los Angeles: U of California P, 1993), 152. Other prototypical Francoist films include, *Raza* (Race, 1941), *Inés de Castro* (1944), *A mí la Legión* (The Legion Forever, 1942), and *Escuadrilla* (Squadron, 1941). Considered by John Hopewell as parody of Francoist cinema, on the other hand, are *La princesa de los Ursinos* (The Princess of the Ursines, 1947), *Locura de amor* (Madness of Love, 1948), *Agustina de Aragón* (1950), *La leona de Castilla* (The Lioness of Castile, 1951), *Alba de América* (Dawn of Freedom, 1951), and *Lola la piconera* (Lola, the Charcoal Vendor, 1951). These "six historical super-productions [were] made by Cifesa in a doomed attempt to rival American cinema at home and abroad." John Hopewell, *Out of the Past: Spanish Cinema after Franco* (London: British Film Institute, 1986), 42.

2. Nationalist historian Renato Constantino writes, "By the time the Treaty of Paris through which Spain ceded the Philippines to the United States was signed on December 10, 1898, Spain actually controlled only a few isolated outposts in the country. The Filipino people had won their war of liberation." In collaboration with Letizia R. Constantino, *The Philippines: A Past Revisited* (Quezon City: R. Constantino, 1975), 219.

3. What have been disseminated are "imperialist nostalgia" (see Renato Rosaldo, *Culture and Truth: The Remaking of Social Analysis* [Boston: Beacon, 1989], 68–87) and "colonial desire" (see Robert Young, *Colonial Desire: Hybridity in Theory, Culture and Race* [London: Routledge, 1995]). Related to the colonialist nostalgia for "the colonized culture as it was 'traditionally' (that is, when they first encountered it)," imperialist nostalgia, according to Rosaldo, refers to a situation "where people mourn the passing of what they themselves have transformed" (69). Colonial desire as defined by Young, on the other hand, refers to "a covert but insistent obsession with transgressive, inter-racial sex, hybridity and miscegenation" (xii). I take a shifting correlation to refer to Spain's colonial legacy and imagined imperial history.

4. For a discussion of the historical development of the term "imperialism," see Eric Hobsbawm, "Age of Empire," in *The Age of Empire 1875–1914* (New York: Vintage Books, 1987), 56–83; and of "colonialism," see J. Jorge Klor de Alva, "The Postcolonialization of the (Latin) American Experience: A Reconsideration of 'Colonialism,' 'Postcolonialism,' and 'Mestizaje,'" in *After Colonialism: Imperial Histories and Postcolonial Displacements,* ed. Gyan Prakash (Princeton: Princeton UP, 1995), 241–75.

5. Kinder, 150. See also Peter Besas, *Behind the Spanish Lens: Spanish Cinema under Fascism and Democracy* (Denver: Arden, 1985), 27–28.

6. The proclamation of independence was made on June 12, 1898, which marked the first public display of the Philippine flag and the first public playing of the national anthem. However, "while the June 12 [proclamation]

was a declaration of independence from Spain, it put the United States in the special position of protector of that independence." Constantino, 211.

7. Benedict Anderson, *Imagined Communities* (London: Verso, 1991).

8. Ernest Renan, "What Is a Nation?" in *Nation and Narration,* ed. Homi K. Bhabha (London and New York: Routledge, 1990), 19.

9. Anderson, 6.

10. For a discussion of the correlation of women and melodrama in an allegorical context, see Ana M. López, "Tears and Desire: Women and Melodrama in the 'Old' Mexican Cinema," in *Mediating Two Worlds: Cinematic Encounters in the Americas,* ed. John King, Ana M. López, and Manuel Alvarado (London: British Film Institute, 1993).

11. By "Third World," I am referring to both ideology and neocolonized formations as imbricated by colonialism and late capitalism, as well as by indigenous modes of production.

12. Partha Chatterjee, "Whose Imagined Community?" in *The Nation and Its Fragments: Colonial and Postcolonial Histories* (Princeton: Princeton UP, 1993), 5.

13. Anderson, 35–36.

14. Chatterjee, "Whose Imagined Community?" 5.

15. Eric J. Hobsbawm, *Nations and Nationalisms Since 1780* (Cambridge: Cambridge UP, 1990); Ernest Gellner, *Nations and Nationalism* (Ithaca, N.Y.: Cornell UP, 1983).

16. Renan, 19.

17. Quoted in Anderson, 6.

18. Gellner, 20.

19. Partha Chatterjee, *Nationalist Thought and the Colonial World: A Derivative Discourse* (Minneapolis: U of Minnesota P, 1986), 21.

20. Raymond Carr, *Modern Spain, 1875–1980* (Oxford: Oxford UP, 1980), 164.

21. Emilio Sanz de Soto, "1940–1950," *Spanish Cinema, 1896–1983* (Madrid: Ministerio de Cultura, Instituto de Cine, 1986), 124–25.

22. A. Rigol and J. Sebastian, "España: Los últimos de Filipinas (1945) de Antonio Román," *Film Historia* 1, no. 3 (1991): 182. My own essay builds on several issues raised in this article.

23. Voice-over in film's opening sequence, quoted in A. Rigol and J. Sebastian, 176.

24. A. Rigol and J. Sebastian, 176–77.

25. Quoted in A. Rigol and J. Sebastian, 176.

26. Kinder, 150 and 153.

27. Such fetishization of the flag is also reproduced in Carlos Saura's film *¡Ay, Carmela!* (Iberoamericana Films, 1990).

28. See Eric Hobsbawm, "Introduction: Inventing Traditions," in *The Inven-*

tion of Tradition, ed. Eric Hobsbawm and Terence Ranger (Cambridge: Cambridge UP, 1983), 13–14.

29. Carlos Quirino, "Epic Stand in Baler," in *Filipino Heritage,* vol. 10, ed. Alfredo Roces (Manila: Lahing Pilipino Publishing, 1978), 2156.

30. Quirino, 2156.

31. Carr, 156. He goes on to define "conditions" as "the creation in Spain of a market economy where prices would control the allocation of resources, and the integration of that market into the capitalist economy of the West" (156).

32. Carr, 148. The premise "state of progressive despair" is coined by Spanish historian Americo Castro.

33. Hobsbawm, *The Age of Empire,* 150.

34. Hobsbawm, *The Age of Empire,* 151.

35. Carr, 169.

36. Carr, 169.

37. Bienvenido Lumbera and Cynthia Nograles Lumbera refer to a hierarchization of the native population and their cultures in the pueblo system: "A distinction would be made between those Filipinos who settled where they were within easy reach of the power of the Church and State in *pueblos* (*taga-bayan*), and those who kept their distance from colonial administrators and their colonial agents . . . (*taga-bukid, taga-bundok*). . . . In time, *taga-bayan* came to be a flattering term for the Hispanized and, therefore, 'urbane and civilized' Filipino, while *taga-bukid/taga-bundok* was to mock the indio who had not learned the ways of the colonial masters. . . . In this way did the non-Christian Filipinos come to be regarded with condescension, if not outright contempt and suspicion, by lowlanders who soon began to think of themselves as more 'genuine' Filipinos." "Literature under Spanish Colonialism," in *Philippine Literature: A History and Anthology* (Metro Manila: Kalayaan Press, 1982), 31.

38. Only after two hours of battle, Admiral Partricio Montojo y Pasarón's flagship was already destroyed. General Basilio Augustín Dávila, the Spanish governor, issued a call to the Spanish population in the Philippines using a similar "Catholic nationalist" rhetoric against the Americans: "The aggressors shall not profane the tombs of your fathers, gratify their lustful passions at the cost of your wives and daughters, appropriate the property that our industry has accumulated to provide for your old age. . . . Prepare for the struggle! Let us resist with Christian resolve and the patriotic cry of Viva España!" Quoted in Stanley Karnow, in *In Our Image: America's Empire in the Philippines* (London: Century, 1990), 103.

39. Carr, 169.

40. Senator Alfred J. Beveridge, "Our Philippine Policy," in *The Philippines Reader: A History of Colonialism, Neocolonialism, Dictatorship, and Resistance,* ed. Daniel B. Schirmer and Stephen Rosskamm Shalom (Quezon City: Ken, 1987), 23–26.

41. Kinder, 153.

42. Neferti Xina M. Tadiar, "Sexual Economies in the Asia-Pacific Community," in *What Is in a Rim? Critical Perspectives on the Pacific Region Idea,* ed. Arif Dirlik (Boulder: Westview, 1993).

43. For a discussion of "colonial mentality," see Virgilio G. Enriquez, *From Colonial to Liberation Psychology: The Philippine Experience* (Quezon City: U of the Philippines, 1992). In Maria Luisa Canieso-Doronila's survey and analysis of national identity formation among elementary students, only 10 percent ranked the Philippines as their first preference as mother country. American, Japanese, and Saudi Arabian nationalities were more preferred. "The present finding is in accord with a 1979 content analysis of the Grade IV World Bank–funded textbook in Social Studies which showed that the Philippines ranked third, after the United States and Japan in the degree of esteem in which it is held by Filipinos, as indicated by the frequency of favorable mention in the textbook." Doronila, "The Nation in Its Relationship with Other Countries: A Content Analysis of an EDPITAF Textbook in Social Studies," *Philippine Social Science and Humanities Review* 45; nos. 1–4 (1981): 67–83, quoted in her *The Limits of Educational Change: National Identity Formation in a Philippine Public Elementary School* (Quezon City: U of the Philippines P, 1989), 72.

44. Among the body of works that discuss the patron-client relationship in Philippine political culture are Anderson, "Cacique Democracy in the Philippines: Origins and Dreams," *New Left Review* 169 (May/June 1988): 3–33; Vicente Rafael, "Patronage and Pornography: Ideology and Spectatorship in the Early Marcos Years," *Comparative Studies in Society and History* 32, no. 2 (1990): 282–304; and Alfred W. McCoy, ed., *An Anarchy of Families: State and Family in the Philippines* (Quezon City: Ateneo de Manila UP and Center for Southeast Asian Studies, U of Wisconsin, Madison, 1994).

PART 2

Sexual Reinscription

STEPHEN TROPIANO

Out of the Cinematic Closet:

Homosexuality in the Films of

Eloy de la Iglesia

One of Spain's most prolific filmmakers of the post-Franco period, Eloy de la Iglesia broke new ground in Spanish cinema with his frank, explicit depiction of homosexuality. From the mid-1970s through the early 1980s, de la Iglesia's treatment of such subjects as sex, crime, violence, drugs, and politics translated into financial success at the box office.[1] Despite his success, the Basque director has received limited critical attention because his style of filmmaking is considered sensationalistic and commercial in comparison to the more "artistic" work of Spanish auteurs like Carlos Saura, José Luis Borau, Manuel Gutiérrez Aragón, and Luis García Berlanga.

Only recently have critics begun to assess the importance of de la Iglesia's work and give his films the full critical and historical consideration they deserve. Marsha Kinder includes de la Iglesia in her list of "Spanish mavericks" (along with Luis Buñuel, Pedro Almodóvar, and José Juan Bigas Luna) who utilize melodrama subversively. She also credits the Basque filmmaker for successively "breaking through to an international market by politicizing marginality."[2] In the second edition of *El cine español después de Franco* (The Spanish Cinema after Franco), John Hopewell offers an expanded discussion of de la Iglesia's films, which outlines their historical importance in their depiction of marginalized sexuality within the newly democratized Spain.[3] Paul Julian Smith, who has written the most extensive appraisal of the director, finds de la Iglesia's exclusion from national and regional histories disturbing because his films "represent what is perhaps a unique moment during the transition to democracy when the topic of homosexuality and the mass audience coincided in the Spanish cinema."[4]

The unprecedented popularity of gay-themed films by a mass audience during Spain's democratic transitional period (1975–78) was due to de la Iglesia's ability to link homosexuality as a marginalized form of sexuality to current sociopolitical issues. Although his best-known films of this period—*Los placeres ocultos* (Hidden Pleasures, 1976) and *El diputado* (The Deputy, 1978)—focus on the plight of the homosexual living in an oppressive society, de la Iglesia, a committed Marxist, is equally concerned with other forms of "difference"—economic, political, and social—which marginalize individuals in patriarchal Spain. Thus by politicizing homosexuality, the writer/director broadens the appeal of a subject matter that had been virtually absent from Spanish cinema until the early 1970s.

Historically, this link between male homosexuals and other marginalized groups played an integral role in the development of the Spanish homosexual rights movement, which officially began in 1972 in response to the enactment of the most severe antihomosexual legislation in modern Spanish history. The 1970 Peligrosidad y Rehabilitación Social (Social Danger and Rehabilitation Law) criminalized homosexual acts and empowered the police to arrest any man suspected of homosexuality because of the potential threat he posed to society.[5] The law prohibited homosexuals from living in a "designated place or territory" and visiting "certain public establishments or places" as well as requiring them to submit to the "vigilance of the deputy."[6] In addition, the law included a reeducation component for those who commit homosexual acts in order to "guarantee the reform and rehabilitation of the dangerous with more technical means of purification."[7]

In *Epistemology of the Closet*, Eve Sedgwick identifies one of the contradictions internal to the twentieth-century understandings of homo/hetero definition as the difference between "seeing homo/hetero definition on the one hand as an issue of active importance primarily for a small, distinct, relatively fixed homosexual minority (which I refer to as a minoritizing view) and seeing it on the other hand as an issue of continuing, determinative importance in the lives of people across the spectrum of sexualities (which I refer to as a universalizing view)."[8] The minoritizing versus universalizing binarism proposed by Sedgwick is played out historically in Spain in terms of the difference between the Spanish government's perception and treatment of male homosexuals as a distinct, fixed minority (minoritizing) versus the Spanish gay rights movement's inclusion of a wide spectrum of sexual identities as well as membership in a democratic coalition of social and political minorities challenging the hegemony of the Franco regime (universalizing). The antihomosexual legislation enacted by the Franco regime was specifically designed to marginalize homosexuals by rendering them "invisible": they were prohibited from holding public meetings, publicly voicing their opposition, and participating in government. The Peligrosidad y Rehabilitación Social prevented homosexuals from achieving any form of self-identification as a minority, yet as Michel Foucault suggests, the prohibition of sexuality through civil law had the reverse effect: through antihomosexual legislation, homosexuals were identified by the government as a distinct social minority.[9]

In response to legal and societal oppression, the official agenda of the gay rights movement, the Common Platform of the La Coordinadora de Frentes de Liberación del Estado Español (COFLHEE, The Coordinated Homosexual Liberation Fronts of the Spanish State), aimed to eliminate all forms of discrimination that marginalize an individual on the basis of gender or sexual identity. One way to completely demarginalize homosexuals would be to abolish all "ideological categories" such as "homosexual" and "heterosexual," since "its maintenance goes hand in hand with the repression of homosexuality. In this sense, we propose the abolition of "roles"—whether they be man/woman, masculine/feminine, or active/passive, as they prevent an individual's becoming aware of his/her sexual identity, adding instead to feelings of shame, guilt, and self hatred."[10]

Moreover, the underlying goal of the COFHLEE Common Platform was to dismantle all legal, semantical, and social barriers that marginalize the male homosexual and the homosexual community as a whole. They proposed a series of social reforms designed to eliminate all forms of discrimination based on gender, sexual orientation, and public morality. Their demands included the reduction of the minimum age of consent to fourteen, the total separation of church and state, the end of censorship, the introduction of looser divorce laws, the decriminalization of abortion, and the avocation of equal rights for women, prostitutes, and transvestites. Homosexual leaders recognized that they could achieve their goals only by becoming an active part of the larger, unified social movement struggling to maintain democracy: "Our struggle will only attain its objective when closely united with those movements

being developed by feminists, young persons, prisoners, and the marginalized, which together with the working-class movement can make
possible a society without classes and with full democratic freedoms for
all, including the national minorities."[11] Gay activists formed strong
alliances with other political and social groups who experienced similar
marginalization under thirty-nine years of fascist rule. Consequently,
when gay men, lesbians, transvestites, and transsexuals defied a government ban and marched through the Ramblas section of Barcelona in
1978, they were joined by Communists, Socialists, labor union leaders,
feminists, and Catalan nationalists.[12]

   In exposing the oppression male homosexuals continued to face during Spain's democratic transition, de la Iglesia situates sexual issues
within a universalizing context of economic and political oppression.
For this reason, de la Iglesia's work has been dismissed by American and
British gay critics, who feel his films never offer any substantial investigation of homosexual oppression because the homosexual issue is often
diluted and displaced by other social concerns. Vito Russo rejects the
coalition of the economic oppression created by capitalism and homophobia in *Los placeres ocultos* as the source of mainstream audience's "all-
too-familiar spectacle . . . of the contradictory forces of money, class, sex,
intellect, convention and muscle resolving themselves in age-old violence."[13] Richard Dyer labels *El diputado* as "straight cinema" in which
positive images are curtailed by social repression and homosexuality is
associated with "problems" and "tragedy."[14] Even Smith, who acknowledges that although homosexuality in de la Iglesia's films is "qualified
by factors such as class, national politics and regional identity and not
exiled to some space outside history," argues it [homosexuality]

exists primarily as a disturbance in heterosexual and familial relations; it thus
follows that a homosexual hero must be a special case, cannot be representative
of the totality of social circumstances at any moment in a nation's history.
Moreover, this disturbance at the heart of the family resists naturalistic expression, is best served by the conventions of melodrama. For all their love of the
referent and passion for topicality . . . these films are small-scale romances of the
private sphere.[15]

What Smith (and to some extent Russo and Dyer) fail to understand is
that by positioning his investigation of homosexuality within the con-

text of "small-scale romances of the private sphere," de la Iglesia is employing melodrama as a strategy in the Spanish melodramatic tradition.

As Kinder demonstrates in her discussion of the Spanish oedipal narrative, the oedipal conflicts that characterize the Spanish family melodrama were the means by which current political and historical issues were investigated during the Franco period and "with even greater flamboyance in the post-Franco period after censorship and repression had been abolished."[16] The Spanish oedipal narrative consists of an absent father, who is usually idealized or replaced by a surrogate father; a patriarchal mother (a stand-in for the father), who often has contradictory functions as the object of desire for the son and an instrument of his repression; and an emotionally stunted child with patricidal tendencies.[17] The child struggles "against his patricidal destiny—i.e., against replacing his murderous father, who is the structuring absence of the Sophocles play."[18] The absence of the father often results in a displacement of the blame of the violent father onto the mother.

A homosexual variation of the Spanish oedipal narrative focuses on the relationship between the son and his surrogate father, who is both a desirable and threatening figure. The son's desire to imitate the father and assume his place in the patriarchal order becomes more central in the text than his attraction to the mother. The father is desirable because he provides the son's entrance into the patriarchal order via economic stability and by offering him a place within a family unit, which is often times mimetic of the traditional nuclear family structure. On the other hand, the father is a threatening figure because he unleashes the son's repressed homosexual desire, which will prove to be a barrier in the son's entrance into the patriarchal order.

The "father-son" version resembles the homosexual backstory of the oedipal myth involving the kidnapping of young Chrysippus by Oedipus's father, Laius. As an infant, Laius goes to live with King Pelops when his own father, King Labdacus, dies. When Laius grows older, he falls in love with King Pelops's son, Chrysippus, and kidnaps him without the king's consent. As punishment, King Pelops curses Laius, warning him that if he ever bears a son (which he does), his son would kill him (which Oedipus does).

The homosexual backstory has been interpreted by psychoanalysts George Devereux and Marie Balmary as evidence that the true fault behind Oedipus's crime is homosexuality.[19] Yet Devereux and Balmary's homophobic misreading of the story fails to consider that homosexuality in ancient Greece was an institutionalized practice. Devereux also rejects Hans Licht's suggestion that King Pelops's reason for cursing Laius was not due to the homosexual aspect of Laius's relationship with the king's son, but to the violence employed by Laius and his violation of the king's hospitality.[20]

Bernard Sergeant argues, in contrast, that Pelops's reaction may be due to the repression of the king's own homosexual abduction as a boy by Poseidon. Devereux characterizes Pelops's relationship with Poseidon as an "anxiously eroticized submission to a divine homosexual father figure," whereas Sergeant argues there was no anxiety evoked in the pederastic love relationship.[21] Thus, the lesson to be learned from the homosexual backstory is that it is not homosexuality, but the *fear of and desire for the father* that poses a threat to the son and generates sexual repression and violence. As Laura Mulvey suggests, the threat of the primal father is perhaps what the desire of the mother is concealing in the Oedipal story: "Perhaps desire for and fear of a powerful mother and the misogyny it generates conceals something more disturbing, desire and fear of a violent father. Perhaps it is the "unspeakable" ghost of Laius that haunts relations between men, generating homophobic anxieties and an attraction bonded by physical violence."[22]

In the films of de la Iglesia, homosexuality is represented in the context of father-son relationships with pedagogical overtones. The male homosexual couples in *Los placeres ocultos* and *El diputado* are characterized by disparity in the individuals' ages, social status, income, education level, and politics. In order to fully comprehend the dynamics of homosexual relationships in the context of Spanish culture, one must understand the Greek context from which the intergenerational homosexual model originates. The intergenerational relationships in de la Iglesia's films closely resemble the Greek model of pederasty, an integral part of sexual relations in fifth century B.C. Athens. The sexual practices of the classical Athenians, far from being independent and detached "from politics (as we conceive sexuality to be), . . . [were] constituted by the very principles on which Athenian life was organized."[23] The most powerful members of Athenian society, adult male citizens could hold office, participate in the state assembly, and have sex with any member of a subordinate group who was inferior in social and political status (namely, women, boys, foreigners, and slaves). Social status directly determined the role one assumed in the sexual act. Adult males, who were empowered by their citizen status to initiate sex, assumed the dominant "active/insertive role," while members of the subordinate group were "passive" and the recipients of penetration. Even when penetration was not involved, it was assumed that the partner whose "pleasure was promoted" was "active."[24]

Labels commonly utilized today to categorize an individual's sexual preference are not applicable because there was no distinction in ancient Athens between heterosexuality and homosexuality. For Foucault, the categorization of Greek male love as "homosexuality" is inadequate because "the Greeks did not see love for one's own sex and love for the other sex as opposites, as two exclusive choices, two radically different types of behavior."[25] "Bisexuality" is an unsuitable term as well because the option of choosing between females and boys did not refer "to a dual, ambivalent, and 'bisexual' structure of desire."[26] In other words, a male citizen's desire for women and boys were the two sides of the same coin: the gender of the passive partners was of secondary importance to their subordinate status, which was the sole determinant of their receptive role in the sexual act.

In terms of pederastic relationships, an adult male citizen (the *erastes*) would take a young boy (the *eromenos*) as his lover. As social status directly determined the role one assumed in sexual relations, the erastes would assume the active position, while the eromenos would assume the passive. The origin of the erastes-eromenos relationship can be tracked back to the pedagogical homosexual initiation rituals of ancient Crete, in which an erastes would take his eromenos away from the city for several months of hunting, feasting, and homosexual sex. The eromenos would then return home and become a full-fledged member of the patriarchal order and would one day have an eromenos of his own.[27]

In the films of de la Iglesia, homosexual relationships mirror the Greek model of pederasty, as the respective roles each partner assumes are defined in terms of economic and political differences. In *Los placeres ocultos,* a homosexual banker attempts to seduce a heterosexual college student by offering him economic security. *El diputado* focuses on a socialist congressman who falls in love with a teenager who has been hired by the fascist underground to destroy the politician's career. The "oedipalization" of homosexuality is thus employed by de la Iglesia as a strategy consistent with the political agenda of the Spanish homosexual rights movement to demonstrate how homosexual desire continues to be constructed and controlled by patriarchal capitalism and the legacy of Spanish fascism.

Los placeres ocultos (1975)

Eduardo is a closeted homosexual and bank president from an upper-class family who pays young hustlers for sex. He falls in love with a heterosexual college student named Miguel, who, oblivious of Eduardo's sexual interest in him, accepts a trainee position at his bank. As the two become close friends, Eduardo showers Miguel with attention and buys him expensive dinners and gifts. When Eduardo finally confesses his love, a disgusted Miguel ends their friendship, only to return when Eduardo is beaten and robbed by a group of hustlers from Miguel's barrio. Miguel introduces Eduardo to his girlfriend, Carmen; the trio become a "family" and enjoy good times together. Meanwhile, Miguel's former mistress, Rosa, thinks Miguel is sleeping with Eduardo and becomes jealous. Rosa convinces Carmen's father that Miguel is performing sexual favors for Eduardo. The father forbids Miguel to see his daughter. Having lost Carmen because of his friendship with Eduardo, Miguel publicly confronts Eduardo in the bank and "outs" him in front of his employees and customers. Eduardo is once again left alone, until there is a knock at the door. A smile comes to Eduardo's face as he (but not the spectator) sees who is behind it.

The story of a son's struggling relationship with his desirable/threatening father, *Los placeres ocultos* displaces the subject of homosexuality onto a discourse of power, capitalism, and class difference in an impoverished Spain. In his relationship with the fatherless Miguel, Eduardo assumes the role of surrogate father, fostering Miguel's entrance into the patriarchal capitalistic order via materiality and financial security and simultaneously destabilizing Miguel's heterosexuality. Instead of focusing exclusively on the personal plight of a homosexual in a homophobic society, the text employs an oedipal narrative to expose how desire—homosexual and heterosexual—are economically determined and controlled by patriarchal capitalism.

The link between homosexual desire and capitalism is established in the opening sequence, in which Eduardo pays a prostitute after their sexual encounter. Eduardo's bourgeois background and his bank president title (most appropriate within the context of the narrative) situates him in a position of power in his sexual relationships with men. His initial seduction of Miguel is economic: he sends Miguel a phony letter from a fictional organization offering to sponsor him for a training program at Eduardo's bank. "I represent an organization dedicated to finding people with potential," Eduardo tells him, "Promoting young people. We have observed you on several occasions . . . you have earned out support." The "observer" is, of course, Eduardo, who first spots Miguel admiring a motorcycle in a store window. We later learn that Eduardo's economic seduction of young men, like Greek homosexual initiation rites, is ritualistic behavior. When he later confides in his co-worker/ex-lover Raoul his uncertainty about Miguel's sexual interest in him, Raoul assures Eduardo that Miguel will eventually give in: "They always perform well. I'm living proof."

In the tradition of the Spanish oedipal narrative, both Eduardo and Miguel have absent fathers whom they hold in contempt: Eduardo's fascist father is deceased; Miguel's father abandoned his family. Their mothers are sympathetic, saintly figures whose relationships with their respective sons are economically determined. Raising her three children by herself, Miguel's mother works as a laundress to support her family. On her deathbed, Eduardo's mother, who embodies the traditional, religious Spanish values, admits to Eduardo that she always knew he was different but that a mother, particularly a woman of her class, didn't probe their children about such matters.

Eduardo assumes the role of surrogate father for Miguel by buying him the motorcycle in the window and expensive nights out on the town, which even include heterosexual desire in the form of a female prostitute. When they first meet, Miguel ironically mistakes Eduardo for a college teacher. More significant, Eduardo is repeatedly mistaken for Miguel's father, which pleases the youth. "I like the idea," Miguel admits, "I can imagine whatever I want. I can invent a father who is rich and understanding." Like a Greek erastes, Eduardo prepares his eromenos Miguel for adulthood by instructing him in the harsh economic realities of desire. This lesson is first articulated in the form of *Los heridos* (The Wounded), a novel Eduardo pretends to be writing so he can spend more time with Miguel, whom he hires as his typist. Eduardo explains that the book is not about the physically wounded (Miguel thinks it is about the Civil War), but one wounded by failure. He reveals his pain and frustration at not being able to arouse Miguel's sexual interest by positioning himself as the masochistic protagonist of his novel: "Only then did he comprehend. He saw that with each moment it became more distant and unattainable. Everything, absolutely everything, was lost."

When Eduardo finally reveals his true feelings, Miguel is repulsed and accuses his "fag" employer of trying to corrupt him. Raoul, who serves as de la Iglesia's mouthpiece for the more progressive, Marxist faction of homosexuals who advocate collective action and support, explains to Miguel that the blame should not lie with homosexuality, for *capitalist* seduction, not homosexual seduction (as Devereux and Balmary would suggest), is the true "fault" of the father. "You should get ready for the struggle," Raoul warns him, "Not only against a gay who offers you money. Maybe you've been selling more important things and you don't already know it."

The truth in Raoul's warning also applies to heterosexual desire, as exemplified by Miguel's relationship with his married neighbor Rosa, who invites Miguel over to "fix the plumbing," a comical metaphor they use to hide their affair from Miguel's unsuspecting mother. After making love in the darkness of Rosa's room, Miguel is paid for his services. Their sexual relationship thus mirrors the economic conditions of Miguel's friendship with Eduardo. Rosa is an example of what Kinder identifies in her discussion of the Spanish oedipal narrative as the excluded, vengeful woman whose "sexual power is deemed inferior to the homosexual alternative."[28] When Rosa discovers that Eduardo is her rival for Miguel's affection, she accuses him of using Miguel as his "parasite" and then tries to negotiate with Eduardo, asking him if Miguel can continue sleeping with her ("once a week or every fifteen days"). "You know what it is to love him," she pleads, "and what love makes one do." Heterosexual desire thus functions under the same economic rules, but while Eduardo repents and recognizes that his attempt to seduce Miguel was misguided, Rosa becomes increasingly more jealous and spiteful.

Eduardo's solution for maintaining his relationship with Miguel is to rechannel his desire and assume his role of surrogate father for both Miguel and Carmen. The threesome now begin to relate as a reformulated version of the nuclear family. Eduardo takes the couple on outings and soon begins to talk of starting his own family to "find a way to escape the solitude to which we are condemned." By having a family (or even a pretend one), he can, in his words, "stop being alone, being an outsider." Consequently, the politicized Raoul dismisses the suggestion that having a false family is the way out; he views it as also part of the capitalist system and another way of "paying" for a lifetime of satisfaction. His radical views would later be echoed by the COFHLEE Common Platform, which advocated the "creation of free human relations as a substitute" for oppressive institutions such as marriage and the patriarchal family.[29]

As Smith suggests, de la Iglesia inverts the "homosocial triangle" identified by Sedgwick in her study of the nineteenth-century novel. According to Sedgwick, male homosocial desire excludes female desire, as a woman (in this case Carmen) can serve only as a vehicle for two men to explore their relationship with one another.[30] In the case of Eduardo/Miguel/Carmen, as Smith argues, "this relationship is desublimated, openly acknowledged to be based on erotic desire."[31] The similarity between *Los placeres ocultos* and the novels analyzed by Sedgwick is more extensive than Smith acknowledges, for female desire is excluded in the film not at the expense of homosexuality, but patriarchy. As Sedgwick herself asserts:

Clearly, however convenient it might be to group together all the bonds that link males to males, and by which males enhance the status of males—usefully symmetrical as it would be, that grouping meets with a prohibitive structural obstacle. From the vantage point of our society, it has apparently been impossible to imagine a form of patriarchy that was not homophobic . . . the historical manifestations of this patriarchal oppression of homosexuals has been savage and endless.[32]

De la Iglesia is struggling against the patriarchal forces that both repress homosexuality and define homosexual (Eduardo's love for Miguel) and heterosexual (Rosa's love for Miguel) desire in capitalistic terms. Equally problematic is the marginalization of female desire in the narrative. The female characters are represented in Manichaean terms in the traditional female Spanish oedipal narrative roles of saint (Miguel and Eduardo's mothers and Carmen) and whore (Rosa). Moreover, de la Iglesia displaces the blame for Eduardo's economic seduction of Miguel

Miguel (Germán Cobos) is controlled by the vengeful Rosa (Charo López) in
Los placeres ocultos. (Photo courtesy: Award Films)

onto the vengeful Rosa, who instigates Miguel's tragic loss of Carmen
and his rabid public revenge on Eduardo. There is, in fact, a double
displacement leading back to patriarchy because Rosa can only achieve
her revenge by going to Carmen's father. More important, Rosa's behavior is not perpetuated by Eduardo's homosexuality, for both homosexual desire and female heterosexual desire are clearly determined in
the narrative by the same patriarchal, capitalist system. As Gayle Rubin
suggests, "the suppression of the homosexual component of human
sexuality, and by corollary, the oppression of homosexuality, is . . . a
product of the same system whose rules and relations oppress women."[33]
This is not to suggest that homophobia and female oppression are one in
the same nor to promote *Los placeres ocultos* as a feminist alternative to the
nineteenth-century novels exposed by Sedgwick. De la Iglesia unfortunately never ventures into the same territory Almodóvar later explores
in films such as *La ley del deseo* (Law of Desire, 1987), in which both
homosexuals and women share a common bond on the basis of their
marginalization in Spanish society.

Miguel and Eduardo's relationship never extends beyond the pla-

Miguel (center) avenges the "fault" of homosexual "father" Eduardo (Simon Andreu) in *Los placeres ocultos*. (Photo courtesy: Award Films)

tonic, yet Eduardo continues to play the "good father" and fulfill Miguel's material needs. When Miguel loses Carmen after Rosa tells Carmen's father that Miguel is being kept by a man, Miguel still mistakenly assigns the blame to homosexuality. "You took me away from my environment, my world," he declares, "and dropped me into yours." He lashes out at Eduardo by publicly exposing his crimes. "Your boss is a queer," he shouts in the bank lobby, "He's a fag! He pays kids to go to bed with him!" Still failing to comprehend the ramifications of allowing himself to be bought by both Eduardo and Rosa, Miguel (like Devereux and Balmary) assigns the blame to homosexuality, never understanding that he is a victim of a class system created by capitalism and which ultimately controls heterosexual and homosexual desire.

Because the film focuses on a homosexual's unrequited love for a heterosexual man, homosexual desire cannot be played out in narrative terms. The spectator is left to speculate on the film's ambiguous final moment. Has Miguel returned to Eduardo for forgiveness? To declare his love? As constructed within the confines of capitalism, both homosexual and heterosexual desire are reduced to the cinematic representation of the male and female body as the object of the voyeuristic gaze. In the first shot of the film, a young male hustler towels off his naked body as he steps out of the shower and walks into Eduardo's bedroom. Through a series of shots, Eduardo sits to the right, watching the hustler get dressed. As Smith concludes, de la Iglesia "implicates the spectator in a traffic of homosexual voyeurism which is overtly commercial. The man and the audience have paid to look; the boy is paid to be looked at."[34] Smith fails to fully address, however, de la Iglesia's thematic treatment of voyeurism on the narrative level and how his cinematic use of shot/reverse shot operates similarly for heterosexual desire. De la Iglesia involves the spectator in both the homosexual and heterosexual gaze through shot/reverse shot when Eduardo gazes at Miguel (when he first spots him on the street, watches him sleep, and so on) and when Miguel casts his gaze on Carmen's face (before their first sexual encounter) and Rosa's naked body (after they make love).

Smith inaccurately claims that the change in perspective attained by de la Iglesia in his use of the cinematic technique of rack focus "is an emphatic means of underlining the irreconcilability of the two gazes in the film: the man's amorous regard for the youth, and the youth's erotic pleasure in his girlfriend."[35] Smith cites two examples from the film. The first involves Eduardo spying on Miguel and Carmen in the park. According to Smith, de la Iglesia racks the focus from the kissing couple in the distance to the green leaves in the foreground behind which Eduardo is hiding. The second involves a rack focus from a photograph of Eduardo in the foreground to the naked bodies of Miguel and Carmen in the background. The second shot does not appear in the print of the film I viewed; the first example is inaccurate. The shot is not a rack focus; a cut reveals that the camera's gaze on Miguel and Carmen kissing on a park bench is from Eduardo's point of view. In contrast to Smith's claim, the homosexual and heterosexual gazes are not cinematically represented as irreconcilable, for both the male and the female body are positioned as the object of the cinematic spectator's voyeuristic gaze.

The point is underlined further by bringing the spectator into the act of voyeurism in the park, where Eduardo encounters a self-professed voyeur, who spies on couples having sex. The voyeur implicates not only Eduardo in his voyeuristic activities, but the cinematic spectator as well. "There aren't many of us left," the voyeur admits, "Everyone is going to the movies. I still prefer the real thing." By including the spectator, de la

Iglesia refuses to differentiate along the lines of gender and sexuality, because both the positioning of the male and female body as the object of the gaze, regardless of who is gazing at whom, is central to the film's theme: heterosexual and homosexual desire are part of the same economically determined power system. More important is that through his use of the double gaze, de la Iglesia threatens to destabilize the clear-cut binary opposition between heterosexuality and homosexuality, a dynamic that Almodóvar takes much further.

El diputado (1978)

While serving time in jail as a political prisoner, Roberto Orbea, a leftist lawyer and a leader in the fictional Partido Radical Socialista (Radical Socialist Party), has a homosexual encounter with Nes, a street hustler imprisoned on a morals charge. Upon his release, Roberto confesses what happened to his wife, Carmen, who, knowing that her husband had homosexual relations prior to their marriage, is sympathetic and understanding. Meanwhile, radical changes occur in the Spanish government. Adolfo Suárez replaces Arias Navarro as prime minister (on July 3, 1976) and the Spanish Communist Party is officially legalized the following year (April 9, 1977). Roberto is elected as a congressman to the new democratic government and continues to have homosexual relations with young boys supplied by Nes. With Nes's help, the fascists plan to blackmail Roberto by paying a young hustler, Juan, to become involved with him. Juan agrees to the plan but soon falls in love with Roberto. When the fascists discover that Juan has disclosed their plan to Roberto, they murder Juan in Roberto's apartment, thus ending the congressman's political future as the newly elected head of the Spanish Socialist Party.

In *El diputado,* Franco's legacy and the contradictions in current Marxist politics continue to marginalize homosexuals in the newly formed democracy. Once again, de la Iglesia refuses to deal exclusively with the homosexual struggle, but instead relates sexuality to broader social issues by addressing the subject of sexual oppression within the context of national politics. When Adolfo Suárez legalizes the Spanish Communist Party, Roberto and his comrades are allowed for the first time to hold public meetings and demonstrations as well as participate in government. Concurrent with his political liberation is the unleashing of his repressed homosexual feelings, which Roberto must keep hidden, as he once did his politics, in order to maintain his position as an elected official. At the start of his relationship with Juan, he uses for their clandestine encounters the apartment where underground Communist meetings were once held. Carmen finds this strange, but as Roberto explains to her, it is most appropriate: "I still need this place for certain aspects of my life. I still need the secrecy."

Roberto soon discovers he is unable to keep the private/sexual and his public/political aspects of his life separate. He is thus forced to face his oppressors from opposite sides of the political spectrum. On the right, the fascist underground, a remnant of oppression under Franco's regime, hire Juan to destroy Roberto's political career. The political Left, despite sharing common ground with the gay liberation movement, failed to deliver on their promise and include homosexual rights in their agenda. One of the first and most active gay rights organizations, the Frente de Liberación Gay de Cataluña (The Gay Liberation Front of Catalonia), had to wait five years to be legally recognized by the Spanish Ministry of the Interior, three years after democracy was established. The legalization was viewed by one gay activist as "not more than one point in the fight of the gay movement" because of the continual existence of "a century old oppression generated by the dominant ideology and extended to the whole social milieu."[36] De la Iglesia, a former member of the Spanish Communist Party, is thus critical of his party for failing to address sexual issues, but the Left's rejection is never fully played out in the narrative. The contradictions of the leftist agenda, which force Roberto to treat his sexuality as he once did his politics, are instead displaced in the Spanish melodramatic tradition onto the homosexual oedipal relationship of Roberto and Juan.

The parallel between sexual and political liberation is first introduced in the film's opening title sequence, in which paintings depicting Communist revolutionary scenes are intercut with extreme close-ups of body parts from Michaelangelo's David. On the soundtrack, Manuel Gerena sings "Canto de la Libertad" (Song of the Revolution), a musical motif heard through the film and which later serves as the underscoring of Robert and Nes's sexual encounter. After a brief prologue, which establishes the narrative as Roberto's flashback on the morning following

Juan's murder, a montage tracing Roberto's political history features a series of government officials reading from his police file. They recount Roberto's early days as a radical, a college professor, and a defense attorney for political prisoners. As he imagines how he would defend his homosexuality, a similar montage recounts Roberto's sexual history, including a series of sexual encounters in subway cars, movie houses, public lavatories, and army barracks.

As an adult, Roberto's homosexual desires are unleashed while he serves a short sentence as a political prisoner. When confessing to Carmen about his sexual experience in prison, he describes how he found himself in that "strange environment again . . . all of a sudden I recalled the lavatories from when I was a student, the army barracks . . . my homosexuality was just like that, dirty and persecuted—something I had to overcome that is back again, perhaps stronger than ever." As Roberto recalls, his homosexuality is constantly resurfacing when he is subjected to patriarchal control in social institutions such as schools, the military, and the prison system. Thus, the state ironically assumes a contradictory role as both oppressor and generator of homosexual desire.

Unlike in *Los placeres ocultos,* the attraction between Roberto and Juan is mutual. There are, however, several similarities between the two couples. Like Eduardo and Miguel, both characters have absent fathers: Roberto has renounced his late fascist father, while Juan is the illegitimate son of a barmaid. The parameters of homosexual desire are also once again determined by capitalism and economic power. De la Iglesia creates a dichotomous homosexual milieu inhabited by bourgeois-buyers and proletariat-sellers. Like Eduardo, Roberto pays hustlers for sex; his relationship with Juan is initially a financial arrangement. Juan and Nes agree to help the fascist underground blackmail Roberto for financial gain; they are motivated by their economic interests, not political ideology. When Roberto asks Nes why he sold him out to the fascists, he replied in a matter-of-fact fashion, "Well you bought me, didn't you? So did they."

Unlike the relationship between Eduardo and Miguel, Roberto and Juan's relationship is not only sexually mutual, but it transcends its capitalist base. There is a pedagogical aspect to their relationship: erastes Roberto introduces his eromenos Juan to art, literature, and

The nuclear family is transformed in *El diputado:* Carmen (María Luisa de San José, left), Roberto (José Sacristán, center), and Juanito (José Luis Alonso, right). (Photo courtesy: Award Films)

socialism. Roberto and Carmen take Juan to museums and in a scene mirroring a Cretan initiation ritual, Roberto takes Juan camping in the woods, where he reads Marxist theory to him. Like a Greek eromenos, Juan is indoctrinated into the social order through his relationship with Roberto. After hearing the congressman speak at a Socialist rally, Juan, who has declared earlier that he has "no opinion at all" when it comes to politics, gets caught up in the moment, raises his hand in the Communist salute, and later joins the youth movement.

The nuclear family once again undergoes a radical transformation as Roberto and Carmen both become surrogate parents to Juan. When Juan at first has trouble dealing with his feelings for Roberto, he tries to have sex with a woman at a party, but the encounter is disrupted by the male host, who insists on watching and participating. A situation that disgusted Juan is later repeated and eroticized when Carmen, Roberto, and Juan have a ménage à trois. In his attempt to duplicate, yet sexually reconfigure the traditional father/mother/son family structure, the representation of female desire exists solely within the confines of the patriarchal familial system: it is through the presence of Carmen that

The desire and fear of the homosexual father: Juanito (José Luis Alonso) lashes out at Roberto (José Sacristán) in *El diputado*. (Photo courtesy: Award Films)

Roberto and Juan can maintain the public facade of father and son. The suggestion that Juan is their son is in fact not made by Roberto, but Carmen, who worries that she will get left behind if her husband continues to lead a double life. Once again, it is patriarchy, not homosexuality, that confines female desire to the nuclear family, as it is the source of oppression that forces Roberto, Carmen, and Juan to publicly assume their respective father/mother/son roles.

In his discussion of *Los placeres ocultos,* Smith argues that "male homosexual desire is present as a disturbance in existing heterosexual and familial relations," which prevents the "re-evaluation of female desire, whether hetero- or homosexual."[37] What Smith fails to understand is the larger issue at stake: de la Iglesia's infusion of homosexuality, within heterosexual/familial relations, whether it be warranted, as in *El diputado,* or unwarranted, as in *Placeres ocultos,* is a strategy by which he disrupts and reconfigures patriarchal institutions such as the family and heterosexual romance. Once again, it is homophobia generated by patriarchal capitalism and not the homosexual "fault" of the father that destabilizes Miguel's heterosexuality in *Placeres ocultos* and draws Roberto and Juan's relationship to a tragic conclusion.

Notes

1. Eloy de la Iglesia's popularity extends to an international gay audience, mostly through the gay film festival circuit and home video market. Five of de la Iglesia's films, *Los placeres ocultos* (Hidden Pleasures, 1976), *El sacerdote* (The Priest, 1978), *El diputado* (The Deputy, 1978), *Navajeros* (Knife Fighters, 1980), and *Males* (Pals, 1982), are distributed in the United States by Award Films, a Los Angeles–based gay video company.

2. Marsha Kinder, *Blood Cinema* (Berkeley and Los Angeles: U of California P, 1993), 55, 430.

3. See John Hopewell, *El cine español después de Franco* (Out of the Past: Spanish Cinema after Franco), 2d ed. (Madrid: Ediciones el arquero, 1989), 233–42.

4. Paul Julian Smith, *Laws of Desire: Questions of Homosexuality in Spanish Writing and Film, 1960–1990* (Oxford: Clarendon; New York: Oxford UP, 1992), 129.

5. Lesbianism was not illegal under Franco law, though lesbians were subjected to harassment by the police. See Peter Tatchell, *Europe in the Pink: Lesbian & Gay Equality in the New Europe* (London: GMP, 1992), 131; Shelly Anderson, *Out in the World: International Lesbian Organizing* (Ithaca, New York: Firebrand, 1991), 47. For a discussion of the lesbian movement in Spain, see Armand de Fluvàa, *El homosexual ante la sociedad enferma* (The Homosexual before a Sick Society), ed. José Ramón Enríquez (Barcelona: Tusquets, 1978), 170–82.

6. Antoni Mirabet i Mullol, *Homosexualidad hoy* (Homosexuality Now) (Barcelona: Editorial Herder, 1985), 164.

7. Mirabet i Mullol, 165.

8. Eve Kosofsky Sedgwick, *Epistemology of the Closet* (Berkeley and Los Angeles: U of California P, 1990), 1.

9. Michel Foucault, *The History of Sexuality Volume 1: An Introduction,* trans. Robert Hurley (New York: Vintage, 1980), 6.

10. COFLHEE, Platform, 205.

11. COFLHEE, 207–8.

12. Barry D. Adam, *The Rise of the Gay and Lesbian Movement* (Boston: Twayne, 1987), 138.

13. Vito Russo, *The Celluloid Closet* (New York: Harper & Row, 1987), 322.

14. Richard Dyer, *Now You See It: Studies on Gay and Lesbian Film* (New York: Routledge, 1990), 267.

15. Smith, 322.

16. Marsha Kinder, "The Spanish Oedipal Narrative from *Raza* to *Bilbao*," *Quarterly Review of Film and Video* 13, no. 4 (1991): 67.

17. Kinder, "The Spanish Oedipal Narrative," 67–72.

18. Kinder, "The Spanish Oedipal Narrative," 73.

19. George Devereux, "Why Oedipus Killed Laius," *Oedipus: a Folk Lore Case-*

book, eds. Lowell Edmunds and Alan Dundas (New York and London: Garland, 1984), 215–33; Marie Balmary, *Psychoanalyzing Psychoanalysis: Freud and the Hidden Fauly of the Father* (Baltimore: Johns Hopkins U, 1979), 8–9.

20. Hans Licht, *Sexual Life in Ancient Greece* (London: Routledge, 1932), as quoted in Devereux, 222.

21. Devereux, 224.

22. Laura Mulvey, "The Oedipus Myth," *Visual and Other Pleasures* (Bloomington: Indiana UP, 1989), 199.

23. David Halperin, *One Hundred Years of Homosexuality* (New York: Routledge, 1990), 31.

24. Halperin, 31.

25. Michel Foucault, *The Use of Pleasure: The History of Sexuality,* vol. 2, trans. Robert Hurley (New York: Vintage, 1990), 187.

26. Foucault, *The Use of Pleasure,* 188.

27. Bernard Sergeant, *Homosexuality in Greek Myth* (Boston: Beacon Press, 1984), 7–15.

28. Kinder, "The Spanish Oedipal Narrative," 73.

29. COHFLEE, 205.

30. Eve Sedgwick, *Between Men: English Literature and Homosocial Desire* (New York: Columbia UP, 1985).

31. Smith, 140.

32. Sedgwick, *Between Men,* 3.

33. Gayle Rubin, "The Traffic in Women: Notes toward a Political Economy of Sex," in *Toward an Anthropology of Women,* ed. Rayna Reiter (New York: Monthly Review, 1975), 180.

34. Smith, 137.

35. Smith, 142.

36. Mirabet i Mullol, 340.

37. Smith, 140.

PAUL JULIAN SMITH

Pornography, Masculinity, Homosexuality:

Almodóvar's *Matador* and

La ley del deseo

In 1993 the British Board of Film Classification published *Video in View: Public Attitudes to Video Classification.* In the section entitled "Attitudes to 'Offensive' Elements" we find the results of test data on a sample of viewers. Whereas "drug use" was considered offensive by a large number of viewers (27 percent), "nudity" and "sex" were cited by a small minority (2 percent and 9 percent, respectively). The specific attitudes toward these two categories are, however, revealing. The report claims: "It is clear that nudity was not a major issue . . . [but] inevitably, male nudity, even when as natural and innocent as that in [Merchant/Ivory's] *A Room with A View* [1986], produced a more uncomfortable viewing experience for many."[1] The sample was also shown a "homosexual kiss" from Stephen Frears's *My Beautiful Laundrette* (1985). I cite the report: "The great majority reacted with extraordinary vehemence to this extract, with many either unable to watch or expressing themselves 'sickened' by what they saw. Men, in particular, found this rather mild demonstration of homosexual affection unacceptable for both themselves and their families. . . . 'It's disgusting . . . I don't need to see it and I don't even want to hear about things like that' (Female BC1, young children) . . . 'It's perverted, made me feel sick' (Male CD2, young children)."

It would be easy to contest these experimental data, which are clearly compromised by the board's procedures and preconceptions. Viewers were shown a single tape of extracts edited together and were thus deprived of the narrative context that would have framed audience responses to sex or nude scenes when they watched the film as a whole. Moreover, the diversity of audiences for film and video is not addressed.

Laundrette was funded by Channel Four, whose remit was precisely that of addressing minority concerns; and there could be few members of the film's original audience, who had paid to see the film in a theater or at home (unlike the board's guinea pigs), who were not already aware of its gay theme. Also, the definition of respondents in the report (by marital and domestic status, by dint of which men are granted the right to speak on behalf of their children) presupposes a familial setup from which lesbians and gay men are unthinkingly but definitively edited out. Note also the aesthetic bias toward the "quality" cinema of Merchant/Ivory and the supposed naturalness of its male nudes, reassuringly "innocent" and sexless.

More important, however, is to examine the conclusions of the report in these sections: Why is it "inevitable" that male nudity should produce a "more uncomfortable viewing experience"? Why did blameless heterosexual viewers respond with such extraordinary vehemence to the same-sex kiss, with nausea and disgust from which they hoped to shield their innocent offspring? I shall address these questions from a somewhat oblique angle in this essay by working through three different theoretical strata in versions of cinema and sexuality. The first is the gendering of spectatorship (that is, the exploration of male and female viewpoints inscribed in dominant cinema) associated with a psychoanalytically derived feminism, which is itself derived from Laura Mulvey's hugely influential article "Visual Pleasure and Narrative Cinema."[2] The second is revisionist accounts of that gendering by anticensorship or pro-pornography feminists such as Linda Williams, Gaylyn Studlar, and Carol Clover. The achievement of these scholars is both to disrupt sometimes monolithic gender polarities by introducing a certain bisexuality and to introduce history into psychoanalysis, through a close attention to the social reception of specific genres, such as hard-core and slasher films. Finally, I will give an account of Slavoj Žižek's essay "Pornography, Nostalgia, Montage," which, in its reversal of gendered roles, is particularly relevant to the analysis of Pedro Almodóvar's films: for Žižek it is not the pornographic performer who is objectified but rather the spectator, betrayed by a desire that always fails to coincide with the pleasure promised by voyeurism.[3] I suggest, then, that the redefinition of sexualities functions in two ways in Almodóvar: first, by proposing a displacement of the binaries of gendered spectatorship; and second, by suggesting that at the formal or technical level this displacement is effected in the films themselves by a certain dislocation or incommensurability between dialogue and image.

Much film criticism in the '70s and early '80s took it as read that the male gaze was the subject of dominant Hollywood cinema and that it could be described as active, sadistic, voyeuristic, and fetishizing. Its necessary counterpart was the feminine object, held to be passive, masochistic, exhibitionistic, and fetishized. Hence, if Mulvey used the masculine pronoun (*he*) to represent the viewer consistently throughout her article, it was because cinema was founded on the male castration trauma: as in fetishism, the man's perception of the woman's lack of a penis is denied or disavowed, displaced on to a substitute object (nose or shoe) or a substitute practice (perverse cutting of a woman's hair or caressing of her undergarments). Smooth, firm, and impossibly glamorous, female stars such as Marlene Dietrich embodied the phallus, frozen rigid and suspended outside the narrative, a static icon provoking and assuaging male castration anxiety.

It is important to stress here that Mulvey's gendered spectator positions should not be reduced (as they frequently have been) to empirically sexed individuals on the cinema seat. If the spectator is "he," it is because women too have learned to identify with a male gaze; and spectator positions are precisely positions and not implacably immobile identities. However, more recent feminist critics have contested the apparently deterministic implications of Mulvey's argument. As Linda Williams puts it in *Hard Core:* "In this formulation, male pleasure-in-looking struggles against the displeasure of castration in a static realm of iconicity that always constructs the image of the woman as an ultimately reassuring mirror of the man. Patriarchal power invariably wins; the struggle is over before it begins. Power . . . is understood only as the narrative power of action, . . . a realm that already excludes the woman. In both cases we observe the negative operation of a repressive and prohibitory power, but not the positive operation of a power that feeds off of and constructs further pleasures."[4]

One of the areas in which this productive operation of power operates is, for Williams, hard-core pornography. Of all the cinematic genres, this is the one in which women are not punished for being active; far from being the passive victims of the male gaze, female performers frequently initiate action within the films and are the dominant players in their narratives of desire, however vestigial.

Gaylyn Studlar's *In the Realm of Pleasure,* meanwhile, calls attention to Mulvey's stress on the masculinization of the woman watching narrative cinema. What psychoanalytic film theory has failed to address, however, is the possible feminization of the male: "Psychoanalytic film theory has operated on the assumption that the cinematic apparatus and the classical narrative structurally close off the male's possible identification with the represented female or the kind of dialectical viewing experience attributed to women. . . . [However] through the mobility of multiple, fluid identifications, the cinematic apparatus allows the spectator to experience the pleasure of satisfying the drive to be both sexes and of reintegrating opposite-sex identification repressed in everyday life."[5]

Studlar argues, in opposition to Mulvey, that the fetishizing look corresponds more closely to a masochistic than to a sadistic viewpoint; and that the Dietrich films cited by Mulvey as evidence for the fetishization of woman also point repeatedly and unambiguously to the masochistic pleasure of men humiliated by a sadistic woman.

Likewise, Carol Clover's *Men, Women, and Chainsaws* argues against Mulvey's description of the male "sadistic-voyeuristic" gaze, drawing on the apparently unlikely example of the slasher genre: "Horror movies spend a lot of time looking at women, and in first-person ways that do indeed seem well described by Mulvey's 'sadistic-voyeuristic' gaze. But the story does not end there. A standard horror format calls for a variety of positions and character sympathies. . . . Horror is far more victim-identified than the standard view would have it—which raises questions about film theory's conventional assumption that the cinematic apparatus is organised around the experience of a mastering, voyeuristic gaze."[6]

One apparent anomaly in the horror movie is the figure of the "final girl": the resourceful young woman who survives the slaughter and dispatches the monstrous murderer, until the next sequel at least. Given the overwhelmingly male audience for such films, Clover argues (like Studlar also) for a cross-gender identification, with young men taking masochistic pleasure in the triumph of a castrating woman over a spectacularly sadistic man. Twin teenagers, the final girl and the male horror fan, participate in a certain bisexuality, sharing the drive to be both sexes, which is normally confined to fantasy and dream. It thus follows that what is important about these revisions of cinematic gender theory by Williams, Studlar, and Clover is not only that they shake the fixed polarities of male-sadist-voyeurist-fetishist versus female-masochist-exhibitionist-fetishized; it is also that they open up a space for non-literal, fantastic readings of films (in which, say, the gender of participants need not be the same as that assigned on screen), while at the same time historicizing those same fantasies and films, showing the complex ways in which pornography, Hollywood classics, and horror movies are actually read by concrete consumers.

I shall argue later that Žižek goes perhaps even further in linking pornography and its opposite (nostalgia) to precise practices of montage or editing. But let us first offer a provisional reading of Almodóvar, one that addresses the following questions: To what extent does Almodóvar reproduce a traditional gendered division of roles and spectator positions? To what extent does he revise that division, offering more complex views of such elements as female fetishism and male masochism? How does the question of homosexuality further complexify Almodóvar's relation to the pornographic mode and to new versions of masculinity?

I will start with thumbnail plot-synopses. In *Matador* (1986), Almodóvar's fifth feature, Diego (Nacho Martínez) is a retired bullfighter; María (Assumpta Serna) is a successful lawyer who is obsessed with Diego and who imitates his mode of killing, but with human victims sacrificed at the moment of orgasm; Angel (Antonio Banderas) is Diego's virginal and repressed pupil, who also attempts to imitiate Diego and is defended by María. When this triad of characters obsessed by sex and death come into conflict, none of them can resist the inevitable. *Matador* features fluid photography from Angel Luis Fernández and virtuoso editing from José Salcedo.

In *La ley del deseo* (Law of Desire, 1987), Pablo (Eusebio Poncela) is a successful gay film director; Antonio (Antonio Banderas) is his obsessive lover, who will stop at nothing to possess the object of his desire; Tina (Carmen Maura) is Pablo's transsexual sister, who is concealing a dark secret. When the ironic and manipulative Pablo is confronted by the absolute demand of *amour fou,* destructive passions are unleashed. This, Almodóvar's sixth feature, is his only gay-themed narrative to date. Crosscutting between comedy and pathos, it offers gorgeous costumes and art design (by Cossío), memorably extravagant performances, and an outrageously improbable storyline. The central triangle of characters is supplemented in both films by somewhat pallid erotic rivals: Eva (Eva Cobo) is Diego's petulant fiancée in *Matador;* Juan (Miguel Molina) is Pablo's chaste boyfriend in *La ley del deseo.* Neither can compete with the deadly passions of amorous interlopers María and Antonio, respectively. The triangle is thus stretched somewhat awkwardly into a quadrilateral, betraying a diegetic excess or remainder typical of Almodóvar.

Let us compare the opening scenes of the two films. *Matador* begins with unidentified footage from slasher videos. Almodóvar cuts back to a close-up frontal shot of Diego's fevered face in an unestablished location. Crosscutting between video and voyeur gives us a brief objective shot from the side, which reveals that Diego is in an armchair, and is furiously masturbating, just out of frame. We cut without explanation or motivation to what we later recognize as the bullfighting academy in which Diego is lecturing a class on the art of killing. The camera lingers in close-up on Angel, a young student whose gaze is directed at an unseen object. The schoolroom is crosscut with another unestablished series of locations in which María picks up a young man in a square and initiates sex with him in an unknown interior. The sex play is now crosscut with an exterior of the students practicing their moves with dummy bulls. There is a fake match on action here as a student's lunge from left to right is continued by María's pushing of her victim in the same direction on to the bed. As the soundbridge of Diego's lecture dies away, the crosscutting becomes faster and more rhythmic, culminating in María's plunging of the hairpin into the nape of the man's neck, shown in extreme close-up. As dreamlike music, from Satie, begins, she continues mounted on him in long shot, achieving a solitary orgasm.

The discontinuity editing in this opening sequence is wholly unlike Hollywood norms. With reference to place, there are at least five unestablished locations here whose relative positions are impossible to determine: the video voyeurism room; the classroom; the practice ring; the square and apartment of María's murder. With respect to time, there is an unquantified lapse, or ellipsis, between the scene of the video and that of teaching. Moreover, the crosscutting between bullfight practice and murderous seduction implies a simultaneity of action that is at no point clearly confirmed. As far as person is concerned, the opening shot of the video material is only subsequently confirmed as a *pov* (subjective view) from Diego's perspective; the murder sequence, on the other hand, is shot with an objective camera, which denies us identification with either María or her victim. Finally, and most disruptively, the close-ups of Antonio that precede the views of the murder scene might suggest a subjective framing of that scene, but he, however, is not present. This is later confirmed when we learn that he is a psychic obsessed by sadistic visions over which he has no control. In each of these areas, then (of place, time, and person), there is an expressive surplus or remainder that resists assimilation to narrative sequence: most disturbing, perhaps, is the brief and curious shot in which a troubled Diego stands in the practice ring, as if aware of being observed, while behind him Angel looks on, out of focus, his gaze unverifiable. Moreover, the discontinuity of image is overlain with an incommensurability of image and sound, which is equally disorienting: the use of the soundbridge implies a subjective merger or fluidity (the drive to be in two locations or times simultaneously) that transcends individual experience.

How do the characters established in this sequence respond to Mulvey's gendered divisions of roles and spectatorship and to feminists' later revisions of her account? Diego would appear to be set up as the male gaze par excellence: voyeuristic, fetishistic, and sadistic, he reconfirms that unthinking and generally incorrect equation of pornography with the slasher or video nasty, enjoying the penetration of female flesh by male weapons. Taking pleasure in women's victimhood, he might also, however (and this is confirmed by the subsequent narrative), identify with those victims and crave a similar fate for himself. María would appear at first to be the mirror image of the gender stereotypes: the woman with the weapon, who initiates a violent sexual encounter, she is also a voyeur who takes pleasure in male nakedness and a fetishist who eroticizes the substitute object of the hairpin and perverse goal of murder, rather than the genital object and aim assumed by Freud to be standard.[7] However, to reverse the polarities is to leave the gendered division itself in place: in the theory of fetishism, this smooth, hard woman with her elevated hairstyle is quite clearly the traditional phallic woman whom men love and fear; as femme fatale María here embodies Freud's account of classical castration anxiety in which men both project on to and deny the supposed threat of the female anatomy in the figure of a cruel woman. María will alternate in the film between virilized black-and-white business suits (she is, after all, a lawyer) and extravagantly "feminine" costumes. Just as the mild-mannered Diego oscillates between male rapacity and female fragility, so the defiant María seeks also to be two sexes, to enjoy voyeurism and exhibitionism at once and alternately.

More difficult to account for is the third character in the sequence, Antonio Banderas's Angel. As we have seen, Angel's viewpoint is as hard to establish as his gender or sexual identity. The unwilling witness to both male and female sexual violence, he identifies with his master Diego to such an extent that he attempts to rape the latter's girlfriend, Eva. Consistently asked if he is himself homosexual (by Diego and the police inspector), Angel represents an impossible bisexuality that can only lead beyond gender identity to rapture and unconsciousness: gazing up at the sky, he falls in a fainting fit.

What we see in the three main characters of *Matador* is a fantasy of the suspension of sexual difference. Feminized man, virilized woman, and bisexual visionary, each points in their different ways to a cross-gender identification open also to spectators in the cinema. But if Almodóvar shifts the cinematic apparatus toward the unaccustomed spheres of male masochism and female fetishism (María collects mementos of Diego's bullfighting career), he also acknowledges the extreme difficulty of shifting gender polarities. As we see with the *Liebestod* in the final sequence of the film, it is only in death that sexual difference can be subject to a final and definitive suspension; and the bisexual Angel remains a chaste and immaculate visionary to the very end.

The alternative models of masculinity suggested by *Matador* are effected to a large extent by modes of performance: the anemic Nacho Martínez is unlikely to be many directors' first choice for the role of a sadistic murderer. Both he and Assumpta Serna's sympathetic María reconfirm Freud's suggestion in his essay on fetishism that fetishists are unlikely to experience their behavior as "the symptom of an ailment": "Usually they are quite satisfied with it, or even praise the way in which it eases their erotic life" (351). Almodóvar effects a certain banalization of the perverse in *Matador:* it is Angel's neurotic mother who is stigmatized for her unacceptable behavior in rejecting her son. If Almodóvar seems to challenge gender polarities ascribed to pornography and masculine modes of viewing, how then does this intersect with the question of male homosexuality addressed most directly in *La ley del deseo?*

The opening sequence of this second film raises similar questions to that of the first. It begins with a long shot of a youth in an unestablished location, apparently a bedroom. As the camera tracks in, an unidentified voice instructs the youth to remove his clothes. The youth rubs his groin in a mirror, a high angle briefly aligning itself with his point of view. Returning to the bed he removes his underpants, turns over, and instructed by the voice once more, masturbates or simulates masturbation: in medium long shot his buttocks are visible but not his penis. Almodóvar now cuts away to another unestablished location in which two older, bald men are reading from a script into microphones. The repetition of the phrase "Fuck me" by the youth and one of the men reveals that the men are postsynching the sound for the opening shots we have just seen. Quick cuts after this cinematic orgasm reveal that the sequence forms part of the new film by director Pablo, who is greeted by his transsexual sister Tina at the premiere, as future lover Antonio comes into frame on the left.

Once more we have dislocation of place, time, and person. It is never established whether the bedroom is a studio set or an authentic location; the pencil line is drawn in an editing suite we are never shown; the theater may or may not be the one at which Pablo and Tina present *La voix humaine* later in the film. There is clearly some elapse of time between the shooting of the youth and the premiere; the length of the period is not specified. More important, the status of the opening shot is undecided: it might appear to be a subjective viewpoint of the first Voice to speak; but we later learn that they are in a dubbing studio, not immediately present off-camera to the youth. The repeated instruction that the youth not look at "me" suggests a sabotaged attempt at objectivity. It remains unclear, however, how much of the dialogue we hear will be present on the sound track of Pablo's film. The instructions to the youth, which we assume to be sotto voce direction to the actor, are in fact (like the voice of the young man himself) being dubbed elsewhere. There is thus a disorienting incommensurability or dislocation between sound and image, which remains despite the reassuring deflation of sexual tension brought about by Almodóvar's use of comic relief.

In spite of the youth's protestations, it seems likely that this soft-core scene disables voyeuristic spectators rather than its actor. The sweating and shuddering dubbers appear more vulnerable than the polished performer, shielded by his youth and beauty. It seems significant, however, that the most graphic sex scene in the film should (like the video voyeurism of *Matador*) be placed in quarantine, as it were, detached structurally and formally from the rest of the film. For as Žižek notes, the reconciliation of graphic sexuality and narrative coherence is impossible in the same work: one must exclude the other. Moreover, the sexual charge of this particular sequence will be much greater in a country such as the United Kingdom, in which (unlike in Spain) hard-core pornography is prohibited by law.

As *La ley del deseo* develops, its central triangle of homo- or transsexual characters displays a similar evolution to the overtly heterosexual figures of *Matador*. Thus Pablo (Eusebio Poncela), the director, is initially masterful and detached, like Diego, a voyeur-sadist who manipulates his male lovers and sister, Tina. However, by the end of the film he who, we are told, has "taught" Antonio how to make homosexual love, is forced to obey Antonio, the willing pupil now a forceful teacher. Transsexual Tina (Carmen Maura) is like María: ostentatiously feminine in costume and manner, she is also masculine identified and has no difficulty punching out a disrespectful detective who gets in her way. Finally, Antonio the obsessive lover has much in common with *Matador*'s Angel, played by same actor, Antonio Banderas. Unable to distance himself from his erotic obsessions, he gives himself up to psychosis, the unmediated incursion of fantasy into the real.

The moral of *Matador* is that there is no sexual relation: heterosexuals can achieve reciprocity only when sexual difference itself is suspended in fantasy or death. The moral of *La ley del deseo* is similar but equally dispiriting. It is that reciprocity is equally problematic for gay men: Pablo claims to love Juan, who does not love him in the same way; and he only comes to love Antonio when it is too late and the latter is on the brink of suicide. Almodóvar would thus appear to coincide with theorists such as Guy Hocquenghem in suggesting that there is no such thing as homosexual desire, only desiring subjects whose objects invariably fail to meet their demands.[8] If *Matador* points toward an impossible, utopian bisexuality (in which we can be, for a moment, both sexes), then *La ley del deseo* points to the necessary insatiability of sexuality, its continuous and repeated failure to hit the mark.

This is a point stressed by Žižek in his "Pornography, Nostalgia, Montage," which underlies this essay. It is an argument that not only sheds light on Almodóvar's use or abuse of these modes; but also points to a concrete analysis of his technique. Žižek starts with a reference to Michael Mann's thriller *Manhunt* (1986), in which a detective finally realizes that what unites a number of murder victims whose home

Pablo (Eusebio Poncela,
right) is initially masterful
with his male lovers in
La ley del deseo.

Carmen Maura
plays the transsexual
Tina in *La ley del deseo.*

Tina nurtures her adopted child Ada in *La ley del deseo.*

Antonio Banderas plays a young man trapped by erotic obsession both in *La ley del deseo* and *Matador.*

Diego and María partake in a final murderous embrace in the finale of *Matador*.

movies he has watched is not the content of these movies but the medium itself. They had previously been viewed by the murderer, who proves to be a laboratory technician: "[the detective] is already identified with the murderer. . . . His obsessive gaze, surveying every detail of the scenery, coincides with the gaze of the murderer."[9] This coincidence of our own gaze with the perverse-sadistic gaze of the Other is one exploited by Almodóvar in the opening sequences of *Matador,* and to a lesser extent, of *La ley del deseo*. But it is precisely this identification of the perverse gaze with the gaze of the Other that, according to Žižek, renders pornography unsatisfactory: as Almodóvar's impotent and feminized voyeurs also reveal, "contrary to the commonplace according to which in pornography, the other . . . is degraded to an object of our voyeuristic pleasure, . . . it is the spectator himself who effectively occupies the position of the object. The real subjects are the actors on the screen trying to rouse us sexually, while we, the spectators, are reduced to a paralysed object-gaze" (110).

I have already referred to one consequence of this "failed encounter": the structural impossibility of "congruence between the filmic narrative (the unfolding of the story) and the immediate display of the sexual act" (110), which functions as "an intrusion of the real undermining the consistency of this diegetic reality" (111). While Žižek's hypothetical example of genuine, hard-core coupling between Meryl Streep and Robert Redford in *Out of Africa* (1985) proves his point perfectly, even Almodóvar's softer sexual moments are exiled outside of the main body of his narrative, whether hetero- or homosexual, and resist integration within it. But there is another mode at work in Almodóvar; the opposite of pornography, which Žižek calls "nostalgia." Whereas pornography implies an identification with the perverse view of the Other (as when we discover that our perspective has been aligned with sadistic murderer Diego), nostalgia suggests, to the contrary, a "split between fascination and ironic distance: ironic distance toward . . . diegetic reality, fascination with [the] gaze" (112). Žižek's examples here are the rereading of film noir from the '50s onward, in which the modern viewer presumes a contemporary innocent viewer through whom she or he experiences the text; and Westerns since the same decade, where modern audiences contemplate not the content of the genre itself, from which we are ironically distanced, but the "gaze of the naive other absorbed, enchanted by it" (114). This domestication of the gaze of the other is a fine model for Almodóvar's "gentrification" of provocative sexual material in these films because sequences clearly allusive to pornography are framed within repeated allusions to Hollywood melodrama of the '40s and '50s. Associated at first, and most troublingly, with the perverse sadism or manipulation of Diego or Pablo, we are later seduced into an ironic and amused contemplation of the naively romantic frame tale. Shamelessly sentimental, *Matador* and, more particularly, *La ley del deseo* capture our fascination not so much through their content, but through the nostalgic longing they imply for the untrammeled excesses of melodrama.

But that excess is cinematic as well as narrative. And Žižek has, finally, offered a typology of editing that shows how the "transformation of fragments of the real into cinematic reality produces . . . a certain leftover, a surplus that is radically heterogeneous to cinematic reality but nonetheless implied by it, part of it" (116). In his analysis of sequences such as Lilah's approach to the uncanny house (or Thing) at the end of Hitchcock's *Psycho,* Žižek shows how the play of shots effects identification in montage: "Two kinds of shots are . . . permitted and two forbidden. Permitted are the objective shot of the person approaching a Thing and the subjective shot presenting the Thing as the person sees it. Forbidden are the objective shot of the Thing . . . and—above all—the subjective shot of the approaching person from the perspective of the uncanny object itself" (117).

Almodóvar follows these prescriptions in the sequences we saw. In *Matador* we find the subjective shot of the video screen from Diego's pov and the objective shot of Diego himself from the side; in *La ley del deseo*, the subjective shot of the youth from the Voice's viewpoint and the objective shot of the Voices shown at work in the dubbing theater. What Almodóvar does not allow us (or only allows us momentarily) is an objective shot of the screen or the youth unanchored to a subjective pov; and (most particularly) a subjective shot from the object's viewpoint, with the screen or the youth looking back at their respective voyeurs. However, this does not for Žižek imply the sadistic dominance of the voyeur: it is only because the object is already looking back at the voyeur that the filmmaker need not or cannot show it doing so; in both Hitchcock and Almodóvar, voyeurism implies not dominance but a subject seduced by the death drive, aiming straight for oblivion.

We have seen, then, that gender positions are not fixed in cinema: as in fantasy, we may find female fetishism and voyeurism, male masochism and exhibitionism. And although pornography may reinforce gender polarities, it may also unfix them, promoting new modes of masculinity: victim- or cross-gender-identified, male spectators may be getting off on the pleasure and terror of letting go of identity, or of giving in to active, sadistic women. What is more, homosexuality is no asylum from the straight sexual fix, revealed in Almodóvar at least to be as prone to delusion and dissatisfaction as heterosexuality. Almodóvar himself has practiced a double disavowal with these films, claiming in interviews that *Matador*, ostensibly concerned with straight passion, is about two "homosexuals," creatures of the same species who desire one another; and that *La ley del deseo*, ostensibly concerned with homosexuals, is a story of love between brother and sister, between brother and brother.

Rather than criticizing Almodóvar for mystification or closetry, we should note that this flexibility in the narrative scheme is also present at the technical level: crosscutting between subjective and objective viewpoints, between established and unestablished locations, dislocating the image and sound tracks through soundbridges that "bleed" over the cuts, Almodóvar points through purely cinematic means to the fluidity of gender identity, which (as Gaylyn Studlar suggests) we would rather not acknowledge in waking life. Just as Freud noted that any challenge to narcissistic investment in the penis could be read hysterically as an attack on "Throne and Altar,"[10] so the apparent challenge to sexual difference staged by a homosexual kiss may be enough to threaten the stability of the family values enjoyed by those members of the public who responded with such "extraordinary vehemence" to the inquiries of the euphemistically named British Board of Film Classification. What Almodóvar shows us, however, both here and elsewhere, is that it is by no means easy to introduce the freedom of filmic fantasy into the constrictions of everyday life. In both *Matador* and *La ley del deseo,* the suspension of sexual difference, the quest for a love without limits, leads inevitably to death.

I began by asking why British video audiences found male nudity and a homosexual kiss so offensive. From anecdotal evidence, it might appear that Spanish audiences have stronger stomachs. Hard-core pornography is openly sold on the street, with "bizarre" material such as coprophilia or bestiality available in some sex shops. Moreover, an enlightened Constitution guarantees equality for all citizens, including lesbians and gay men.

It is in this context that any redefinition of sexualities in the work of Almodóvar is to be examined. As is well known, both *Matador* and *La ley del deseo* benefited from healthy government subsidies;[11] and the latter, Almodóvar's first self-production for his homonymous company El Deseo, was the film that most represented Spain at foreign festivals in the year of its release.[12] As late as 1993 the first Spanish cultural festival in Israel included *La ley del deseo* among the small number of films to be exhibited. The film was thus fully incorporated into the Government's cultural policy, and, as I have argued elsewhere,[13] its homosexual theme may be read in post-Franco cinema as a synecdoche for the modern, secular Spain that was to be marketed around the world.

Of course, official policy need not mirror changes in popular attitudes. And for all the overt liberalism of the socialist ethos, deviant desires have found relatively little symbolic representation: the period has seen little increase in social organization or visibility for either feminists or gay men. Likewise, theories of gendered spectatorship (or their various revisions) have produced little response in Spanish universities, where women's studies remain undeveloped and lesbian and gay studies inconceivable. Ironically, however, that fluidity of gender cate-

gories and sexual identities explored by psychoanalytic film theory outside Spain may correspond to some degree to sexual behavior within
Spain. Lacking, to a large extent, publicly visible communities organized around sexual identity, Spaniards may experience more flexible
"cartographies" of desire than Anglo Americans, formations such as
those that have also been identified by sociologists for Spanish-speaking
America.[14] Once more, then, Almodóvar would seem to reconfirm
rather than redefine sexual experience, just as he falls into line with the
sociodemocratic ethos of his time. This is not to propose that Spaniards
can publicly adopt comparable personae to the feminized man, virilized
woman, or bisexual visionary familiar from *Matador,* but rather that in a
private sphere defined more widely than elsewhere there may be more
space to play with such categories than stereotypes of Catholic morality
would suggest.

A recent French collection of interviews with Almodóvar is similarly
open ended. In his unwillingness to pin the director down in his introduction, Frédéric Strauss situates Almodóvar in a zone of implicitly pre-
oedipal drives and indifferentiation: his is a cinema that neglects logical
sense for aesthetic sensation, produces inexplicably powerful emotions
in the unsuspecting spectator, and deploys a formal power that goes
beyond mere formal technique.[15] Strauss's is a psychic model of creation
and spectatorship that neglects the historical conditions of film production explored in the interviews that form the body of his book. But in his
brave and naive stress on the emotional transference between cineaste
and audience, Strauss suggests an important point: the visual and libidinal pleasures of Almodóvar's cinema can never be wholly exhausted by
the liberal ideology that funded and marketed them, and there are
inexplicable excesses of both narrative and technique that remain irre-
cuperable. It is those Things that most fascinate the spectator or critic,
those Things which leave us objectified, even paralyzed, as we approach
the screen, caught (like Žižek and Almodóvar) between nostalgia and
pornography.

Notes

1. British Board of Film Classification, *Video in View: Public Attitudes to Video
Classification* (London: BBFC, 1993), 9.

2. Laura Mulvey, "Visual Pleasure and Narrative Cinema," *Screen* 16 (1975): 6–18.

3. Slavoj Žižek, "Pornography, Nostalgia, Montage," in *Looking Awry: An Introduction to Jacques Lacan through Popular Culture* (Cambridge: MIT Press, 1992).

4. Linda Williams, *Hard Core: Power, Pleasure, and the "Frenzy of the Visible"* (Berkeley and Los Angeles: U of California P, 1991), 43.

5. Gaylyn Studlar, *In the Realm of Pleasure: Von Sternberg, Dietrich, and the Masochistic Aesthetic* (New York: Columbia UP, 1988), 34–35.

6. Carol Clover, *Men, Women, and Chainsaws: Gender in the Modern Horror Film* (London: British Film Institute, 1992), 8–9.

7. Sigmund Freud, *On Sexuality* (Harmondsworth: Penguin, 1977), 351.

8. Guy Hocquenghem, *Homosexual Desire* (London: Allison and Busby, 1978).

9. Žižek, 108.

10. Freud, 352.

11. Paul Julian Smith, *Desire Unlimited: The Cinema of Pedro Almodóvar* (London: Verso, 1994), 74, 80.

12. "*La ley del deseo,* película que más veces representó a España en festivales extranjeros en 1987," *La Vanguardia* 13 (October 1987).

13. Paul Julian Smith, *Laws of Desire: Questions of Homosexuality in Spanish Writing and Film, 1960–1990* (Oxford: Clarendon; New York: Oxford UP, 1992), 138.

14. Tomás Almaguer, "Chicano Men: A Cartography of Homosexual Identity and Behaviour," in *The Lesbian and Gay Studies Reader,* ed. Henry Abelove, Michele Aina Barale, David M. Halperin (New York and London: Routledge, 1993), 255–73. For Spain, see Oscar Guasch, *La sociedad rosa* (Barcelona: Anagrama, 1991).

15. Frédéric Strauss, *Pedro Almodóvar* (Paris: Cahiers du Cinéma, 1994), 8–9.

MARVIN D'LUGO

La teta i la lluna: The Form of Transnational

Cinema in Spain

Becoming European is a process of *endless* becomings and divisions; . . . it is a process marked by a multitude of histories of uneven development defined by difference and by quite difficult instability at both the personal and the collective level.—John Caughie[1]

In the end, nationality becomes the costume worn by cosmopolitan agents of the transnational phenomenon.—Richard Maxwell[2]

Renegotiating Ideas of Spain and Europe

José Juan Bigas Luna's *La teta i la lluna* (*The Tit and the Moon,* 1994) is a strikingly new kind of Spanish film, one that engages both Spanish and foreign audiences in playful reflections on many of the clichés of Spanish cultural identity while bringing those very audiences to confront the process through which that identity is being reshaped by multinational capitalism. Conceived of as the third part of a cycle of Retratos ibéricos (Iberian Portraits), following *Jamón, jamón* (1992) and *Huevos de oro* (Golden Balls, 1993), *Teta* is distinctive within the trilogy by virtue of the emphasis it gives to the complex regional, national, and transnational forces reordering Spanish culture.

Unlike the dark urban settings that marked many of Bigas's earlier films, *Teta* is set in a space populated by a number of picturesque images of Catalan culture. The most central of these is the traditional Catalan *castell* (castle), a competition in which teams of young men form human pyramids in the main squares of towns and cities. This folkloric custom

The Catalan *castell* is
prominently featured
in *La teta i la lluna.*
(Photo courtesy: José
Juan Bigas Luna)

is not, however, merely some quaint detail to add local color to the story
but rather a defining moment for the film's young protagonist-narrator,
Tete. It becomes, as well, a central visual narrative motif for the film and
thus brings the audience to interrogate an idea of national culture that
has seldom been so problematically posed in Spanish cinema.

As the film opens, the eight-year-old Tete, an *anxaneta* (the small boy
whose task it is to climb to the very top of the castle and declare victory),
is tenuously perched on the shoulders of several of the young men who
form the upper tiers of the castle. Gripped by fear as he looks down at the
sea of people below, Tete is urged on by his father who, as coach of the
castell team, tells him he must keep climbing to the top. It soon
becomes apparent that to ascend to the peak of the castell is a macho rite

of passage, a proof of manhood not only to the assembled community but, more important for the young Tete, to his father. It is precisely this narrative conflation of personal and social scenarios that helps bring into focus Bigas's larger conceptual plan in which narratives of the community and those of the individual are woven into a national allegorical text. Indeed, within the broader context of cinematic culture, Tete's precarious position dramatizes just how the film as a whole self-consciously situates itself in the unstable space of a national community in the throes of reshaping itself around a series of radical economic, social, and political changes.

Some audiences may mistake the use of Catalan symbols and objects, including the Catalan flag, as another example of the reverential cultural boosterism the Catalan government has long supported through its generous film production subsidies. Bigas's playful sense of parody, however, is never far from the surface. For instance, he has his little hero imagine himself to be the first Catalan astronaut on the moon, planting the regional flag along with that of the European Union (EU) on the lunar surface. Just as in *Jamón, jamón,* where the icons of Spanishness were wildly lampooned to deflate the commonplaces of a sacrosanct "Spanish" culture, in *Teta* the notion of some profound regional subculture, linked in little Tete's mind with his position in his own immediate family, is derided as merely a transitory stage of communal allegiance to be superseded in time by other forms of social affiliation. In the parodic style of these Retratos ibéricos Bigas and his co-scriptwriter, Cuca Canals, do not merely mock the solemnly self-important but finally provincial notion of subnational identity. They exploit it comically in order to focus on the complex shift in cultural logic in recent years that has brought Spaniards of all regions to acknowledge what amounts to the transnational formulation of their culture in relation to Europe and the world.

In making Catalan symbols the target of parody, Bigas effectively poses a broader cultural scenario in which Catalonia functions synecdochically for a more expansive Iberian scenario characterized by the progressive wearing down and reshaping of traditional Spanish cultural stereotypes. Such a treatment explicitly situates Catalonia as a micro-regional culture, defined between the oppositional terms of Spain and Europe. As Marsha Kinder has argued, the microregion functions to challenge the national hegemony of Castilianized Spanish culture by positioning that culture within a regional/national/global interface that effectively reveals the relativistic nature and shifting centers involved in such formulations of cultural communities.[3] This interface, as Homi Bhabha observes, partakes of a postmodern sense of national cultures whose "implicit critique of the fixed and stable forms of the nationalist narrative makes it imperative to question those theories of horizontal, homogeneous empty time of the nation's narrative."[4]

Such a project comes at a critical historical juncture for Spanish cinema, when the very idea of Spain as a national cultural entity is ceding rapidly to the realities of transnational capitalism,[5] and is producing alarming results in the always volatile Spanish film industry. For well over a decade now, media historians and cultural theorists have been describing aspects of the realignment process in European mass media in which the growing presence of macroregional or transnational audiences have come to defy the traditional boundaries of nation-states.[6] This literal remapping of cultural boundaries by the mass media has been called "cultural synchronization" and described as "a canny reorientation of national cultural industries in line with . . . the core of capitalist cultural production."[7] Inevitably, such realignments of audience have spawned a series of works that can no longer respond to what is assumed to be the fixed boundaries of national cultures, nor be read within the context of immutable cultural identities. Rather, they are marked by a complex textual hybridity as well as a heterogeneity in the projection of their audience. *La teta i la lluna* positions itself in that dialogical space of overlapping national and transnational formations as it engages a European audience in the process of reassessing its own clichéd images of Spaniards and Spanish culture, while at the same time renegotiating the coherence of Spanish cultural identity for Spanish viewers.

Bigas's emphasis on the folkloric marks of identity of Catalan culture, while coinciding with claims by regional chauvinists of a historically distinctive cultural tradition, also advances a contrary project: a conceptualization of Spanish identity in which Catalonia, because of its strategic geographic position "near Europe," serves as a mediation between as well as the paradigm of economic and cultural modernization for Spain's potential shift toward Europe. Traditionally, Europe has been viewed as a model for certain intellectual ambitions identified with the modernization of Iberian culture dating back at least three centuries. The dominant models of eighteenth- and nineteenth-century liberal social thinking for Spaniards were explicitly rooted in the contrast between the ideal of enlightened European cultural development and the fortress-like mindset that characterized the Spain that evolved out of Counter-Reformation ideology. With the rebirth of Catalan nationalism at the end of the last century, the effort to construct a sense of an independent Levantine tradition identified more strongly with the European avant-garde than with peninsular cultural developments became a prominent tendency in a variety of fields.

Although the attraction of Europe as the harbinger of cultural modernization has long been a theme in Spanish intellectual circles, beginning in the 1960s a distinctive rapprochement with Europe began to be advocated, one to be shaped by economic rather than intellectual or artistic forces. Its origin may be traced to a redirection of Francoist governmental policy starting in the late 1950s that sought fundamental economic and social transformation through commercial integration. That movement ran through governmental policies of both the dictatorship and the fledgling democracy and reached its fruition in the mid-1980s with Spain's entrance into the EU. It is this market-driven notion of an economic realignment of Spain with Europe that provides the backdrop for the Retratos ibéricos.

Though each part of the trilogy operates as an autonomous film, all three works are pointedly cast within the reordered commercial space of transnational European cinema. To that end, Bigas has followed a distinctive enunciative strategy, first crystallized in *Jamón, jamón,* in which the narrative is elaborated around certain cultural stereotypes that serve transnationally as a lingua franca through which a beguiling and familiar image of Spanish social and sexual identity is played out. Those very same clichés also work as a shorthand through which the narrative of an emerging Europeanized Spain is formulated for a specifically "national" audience. For this latter audience, the idea of a Spain resemanticized by the forces of transnational capitalism poses a very potent and polemical theme. Here the medium is indeed the message as that national audience is led through each successive part of the trilogy to read an exploration of the underlying tensions in Spanish culture that have effectively forged for Spain a new relation to European art and commerce.

History as Allegory

La teta i la lluna poses what amounts to a revisionist reading of the Spanish "national fiction" in that it examines the very nature of the cultural specificity of the national as a relative, shifting signifier in relation to a series of rapidly changing historical contexts.[8] Framed from a truly "eccentric" narrational position of instability, Tete's "story" is enunciated as a first-person narration motivated by the young boy's precarious emotional and physical states. That narration begins as he stands atop the human pyramid in a Barcelona square, frozen by a vertigo occasioned by his view of the mass of people below him. Egged on by his father, who tells him not to look down but to keep ascending, Tete pauses and then falls. A second attempt at climbing to the top of the pyramid proves equally fruitless. A parallel narrative of a more symbolic ascent, told with the trappings of a magical, childlike fairy story rhetoric, ensues after this second fall. This "other" story further details Tete's state of crisis and displacement.

With the birth of his brother, the eight-year-old boy is deprived of the nurturing maternal breast that obsesses him until he begs relief from the moon with whom in his childish reverie he carries on a private dialogue. Relief comes in the form of a substitute breast, that of Estrella, a dancer in a traveling carnival, who arrives in Barceloneta. Rather than resolving the longing for the breast, however, Estrella's presence only leads Tete to a new form of manly competition. Her body is also coveted by two other males: her husband, Maurice, some twenty years older than she, a *pedoman,* whose carnival performance consists of modulating his flatulence as though it were a musical instrument, and Miguel, a young Andalusian who falls passionately in love with Estrella at first sight and wins her over when he breaks into Andalusian song in the middle of the street to court her. Thus Tete can only fantasize that Estrella has given him milk. It is Miguel on whom Estrella takes compassion and with whom she makes love. Subsequently, Maurice and Estrella disappear, and Miguel, so distraught by the loss, attempts but fails to drown himself in the Mediterranean. Tete finds himself once again perched atop the human castle, again urged on by his father. Only this time, Estrella magically appears next to Tete's father in a balcony overlooking the square and entices the anxaneta to the top. Tete succeeds and is cheered by the crowd. His father now boasts that his son has "the balls of

Bigas Luna stands underneath the image of the bull, which is prominently featured in the opening of *Jamón, jamón.* (Photo courtesy: José Juan Bigas Luna)

a bull," a comment that may bring the audience to discern an underlying circularity to the trilogy as it recalls the opening image of *Jamón, jamón.* Tete's story concludes with a coda that repeats the credit sequence of the film in which Estrella appears in the staged performance as a dancer coming out of a box, now joined harmoniously by both Miguel and Maurice as Edith Piaf's voice is heard intoning *"Les mots d'amour."*

The visual style of *La teta i la lluna,* its nostalgic ambience, and carnival setting all contribute to emphasize a certain Felliniesque quality, effectively "Europeanizing" the story by transposing it from its narrow Catalan context to a larger, "Mediterranean" milieu.[9] Like *La Strada* (1954), upon which it is inspired, and *Amarcord* (1974), with which it shares certain narrational and thematic affinities, *Teta* is posed as a tale of nostalgia, foregrounding the process of looking back from a moment of contemporary crisis to the presumed security of an "age of innocence." In interviews Bigas suggests that *Teta,* though made after the other two parts of the trilogy, should precede those two parts in a viewing, to be followed by *Jamón, jamón* and concluded with *Huevos de oro.*[10] Through this ordering one may readily discern the temporal progression of the trilogy from the simple world in which love, rather than eroticism or an aggressive sexuality, dominates, to progressively more brutal stages of sexual desire and its manipulation. Indeed, a number of elements in the film function both to secure the sense of a national allegory and to historicize that symbolically charged narrative.

The most striking of these is the rhetorical prominence given to the act of remembrance, underscored by the frequent use of Tete's voice-over narration. Speaking of the patterns of so-called nostalgia films and the popular cinematic use of a "retro style" in movies, Fredric Jameson notes that what is at stake in establishing this historical perspective through narrative and images is "essentially a process of reification whereby we draw back from our immersion in the here and now (not yet identified as a 'present') and grasp it as a kind of thing . . . producing what one might call the trope of future anterior—the estrangement and renewal as history of our own reading present as the past of a specific future."[11]

This complex "reading present" is clearly evidenced in the way the Retratos ibéricos effectively overlay upon a series of contemporary narratives a cluster of symbolic historical meanings, transforming these stories into an elaborate allegory. The pivot of that process of "estrangement and renewal" of which Jameson speaks is a formulation of each story so as to address simultaneously the anxiety of individuals, of the local community, and of the nation, all in the throes of realigning allegiances. The implications of that allegorical weight may best be assessed by considering the spatial logic of the expanding mise-en-scène produced by the chronological reordering of the three parts of the trilogy. *Teta* begins in the Barceloneta port district of Barcelona, which represents the point of encounter between Andalusians seeking economic improvement and Europeans wanting to exploit a Spanish market. *Jamón, jamón* moves to a more expansive and more stereotypical "Spanish space," initially viewed as linked to the atavistic images of bullfighting. Such icons, however, are insistently displaced by the signs of economic development as evoked by shots of trucks and highways that punctuate the narrative. *Huevos* reflects an intensification of that economic trajectory by its spatial movement. Opening in Melilla, one of Spain's last two African colonies, the action quickly moves to the Costa Brava resort city of Benidorm, the site of unbridled touristic speculation in the 1980s, then finally ends in Miami, a "new frontier" for Spanish

In *Huevos de oro,* Javier Bardem plays Benito González, an aggressively entrepreneurial Spanish Everyman of the 1980s. (Photo courtesy: José Juan Bigas Luna)

international business development. Thus the trilogy charts the flow of Spanish commercial empire-building from the last century right up to the present.

These expanding sites of Spanish economic history form a mise-en-scène that parallels the shifting stages of consciousness. The trilogy charts the evolution of masculine consciousness from the maternal breast that obsesses the protagonist of *Teta* to the final image of *Huevos de oro,* in which Benito González, an aggressively entrepreneurial Spanish everyman of the 1980s, sits in his Miami bungalow acknowledging his own impotence. Coming right after *Huevos de oro, Teta* might well be read as a manifestation of the longing for a return to simpler times motivated by the Iberian male's recognition of his ensnarement in the self-deluding myth of his own power and virility. Looking back, as if in a nostalgic flashback, *Teta* begins with the image of the child in the process of ascent. Yet the "age of innocence" evoked in *Teta,* similar to that of *Huevos de oro,* is fixed on the image of male anxiety and immobility, this time atop the human pyramid.

Bigas has further explained the logic of the film's apparent historical allegory in terms of generational outlooks. Maurice represents the generation of the 1970s, Miguel and Estrella, the generation of the 1990s. Tete, according to Bigas, is the central character of growth, representing the world of the year 2000.[12] In such a context, *La teta i la lluna* becomes the millennial tale in which the little hero passes through progressive stages of cultural allegiance and consciousness as he sheds the old marks of identity of Catalanism and Spanishness and looks toward a Europeanized Spain of the future.

Sexuality and Nationness

As in other of Bigas's films where a sexual discourse serves to articulate political themes, in *Teta* sexuality becomes a way through which the film dramatizes the refiguration of the national community in relation to Europe. This is achieved through a conspicuous reinscription of the Spanish oedipal narrative by means of which patriarchal order has traditionally been reasserted in Spanish cinema. Marsha Kinder has pointed to a number of modifications in the oedipal scenario in Spanish films as they have worked either to affirm Francoist ideology or else to oppose it.

One of the most striking of these has been an elaboration of "mimetic desire" that, instead of emphasizing the attraction of the son to the mother in the myth, stresses the son's impulse to imitate the father.[13] In emphasizing this variant of the oedipal tale, the narrative of *Teta* effectively reorders patriarchal law by defining family and social ties exogamously. The oedipal scenario initially appears to be forming as a rivalry for patriarchal power, symbolized in the desire by both mother and son for *leche* (milk), here an ambiguous term that signifies the father's semen as well as the mother's milk. That rivalry is avoided, however, when Tete is displaced from the maternal breast and led to covet the breast of a young woman. That other woman, tellingly embodied by the French dancer, Estrella, pushes the son toward a refigured notion of Spanish family ties within a larger, "European" context. Tete's story of his displacement from the maternal breast and his subsequent quest for Estrella is told with the linear simplicity of a folkloric parable in which the questions of personal sexual desire parallel a more symbolic narrative with import for the community.

The central tension of the community's narrative is the struggle against the old scenarios of confining cultural values and the emergence of a new and broader conception of communal ties. In the process of this transformation of the sexual story into a narrative of quest, the anxaneta's movement from the most intimate of sites of identity (the maternal breast and the paternal call to manhood) through various stages of psychic growth beyond the family (the neighborhood, the city, the region, and finally to the nation in relation to the world), describes a symbolic trajectory whose psychic-social dimensions effectively redefine the national community. Indeed, the idea of the quest seems to be underscored by the very title of the film.

The plot of *Teta* evolves through a series of conflicts and tensions formed around the allure of the sexual body. On the level of the cinematic image, we may clearly see how those tensions are both elaborated and resolved narratively. The film begins and ends with the same pair of images: In the credit sequence we see a music-hall presentation of Estrella's coming out of a box and dancing on stage, followed in the opening narrative sequence with Tete atop the castell. The narrative ends with Tete reaching the top of the castle, thereby achieving his manhood in the eyes of his father, then shifts to a coda in which Estrella, Maurice, and then Miguel appear, with Estrella returning to her box for the scrolling of the credits. In effect, *Teta* is constructed around the gendered opposition between images of the phallic castle and the female dancer in her theatrical space as each spectacle is imbued with culturally specific details that, together, effectively articulate the film's theme of cultural realignment. As noted earlier, the festive ritual of the castell embodies traditional Catalan culture. The theatrical setting for Estrella's final dance is identified as Stuttgart, and her entire performance is accompanied by the background music of Edith Piaf's "Les mots d'amour." The scopic enticement that moves the film's audience from the *castell* to the music hall stage thus mirrors Tete's story of quest as it has led viewers through its narrative and cultural logic from the phallocentric regionalism of the human castle to an enticingly feminized Europe embodied by Estrella.

Catalanitat

Sexuality clearly appears to be the narrative "bait" through which to engage an audience in a reading of the film. It is ultimately the scenario of cultural and economic realignment, however, that drives the story. In a certain respect, the character of Tete is fashioned as an updated version of Ana from Víctor Erice's 1973 film, *El espíritu de la colmena* (The Spirit of the Beehive). As the vulnerable subject of a cultural discourse, he is positioned between historical epochs and therefore ideally suited to interrogate the cultural order ending and to pursue the new order just beginning. Like Erice's protagonist, Tete possesses a precocious heterogeneity: he is at once the child, but also the adult; he embodies innocence, but at the same time he is the sexual pursuer of his "Estrella."[14] The Catalan culture here presented to Tete is a discursive formation into which he has been born, but, as with Erice's Ana, into which he must also be interpellated: that is to say that *catalanitat,* the traditional marks of Catalan cultural identity, is perceived as an arbitrary social construction. Characterized through the filter of the child's consciousness, catalanitat comes to be viewed by the audience as a national "imaginary" through which the individual and the community must pass in the process of maturation. This cultural imaginary tellingly emerges out of the child's enunciation that conflates personal imaginings with physical reality, as when Tete imagines his newborn baby brother, who has taken

Mathilda May plays Estrella, the elusive object of collective desire in *La teta i la lluna*. (Photo courtesy: José Juan Bigas Luna)

all of his mother's breast milk, to be a pig and we see a piglet dressed as a baby in the child's cradle. In a similar reverie, Tete imagines receiving milk from the breast of Estrella and the stream of milk pours from her nipple like water from a spigot.

Such fantasies are gradually elided with the representation of certain conspicuous Catalan "marks of identity," as when Tete's brother appears with a tiny scullcap in the Catalan national colors, or when his father, a rabid Catalan nationalist who boasts of the Roman origins of Catalan culture, is viewed in gladiator's garb. In this way, the text humorously depicts Catalan folklore and culture as part of a transitory state identified with the community's age of innocence, out of which Tete must eventually grow.

Bigas advances his larger European thematic by destabilizing the conspicuous figures of Catalan culture. He first stages a series of almost parodic simulations of Catalan motifs, then exposes the transcultural spaces within which that overstated cultural cluster is located. This elaboration begins with the situating of the narrative within a highly stylized culturally specific locale, the Barceloneta port district, as mise-en-scène. This is the first time, in fact, that Bigas has been so explicit within the trilogy by calling attention to a precise Catalan space. The presumed regionalist thematic is further underscored by the repeated appearance of the Catalan flag or combinations of yellow and red stripes. As well, Tete defines each of the other characters as functions of a traditional Catalan identity. Miguel is a *charnego* (a person from another part of Spain living in Catalonia), Maurice is a *gabacho,* the Catalan term for a Frenchman. Such epithets define these characters in function of and yet peripheral to a world whose center is insistently marked as Catalonia.

Growing out of this ethnocentric mental mapping is the implicit backstory of the film, the dramatization of the Catalan *marca,* or economic frontier, precisely as it describes the point of convergence of national and transnational cultures. The filmic mise-en-scène evokes an image of Catalonia as a creative frontier in Iberian social space that, like its North American counterpart, appears to facilitate a reformulation, even a renegotiation of identity within peninsular economic and cultural history. As the Spanish region that historically has experienced the most intense industrial development, Catalonia became the site of continued internal migrations as well as the logical "gateway" for European mercantile and industrial development, principally around the city of Barcelona.[15] That is why Tete's world so naturally comes to be populated by Andalusian workers and French carnival performers.

The alignment of catalanitat with these economic mini-narratives serves to foreground the historical scenario within which culture is intimately shaped by a dynamic commercial spirit. Catalonia is the place to which Andalusian workers looking to improve their economic lot have long gravitated and, as well, the locus of a sensual Mediterranean culture that tacitly opposes the austere elements of Castilianized Spain while connecting the peninsula with Europe. The evocation of that popular construction of Catalan specificity, however, does not work merely to mythify anew some privileged regional space. Rather, the interaction of Spaniards and Europeans within this locale suggests that the Catalan mise-en-scène is really the catalyst for the refiguration of Iberian identity precisely in the face of rapid economic transformation of Spain in a global context. Indeed, once Tete leaves the maternal breast

within this symbolic narrative, he easily assimilates into the micro—
social order that forms around the carnival site on the seashore—Miguel;
his motorcyclist friend, Stalone; Estrella; and Maurice. The hero's "migration" thereby restates the larger paradigm of the shift from the static
forms of Iberian identity (the patriarchal, phallic world symbolized by
the Catalan family), to the alluring images of a Europeanized future.
What ultimately emerges is a conception of identity for the Spaniard in
which Tete's catalanitat is symbolically figured as being shaped, eroded,
and continually redefined within the shifting order of economic culture.
Thus, what began iconographically as the most striking marker of catalanitat, the little anxaneta atop the castell amidst a sea of Catalan bodies,
comes ultimately to be read as a new cultural identity in process, shaped
critically not against any one particular cultural mark or regional identity but rather as the result of a dynamic process dramatized through the
elaboration of Tete's narrative.

Refiguring Spain for Europe

This sense of a refigured Spanish identity metaphorically stated through
a Catalan intertext has its roots in Bigas's 1986 film, *Lola,* his first
popular commercial success in Spain and, significantly, his first conspicuous effort to pose a Spanish cultural message in an accessible, "popular"
style.[16] Key to *Lola's* development is its formulation of a "national"
allegory focusing on a certain stereotypical notion of Spanishness refigured through the narrative reinscription of Catalonia as a symbolically charged space. Spanishness is specified in the film by the
characterization of the mythic Iberian femme fatale, embodied in the
actress who, in the mid-1980s, appeared most closely identified with
that sensuous myth, Angela Molina.[17] The film evolves a simple plotline
that begins by reducing to an unnuanced polarity the cultural relations
between Spain and Europe. The opening sequence presents a stylized
view of an elegant Parisian skyline at night as the setting for a highly
civilized dinner party that is then quickly juxtaposed against the arid
highways of Alicante. In this way, the discussion among French businessmen about Spanish women is quickly transformed into a visual
parody of cultural stereotypes: the rational, mercantilism of the north
versus the passionate affect of the south. The narrative then sets up an

intermediary space between these two extremes—Barcelona, where Lola, fleeing from her violent lover, Mario, will meet and seduce (or be seduced by) Robert, the French businessman. In this culturally inflected narrative, Barcelona tellingly becomes the site of a dynamic repositioning for each of the characters but also, symbolically, for Spain as well.

The allegorical narrative of sexual and commercial exploitation inevitably breaks down the stereotypical polarities of Europe and Spain and begins to suggest something of a cultural hybridization ultimately embodied in the child produced by the union of Lola and Robert. It is this renegotiation of national identities, the allegorical playing out of certain reified scenarios of national culture in Spain against the catalyst of a Europe figured not as culture but as commerce, that eventually shapes Bigas's conceptualization of his Retratos ibéricos.

Teta continues that refiguration process by foregrounding the dialogism by which Spanish identity is reshaped. The picturesqueness of Catalan customs and social stereotypes, especially those that connect regional identity with a broader series of clichés about Spanish sexuality, are the most salient examples of this process. From a Spanish perspective, these are easily recognized as the cultural caricatures that have long been the mainstay of the outside world's stereotyped image of Spanish culture. From Buñuel's *Cet obscur objet du désir* (That Obscure Object of Desire, 1977) to Almodóvar's *Matador* (1986), the clichés of an overstated Spanishness have been used as a marketing strategy through which to capitalize on the narrow expectations of foreign audiences. Bigas exploits these very same foreign views of Spain while playing with Spaniards' recognition of the commercial power of such stereotypes. Unlike earlier films, however, the objective of Bigas's textual manipulation is to break down the simplistic barriers that have defined the fixed borders between cultures.

This renegotiation of cultures is captured within the film by means of three pivotal narrative images. The first of these, the castell, provides the dominant narrative image that guides the early parts of the film; Estrella's magical breast as fountain for Tete constitutes the midpoint; but it is finally the spectacle of the maternal Spanish figure now transformed into the seductive "European" dancer, an homage, as Bigas has said, to a Felliniesque world, that effectively links this sexual spectacle with a refiguration of national identity.

It is through this last narrative image, the dancer luring her extratextual audience to view her "European performance," that we come to understand Estrella's role as the elusive object of collective desire that transforms the cultural fetishization of sexual identity into a constructive energy. This transformative function is textually stated in the final moments of the film as Estrella is seen guiding Tete away from the confining identification with the family and the narrow ethnic community. She first appears as a guiding star, leading Tete to his triumphant mounting of the castell. But after offering her breast to the child, the scene rapidly cuts to the film's coda in which this very same Estrella appears in the theatricalized space of a Stuttgart theater with Maurice and Miguel. The effect of this shift of images is to transform the child's story of a sexual and communal quest into the narrative of a larger communal enterprise: the integration of Spain into Europe.

As the intertextual marker of an enticing Mediterranean Europeanness for Spaniards, Estrella comes also to be seen metacinematically as a means of engaging a European audience with a film that is an example of the very exogamy to which Spanish cinema, as well as Spanish culture, must attend. The final result of that dialogical imaging, now not only Maurice, Miguel, and Tete transfixed on Estrella, but Spanish and European audiences as well, is that the borders between Spain and Europe necessarily dissolve, the ultimate effect of a reciprocal fetishization of the sensuous and commodifiable images of each other.

Notes

1. John Caughie, "Becoming European: Art Cinema, Irony, and Identity," in *Screening Europe: Image and Identity in Contemporary European Cinema,* ed. Duncan Petrie (London: British Film Institute, 1992), 35.

2. Richard Maxwell, *The Spectacle of Democracy: Spanish Television, Nationalism, and Political Transition* (Minneapolis: U of Minnesota P, 1994), 151.

3. Marsha Kinder, *Blood Cinema: The Reconstruction of National Identity in Spain* (Berkeley and Los Angeles: U of California P, 1993), 389.

4. Homi K. Bhabha, "DissemiNation: Time, Narrative, and the Margins of the Modern Nation," in *Nation and Narration* (London: Routledge, 1991), 303.

5. Maxwell, 150–52.

6. See particularly the discussion of this process by David Morley and Kevin Robins, "Spaces of Identity: Communications Technologies and the Reconfiguration of Europe," *Screen* 26, no. 1 (1985): 10–34.

7. C. J. Hamelink, *Cultural Autonomy in Global Communications* (London: Long-man, 1983), quoted in Maxwell, 151.

8. I borrow the term "national fiction" from Graeme Turner's book of the same title in which he studies the textual and contextual construction of Australian narrative. Turner's argument is that there exists a cultural specificity of narrative meaning within given texts so that a focus on a nation's narrative, in his case, a body of texts designated as "Australian narrative," will not be merely an "exercise in nationalism but an enquiry into those determinants of narrative which are culturally specific" (10). See Graeme Turner, *National Fictions: Literature, Film, and the Construction of Australian Narrative* (Sydney and London: Allen & Unwin, 1986), 8–11.

9. Bigas openly acknowledges his effort to present an homage to a certain dimension of Fellini's films. See Pablo Llorea, "Lucho contra mi propia estética," *Babelia: Revista de Cultura* no. 149, *El País,* August 27, 1994, 15.

10. Esteve Riambau, "La teta de Tete y la luna de Bigas," *Dirigido Por,* no. 228 (October 1994): 38.

11. Fredric Jameson, "Film: Nostalgia for the Present," in *Postmodernism, or, The Cultural Logic of Late Capitalism* (Durham, N.C.: Duke UP, 1992), 284–85.

12. Bigas Luna, interview by author, October 20, 1994.

13. See Kinder, 197–275, especially her discussion beginning on p. 221, which deals with the ways in which the oedipal myth has been used to subvert the traditional cultural messages of the patriarchy.

14. There is an obvious symbolic quality to Bigas's naming the driving force of exogamy in the film "Estrella," suggesting a guiding star. One recalls the heroine of Erice's second film, *El sur* (The South, 1983), who is also called Estrella. She too is a figure situated in a subversive variation of the oedipal narrative, leading her to move beyond the confines of a past closely aligned with traditional Spanish patriarchy and toward the "south," a site identified, as Bigas's Europe is, with the allure of a revivified world for the individual.

15. The intensity of that condition of the economic *marca* is perhaps best captured cinematically in Josep María Forn's 1964 film, *La piel quemada* (Burnt Skin), which traces the fortunes of an Andalusian family in its pilgrimage to Catalonia in search of economic improvement. For a detailed discussion of this film in relation to the larger theme of Catalanitat, see my essay, "Catalan Cinema: Historical Experience and Cinematic Practice," *Quarterly Review of Film and Video* 13, nos. 1–3 (1991), especially pp. 136–38.

16. Up to this point Bigas's films had either been set in a noir version of Barcelona or, in his failed American debut, *Reborn* (1981), in the United States: "Con Lola he pretendido hacer una película con una narración directa, de fácil lectura, en la que los personajes han sido escogidos porque están muy cerca de nosotros. Es una película que puede llegar a gustar a mucho más público que mis trabajos anteriores." (With *Lola* I tried to make a film with a direct story

line, easily read, in which the characters have been chosen because they're close to us. It's a movie that can please a much larger audience than my earlier works.) Bigas, interview with Susa Dasca, *Diario 16* February 2, 1986, as cited in Antonio Weinrichter, *La línea del vientre: El cine de Bigas Luna* (The Line of the Belly: The Cinema of Bigas Luna) (Gijón: Festival de Cine de Gijón, 1992), 49.

17. Weinrichter, 49.

JAUME MARTÍ-OLIVELLA

Regendering Spain's Political Bodies:

Nationality and Gender in the Films of

Pilar Miró and Arantxa Lazcano

The Female Gaze and/or the National Debate:
Regendering Spain's Political Bodies

Within the contemporary cultural and political debate concerning the redefinition of Spain, there is a need to rethink the traditional notion of nationalism in light of the expanded historical and theoretical models at work in the world today. This essay will focus on the cinematic contribution to that process of cultural refiguration and, more specifically, on the most recent work done by two women filmmakers, Pilar Miró and Arantxa Lazcano (one Castilian and one Basque, one "central" and one "marginal"), each of whose work may be seen as a representational site for this debate. Miró's *El pájaro de la felicidad* (The Bird of Happiness, 1992) and Lazcano's *Urte ilunak* (The Dark Years, 1992) illustrate how Spanish cinema is renegotiating the traditional boundaries between "nation" and "narration," the concepts that Homi Bhabha has so persuasively reelaborated.[1] Both films present stories that reconstruct a personal and private world and that ultimately become tales of a collective, national significance. Both films invite the viewer to share in the "allegorical double vision" described by Doris Sommer when she refers to "Latin America's national novels as an interlocking, not parallel, relationship between erotics and politics."[2] Despite their avowed distance from any feminist agenda, Miró's and Lazcano's common gesture of making the private into a public story, of telling a personal tale of female bonding charged with political overtones, clearly aligns them with the goals of other feminist and postcolonial discourses. This set of discourses are, as stated by the editors of *Nationalisms and Sexualities*, expanding and critiquing the homosocial base of the traditional national narrative, as it has been described by the pioneering studies of George Mosse and Benedict Anderson.[3] What I would like to suggest here is that Miró's and Lazcano's representations of the nation as a "passionate sisterhood," different as they are, clearly contribute to those discourses while becoming, at the same time, powerful models for how to regender Spain's "political bodies."

Television and cinema have taken the place of newspapers and novels as ideal sites or locations for the production of those ambivalent and simultaneous voices that constitute our migrant national narratives. It is primarily in the context of these decentered "imagined" discourses, I would argue, that any individual voice or desire may be culturally inscribed and circulated against the monoglossic constraints of the national or transnational hegemonic narrative.

In the case of Spain under Franco, it seems obvious that cinema played this crucial role. Against the dictator's construction of an exalted Spanish epic as the only vision of the nation, a vision entirely dependent on his violent reinforcement of a general *oubli* or amnesia, many voices struggled to provide a series of alternative narratives. In fact, historical memory became the central concern of a large group of Spanish filmmakers including Juan Antonio Bardem, Luis García Berlanga, Basilio Martín Patino, and Carlos Saura, the last arguably the leading figure in the anti-Francoist new Spanish cinema movement.[4] The historical responsibility of Spanish cinema is perhaps even greater today with the rise to power of another political force whose essential banner seems to have been a revival of that Francoist amnesia. I am referring to the victory of Manuel Aznar's Partido Popular (Popular Party, PP) in the last general elections—a party that has campaigned on the platform of Spain's "unity," one of Franco's most damaging and enduring political principles.[5] Against the return of such a monoglossic concept of Spain, there is a vital need to reimagine our political community as a multicultural and heteroglossic space wherein both national and gender differences may be constantly negotiated. What is at stake, ultimately, is what Xavier Rubert de Ventós aptly called "our access to a democratic culture."

Hasn't it been said that political democracy requires as its foundation a "democratic culture," a series of implied conventions on which it is based? Well, then this "democratic culture" is nothing else but the reconstruction at a "political" level of the traditional or metropolitan coherence on which the freedom of the smallest and/or homogeneous communities is based, a "democratic culture" with which the State has to compensate and supplement—not to substitute— that coherence in order to turn those small islands of autonomous identity into a continent of democratic freedom.[6]

In the Spanish context, Rubert de Ventós's "continent of democratic freedom" implies the political recognition and "reconstruction" of those autonomous identities that have a "coherence" of their own. Simply put, the recognition and reevaluation of a multicultural and a plurinational state may ultimately destroy those limitations that were imposed by a Spain conceived as a nation-state. It is within this context that I see the collective significance of Miró's *El pájaro de la felicidad* and Lazcano's *Urte ilunak*. These two films constitute the most powerful illustrations of a new gendered discourse—one that establishes the visual foundations for an urgent dialogue across Spain's diverse languages and cultures.

The work of Miró and Lazcano provides a representational site for the national debate inasmuch as they themselves embody the dialectics of margin and center that lie at the core of Spain's cultural redefinition. First, as women filmmakers, they occupy a marginal position inside a cinematic discourse that structures itself around the sexual and textual politics of the male gaze. Paradoxically, though, in Miró's case, the concept of marginality is problematized by her central role in redefining Spain's cinematic politics during the heyday of Felipe González's now ailing Socialist Party (PSOE). Miró was appointed general director of cinematography in Felipe González's first Socialist government and in that capacity devised a policy to protect Spanish cinema. Termed "ley Miró" (the Miró Law), this policy provided pre-production subventions for those projects deemed good enough to merit official funding. Although helping the overall aesthetic quality of Spanish films, this policy was viewed negatively by the Spanish cinematographic industry, which accused it of being elitist and politically partisan.[7] What is crucial to my argument, however, is not so much the validity of Miró's cinematic policies but rather the fact of her personal embodiment of political power and her regendering of Spain's political body. It is this direct experience of political power that profoundly affects her own personal representation.

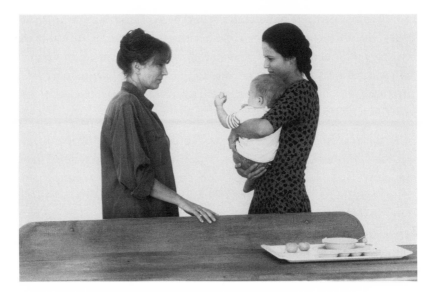

In *El pájaro de la felicidad* the homoerotic bonding between Carmen
(Mercedes Sampietro) and her daughter-in-law Nani (Aitana Sánchez-Gijón)
threatens the fraternal model of Spain's national narrative. (Photo courtesy:
Ministerio de Cultura)

El pájaro de la felicidad is especially important in this context because
it represents Miró's most daring inscription of an alternative desire that
brings "on-stage" what Spain's traditional powers had always erased.[8]
The homoerotic bonding between Carmen and Nani clearly threatens
the stability of the fraternal (even the fraticidal/Cainite) model of Spain's
national narrative. And yet, as I will argue, it also presents itself as a story
that dreams of a "national conciliation," or, given Carmen's emblematic
profession as art restorer, of a "national restoration." In fact, Miró's entire
production to date seems constantly to negotiate the boundaries between her private and her public spaces and to render visible her dream
of reconciling opposing discourses in herself and in her nation.[9]

In contrast to Miró, Arantxa Lazcano, a young Basque woman from
Zarauz, represents the double marginality of her gender and her "regional" culture. *Urte ilunak,* her first feature film, presents a powerful
refiguration of a Basque society trapped in the violent clash of two
patriarchal discourses fighting for hegemony. *Urte ilunak* introduces a
(re)vision of the Basque cultural reality by presenting the story of Itziar,
a girl growing up in the household of Juan Laza and Gloria Artegui, a

family tormented by a sense of defeat and betrayal. Itziar's development is portrayed in powerful poetic images that illustrate her difficult and yet stubborn negotiation of a society that is oppressive in its linguistic polarization. Itziar's central question "zergatik?" (Why?) becomes Lazcano's own interrogation of the strictures of a historical past that still looms large in the struggle for cultural and political identity within the Basque country today.

Miró's Carmen, the female protagonist of *El pájaro de la felicidad*, on the other hand, is an uprooted Catalan woman who has become a prestigious art restorer. Living and working in Madrid when we first encounter her, this divorcée has an estranged son and a faltering relationship with a Catalan architect. Soon, she will be raped, an aggression she will try to overcome by means of a complete withdrawal into herself and her own troubled past. In the end, Carmen's return to her Catalan origins and the expression of her submerged homoeroticism will allow her to reach a deeper understanding not only of herself but of her historical context. There is, however, no closure in Miró's film, since it constantly foregrounds the ambivalence of the traditional spaces represented. This aspect is most clearly visible in the construction of the "Catalan" family to which Carmen returns. This family becomes a true "nation-in-miniature,"[10] which allows Miró to inscribe the clashing discourses of traditional patriarchal values embodied in the Catalan landowner father, the Francoist rhetoric of the Spanish-speaking mother, and the collapse of the Socialist Party "family," which Carmen herself incorporates. Perhaps unself-consciously, the entire Catalan sequence of *El pájaro* seems to betray another of Miró's significant needs. To say it in the words of the editors of *Nationalisms and Sexualities,*

Though undeveloped in his analysis, Anderson's comparison enables the crucial recognition that—like gender—nationality is a relational term whose identity derives from its inherence in a system of differences. . . . But the very fact that such identities depend constitutively on difference means that nations are forever haunted by their various definitional others. Hence, on the one hand, the nation's insatiable need to administer difference through violent acts of segregation, censorship, economic coercion, physical torture, police brutality. And hence, on the other, the nation's insatiable need for *representational labor* to supplement its founding ambivalence, the lack of self-presence at its origin or in its essence.

The female gaze in *El pájaro de la felicidad* is controlled by both Carmen and Nani. (Photo courtesy: Ministerio de Cultura)

The very choice of the term "representational labor" betrays a conflation between nationality and motherhood, which the authors of the piece already acknowledge in their discussion of the traditional trope ("nation-as-woman") embodied in the figure of the ideal mother. What interests me here is how Miró may also be conflating these levels in her allegorical construction of Carmen's Catalan family. This construction becomes especially paradoxical if one thinks of the double displacement of the maternal role. Carmen's mother is certainly not "idealized" as in traditional national narratives; she is in fact presented as "out of place." Speaking Spanish in the midst of Ripoll, at the very heart of Catalonia, and disavowing her daughter's life as part of the disarray brought about by "esa gentuza que gobierna en Madrid" (that populace that governs in Madrid), her inclusion in the film speaks to a general rejection of the Socialist government uttered from a personal nostalgia for the Francoist past. Whose position is that? Why is it located in the segment that represents "Catalan-ness"? Why is Miró crossing the linguistic and symbolic boundaries of traditional (and maternal) representations? Mostly, I believe, because of that very "need for representational labor." Like the nation(s), Miró seems to be (re)presenting herself in order to exist.

Itziar wields the female gaze in *Urte ilunak.* (Photo courtesy: Arantxa Lazcano)

Ultimately, what Miró and Lazcano share is a female gaze that allows them to regender the national debate in the private sphere of their female bonding tales. And, in so doing, they dis-locate the traditional stories of national conciliation. Moreover, *Urte ilunak* and *El pájaro de la felicidad* become significant examples of a cinematic return to music, poetry, and intertextuality, a move that seems to characterize an emerging European cinematic idiom, an (inter)national dialogue that is expanding our imagined communities while disseminating national and narrative boundaries.

Between Micro- and Macroregionalism: Arantxa Lazcano's *Urte ilunak* and Pilar Miró's *El pájaro de la felicidad*

Within Spain's process of refiguration, Miró's and Lazcano's most recent films provide interesting examples of the new dynamics of micro- and macroregionalism, as they have been delineated by Marsha Kinder.[11]

While the United States has successfully marketed and naturalized its own national product as a global mass culture capable of colonizing the world, the Japanese have perfected the opposite strategy—the ultimate postmodernist simulacrum that imitates, improves, and thereby conquers and replaces the alien Other. Yet both models eradicate difference. In contrast, the European Community is developing a strategy that retains and highlights cultural diversity, and that is why the combination of micro- and macroregionalism is so central to its enterprise.[12]

In order to achieve or retain a personal idiom that can confront the hegemonic language of Hollywood, European cinemas try to reemphasize their particularities. Among these particularities is one I have already suggested when describing Lazcano's and Miró's films: the return to music and poetry. As if returning to a kind of cinematic origin, this strategy creates very intimate, almost confessional narratives, which, nevertheless, seem capable of reimagining the national communities that they allegorically represent. Among the most interesting recent examples that come to mind are the German films *The Nasty Girl* (1990), directed by Michael Verhoeven, and *Nobody Loves Me* (1994) by Doris Dorrie; the Italian films *Ciao Professore* ('Bye, 'Bye Professor, 1993), by Lina Wertmüller, and *Stanno tutti bene* (Everybody Is Fine, 1990) by Giuseppe Tornatore, the director of *Cinema paradiso* (1989); the internationally acclaimed French-Polish Krzysztof Kieslowski's Three Colors trilogy and *Antonia's Line,* the Dutch film directed by Marleen Gorris that received the 1995 Oscar for Best Foreign Film. When considered together, these and other films may be seen as part of a new European filmic idiom.

It seems clear that Miró was consciously trying to ally herself with this new idiom when she hired the Catalan composer Jordi Savall to write the excellent musical score for *El pájaro de la felicidad.* Two years earlier, Savall himself had been responsible for the musical sound track of Alain Corneau's intensely lyrical *Tous les matins du monde* (All the Mornings of the World, 1991). The leading poetic motif of that film, "tous les matins du monde sont sans retour" (all the mornings of the world never come back), is a clear influence on Miró's own nostalgic retrospection. The rich intertextuality of Miró's film encompasses, besides Alain Courneau's film, several poetic and musical references,[13] among which, I find particularly significant the use of Dido's beautifully dramatic aria from Henry Purcell's opera *Dido and Aeneas.* The last sequences of the film are a poetic and even parodic reversal of Purcell's (and Virgil's) patriarchal *Liebestod* motif, which becomes transfigured into

Miró's affirmative version of the sacrifice of love. Indeed, Carmen's reclaiming of her own body, her newly accepted maternal role, and her new life beyond her "social death" are all brilliantly counterpointed through Purcell's operatic intertext. Carmen's rich and difficult solitude, moreover, resonates throughout the film by means of another poetic intertext: Angel González's lyrical intensity—"La soledad es como un faro certeramente apedreado, en ella me apoyo" (Loneliness is like a lighthouse deftly stonewalled, on which I lean). These lines amount to a visual and textual inscription of Carmen's (and Miró's) personal split between the need for silence and introspection and the commitment to public action, a contradiction that informs many of Pilar Miró's films and, most especially, *El pájaro de la felicidad.*

Having thus established Miró's inscription in the context of this new European idiom, I need to return briefly to Marsha Kinder's argument. She writes: "Most important, because micro- and macroregionalism function codependently, fluidly shifting meaning according to context, they thereby serve as an effective means both of asserting the subversive force of any marginal position and of destabilizing (or at least redefining) the hegemonic power of any center. Once regional structures and the "center" come to be seen as sliding signifiers, then there is movement toward the proliferation and empowerment of new structural units both at the micro and macro levels."[14]

Concerning the two films considered here, I would argue that Lazcano and Miró may be doing the same thing within the Spanish context. By inserting a local story into a national context and by bringing a "regional" language into a national circuit, they are both "sliding the signifiers" of center and margin. It is interesting that one of the few reviews published in Madrid of Lazcano's *Urte ilunak* called this film "historia local" (a local story); Esteban Hernández writes: "Shot in direct sound in Castilian and Basque in the area of Guipuzcoa, it is a local production that now enters a national market."[15] The reviewer, therefore, wants to marginalize the film by alluding to its "local" origin while reinforcing the notion of "national" as only belonging to films shot in Castilian Spanish. The contestations over language, nationality, and hegemony are vividly illustrated by the extremely opposite reactions the film elicited from a Basque viewer and two expatriate Spanish women at the Montreal International Film Festival, as reported by Fernando Bejarano: "The film is spoken mostly in Basque. This fact generated interesting opposite reactions in the viewings here in Montreal. On the one hand, a Basque viewer got very moved while listening to his language and gave a Basque flag to the director. On the other, two women, of a conservative outlook, complained bitterly. Those irritated women belong to the Spanish colony of Montreal and they said they came to see Spanish cinema. They found, instead, that part of *The Bilingual Lover* [*El amante bilingüe*, 1993 film by Vicente Aranda] is spoken in Catalan. *The Dark Years*, however, was too much for them to handle."[16]

Similar and perhaps more symptomatic reactions were previously elicited by the films of Eloy de la Iglesia, another Basque director who brought the "marginal" and the "regional" into the "national" mainstream. In his pioneering study *Laws of Desire*, Paul Julian Smith observes:

In spite of his espousal of the newspaper form, de la Iglesia's treatment at the hands of the press during this period was brutal. . . . Some of the abuse is also motivated by anti-Basque racism: one squib mocks de la Iglesia for a project (later to metamorphose into *El pico* [The Shoot]) featuring a gay love set in the Basque country complete with dialogue in "euskera." The anonymous journalist states that other countries seek to conquer the international market, implying that Spanish directors waste their time on such minority projects. This was a curious complaint to make against the most commercially successful director of his time: homosexuality and regional identity would thus always seem to be marginal even when placed at the center of mass culture.[17]

Lazcano's and Miró's films not only follow that tradition but they also clearly problematize the common notion of a Spanish film by incorporating "marginal" languages into "nonmarginal" contexts. Thus they present a new alternative means of recognizing our multicultural reality. A remarkable common point between these two films produced in 1992 is that they use subtitles in their original versions, thereby presenting the transition between Basque and Spanish or Catalan and Spanish as if it were already a normalized plurilingual reality when, in fact, they are themselves trying to normalize that reality through these very representations. Moreover, both films thematize the linguistic tension in their construction of allegorical families that are also linguistically split. I already mentioned Carmen's Spanish-speaking mother in *El pájaro de la felicidad*. Lazcano also introduces us to the contradictory fact of having Itziar's parents speak in Spanish while trying to impose Euskera

(Basque) on their children. Thus, the linguistic boundaries of the nation are already problematized in the microlevel of the familial unit.

My last remarks bring me full circle to the beginning of this essay: What is the reality that these two films try to "normalize"? It is the reality of a shared political space, Spain, that still resists being reimagined and thus represented as a plurinational, multicultural, and heteroglossic community. The bilingual realities of both films serve as a strong political statement on our current historical moment, still characterized by the bitter debates surrounding the acceptance of such a multicultural reality. They underline a common goal to reimagine the different languages and cultures of Spain as an essential richness rather than a constant source of national struggle. Miró, whom nobody thinks of as having Catalan inclinations,[18] has been very clear in this respect. When talking about the incorporation of Catalan into her film, she said: "In Catalonia I have wanted to explore a landscape, a language and an atmosphere that I consider very beautiful. Often from Madrid, Catalan culture is perceived as something very remote and I think that is not the case."[19]

Both Miró and Lazcano flatly object to their films being considered as representatives of a feminist or feminine cinematic discourse.[20] I think that their resistance betrays, on the one hand, a misconception of the very term "feminism" and, on the other hand, a defensive mechanism to oppose any essentialist reduction that might render them even more vulnerable in a male-dominated milieu. As for the misconception, I see it as an example of their fixation on an outdated historical position concerning feminism. That this is a rather common position held even by progressive and intellectual women in Spain may be corroborated by the following observations by Martha A. Ackelsberg in her book *Free Women of Spain:*

But I was most fascinated, intrigued, and perplexed by her attitudes toward feminists and feminism—attitudes which were, in many ways, the mirror image of those which the young ones had of Mujeres Libres: "We are not—and we were not then—feminists," she insisted. "We were not fighting against men. We did not want to substitute a femininst hierarchy for a masculine one." . . . I was surprised by her assumption that "feminism" meant opposition to men or the desire to replace male hierarchy with female hierarchy. A product of the early feminist movement in the United States, I had always assumed that feminism meant opposition to hierarchies of any sort.[21]

Elsewhere I have argued that one of the most interesting and challenging developments in Spanish fiction written by women is their
specular transgression of the traditional mirror repetition imposed by
general patriarchal models and rigorously reinforced by Francoist ideology.[22] It is my contention that such a gesture has finally arrived to the
Spanish screen. Despite their disavowals, both Miró and Lazcano create
their own mirror images that perform a transgressive—and indeed a
feminist—gesture, one that represents the personal as political and that
constructs a national allegory through the inscription of their most
private emotions.[23]

Of significance is that both films are told from "the perspective of the
nation's margin and the migrant's exile," the perspective chosen by
Bhabha's own retelling of "the history of the modern western nation."[24]
Miró's Carmen is a marginalized "central" figure and Lazcano's Sofía is a
migrant exile whose freely chosen sisterhood with Itziar, the protagonist
of *Urte ilunak,* disseminates the patriarchal boundaries of the Basque
national narrative. And yet, both films may be also read as allegorical
love stories of national conciliation, in the sense given to this concept by
Doris Sommer when she interprets Latin American nineteenth-century
romances as "projections of national conciliation through lovers' yearn-
ings across traditional racial and regional barriers."[25]

In the case of Lazcano's film, this seems to be the implication of the
allegorical scene in which the two girls, the Basque Itziar and the Extremaduran Sofía, unite their blood in ritual sisterhood under the emblematic tree.[26] The collective significance of Lazcano's *Urte ilunak* was readily perceived in the Basque country, whereas it was mostly ignored or
criticized elsewhere. For example, in a review significantly titled "Demasiada poesía" (Too Much Poetry), which appeared in the Madrid daily
El Mundo, Francisco Marinero writes: "The first and most obvious excessive thing of the film is to resemble a historical chronicle." In contrast,
Felipe Rius, writing in Basque for *Egin,* reports: "Arantxa Lazcano in her
first film not only frames the events that happened to a girl, but some
facts of the history of an entire people."[27] This awareness of the film's
collective significance did not preclude, however, a certain degree of
marginalization "within the nation" as a response to the threatening
"cultural liminality" of Lazcano's film. As Bhabha formulates it: "Once
the liminality of the nation-space is established, and its 'difference' is
turned from the boundary 'outside' to its finitude 'within,' the threat of

cultural difference is no longer a problem of 'other' people. It becomes a question of the otherness of the people-as-one."[28]

Despite Miró's and Lazcano's great reluctance to be identified with a gendered discourse, one should consider the fact that sex and gender are not regulated according to any specific identity politics and, therefore, their rejection of an official feminist label doesn't necessarily entail a lack of feminist concerns. Both films offer a conflation of nation and narration that apparently springs from the most personal and productive of their directors' own contradictions. It is precisely in assessing one of Miró's most significant contradictions that Juan Antonio Pérez Millán, in his text *Pilar Miró: Directora de cine* writes:

Pilar Miró's cinema could not be understood were it not intimately connected to her global attitude towards life. An attitude that is determined, among other factors, by her visceral rebelliousness in the face of anything imposed on her; by a peculiar need for self-assertion that pushes her to frontally oppose anything that is felt as an arbitrary imposition. That characteristic reaction . . . solidified . . . in a position that was then termed "engaged" and that became compatible with a radical and rather contradictory individualism. As . . . is also contradictory her capacity to combine her tendency to rationalize everything, to present her arguments in a cold, even ruthless way, with her admiration for genuine tenderness and her recourse to emotion and feeling as the privileged form of communication. . . . Six feature films have emerged from that constant struggle between ideas presented with a stubbornness that borders on obstinacy and emotions that tend to surface as if they had been repressed, as if belonging to an old seated dream.[29]

Millán's perceptive analysis proved especially significant in Miró's seventh film, *El pájaro de la felicidad,* for it is not until this work that Miró directly confronts those "old seated" emotions in herself. Never before had the Spanish director been able to embody her critique of the surrounding violence in a format that allowed so clearly the inscription of her (homoerotic) desire. In fact, as suggested earlier, Miró's production to date seems to embody the struggle of opposing drives in herself, an opposition that translates into two rather distinct cinematic discourses. On the one hand, there are those films that confront political violence directly, such as the polemic *El crimen de Cuenca* (The Cuenca Crime, 1979), a film that bluntly represents political torture and indicts the Guardia Civil, Franco's paramilitary police force, and *Beltenebros*

(1991), Miró's forceful rendering of Antonio Muñoz Molina's homonymous narrative of political intrigues and betrayals in the context of the expatriate anti-Franco struggle. On the other hand are the films that inscribe the political through the personal. Among these, *Gary Cooper que estás en los cielos* (Gary Cooper Who Art in Heaven, 1980), *Werther* (1996), and *El pájaro* (1992) are films that share a confessional tone, a poetic visual style, and the specular gesture of inscribing Miró's own private story in social contexts of general and collective significance. More important for my argument here, they all have the same leading actress—Mercedes Sampietro—who has been referred to by some critics as Miró's "fetish" actress. Sampietro does, indeed, play Andrea Soriano, the television producer in *Gary Cooper;* Carlota, the pediatric neurosurgeon who will fall in love with her almost-autistic son's tutor in *Werther;* and Carmen, the art restorer of *El pájaro.* This reappearance constitutes, in my view, Miró's perhaps unself-conscious attempt to recreate her own image, for Sampietro does in fact bear a resemblance to the director. It points toward Miró's need to supplement the fraternal national narrative with an alternative passionate sisterhood, without any implication of a symmetrical substitution, since most of Miró's characters are portrayed as inner exiles whose isolation is never fully overcome.

One of the most blatant examples of Miró's inscription of the personal as political is her film *Gary Cooper,* in which Miró's own open-heart surgery is represented in Andrea Soriano's discovery of an illness that forces her to confront the fact of her radical isolation in terms of the sudden decay of her own body. Similarly, *El pájaro* presents a strong and independent woman suddenly brutalized by an external, collective aggression. Carmen's rape, in fact, becomes emblematic of the decay of the body politique. Technically, Miró employs several significant "dissolves" in order to establish visually the notion of the progressive dissolution of a national discourse that had constituted her own,[30] that of the Socialist Party. Carmen's return is not so much back to a "real" but to an "imagined" and, perhaps, given its (im)permanence, a utopian home.[31] Or, to put it again in Bhabha's terms, Carmen's marginal status, her own migrant condition "articulates the death-in-life of the idea of the 'imagined community' of the nation."[32] Before that emblematic and impossible return, however, Miró shows us Carmen's desolate (self) questioning. In that "¿qué pasa?" which is addressed to the camera more than to Fernando (Carmen's lover) and which recalls Itziar's "zergatik" (why?) in Lazcano's *Urte ilunak,* Miró condenses a personal and a collective crisis. The "dissolve" of Miró's public narrative echoes the dissolution/disillusionment of the alternative official narrative brought about by the Socialists' own decay. Carmen's sexual abuse is, therefore, a visible figuration of Miró's political victimization.[33]

At the end, however, Miró highlights the new vision, or the revision, of her most tender emotions. As Millán has it: "In fact, Carmen's discovery of a new dimension in her interpersonal relationships, at the end of the script of *The Bird of Happiness,* points toward the development of a different alternative."[34] In Carmen's embrace of Nani, her daughter-in-law, Miró seems to have embraced a different desire, a different tenderness, a newly recovered sense of human contact and pathos. Her quasi-ekphrastic use of the Murrillo rendition of the Virgin Mary and of Saint Elizabeth amounts to a reversed "pietà." When Mercedes Sampietro tells Aitana Sánchez-Gijón that Murrillo wanted to portray the positive side of life, Miró seems, through these two actors, to be telling us and herself that the only way out is to try to find the nonconfrontational other in the others and in ourselves. What this crucial sequence betrays is that "mystical inflection" that Benedict Anderson identified in the Western national discourse. Sommer summarizes it this way: "Specifically, Anderson asks how we can account for the passionate charge of nationalism even, or most especially today, in marxist regimes that should have gotten beyond the limits of national bourgeois culture. In part it is because nationalism is not 'aligned' to abstract ideologies such as liberalism or marxism but is mystically inflected from the religious cultural systems 'out of which—as well as against which—it came into being.' . . . The imagined community of a nation, he suggests, inherits or appropriates a spirit of sacrifice that would be unimaginable from the kind of cost-benefit calculations that self-conscious ideologies assume."[35]

It is this "mystical" trace that we see in Carmen's "sacrifice of love," when she lets Nani go to meet her own unfulfilled desire. And yet, the transformative and unsettling power of the female homoerotic bonding has already been inscribed in that national discourse that has always either erased the desire or marginalized it by framing it "mystically."[36] Ironically, Carmen's profession hypostatizes the maternal in her restorative care of the iconographic national treasure.

The gesture that unites Itziar and her newly found Extremaduran friend, Sofía, as "blood sisters" in *Urte ilunak* is not a biological sister-

Sisterhood is represented in *Urte ilunak*. (Photo courtesy: Arantxa Lazcano)

hood but a bond freely chosen, and, as such, it becomes a direct rejection of what Anderson described as "the appropriation of a spirit of sacrifice" inherent in modern imagined communities. Itziar and Sofía's encounter points toward a liberated space, neither central nor marginal but located in the fissures of nationalist ideologies, in that cultural liminality alluded to by Bhabha. Lazcano's film, therefore, articulates not so much the illusion of a stable (Basque) imagined community but the fragile communal dream of children at play in the midst of oppressive national discourses. Itziar and Sofía's sisterhood is ironically counterpointed with the Francoist sisterhood of the Catholic nuns who imposed a linguistic union by violent coercion. Thus, the embrace of Itziar and Sofía constitutes the culminating moment in Lazcano's rejection of a violent society that scapegoats its children. In their moment of bonding, the two girls are initiated not only to the secret hidden by the allegorical tree—a clear allusion to the Basque national emblem, the Guernica tree—but to their own secret desire. In that new emotional and psychological context of female contact, the healing hands reaching out constitute a rich and radical gesture of self-affirmation, one that becomes the common signature of these two films and their gendered discourse.

Another important common signature is Miró's and Lazcano's similar treatment of what Catherine Russell has called "narrative death" and its relation to the concept of closure.[37] In both films, the ending becomes a strong affirmation of an inner language that endures and transgresses the "social death" of the protagonist. Indeed, death figures largely in those endings, which resist closure by reopening the most vital tensions of the films' narratives. Thus, as Meri L. Clark has it:[38]

The "true" death of which Carmen speaks is the closure of another element of the old narrative of her life, the narrative that had been interrupted with her rape. Carmen lives again "after" the rape—a social death that re-opens the narrative. . . . The language that Carmen has been taught to speak throughout her life is an elaborate social construction that upholds a social order that commits violence against her. The infinite, silent space of the individual is the realm that Carmen actively seeks. . . . The conscious and incessant performance of death, the silencing of the performative language of violence, of life, is the only recourse to change, to hope for the future. Having found peace within herself and, to a certain extent, with the external world at the "end" of "El pájaro de la felicidad," Carmen at once crystallizes and reopens narratival possibilities: the future is that which has already been lived, she says, and peace is that which is found in death.

Itziar's "peaceful death" has an identical value in Lazcano's *Urte ilu-nak.* In the final sequence of the film, as the now adolescent Itziar lies down by the tree that harbors her hidden treasures (the treasures of her imaginative self and of her private communal dream), we are reminded that it was under this very tree that Itziar and Sofía became blood sisters, for we hear her voice-over that repeats the same magical lines of the initial sequence: "Si el tiempo, en sucesión única, no fuese tan injusto, llegaría hasta la niña que un día fuí y desnudaría, lentamente, el cuerpo que un día tuve, acariciándolo, luego, centímetro a centrímetro, hasta que aquellos ojos, tras los cuales un día miré, se cerraran en el más dulce de los sueños" (If time, in its linear succession, were not so unfair, it would arrive onto that girl that I once was and it would slowly undress that body that I once had, caressing it, then, inch by inch, till those eyes behind which once I looked, would close in the sweetest of dreams).[39]

This "dream" is *Urte ilunak,* for the dream imagery of film is a perfect vehicle for reimagining one's own past and re-creating one's own (national) identity or one's own "imagined community." Lazcano's poetic retracing of her historical time fulfills Itziar's impossible wish at the end of *Urte ilunak* without providing any narrative closure to the crucial questions raised about the violent Basque society that brought about her social death. The film's ending reads as Lazcano's strongest "allegorical double vision," both her visual embodiment and her rejection of Itziar's national "sacrifice." As the spectator sees a medium shot of Itziar's body lying on the ground, with arms outstretched in a Christlike position, with her father's razor in one hand and her Basque boyfriend's poem in the other, she hears her imaginary voice-over narrating the dream of reappropriating her own body. This striking image of her historical violent sacrifice is Lazcano's most persuasive conflation/confrontation of the Basque imagined-community and her own private communal dream.

In bringing these two films together, I have shown how they articulate alternative narrative desires that challenge Spain's master narrative of Cainite violence. In their common gesture of reclaiming the historical times and physical bodies of their female protagonists, both Pilar Miró and Arantxa Lazcano have opened new grounds in the filmic representation of gendered nationalisms both within and outside of Spain.

Notes

A previous version of this essay, titled "Towards a New Transcultural Dialogue in Spanish Film," was presented in the context of the conference "Spain Today: Literature, Culture, and Society," held at Dartmouth College in the fall of 1994. It has been published in *Spain Today: Essays on Literature, Culture, Society,* José Colmeiro, Christina Dupláa, Patricia Greene, and Juana Sabadell, eds. (Dartmouth, Mass.: Dartmouth C, 1995), 47–66. I want to thank my colleagues Mona Fayad, Joseba Gabilondo, David Miller, Fernando Valerio, and Charlotte Wellman, who each offered very valuable suggestions in the process of revising this essay.

1. See Homi Bhabha's *Nation and Narration* (London: Routledge, 1990), for an expanded analysis of the postcolonial discourse on "nation" as a site of cultural constructions. For the purposes of this essay, I am especially interested in Bhabha's essay "DissemiNation: Time, Narrative, and the Margins of the Modern Nation," which emphasizes the concepts of migration and marginality in the construction of the modern nation. Both concepts are at the heart of Miró's and Lazcano's transgressive representation of the Spanish national narrative.

2. In her groundbreaking analysis of early Latin American national narratives,

Foundational Fictions: The National Romances of Latin America (Berkeley and California: U of California P, 1991), Doris Sommer articulates Walter Benjamin's dialectics with Fredric Jameson's notion of "national allegory" to argue that "I take allegory to mean a narrative structure in which one line is a trace of the other, in which each helps to write the other, . . . If I read a double and corresponding structure between personal romance and political desiderata, it is not with any priority of either register. I am suggesting that Eros and Polis are the effects of each other's performance" (42–47). My approach to Miró's and Lazcano's films as both traces of their personal desire and inscriptions of national histories is taken much in the same vein as Sommer's own.

3. Andrew Parker, Mary Russo, Doris Sommer, and Patricia Yaeger, the editors of *Nationalisms and Sexualities* (New York: Routledge, 1992), are very clear concerning the homosocial bonding as the crucial component of the traditional national narrative when they write: "George Mosse and Benedict Anderson both second this view that nationalism favors a distinctly homosocial form of male bonding. Mosse argues that 'nationalism had a special affinity for male society and together with the concept of respectability legitimized the dominance of men over women.' For Anderson this recognition is deeply implicit: 'The nation is always conceived as a deep, horizontal comradeship. Ultimately, it is this *fraternity* [emphasis ours] that makes it possible, over the past two centuries, for so many millions of people, not so much to kill, as willingly to die for such limited imaginings.' Typically represented as a passionate brotherhood, the nation finds itself compelled to distinguish its 'proper' homosociality from more explicitly sexualized male-male relations, a compulsion that requires the identification, isolation, and containment of male homosexuality" (6). The authors are referring to Benedict Anderson's renowned work *Imagined Communities: Reflections on the Origin and Spread of Nationalism* (London: Verso, 1983) and to George L. Mosse's *Nationalism and Sexuality: Middle-Class Morality and Sexual Norms in Modern Europe* (Madison: U of Wisconsin P, 1985).

4. For a lengthy discussion of Carlos Saura's excellent use of the amnesia motif in his allegorical *El jardín de las delicias* (Garden of Delights, 1970) see Marvin D'Lugo's *The Films of Carlos Saura: The Practice of Seeing* (Princeton, N.J.: Princeton UP, 1991), especially the section "Film and Lucidity" (102–4). See also my own analysis of that same motif in the essay "Paseo crítico e intertextual por el jardín edípico del cine español," *Letras Peninsulares* 7, no. 1 (1994): 93–118.

5. Prime Minister Felipe González resisted the political pressure to advance the general elections. His basic argument was the need to postpone those elections until the end of Spain's tenure of the presidency of the European Union (December 1995). The series of financial and political scandals involving the Socialist Party (PSOE) have added a public layer of dissatisfaction, which has undoubtedly benefited the PP's rise to power. Against public polls and political

expectations, however, the results of the elections held on March 3, 1996, have only granted partial majority to Aznar's party. This has created a new political situation that has forced Aznar and his party to publically declare their support for Spain's different nationalities. In fact, his investiture as Spain's new prime minister has been possible only after a political deal with the Basque and Catalan nationalist parties.

6. See Xavier Rubert de Ventós's excellent study *Nacionalismos: El laberinto de la identidad* (Nationalisms: The Labyrinth of Identity) (Madrid: Espasa Calpe, 1994), especially 143–147. Quote is from pp. 143–44.

7. For an extended discussion of Miró's role as general director of cinematography, see José Enrique Monterde's *Veinte años de cine español: Un cine bajo la paradoja, 1973–1992* (Barcelona: Paidós, 1993), especially the section titled "La política proteccionista" (Protectionist Policies), pp. 98–113.

8. Both films, but especially Miró's, take female homoeroticism onto the "stage" of representations of nationalism, a stage that, as we are reminded by the editors of *Nationalisms and Sexualities,* was not their own: "By the early twentieth century, new public identities for women as workers, consumers and political leaders emerged with new national and international social movements. But even in this changing historical context, the representation of lesbianism in national discourse remained largely off-stage in that space described by Teresa de Lauretis as 'socio-sexual (in)difference' " (7).

9. For a more detailed treatment of Miró's representational split, see my essay "La piedad profana de Pilar Miró," in *Cine-Lit II: Essays on Hispanic Film and Fiction,* ed. George Cabello-Castellet, Jaume Martí-Olivella, and Guy Wood (Corvallis: Oregon State U, 1996): 137–45.

10. I am referring to the concept coined by Anne McClintock in her essay "No Longer in a Future Heaven," as quoted in the introduction to *Nationalisms and Sexualities,* p. 16, n. 13.

11. Parker, et al., eds., 5; emphasis added.

12. This concept was first presented by Marsha Kinder in her essay "Micro and Macro Regionalism in 'Vida en sombras' and Beyond" published in *Cine-Lit: Essays on Peninsular Film and Fiction,* ed. George Cabello-Castellet, Jaume Martí-Olivella, and Guy Wood (Portland, Oreg.: Portland State UP, Oregon State U, and Reed C., 1992), 131–46. It was later developed into chapter 8, "Micro and Macro Regionalism in Catalan Cinema, European Coproductions and Global Television" in her volume *Blood Cinema: The Reconstruction of National Identity in Spain* (Berkeley and Los Angeles: U of California P, 1993), 388–441. The quote comes from p. 400. Particularly relevant to my argument here is the paragraph that reads, "Since regionality (like nationality) is an ideological construct, 'regional film' and 'regional television' are relativistic concepts. . . . Given this relativism, regionalism clearly may refer to geographic areas that are both 'smaller' and 'larger' than a nation. Thus, the terms 'micro-

regionalism' and 'macroregionalism' help us to understand the regional/national/global interface" (388–89).

13. The obvious intertextual reference is to Pío Baroja's passage: "¿Habré tenido yo la suerte de cazar ese pájaro maravilloso de la felicidad que todo el mundo asegura saber dónde anida y que nadie en último término encuentra?" (Will I have had the fortune to capture that wonderful bird of happiness, the one whose whereabouts everybody claims to know and that nobody ever finds?) From Miró's press book for *El pájaro de la felicidad,* quoted by Juan Antonio Pérez Millán in his volume *Pilar Miró: Directora de Cine* (Madrid: Sociedad General de Autores de España, 1992), 273.

14. Kinder, "Micro and Macro Regionalism," 389.

15. See Esteban Hernández, "Una historia local," *El Mundo,* October 22, 1993, E3.

16. See Fernando Bejarano's "Arantxa Lazcano: 'Al comprobar que mucha gente aquí entiende la película he respirado.' Crónica del Festival de Montreal." *Diario 16,* September 3, 1993, 39.

17. Paul Julian Smith, *Laws of Desire: Questions of Homosexuality in Spanish Writing and Film* (Oxford: Clarendon; New York: Oxford UP, 1992), 130–31.

18. See "Diez años de cine español" (Ten Years of Spanish Cinema), in *La cultura española en el postfranquismo: Diez años de cine, cultura y literatura en España (1975–1985),* Samuel Amell and Salvador García Castañeda, eds. (Madrid: Playor, 1988), 27–32, in which Miró writes: "In the meantime, the development of the Autonomous governments has had an obvious, although very different, impact on their cinematographies. While the Catalan government spends most of its cinematographic budget funding big American productions dubbed into Catalan, with a criterion that resembles the 1941 law that declared forbidden the use of any language other than Spanish, the Basque government is following a much smarter policy of funding with almost 25% of its budget those productions that are filmed in the Basque Country dealing with Basque themes and with a Basque cast and crew" (32). Even if agreeing on the substance of Miró's critique, I find that her comparison of the Catalan policy with the Francoist law of 1941 betrays an embedded anti-Catalan prejudice.

19. See the interview "Entrevista con Pilar Miró" that Salvador Llopart published in the Barcelona daily *La Vanguardia,* May 6, 1993, 33.

20. Miró and Lazcano were both very vocal and adamantly opposed to my own gendered approach to their films during the round table on "New Hispanic Cinema" that took place in March, 1994, in Portland, Oregon, during Cine-Lit II, the Second International Conference on Hispanic Cinema and Literature. More recently, in October 1995, Lazcano reaffirmed her rejection of any gender-specific distinctions in film during her talk at Barnard College in the context of the Sixth International Conference of The Feminine Hispanic Literature Society (ALFH).

21. Martha A. Ackelsberg, *Free Women of Spain: Anarchism and the Struggle for the Emancipation of Women* (Bloomington: Indiana UP, 1991), 2.

22. See my essay "Homoeroticism and Specular Transgression in Peninsular Feminine Narrative," *España contemporánea* 2 (fall 1992): 17–25, where I elaborate on this new feminine/feminist aesthetic. See also the extensive discussion of the topic in Smith's *Laws of Desire.*

23. In using Fredric Jameson's concept of national allegory, as it was first articulated in "Third-World Literature in the Era of Multinational Capitalism," *Social Text* 15 (1986): 65–88, and further elaborated in his *Signatures of the Visible* (New York: Routledge, 1990), I would like to recall here Doris Sommer's qualification, to which I entirely subscribe: "Not long ago, Jameson discovered the possible charms of contemporary 'third-world literature,' thanks to allegory: 'All third-world texts are necessarily, I want to argue, allegorical, and in a very specific way: they are to be read as what I will call *national allegories.*' . . . But Jameson both affirms too much by it (since clearly some 'third-world' texts are not 'national allegories') and too little (since 'national allegories' are still written in the First World, by say Pynchon and Grass among others). I also wonder if Jameson's assumption that these allegories 'reveal' truth in an apparently transparent way, rather than construct it with all the epistemological messiness that using language implies, doesn't already prepare him to distinguish too clearly between Third and First World literatures" (42). Or, in the context of this essay, I would add the problem of the location of a Second World or, better, to borrow the term coined by my colleague Joseba Gabilondo, the location in discourse of a "postnational space."

24. See Bhabha, 291.

25. See Sommer, xi.

26. An interesting problem in Lazcano's film arises precisely from that unresolved friendship between Itziar and Sofía. Why don't they meet again after Itziar's return as an adolescent? What does that imply in terms of that national conciliation? Lazcano was rather evasive when asked a similar question in October 1995 at Barnard College, during the Sixth International Conference of ALFH.

27. See Francisco Marinero's "Demasiada poesía," *El Mundo,* October 29, 1993, 33, and Felipe Rius's "Urte ilunak," *Egin,* September 17, 1993, 57.

28. See Bhabha, 301. In a letter to author (May 16, 1996), my colleague the Basque critic Joseba Gabilondo was very explicit in referring to this "indifferent" response. In commenting on the lack of reception to Lazcano's film, he says: "What I'm saying is that even the official Basque world (male centered and mysoginist) tries to ignore these films which in other non-Basque and more feminist contexts may receive a more favorable reception. That is to say that the marginality of the film reveals itself even inside a marginal national discourse such as that of the Basque Country."

29. Pérez Millán, *Pilar Miró: Directora de cine* (Madrid Sociedad General de Autores de España), 278–79.

30. I want to thank Dona Kercher, whose comments about the way Miró constructed visually her national allegory allowed me to realize the importance of the different dissolves in the film; and, especially, of its most beautiful one. I am referring to the sequence in the Catalan Pyrenees, where the (im)permanence of the Francoist mother's and the conservative landowner father's narrative is "dissolved" in the final fade-out that transports Carmen and the viewer from the soft green lights of the Pyrenees to the sun-drenched white and blue colors of the Andalusian South. North and South (Catalan and Spanish), are not confused but "dissolved" in Miró's beautiful rendering of Carmen's inner resistance to dominant narratives.

31. I thank again Joseba Gabilondo, who is working with this idea in the context of Pedro Almodóvar's films, where the return home is always either impossible or utopian, as exemplified in *¿Qué he hecho para merecer esto?* (What Have I Done to Deserve This? 1984), *Kika* (1993), *La flor de mi secreto* (The Flower of My Secret, 1995).

32. See Bhabha, 315.

33. Miró was forced to resign from her position as general director of cinematography because of a scandal involving accusations of having misappropriated public funds for private (clothing) expenditures. The personal as political adopts here almost a paradoxical and/or grotesque dimension.

34. See Millán, 275.

35. See Sommer, 37.

36. Concerning this process of denial and sublimation as it is inscribed in Western iconography, see Julia Kristeva's "Motherhood According to Giovanni Bellini," in *Desire in Language: A Semiotic Approach to Literature and Art,* ed. Leon S. Roudiez (New York: Columbia UP, 1980), and, especially, the concept that "sublimation here is both eroticizing without residue and a disappearance of eroticism as it returns to its source" (240). The maternal source of Carmen's homoeroticism is doubly poignant in Miró's film given the rejection of her "real" Francoist mother and the suppression of her "imaginary" maternal role.

37. Quite relevant to my discussion of Miró's and Lazcano's "undoing" of the social death of their protagonists is Catherine Russell's definition of narrative mortality. In *Narrative Mortality: Death, Closure and New Wave Cinemas* (Minneapolis: U of Minnesota P, 1995), she writes: "The term 'narrative morality' refers to the discourse of death in narrative film. It is a discourse produced by reading/viewing as much as it is by writing/filmmaking; it is both a critical method and a discursive practice. Narrative mortality is an 'undoing' or 'reading' of the ideological tendency of death as closure. It is a practice of resistance, with aspirations toward a radical politics of filmic narrativity. Narrative mortality is a method of understanding the function of narrative endings in the

politics of representation, a means of moving beyond formalist categories of 'open' and 'closed' endings, as well as mythic categories of fate and romance" (2).

38. I want to thank Meri L. Clark for letting me quote from her unpublished paper "The Death of the Ending" (Reed College, April 10, 1995).

39. These lines are quoted directly from Lazcano's original script. I thank Arantxa for her kindness in letting me have this unpublished document.

PART 3

Marketing Transfiguration:

Money/ Politics/Regionalism

PETER BESAS

The Financial Structure of Spanish Cinema

The economics of film production in Spain and, indeed, in most countries outside the United States, must seem baffling to those accustomed to thinking of filmmaking as essentially a process wherein a picture is produced at a given cost and either makes it or breaks it depending on subsequent revenue received from box-office receipts and sales in ancillary markets such as television, cable, and home video, as well as in offshore outlets.

How can it be that a small country such as Spain can continuously produce over fifty features a year, 90 percent of which prove to be duds upon release or never even see the light of the screen? How is it that producer/director/scripters who fail dismally time and again nonetheless continue to burden cinemas with new aberrations? How can it be that in 1991, $87.7 million was spent on making films, but only $37 million was recouped at the box office (of which the producers received only one-third) and the following year another $82 million was poured into production, with a piddling $32 million return, and so on, year after year?[1] Even the local solons I consulted were hard pressed to shed more than partial light on this conundrum. Certainly, no two films are financed in quite the same manner; the formulas are as varied as schemes on how to get rich quick.

Generally, however, the answer lies in the financing structure of cinema in Spain and in a varied system of subsidies and pre-sales, mostly within Spain, which enable many filmmakers to limit the risk factor to a minimum, if not to nil. The secret, in many cases, is that profits are assured at the *financing* stage and not at the box office.

Only after all concerned have tucked away their profits does produc-

The king of the Madrid comedy, producer and director Fernando Colomo, poses with two of his popular stars, Ana Belén (right) and María Barranco (front), for *Rosa Rosae* (1992).

tion begin. Then, the film is shot as best as one can with whatever remains of the budget. Of course, not all films use this fail-safe system, and the trails of debts left every year from unsuccessful productions testify to the pitfalls of the method and the folly of those providing services to such ventures. Yet this modus operandi certainly prevails for many films made in Spain and elsewhere in Europe, though admittedly there are also producers who put their own money on the line and run financial risks.

This economic cushioning and minimal-risk financing, in turn, conditions the genre and quality of the films made. With audience acceptance treated as an afterthought, the films all too often turn out to be insular, self-indulgent, uninspiredly experimental, pretentious, and, on occasions, hopelessly amateurish. These are the films rarely seen outside Spain and barely within Spain, though occasionally one does surface at a film festival if it is quirky enough. But mostly, they ignominiously end their aborted careers as a government statistic. For example, Title: *La fiebre del oro* (Gold Fever). Budget: $3.16 million. Subsidy from Madrid government: $850,000. (Other subsidies from the Catalan regional government.) Box-office gross: $130,000. Or, Title: *Una estación de paso* (A Passing Season). Budget: $2.36 million. Subsidy: $650,000. Box office: $40,000. These are not rare exceptions. They tend to be the rule for the bulk of production.[2]

Another Catalan ship that sank, *Monturiol* (1993), a period piece about the inventor of the submarine, was directed by Francesc Bellmunt.

Hence, when moving in Spanish film circles, use of the expression "the Spanish film industry" tends to bring a wry, indulgent smile to the lips of those producers hoary with experience and savvy to all the intrigues and vagaries of production. For "industry" is a rather grand term to describe what is often more akin to artisanry.

In a rather telling recent survey conducted by the Instituto Cinematográfico de Artes Audiovisuales (Spanish Film Institute, ICAA) between 1989 and 1992, 41.9 percent of 117 production companies polled declared they had no fixed assets at all. Only 6.5 percent said they possessed cameras and lighting equipment. In the same survey, 35.5 percent answered they had a base capital of less than $10,000. Fewer than 5 percent of the companies were in the over-$500,000 capital bracket.[3] Even the most prosperous producers, such as Pedro and Agustín Almodóvar and Andrés Vicente Gómez, work out of relatively modest offices located in apartment buildings. In addition, since most producers are private entrepreneurs, who often treble as screenplay writers and directors as well (sometimes they'll even do a thespian stint in their own films), the financing of their projects is vitally bound not only to the success of their filmic ventures, but also very much to their personal purse strings and private financial survival.

Popular tough guy Javier
Bardem stars in *Días contados*
(Running out of Time, 1994)
by Imanol Uribe.

The mainstay of financing in Spain for the past fifty years has been the
subsidy system, which continues to provide the wherewithal that enables most Spanish films to be made. Without public funding, Spanish
cinema, like that of virtually all countries outside the United States,
would have long since withered and disappeared, barring perhaps a half
dozen features each year.

With the advent of television in Spain in 1956, a massive influx of
tourism in the late 1950s and 1960s, and growing international and
political and economic pressure on the Franco government to ease up
and be less restrictive, a new kind of film structure came to supersede the
old "classic" studio-type films.

Enter on the one hand new, committed, earnest filmmakers and
"auteurs" such as Luis García Berlanga and Juan Antonio Bardem, some
producing their own films, others seeking out a new generation of
producers who denounced the naive simplicities of earlier productions
and embraced the earthy verities of Italian neorealism.[4]

Simultaneously, on the other hand, a phalanx of producers cranking

Veronica Forqué (left) and Jorge Sanz (right) star in *¿Por qué lo llaman amor cuando quieren decir sexo?* (Why Do They Call It Love When They Mean Sex?, 1993), a modern boulevard comedy directed by Manuel Gómez Pereira.

out simplistic schlock appeared, purveyors of boulevard comedies starring sexy principals and new funnymen. Much of this trite domestic fodder, as thought-provoking as a tortilla, was tremendously popular and successful. It titillated and teased a generation of Spaniards who had been barred from seeing so much as a kiss on the screen. Interestingly, these films, though now dated, are still draws on television, since the dialogue was clever and the acting pithy. These were the films never seen at film festivals or written about in "serious" books on Spanish cinema, though perhaps they better reflect the reality of Spain in those days than the films made by the auteurs.

This spate of comedies was supplemented by dozens of Italian-co-produced spaghetti westerns shot in Almería, and cheaply made horror films suitable for export after being dubbed into English—pictures a few notches below the Hammer films made in England.[5]

Through the 1960s and 1970s, both the serious films and the boulevard pap vied for government subsidies and received them. For a number of years, in addition to the automatic 15 percent of box-office subsidy, an additional 25 percent of box office was heaped on for high-budget films. Still another subsidy was awarded for the nebulous "special quality" category.

The criteria for giving subsidies have always been murky, vague enough so that political and private favoritism could be exercised. Nepotism and influence-pulling overshadowed the system and continue to be a key factor in the subsidy system, whether under Franco or under the Socialists. After all, behind all the laws and legal frippery always hover the human factors. Influence pulling does not alter with political systems. Only the people in it change. Indeed, the tug-of-war for currying favors today is just as fierce as it was in the times of El Cid.

The outcome was that production boomed. In the Uniespaña (official Spanish film-promotion organization of the time) catalogue of 1968, 134 features are listed. The films ranged from Carlos Saura's *Peppermint Frappé* to the singing nun *Sor Yé Yé* to *The Return of the Magnificent Seven* with Yul Brynner and Warren Oates.[6] By 1977, Spanish films culled 29.76 percent of the domestic Spanish market.[7]

The administration's dilemma has always been how to encourage more ambitious films that might stand a chance of chalking up foreign sales and thus not only bring in revenue to Spain but also provide prestige to the *madre patria*. The scales have alternately tilted toward more "commercial" and more "artistic" films. Thus, it is not surprising that during the 1960s and early 1970s the auteurs and schlockmasters were always at daggers drawn. In their personal political attitudes they tended to polarize into Left and Right. The auteurs were staunch opponents to the dictatorship and tried to push the contents of their films to the brink of censorship limits; the "commerce-floggers" were happy to crank out their comedies and teasing sex films and rake in the profits.

When Franco died in 1975, the panorama changed radically. The auteurs suddenly had the upper hand and could now openly excoriate and vilify the producers and directors of the boulevard pap. New legislation increasingly favored the auteurs in detriment to the comedy, gore, boulevard schlock, and "lower" genres that had proved popular mass entertainments.

But neither "auteur" nor schlockmaster could produce if the subsidies weren't forthcoming. Those Ministry of Culture officials involved in film matters began, at the behest of vociferous arthouse producers and directors, pushing "quality" films by reputable writer/directors such as José Luis Borau, Jaime de Armiñán, Manuel Gutiérrez Aragón, Vicente Aranda, Mario Camus, Pilar Miró, Gonzalo Suárez, Víctor Erice, and Carlos Saura. The nods went toward those producers with an affinity to the new Socialist political spectrum such as Elías Querejeta, Andrés Vicente Gómez, Emiliano Piedra, José Luis Borau, Luis Megino, and others.

In 1983, with the Socialist Party in power, a significant fillip was given to this policy of encouraging "quality" fare when film director Pilar Miró was appointed director general of cinematography. Miró, a staunch liberal who had confronted the Guardia Civil in her film *El crimen de Cuenca* (The Cuenca Crime, 1979) and who knew the quirks of the film business and everyone in it, pushed through a new film law, known locally as the Miró Law, which lavished funds upon "serious" filmmakers and virtually turned its back on the traditional "commercial" directors and producers such as Pedro Masó, José Luis Dibildos, José Truchado, José Frade, and others of their ilk. The law provided hefty advance subsidies aimed at encouraging "quality films, the projects of new directors, those directed towards a children's audience or those of an experimental character."[8] In effect, the Miró Law decimated the ranks of those not within the inner circle of "serious" production. It lavished money on new "talent" and on the by-now aging anti-Franco centurions with their penchants for politics, the Spanish Civil War, and "educating" audiences.

The results were not long in manifesting themselves, not terribly different from those in other countries where the commercial targets of films are not adequately taken into account, where an attitude of high-minded didacticism eclipses "crass" business objectives, where, in short, "entertainment" and "commercial" become dirty words. The agelong and perhaps a trifle puerile controversy about whether film should be "art" or "commerce," hotly argued and debated in innumerable smoke-filled cafés and in film festivals and symposiums, was peremptorily decided in favor of the former.

The Miró Law, in retrospect, proved nigh disastrous, which is not to say that some excellent films were not made. But then two or three excellent films have *always* come out of Spain each year, no matter what the subsidy system used or the government in power. Well-intentioned perhaps as are so many idealistic ventures that produce nefarious results, the Miró Law in fact proved so crippling that Spanish cinema is still reeling from it. Miró's coterie has largely faded into obscurity, leaving in their wake dozens of films that simply didn't interest modern audiences. (She herself still directs commercial duds such as the recent *Tu nombre envenena mis sueños* [Your Name Poisons My Dreams] and *El perro del Hortelano* [The Gardener's Dog], both 1996.) Not only did production plummet to about fifty features a year, but, far worse, local audiences were turned off by the majority of Spanish films. The share culled by local pictures in their own market dropped to 10.80 percent in 1991, 9.32 percent in 1992, and 8.52 percent in 1993.[9] Repeatedly disappointed by pictures that had been hyped by film critics, many of whom were often in cahoots with the filmmakers, Spanish audiences started to shun local fare.

The subsidy system in Spain always had two key adjuncts, without which the awarding of subsidies would have been meaningless. Since an important part of the subsidy money may come from the 15 to 40 percent or more of the box-office return, and to assure the Spanish producer ample opportunity to pocket as many pesetas as possible at theaters, two measures were legislated that would complement the subsidies in protecting and promoting Spanish cinema. For decades now these two measures have been a constant source of friction between local producers and the government on one side, and the American majors and local exhibitors on the other. They are as hotly contested today (November 1996) as they were in 1960.

The first is a screen quota, which obliges exhibitors to release one Spanish or one European Union (EU) film for each two non-EU Spanish-dubbed ones in cities with a population greater than 125,000 and in a one-to-three ratio in smaller towns. "Non-EU" essentially means U.S. pictures, which accounted for 72 percent of box-office revenue in 1994.[10] (About 96 percent of the national box office for foreign-language films comes from Spanish-dubbed versions. The remaining 4 percent subtitled fare is generated mostly in Madrid and Barcelona.)[11]

Established January 1, 1942, the first screen quota required one week of Spanish films to be shown for every six weeks of foreign ones.[12] For most of the past two decades, the quota has been one day of Spanish films for every three days of Spanish-dubbed foreign ones. But in the past few years, the quota has been extended to include EU films, which may now be played in lieu of Spanish films. Screen quotas are not unique to Spain. Many countries legislate them to try to assure the release of the local product. However, often when local production drops, the quotas become unenforceable.

The second government safeguard to complement the subsidy system is a law requiring any distributor releasing Spanish-dubbed films to obtain a license. These licenses can only be obtained by releasing Spanish (and now EU) films. The Euro product is usually even less popular than the Spanish films—4.70 percent of box office in 1995 for the *sum* of Italian, French, and German films![13]

The license system dates back to 1943. At that time three to five import licenses were given for a "category 1" Spanish film released by a distributor, two to four licenses for a "category 2" film, and one for "category three" films.[14]

The awarding of dubbing licenses has always been a regulatory weapon wielded by producers against U.S. distributors and their agents. More recently, the licenses were pegged to the box-office results of Spanish films released by these distributors so that the first license was awarded when the Spanish film was contracted for release, the second when the film hit 30 million pesetas gross ($300,000), the third when it hit 60 million ($600,000), and the fourth if and when it hit 100 million gross. Only two or three Spanish films a year ever attain the latter figure.[15] (Note: unless otherwise indicated, dollar equivalents are given at the exchange rate of 100 pesetas. The rate has fluctuated between 90 and 140 during the past decade.)

A new law passed in 1994 brought Spanish legislation into tune with that of the EU. It limited licenses to only two. The first is now issued when an EU or a Spanish film grosses 20 million pesetas and a second when it hits 30 million. A stipulation for obtaining the second license is that it must also be released in a second of Spain's official languages, a sop thrown to the Catalans. Moreover, licenses could no longer be transferred from one distributor to another.[16]

These, then, have been and continue to be the three financial crutches that have enabled the Spanish "industry" to survive: subsidies, exhibit quotas, and dubbing licenses for foreign films issued only when Spanish films are also released. Obviously, the producers' very existences are at stake should any of the three elements slacken. The subsidies alone are not enough to assure their survival because, even if a producer succeeds in completing a film, he must then find a distributor who will adequately push his or her film, promote it, and obtain a good release date. However, because most Spanish films perform poorly at the box office, more often than not the distributor releases the film in order to obtain the dubbing license rather than for the revenue expected from its release. As for the exhibitors, they usually consider Spanish product to be their bane, since the average Spanish film draws about 40 percent less audience than the average American one.[17] The best play dates are usually reserved for Yank blockbusters.

The three legal dispositions have only been partially complied with. Subsidies were often as late as a year or two in being paid to producers; exhibition quotas were frequently winked at by theater owners; and dubbing licenses, until recently, were "sold" from one distributor to another, which is to say arrangements were made for a distributor with a surplus of licenses to release films from one who lacked them.

With all their imperfections, the subsidies and quotas nonetheless form the cornerstone for financing and sometimes amortizing most Spanish films. However, other sources of revenue are needed before a producer can arrive at that felicitous state in which he has brought the risk factor down as close as possible to zero. There are thousands of variations, twists, exceptions, intrigues, swindles, and heartbreaks involved in the arcane methods of raising production money, both in Spain and in every country in the world. The following rundown covers the most common finance sources in Spain.

1. *Government subsidies.* Many films receive their initial impetus when the producer/director/writer sends a screenplay and production and financing plan to the film department of the Ministry of Culture (ICAA) applying for a subsidy to make a film. If this is approved, the filmmaker is guaranteed, say, anywhere between $200,000 and $600,000, though there are cases where far more was given, as with Carlos Saura's *El Dorado* (1988) and Ridley Scott's *1492* (1992), the latter a co-production with Spain for which the local producer received about $2 million in subsidy money. Up to 49 percent of the acknowledged budget of a film may be advanced, usually with a limit of 100 million pesetas. Thus, Saura's *Maratón* (Marathon, 1992) got 80 million pesetas, as did Berlanga's *Todos a la cárcel* (Everyone off to Jail, 1993), whereas José Luis Garci's *Canción de cuna* (Lullaby, 1994) obtained 70 million.[18] Jaime Camino's Catalan epic *El largo invierno* (The Long Winter, 1992) managed to squeeze out 170 million pesetas, though it grossed only 20 million.[19]

In 1993, about $14.1 million were earmarked for subsidies to Spanish films. The ICAA's budget for subsidies in 1994 was 3,174 million pesetas (about $25 million at that year's exchange rate), of which 2,788 million were for features. Of this amount, 1,606 million were destined for advanced subsidies to projects and 1,022 million to *ayudas a la amortización,* that is, to Spanish films made without prior subsidies, but payable upon commercial release. A figure from 1990 illustrates this process: 31.7 percent of the average film's budget officially came from government subsidies (in 1993 that figure was down to 29.5 percent, and in 1994 and 1995 it was 19 percent and 19.1 percent, respectively.) but since the smaller producers are wont to sign "dummy" contracts to ostensibly obtain financing from private sources in order to comply with ICAA demands that a portion of the budget come from their own resources, the real percentage covered by the subsidy is probably vastly higher.

In any case, all producers at present continue to receive the automatic 15 percent-of-box-office subsidy for their films. Those not requesting advance subsidies receive the additional 25 percent, that is, a total of 40 percent of box office. Moreover, in 1994 those who presented three films within a two-year period got 60 percent-of-box-office subsidy for each film. There are also subsidies for scripts (about $25,000), and "special quality" subsidies ($250,000) once the film has been released. Subsidies are usually awarded three times a year.

About two-thirds of films receive advanced subsidies. In 1991, for example, of the sixty-four films produced that year, forty-two received advance subsidies. In 1995, 61.7 percent of films received both state subsidies and TV advances. In any case, no advance subsidies are usually awarded to horror genre films or overt pornographic films; hence, these are rarely produced, though extreme violence is considered okay.

2. *Television.* You can then apply to one of the local television networks for financing. Previously that meant Radiotelevisión Española (RTVE), the government network; as of five years ago, it could also be one of the private channels, mainly Antena 3 TV. RTVE had been especially profligate in providing financing for cinema, and until its recent financial debacle would foot sums of $400,000 to $600,000 per project. In return, the network kept the domestic TV screening rights for the film, in addition to the foreign sales rights. But the latter tended to be negligible because RTVE sold off the bulk of Spain's most prestigious films at a pittance in "packages." RTVE usually helped finance about twenty films a year.

If losses were incurred, no feathers were ruffled, for as a state-owned network RTVE was expected to support local production and, until the private networks came in, was making fortunes in spot advertising, it being the only game in town. (Those were the days—when Pilar Miró went on to become head of RTVE—when the network spent a mind-boggling $40 million to produce a Spanish Civil War series, *La forja de un rebelde;* other series such as *Don Quixote* and one on the last Moorish king, Boabdil, also ran into the $10-million-plus budget range with huge profits to independent producers.)

According to official figures, in 1990, 22.6 percent of the average film's budget came from TV advances. In 1994, it was 24 percent and in 1995, 17 percent. In 1991, thirteen films obtained TV advances, ranging from 8 to 200 million pesetas ($80,000 to $2 million).[20]

Further financing may come from Spain's private pay-TV channel Canal Plus España, which acquired 93 percent of all Spanish films produced in 1993. The pay scale usually runs between $50,000 and $100,000.

3. *Autonomous regions.* The producer will next try to get further financing from provincial authorities. If the film was shot in Aragon, or the Basque provinces, or in Catalonia, for example, an additional $100,000 or $200,000 might be obtained from local sources eager to have their regions promoted. Officially, 6.4 percent of financing came from the regional authorities in 1991. That year ten films received subsidies from regional sources, ranging from $50,000 to $400,000.[21]

4. *Distribution advances and home video.* A relatively minor sum might be obtained as an advance from the distributor of the film in Spain, say $100,000 (5.1 percent of budget, per official sources). However, in 1991, only 42.9 percent of films received distribution advances. Home video rights are usually negligible for most Spanish films, but for a while, before private TV channels came into Spain, there was a big home video boom, making Spain the fourth largest market in the world. At that time some advance money might be obtained from the home video sector as well. In 1991, after the video boom ended, only 0.8 percent of the average film's budget came from home video advances. Three films received from $50,000 to $100,000 each.[22]

5. *Co-productions.* Further financing might be sought by setting up a co-production, usually with France, Germany, Italy, or Portugal, in which case funds could also be obtained from government subsidies in

the co-producing country or countries, provided some token actors or technicians were employed. Each of the participating countries might then apply for local subsidies and benefits.

6. *European Union.* Financing may also come from the EU mechanisms, known as the Media Programme, which had a budget of $300 million over a five-year period (1990–1995) to promote the European audiovisual industry. In 1990 4.2 percent of the average film's budget came from these sources. However, in 1991 only two Spanish films obtained financing from this fund, one $30,000, the other, $420,000.[23]

7. *Eurimages.* Another source of money is the Eurimages organization. This pan-European fund was set up by the Council of Europe in 1989 and has supported the co-production of 144 films between 1989 and 1992, providing about $60 million. In order to obtain Eurimages subsidies, producers from three participating countries must apply jointly.

8. *In-house financing.* According to the official Film Institute statistics, in 1990 only 23.3 percent of financing came from the producers themselves. The real percentage is probably much lower. The turnover in production companies is tremendous and few master the intricacies of survival.[24]

Some outfits, such as PRISA and its filmic offshoot Sogetel/Sogepaq, previously interested mostly in building up a backlog film library and stockpiling negatives for future use in television and eventually cable, do finance their own films. (This is especially the case after the union of Sogepaq with Iberoamericana Films, Polygram, and Canal Plus in 1994, making it now the largest and most powerful production group in Spain.) Others such as ESICMA, Atrium Films, and Cartel also have their own sources of financing.

Private funding can include anything from a generous father who believes in his son's genius as a filmmaker to a rich financier in Bilbao who can be conned into investing in the world of glamour and show business. But mostly, in-house financing is kept to a minimum, and producers are loath to sink their own resources into their films. Better to use other people's money.

9. *Pre-sales.* In rare cases, producers may pre-sell their films to distributors in other countries. Today, about the only producers with enough clout to do this are El Deseo (the Almodóvar brothers) and Iberoamericana Films (Andrés Vicente Gómez), the latter via Sogepaq, the sales arm of Sogetel, Goméz's current corporate sugar daddy.

10. *Official bank loans.* The government's BEX bank in 1991 provided about $600,000 in low-interest loans, but 76.2 percent of producers did not apply because the bank usually asks for personal guarantees and collateral.[25]

11. *Private financing.* At present there are virtually no tax shelters for Spanish producers. A small write-off of from 20 to 25 percent of a film's profit may be obtained, but with a low limit. Otherwise, financing from private venture capital in Spain is negligible, since filmmakers are still considered suspect and the commercial results of most Spanish films are discouraging.[26]

12. *Other sources.* From 1988 to 1992 another important source of financing was the Quinto Centenario organization, which lavished funds on a wide range of Spanish and Latin American projects, in conjunction with the 500th anniversary celebrations of the discovery of America. Saura's *El Dorado* and *Columbus* (1992) of Alexander and Ilya Salkind benefited from this source, as did many projects involving Latin American producers. The organization ceased to exist in 1993.

Financing has also been raised in the past from everything from religious orders (*El hombre que supo amar* [The Man Who Knew How to Love, 1976]) to dubious sources laundering money—but that is a twilight area too touchy to expand upon.

In 1991, sources of financing for Spanish films were officially declared as follows:[27]

ICAA subsidy	26.0%
Regional subsidies	6.4%
European funding	1.4%
Private bank loans	5.8%
Public bank loans	9.3%
Producer's own finance	25.8%
Distribution advance	5.2%
TV advances	16.5%
Pre-sales	2.8%
Home video advances	0.8%

Thus—and this, perhaps, is the critical reason for the failure of so many non-U.S. films—if financing from a part or all the aforementioned sources is obtained before production begins, the commercial success or failure of the film becomes of secondary interest, since everyone involved in making the film has already raked off his or her money. Should the film prove successful upon release, should the producer be able to sell it outside Spain, that is further icing on the cake. But even if the film is a disaster, runs only one week, and dies a quick death, the producer can often go on and start the next project, especially if the producer has a track record that has provided him or her with some prestige. In short, the financial return is often not made at the box office but in the financing stage. And this is why fifty films or more continue to be made in Spain year after year. This system has provided Spain over the past two decades with a handful of exquisite, provocative, brilliantly limned films. But also with a huge number of stinkers that Spanish audiences have turned their backs on.

In 1992, there were fourteen features that never even got released, four of them made with government subsidies. Of the fifty-two films made in 1992, only three grossed more than their production costs (*Belle Epoque, Makinavaja,* and *La marrana* [The Sow]), though the producer's share is usually only a third of the box office.

Some films run for a few days and are then forever forgotten. Still others, shot in Catalan, play in the provinces of Catalonia and after a few runs on regional television are buried, their costs absorbed by the local Catalan government, which has been more interested in pushing its linguistic policies than getting films made that appeal to audiences. After a decade of such filmic folly, the Catalan "industry" is now virtually nonexistent: a dozen titles each year that virtually no one is willing to pay six dollars to see.

In the event that some elements of the financing plan do not pan out for the producer, it is not uncommon for those supplying basic services such as laboratories, lighting equipment, studio space, postproduction facilities, camera rentals, and so on, to be paid either very late or, in some cases, never. It is also not unknown for producers to declare bankruptcy, fold their old banners, and start new companies, after which they run up new debts. Often they do not even bother to move their premises or change their phone numbers.

This financing legerdemain and investment penury inevitably condition the nature of the films made in Spain. Even though the average *declared* budget in 1995 almost doubled to 247 million pesetos, or about $2 million,[28] Spanish producers clearly must stick close to home. Not for them the film boasting flashy special effects; banish the thought of lavish historical reconstructions; eschew expensive stunts or exotic locations or films based on pricey international literary properties or those requiring high-paid foreign actors and actresses. Also strike off those that will receive no subsidies for being too crassly "commercial."

Usually the safest economic bet will prevail: a local comedy or a violent youth picture. Dozens such are cranked out each year. Some of them are big moneymakers, at least in Spain. For here are genres where Spain can hold its own ground: local humor, local celebrities, local slang, local situations that titillate an eye-winking audience, with the current crop of locally popular thespians—Javier Bardem, Aitana Sánchez-Gijón, Penelope Cruz, Antonio Resines, Maribel Verdú, Jorge Sanz, Ariadna Gil, Carmelo Gómez, María Barranco, and Juan Echanove. Rather like the comedies of yore, so vilified at the time by critics and highbrows, these films can sometimes be very funny and well scripted. But they are usually dead ducks outside the country. However, if the production costs are kept down as much as possible, they can be gold mines—well . . . copper mines.

Hence, the top-grossing Spanish film in 1994 was a forgettable comedy called *Todos los hombres sois iguales* (All You Men Are Alike) by Manuel Gómez Pereira, which drew 832,000 spectators and grossed 411 million pesetas (close to $4 million). A close second was *Los peores años de nuestra vida* (The Worst Years Of Our Life), which racked up 310 million pesetas, followed by *Por fin solos* (Alone at Last), with 295 million. But these are exceptions in terms of ticket sales. In all, Spanish films brought in only 7.12 percent of the box-office gross in 1994. The results were somewhat more promising in 1995, when the market share for Spanish pictures rose to 11.88 percent. In 1995, the top-grossing films were Fernando Trueba's *Two Much* (582 million pesetas), Almodóvar's *La flor de mi secreto* (481 million) and Vicente Aranda's *La pasión turca* (414 million). For the first seven months of 1996, the box-office share of Spanish films was 9.93 percent, and local production was booming, mostly in the low-budget, subsidized range.

In an altogether unique category, almost unrelated and certainly not representative of other films made in Spain, are the comic melodramas of Pedro Almodóvar, which of late have risen to the $4 million budget range and are pre-sold worldwide. The last few have been co-financed by the wealthy Ciby 2000 group in France. Almodóvar's *Mujeres al borde de un ataque de nervios* (Women on the Verge of a Nervous Breakdown) was shot in 1988 on a shoestring and in Spain alone grossed an astounding $11 million. Add to that the TV, home video, and foreign sales of the film. Almodóvar now does not need subsidies. Even when not as successful as *Mujeres,* his films do well. Indeed, in Spain Almodóvar has been the butt of envy and dislike in the "industry" and now pretty much goes his own way.

Other genres that are relatively low-risk in Spain range over local adventure films, political thrillers, low budget musicals, and the occasional melodrama using a well-known local celebrity such as Isabel Pantoja. Her lachrymose *Yo soy esa* (I'm That Woman) grossed close to $500,000 in 1990, but a sequel to it died a ruinous death.

Every now and then some more ambitious project does surface, which strives for an international flavor, possibly including a foreign actor, and conceivably even employs an American or British screenplay writer to polish the Spanish version. Such was the case with Fernando Trueba's *Two Much* starring Antonio Banderas and Melanie Griffith. Supposedly budgeted at around $12 million, it did well in Spain, but was a disaster when released in the United States.

In 1994, a few new twists were given to film financing when the subsidy system was modified by the government in an effort to abolish some of the ills heretofore outlined. Advance subsidies, the cornerstone of the Miró Law, have in many cases been replaced by subsidies geared to the commercial results of films, a measure that clearly favors Spain's largest producers. Thus a law passed on June 10, 1994, and amended on October 5, 1994, provides for subsidies of one-third of the money put up by a film's producer up to a limit of 100 million pesetas if and when, upon release, it grosses 30 million pesetas (presently about $250,000). For films of new directors making their first two features, the threshold is 20 million. In addition, if the film is made in a regional tongue (e.g., Basque or Catalan), the amount drops to only 10 million pesetas. That subsidy is in addition to the automatic 15 percent of box office.

But as I write this article, and with a new conservative party government in power, it very much seems again that *plus ça change, plus c'est la même chose.* Quotas and dubbing licenses were to be abolished, subsidies decimated. . . . The twelve years of Socialist film policies were branded as "nefarious" by the new government. But soon the reaction from the vested interests of the film community were heard, the government had second thoughts, and things have more or less returned to what they have been in the past.

Notes

1. Equipo de Investigación de Fundesco, *La industria cinematográfica en España (1980–1991)* (Madrid: ICAA, 1993), 162–63.
2. *Quadre Pel.licules espanyoles per ordre de recaptaciones, segons LICAA,* Barcelona, August 10, 1994. List provided to author by Pérez Coinar.
3. Fundesco, 29–30.
4. See Peter Besas, *Behind the Spanish Lens: Spanish Cinema under Fascism and Democracy* (Denver: Arden, 1985).
5. Uniespaña catalogues (Madrid: Uniespaña), e.g., 1969 through 1975.
6. The Spanish Cinema. Uniespaña catalogue (Madrid: Uniespaña, 1968).
7. ICAA, *Avances cinematográficos* (Madrid: ICAA, 1977).
8. Royal decree of December 28, 1983, and Preamble thereof, Madrid.
9. ICAA, *Avances cinematográficos* (Madrid: ICAA, 1991, 1992, and 1993).
10. Orden ministerial, October 5, 1994; Boletín oficial del estado, Madrid, October 14, 1994.
11. No official statistics are published that break down subtitled and dubbed films. Subtitled films tend to be limited to a cluster of mini-cinemas, mostly in Madrid and Barcelona.
12. Santiago Pozo, *La Industria del cine en España* (Barcelona: Publicacions i Edicions de la Universsitat de Barcelona, 1984), 46.
13. ICAA, *Avance Cinematográfico* (Madrid: ICAA, December 1995).
14. Pozo, 46.
15. Royal decree, sections 2/82 and 12/82, Madrid, 1989.
16. Orden ministerial, October 5, 1994. Madrid.
17. Jaime Tarrazón, interview by author, ACEC (Catalan exhibitors group), Barcelona, July 1993.
18. ICAA, *Subvenciones a proyectos cinematográficos* (Madrid: ICAA, June 2, 1993).
19. *Quadre Pel.licules espanyoles.*
20. Pozo, 138, 140.
21. Ibid., 132.
22. Ibid., 137.
23. Ibid., 140.
24. Ibid., 136.

25. Ibid., 134.
26. J. M. Cunillés, interview by author, November 3, 1995.
27. Pozo, 140.
28. José Angel Esteban and Carlos López, "El trabajo del año," *Revista Academia,* January 1996.

RICHARD MAXWELL

Spatial Eruptions, Global Grids:

Regionalist TV in Spain and Dialectics

of Identity Politics

For most of the twentieth century, the nation-states of Western Europe administered and propagated a territorial ideology of nationality through national broadcasting systems. Although it is doubtless that the media institutions of national states remain strong, they are no longer the only, or primary, players in the field of international communication. For regionalization and transnationalization, the centripetal and centrifugal processes marking the changes in global broadcasting systems have redefined the terms of national culture.[1] Today a resurgent territorial politics of nationality resonates throughout the Europe of nation-states. This political and cultural disruption can in part be attributed to the changing historical significance of the national state within the world economy. The modern nation-state, while becoming more powerful in areas of social control,[2] has to contend with its relative weakness in relation to transnational corporations, which since World War II have become the most powerful agents in the global economy.

This retreat of the state has led to a series of changes that have affected the traditional spaces, and spatial processes, of national culture industries. Among these changes are new regional economic alliances and directives, liberalized transborder commercial communications, a decline in the fortunes of public service broadcasting, and a multiplication of private, profit-making broadcast networks. In addition, and with an entirely different spirit and logic, there has been a boom in small, micro-broadcast adventures: urban radio "pirates" and low-power village TV; community video and bargain-basement cassette reproductions (aka piracy), to name only a few. And somewhere in between these big and small media, there are also those midsized models of broadcasting that have emerged in this European electronic space; meso-broadcasters like those in Wales, or in the Basque and Catalan regions of Spain—the cultural industries in these zones aim to foment national identity of a regional stripe. They may be nations without states, but they have TV networks. In this essay I analyze the significance of the regional TV experience in Spain from the perspective of critical political economy of international media. I identify some of the core policy events and social transformations that gave rise to the institutional framework of regional TV.

The Decline of National Television in Spain

In 1978, after forty years of dictatorship, Spain's new democratic constitution created a parliamentary democracy and ordered the dismantlement of the centralized state. Created in the latter's place was a new "State of the Autonomies," which reorganized the fifty provinces of Spain into seventeen regional autonomous communities. These autonomous communities gained control over administrative powers and social services previously in the hands of the central state. In the wake of this devolution process, the parliaments of the autonomous communities won the right to own and operate their own independent television systems. These television systems exist ostensibly to foment the culture and language within the regions, addressing in particular the needs of distinct nationalities located there. On the economic side, their funding from both advertising and public monies has given important new injections of capital to the communication industries within Spain. Yet their existence is most often touted as a condition for the extension of democracy to regional nationalities in the postdictatorship period in Spain. In the European context of the crisis of public service broadcasting, these regional culture industries are seen also as a necessary corrective to the vicissitudes of centralized state-controlled media.

Three key media policies that arose out of the transition to democracy in Spain were decisive in establishing an institutional framework for regional TV. These are the Statute of Radio and Television (RTVE Statute), the Third Channel Law, and the Private TV Law. The first of these, the RTVE Statute, grew out of a period of compromises, impasse

Madrid
28. Madrid

Extremadura
29. Cáceres
30. Badajoz

Castilla-La Mancha
31. Guadalajara
32. Toledo
33. Ciudad Real
34. Cuenca
35. Albacete

Valencia
36. Castellón
37. Valencia
38. Alicante

Murcia
39. Murcia

Andalusia
40. Huelva
41. Cádiz
42. Sevilla
43. Córdoba
44. Málaga
45. Jaén
46. Granada
47. Almería

Baleares
48. Baleares
(Menorca, Mallorca, Ibiza)

Canary Islands
49. Tenerife
50. Las Palmas

Autonomous Community	Galicia	Basque Country	Aragón	Castilla-León
	1. La Coruña	7. Vizcaya	12. Zaragoza	19. Leon
Province	2. Pontevedra	8. Guipuzcoa	13. Huesca	20. Palencia
	3. Lugo	9. Álava	14. Teruel	21. Burgos
	4. Orense			22. Zamora
		La Rioja	Catalonia	23. Valladolid
	Asturias	10. La Rioja	15. Lérida	24. Segovia
	5. Asturias		16. Tarragona	25. Soria
		Navarra	17. Barcelona	26. Salamanca
	Cantabria	11. Navarra	18. Gerona	27. Ávila
	6. Cantabria			

Autonomous Communities and their provinces.

resolutions, and pacts among the major political parties in the late
1970s. The 1980 statute established norms to ensure a plurality of
political influence over the national network, Radiotelevisión Española
(RTVE), to order state guarantees that broadcasting be treated as an
essential public service, to protect open and free expression, and to
suggest that the autonomous regional communities of Spain might have
new broadcast channels operating in their zones. Two institutional
changes followed. One was the eventual democratization of RTVE (still,
some argue, in transit). The other was the parallel decentralization of
television, an aspect of the wider pattern of political reform associated
with the decline of the centralist state.

Without approved legislation from the central state, the parliaments
of the autonomous communities of the Basque country and Catalonia
approved their own television systems—the Basques in May of 1982,
the Catalans in May of 1983. These actions constituted the first major
institutional change of broadcasting since the Spanish Civil War, when

all broadcast media were nationalized. Together they were also a direct assault on the national legal framework that had controlled broadcasting for more than seventy years, contravening the 1908 royal decree that gave the central state the right to establish and exploit "all systems and apparatuses related to the so-called 'Hertzian telegraph,' 'ethereal telegraph,' 'radiotelegraph,' and other similar procedures already invented or that will be invented in the future."[3] Nevertheless, and missing the mark by many months, the central state approved in December 1983 its own Third Channel Law to regulate the establishment of additional networks in the autonomous communities.

The Third Channel Law came into force in 1984, months after the Basques and Catalans had begun broadcasting (experiments started in December 1982 and September 1983, respectively). Still, it was a very important policy event for the transition to democracy, since it was designed to decentralize the public broadcasting system. In principle, it was meant to cause controlled denationalization of television by creating channels that responded to the plurality of cultures and communities within the Spanish territory. However, the law ordered that decentralization be carried out in line with norms established in the constitution and the RTVE Statute, especially the sections of these that retained the state's control, and RTVE's dominance, over the airwaves. The two regional parliaments in Catalonia and the Basque country, and later the Galician parliament as well, balked at this. Instead, they understood that their separate right to broadcast was not dependent on the state and maintained that their own statutes of autonomy, in combination with relevant clauses in the constitution and the RTVE Statute, protect independent action in this area. For more than a decade now, the contradictory mandates within and between these legal documents have been deployed in endless battles over rights of access to regional airwaves.[4]

Political control over the regional parliaments is another important factor, as evidenced by the limits placed on the development of regional TV in the communities of Andalusia, Valencia, and Madrid. In these regions the Socialist Party (PSOE), the ruling party of the central government at the time, controlled the parliaments and was able to keep the television systems under strict Third Channel Law guidelines, holding their start-up until 1989. (On a smaller scale, a similar battle developed over local, village-level television, which passed from a situation characterized by what some Spanish writers affectionately call "a-legal" broadcasts to one regulated by a posteriori legislation to normalize spectrum use and state intervention.)[5]

By 1990, eleven autonomous broadcast organizations were approved, six of which had already begun broadcasting on a daily basis.[6] In 1989, these systems agreed to merge into a national federation of autonomous broadcasters, known as FORTA, creating a network of public broadcasters to rival RTVE. Participating in FORTA are autonomous systems from the Basque country, Catalonia, Andalusia, Galicia, Valencia, Madrid, and Murcia.

Throughout the transition, RTVE remained a commercial (albeit not-for-profit), state-controlled system with two television channels and two radio networks. For obvious reasons, when the state was the only broadcaster, the private media companies, advertisers, and the advertising agencies saw RTVE's hold over the airwaves as a monopoly over audience attention—a monopoly, moreover, with both economic and political value. The regional autonomous systems broke this monopoly, and with FORTA established a short-lived duopoly of publicly owned, commercial, not-for-profit, television networks. By the late 1980s, with three regional television networks and an expanded national network, the total investment in television advertising had been pushed to more than 1,000 percent over investments in 1975. And private TV hadn't even been activated yet.

The most controversial policy battle during the transition arose over the development of a law of private television. Indeed, in many ways the legalization of commercial, for-profit TV became emblematic of the problems of political transition to democracy. Most commentators argue that privatization was held up for more than a decade because the process became "politicized." (Although it is true in a general sense that official politics took over the process of privatization, restricting decision-making to the closed ranks of a political class, it remains a contentious way of understanding transition politics.) The outcome, however, was the third major media policy event of the Spanish transition: a 1988 law and technical plan for private TV. The law furnished three licenses for the bidding of private corporations, a three-phase framework for the extension of universal territorial coverage, and restrictions on legal ownership to promote multiple partnerships rather than monopoly control.[7] The technical plan created an independent public company, RETEVISION, to manage the technical infrastructure, effectively delinking RTVE from the central source of its economic and political control over the airwaves. Today all broadcasters must pay an access fee to use the public infrastructure. Those regional companies that developed parallel infrastructures—Galician, Basque, and Catalan—have not relinquished control to RETEVISION as far as I know.

At the end of 1989, three new private television channels had begun test broadcasts. By 1991, the market share of national audience attention broke down as follows: two TV channels of RTVE together registered 55.4 percent, FORTA companies got 15.4 percent, two private broadcasters brought in 27.8 percent (Telecinco, 17.0 percent and Antena 3, 10.8 percent), and a third private company, a pay-TV outfit called Canal Plus, reported 1.0 percent. The remainder, 0.4 percent, has been attributed to the municipal and local television systems (over 100 in Catalonia alone).[8] In little over fifteen years, Spanish television made the transition from absolute state control to a regulated, competitive system of national and regional networks of mixed private and public ownership. Except for the occasional strip show or pornographic film, the programming of all channels is very similar to American broadcast television.

Thus the transition to democracy in Spain can be understood in relation to the media transition that give rise to regional TV. A few points should be added to this summary. First, revenues have been slacking off in the past few years. The initial euphoria of promoters, managers, and advertisers has begun to be tempered with doses of the economic reality of rising costs and downward adjustments for regular viewership; and the need for public subsidy for mass media increases at the same time that public budgets shrink. Second, the integration of Spain into the European Union (EU) played a significant role in shaping the legal framework for private TV and the technical plan; related to this were the major reform law of telecommunications (the LOT) and the investments leading up to the Expo '92 (world's fair) held in Seville and the Olympic games held in Barcelona, which placed Spain and two important regions in the international limelight (recall the media baptismal of Spanish democracy in the international coverage of the Olympics). And finally, new channels and new reforms continue to emerge: a second channel each in the Basque and Catalan systems; a third requested by RTVE; further privatization campaigns sponsored by the conservatives of the Partido Popular (PP), who didn't get anything from previous reforms; satellite channels, with and without cable enterprises; and many grassroots alternatives that include—besides local TV and its legalization—closed-circuit community video, urban radio pirates, and video and audio piracy.

What, then, is the significance for contemporary theory of international media of the institutional changes represented by TV in the regional autonomous communities of Spain? Can the Spanish experience alone stand as a decisive moment in the history of international media? I want to suggest that there are at least three salient issues in the Spanish case that raise important questions for international media researchers. These issues can be formulated in relation to the identity politics of the regional networks, globalization (or transnationalization), and the dialectics of local and global connections. And although each of these issues can be identified and analyzed in other locations, the Spanish media experience is theoretically decisive because it is constituted by a clear, if conflict-ridden, articulation of local, national, and transnational media spaces.

Against the Jacobinist Grain

The first issue concerns the identity politics of the regional networks, what more generally we think of in terms of national sovereignty or the rights of self-determination of collective identity and culture. Founded on a cultural politics of nationality, these networks instituted a new daily routine for the construction of a regionalist identity against the centralist culture of the nation-state. Such a routine establishes the boundaries of a distinct cultural space, a national identity framed by the regional TV screen. From the perspectives of cultural studies and what Cornel West calls a "new cultural politics of difference,"[9] the battle to change the cultural industries within the territorial state of Spain represents a progressive, historically significant process. It might even be described as the realization of "the vocation" of cultural studies, which, as defined by Stuart Hall, seeks "to provide ways of thinking, strategies for survival, and resources to all those who are now—in economic, political, and cultural terms—*excluded from anything that could be called access to the national culture of the national community.*"[10] By establishing broadcast institutions to encourage identification with nationality, regionalism in Spain presents a radical challenge to the cultural hegemony of the nation-state, especially to the territorial ideology that omits ethnic and linguistic identities.[11]

This infranational conflict between center and periphery is today manifest in a context characterized by the decline of the nation-state and the media project of national integration. The modern political forms embodying this conflict (small nation nationalism versus state centralism) developed in the late nineteenth century as the political map of Europe became increasingly defined by criteria of nation-statehood. Although the regions of Spain had been integrated administratively as an "early modern state" (absolutist, to be sure) since the sixteenth century,[12] the historic nationalities in Spain (Basque, Catalan, Galician) did not develop a modern politics of nationalism until the late nineteenth century. Like other European nationalities that felt enclosed or cordoned off by the territorial ideology of the modern nation-state, their political aspirations as independent nations crystallized with the wider movement in Europe to establish permanent borders.[13] Apart from the brief periods of cultural and political recognition for the nationalities of Spain prior to the Spanish Civil War (1936–39), these cultural minorities have been subordinated to the nation-state for most of the twentieth century. This repressive centralism achieved its most wicked and brutal form during the forty-year dictatorship of Francisco Franco under the banner of his political coalition, the National Movement.

At this point, I want to suggest that regional politics in Spain demonstrate that an interstate bias of international media research is a weak basis upon which to understand the present-day media space of Europe. The cultural politics of nationality manifest in the regional media systems demonstrate this point with force. Against the grain of the Jacobin cultural politics of the Spanish government, these regional autonomous communities ignored the mandates to coordinate their efforts with RTVE, the national state broadcasting system. Instead they built networks of transmitters and relays running parallel to the national state infrastructure, along with studios, administrative bureaucracies, and creative workforce. Perhaps now room should be made for this kind of identity politics in international media theory. In answering such a theoretical warrant, international media research might contribute new and productive approaches by identifying and analyzing geographical scales divergent with that of the nation-state. For this purpose, the regional autonomous communities of Spain and their television networks provide a clear case study from which to begin.

In that spirit, then, let's assume that research can find a way to look past international relations toward *infra*-national social processes and the way communicative practices are inscribed in them. In this framework, regional and local firms can be found happily trespassing within the cultural borders of national broadcast systems. In terms of defining their publics, regional firms displace the national citizen of the modern nation state. Their mode of address represents a realignment of audience identities with the felt nationalism of the local. Against the culture of the nation-state, which hails its public as citizens of a nationwide community, these regional culture industries call upon their public to act locally. By taking seriously the politics of nationality that erupts on smaller geographical scales, the discourse of international media theory can release itself from the territorial constraints of the nation-state and focus more freely on a range of site-specific media practices. This does not diminish the significance of struggles for cultural sovereignty. On the contrary, such an orientation corresponds to the progressive challenge to the paradigm of the "New World Information and Communication Order"; a challenge aimed basically at the worldview of mainstream international relations.[14] It suggests instead that national culture may not be easily contained within the territory defined by modern nation-states.

There is, however, an important element missing from this account. What has receded from the analysis of the infranational is the global connection. Against the culture of the nation-state, regional broadcasters also hail their publics as global consumers, as shoppers in the EU, as participants in a transnational cultural exchange. For this reason, as later examples suggest, the shift to an infranational analysis is adequate as long as it is carried out in the context of a political economy of international media; that is, as long as we conceive of the plurality of media spaces under conditions of economic domination, political power, and social stratification. At the very least, this cautions international media theory against a romantic account of regionalist movements, and at best it helps identify how regional TV is positioned within the emerging global commercial culture.

Globalization

The second area of concern deals with the conceptual space generated by this alignment of the regional with the global. Basically, the challenge of the previous section was to push existing mental boundaries in international communication theory beyond a focus on relations among national states. Now, I admit that I may have overstated the case for a study of infranational processes. Even with the focus on more "local" problems, international media theory should still recognize the global character and interdependencies of communications systems. Otherwise, there is an inherent danger of "folklorizing" or "anthropologizing" regional cultural movements, or worse, of seeing autonomous regional television in Spain as a treacly and quaint grassroots phenomenon. Stated baldly, the movements of autonomy and decentralization of cultural power are inscribed in the crisis of the nation-state; they are rooted in political nationalism and the conflict between regional authorities and the central government. But they are also affected by liberalized (deregulated) investment of transnational capital in all social, political, and economic spheres. If we are going local, we must avoid being ingenuous.

What the Spanish case illustrates is that a theory about the cultural politics of regionalist television is needed, one that accounts in particular for the evidence that regionalism is both cause and effect of a new international cultural economy.[15] There is no more prominent example of this dual character of regionalism than the programming choice for the opening night of the new Catalan channel, TV-3. In an effort to foment the language and culture of Catalonia to the widest possible audience, TV-3 broadcast the hit episode of *Dallas,* "Who Shot JR?"—dubbed, of course, into Catalan. All the autonomous broadcasters have followed similar programming strategies, choosing to dub the most popular imported series into the local language rather than pursue a strategy based on pure autonomous production. The limits to a dissociative, autonomous cultural industry are obvious in the global political economy. Obvious too is the global character of the anticentralist policies of the regional broadcasters, which created new opportunities for transnational media operations. That most of the broadcasting hardware employed by the regionals is Japanese should not surprise us; however, that the Basques contracted a German firm to set up their system and train its workers instead of going to RTVE in Madrid or Barcelona raises serious questions about the politics of institutional cultural nationalism.

More broadly, such transnationalism resembles what Eric Hobsbawm ventures will emerge as a salient feature of the history of the late twentieth century, which he says "will inevitably have to be written as the history of a world which can no longer be contained within the limits of 'nations' and 'nation-states' as these used to be defined, either politically, or economically, or culturally, or even linguistically. It will be largely supranational and infranational, but even infranationality, whether or not it dresses itself up in the costume of some mini-nationalism, will reflect the decline of the old nation-state as an operational entity. It will see 'nation-states' and 'nations' or ethnic/linguistic groups primarily retreating before, resisting, adapting to, being absorbed or dislocated by the new supranational restructuring of the globe."[16] Internally, regional and local movements for cultural autonomy have put great pressure on the centralized practices of the national state culture to recognize and respect cultural difference. But at the opposite extreme, transnational forces bulk large, pressuring both national state and regional authorities into a secondary role in the international economy.

In this sense, the cultural apparatus of the politics of nationality reflect what Tom Nairn, Hobsbawm, and Phillip Cooke insist is the two-faced nature of nationalism at whatever scale.[17] Cooke puts it this way: "That double profile involves a process of social innovation in which tradition is reappropriated to seek the unification of diverse strata within and across a defined territory and to mobilize a society to support the move forward into an unknown future." The *post*-modern geography of the cultural industries is, in this negative reading, simply "modernism by other means."[18] To admit this makes it easier to see at least one possible future toward which autonomous regional TV in Spain is headed, for it is one that is not new at all. On the contrary, the trends are well known, although quite contradictory given the context in which autonomous regional TV arose.

Spatial Eruptions, Global Grids

The "otherness" and "regional resistances," that postmodernist politics emphasize, can flourish in a particular place. But they are all too often subject to the power of capital over the co-ordination of universal fragmented space and the march of capitalism's global historical time that lies outside the purview of any particular one of them.—David Harvey, *The Condition of Postmodernity*

The third issue takes us to the contradictory links between global media space and media space produced by the politics of nationality. As the empirical and theoretical problems converge, the question raised by Harvey can be more fully interrogated: How does capital reassert its control over regional resistances? The cultural politics defined in opposition to a centralist culture of the national state can be questioned at a point where transnational (supranational) and infranational processes meet. What is at stake are strategies of survival where the cultural politics of nationality erupt onto the global grid of market culture. The question is whether and for how long regionalist movements can occupy this place; whether and in what manner capital reasserts its power to coordinate this geo-cultural disruption.

At the level of discourse, one example already mentioned concerns the institutional mode of address produced by media with crossbred functions of identity politics and commercial advertising. Here the citizen is no longer addressed simply as Basque, or Catalan, or Galician. The use of distinct languages in TV advertisements and imported programming attaches the illusion of national identity to the idioms of marketing and of television genres with a decidedly American accent. By extension, nationality can be said to devolve into the cosmopolitan subject of the market imaginary: act locally, consume globally. What is of concern at this point is how this discursive moment can be traced to wider systemic trends and institutional practices. Among the trends and practices I want to examine here are technological dependency, the growth of big-money transnational advertising, and the extension of audience commodity exchange.

Communications Technology and Dependency

After World War I, Spain had finally come through its industrial revolution with basic industries concentrated in the Basque country and assembly or transformation industries in Catalonia. There was at this time no significant institutional interest in technology, and so by the 1920s Spain established what would become a heavily dependent relation on foreign expertise in communications technology (in transport and capital goods as well). This set a pattern of dependence on imported technology that deepened through three national development plans, the Base Agreement with the United States in 1953, and the market liberalizations of the 1960s. By 1978, Spain's dependency on foreign technology in the sector of electronics components, which includes telecommunications, reached an estimated 93 percent. At the same time, Spain was investing less capital in research and development as a percentage of its wealth than any other European country; and it was notably weak in contracting license agreements and even weaker in assimilating the technology it was licensed to use.[19] These figures contrast dramatically with one of the markers of growth that most economists associate with Spain's "economic boom" in the 1960s: an annual average share of 9 percent of world trade for Spain's manufacturing exports (1962–73). As Casanova reports, "despite all its imbalances" Spain was seen as "a highly diversified, internationally competitive economy."[20]

Nowhere was the internationalization of capital more clearly expressed than in the communication and information technology sector. This sector is usually divided into professional and consumer electronics goods. At the beginning of the transition period in the mid-1970s, Spain's professional electronics market was dominated by affiliates of the transnational firm International Telephone and Telegraph, ITT (Standard Eléctrica, S.A.; Compañía Internacional de Telecomunicacíon y Electrónica, S.A. [CITESA]; and Marconi Española, S.A.). Other important transnational corporations operating in Spain at the time were L. M. Ericsson, Telettra International, and GTE. Of the consumer electronic corporations, the list was topped by Philips, Grundig, Thomson, Sanyo, AEG-Telefunken, Sharp, Matsushita Electric Industrial, and Sony.[21] IBM was, not surprisingly, dominant in the domestic computer market, whereas AT&T would not enter Spain until after divestiture proceedings were complete in the United States in the 1980s.

The enormous power held by transnational electronics firms indicates one of the more influential sectors among the business, as well as political, elites. This pressure was played out most decisively in the formulation of Spain's telecommunication policy,[22] and in political efforts surrounding the union of Spain with the European Economic Community (EC, now called the European Union). In relation to the regional broadcasters, transnational electronics firms were able to expand into new markets when the absolute control of the central government over purchases of communication technology was challenged by the regional authorities in 1982 to 1983. Before that time, the Spanish state regulated capital flows by maintaining total control over purchases of foreign technology. A register of the flows of capital in this sector shows a majority of billings going through the National Telephone Company of Spain (CTNE, or Telefónica), which, as Fregoso has demonstrated, served as the national bridgehead for foreign penetration of information and communication technology in Spain. (Nevertheless, the Socialist Party set out to liberalize this quasi-protected electronic market exchange through its various reindustrialization plans).[23] The share of the gross domestic product attributed to this transnationalized communications sector grew from 1.4 percent to nearly 2 percent between 1975 and 1985.[24]

Transnational Advertising

Advertising is another important sector where transnational firms are dominant in Spain. The penetration of multinational advertising firms began in 1926, with the arrival of J. Walter Thompson during the time of the Primo de Rivera dictatorship, followed by two French agencies, Havas and Publicitas, just prior to the founding of the Second Republic. But like most aspects of the "internationalization of capital" in Spain, the most significant multiplication of firms came on the heels of the 1959 Stabilization Plan, designed in part by Opus Dei technocrats.[25] By 1978, between twenty-five and thirty-one of the leading fifty advertising firms were linked to foreign owners, with four of the top five firms listed as J. Walter Thompson (J.W.T.), McCann-Erickson, Davis Benton Bowles, and a Belgian firm, Univas.[26] J.W.T. and McCann-Erickson as well as five other multinational firms were wholly owned by their "mother" firms, indicating a distinct preference for foreign direct investments in this sector.[27] (Foreign direct investment gives multinational corporations greater flexibility of control and more freedom to move among shifting locations of growth and investment in the global economy without too much attachment to national economies.)

By all accounts, the TV advertising market in Spain had experienced regular annual growth throughout the 1960s.[28] However, the monopolistic relation between the state-controlled Televisión Española (TVE, the television company within RTVE) and the advertising market provoked much ire among private commercial media promoters. Obviously for these businesses, state-controlled TV offered only limited growth potential. For although TVE expanded its advertising throughout the decade following Franco's death, perceived caps on this growth pushed advertisers into other media. Ramón Zallo has demonstrated that marketing strategies receiving the most dramatic investment since 1970 were in fact direct-mail advertising, mail order, and other forms of commercial communication.[29] Nonetheless, record investment in TV advertising in Spain buttressed the power of this sector, while the Spanish state provided the weakest record of any European country in safeguards against outright commercialism of the airwaves. This trend was clearest in the aftermath of the regionalization of the audience commodity in the mid-1980s.

The Audience Commodity

By 1988, *View Magazine* (June 6) had recognized Spain as "Europe's sleeping giant" precisely for the hyperexpansion of its TV program and advertising markets. The growth potential was attributed to the regional autonomous networks and to the regionalized markets these created for advertising and commercial distribution. In the location and identification of the non-mass (or niche) market, Madison Avenue saw in Spain what almost every market researcher or consulting firm would nowadays speak of as business as usual: efficient strategies for communicating with culturally diverse consumers. (The Dow Jones publication *American Demographics* put it this way: "You'll know it's the 21st century when. . . . Everyone belongs to a minority group.")[30] In the

Spanish market, the Basques, Catalans, and Galicians set the parameters of difference along lines of regional identity. To help them, Silvio Berlusconi (Italian-based Euro-media mogul) contracted out the services of Fininvest to the regional federation FORTA to bring their diverse consumers to an advertising market dominated by North Atlantic firms. Fininvest also holds a 25 percent share of the private TV network Telecinco.[31] In the era of transnationalization, the "captains of consciousness" appear to be employing such investment strategies in order to be everywhere at the same time. In other words, global media giants, such as Berlusconi, are striving to become, like transnational corporations in other sectors, "equidistant from all key customers" regardless of their or anyone else's national culture of origin.[32] And most national state governments are obliging by bringing down traditional political barriers through programs of privatization, deregulation, incentives for strategic alliances, and so on.[33]

However, what actually lay behind this market jargon was the expectation of a surge in audience commodity exchange. "The 'war of audiences', as it has become known, has led to across-the-board studies by all parties of the tastes and habits of the Spanish viewer."[34] The groundwork for this battle for attention had already been laid by 1977, when 94.1 percent of TVE's financing came from advertising, with only the purely international firms in Luxembourg and Malta recording higher levels of dependence.[35] In 1984, in reaction to the establishment of regional autonomous television, TVE reconstituted the finance structure of its sixteen regional centers, fragmenting by region the advertising contracts negotiated. After this reorganization, revenues in the regional centers of TVE rose from about $1.1 million to $14.6 million in a brief three-year period.[36] In all, between 1975 and 1985—the first decade beyond dictatorship—TVE recorded an increase in advertising income of more than 1,200 percent, which surpassed that of all European television firms.[37] Separate from this figure, total advertising investment in the autonomous Catalan network (TV-3) between 1984 and 1987 surged from $2.1 million to $10.3 million, while the Basque network's (ETB) earnings rose from a quarter million dollars in 1984 to over three-quarters of a million dollars in 1986, showing a slight decline in 1987 (to $0.73 million). The network of the autonomous community of Galicia (TVG) reported an increase from $0.31 million in 1986 to

$0.81 million in 1987.[38] By 1990, TV-3 was taking in around $170 million and ETB about $23 million; TVG shared with its radio company a total of $19.2 million.[39]

Consider that until 1990, yearly growth in global advertising billings was somewhere around 10 percent. In contrast, a total increase of 156 percent was recorded in the first year following the regionalization of advertising contracts in Spain. In 1986, there was an increase of 239 percent from 1985 revenues, and in 1987 advertising revenues jumped an additional 53 percent. As a percentage of the gross domestic product, total advertising investment in Spain had grown from 0.7 percent to over 1.1 percent between 1975 and 1985; and it reached levels in 1986 equal to the same index in the United States for 1979.[40]

Although minuscule in comparison to global advertising revenues (estimated at $252 billion in 1989), the growth of Spain's regionalized ad market after 1985 proved a profitable example of the international marketing strategy of localization. Yet, by encouraging the regionalization of advertising in Spain, the regional firms helped widen the exchange of the audience commodity form. In addition to realigning audience identity in opposition to national state television and the cultural hegemony of Madrid, autonomous regional TV commercialized its culturally diverse audiences—regional TV made a difference by selling difference.

At first, this is pretty easy to explain. The regional autonomous networks are advertising funded, not-for-profit, companies. However, like other cultural industries, they depend on maximizing their audience in order to cope with increasing costs of production and distribution of their services. As a result, these firms must protect their investment by capturing larger audiences and selling them to advertisers—or risk losing that investment altogether. The situation gets tougher considering that the regional parliaments can afford very little subsidy (Telemadrid receives no subsidy but instead relies on a line of bank credit for its survival).

In order to protect these investments in their locales, these companies must be able to realize growth of their initial investment within their region—as they put it, they seek to become self-financing. Such a regionally bounded turnover of invested capital would allow them to be truly autonomous. Beyond, or even barring, this realization of investments, however, they must look across their borders for further collection of numbers for the ratings game.[41]

Conclusion

This situation tends to support a theory suggesting that the defense of immobilized capital (i.e., infrastructure) alongside the promotion of border-crossing broadcast technology constitute the material basis for interregional factional struggle over exchange of the audience commodity. This would pose neither moral nor pragmatic problems if access to the imaginations of people were not decisively linked to the structures of power in society. In other words, if left to a discourse of cold economic and technical problem-solving, the multiplication of the regional firms and the regionalization of the audience can be seen positively to encourage growth. Competition for viewer attention thus gives rise to a healthy public culture (i.e., one that is growth oriented, technologically innovative, and so on). The key mechanism at work here consists of advertising, which makes feasible the creation, and exchange on expanded basis, of the audience in the form of a commodity.

But once this system is politicized and the power structure revealed, the contradiction arises that in the market economy the regionalist cultural enterprise entails the regeneration of forms of economic organization that privilege the cultural orientations of dominant program and technology suppliers. Paradoxically, quite similar external dependencies were previously the object of regional resistance. However, there was a significant disjuncture between the form these dependencies actually took and the form in which regional decision-makers became conscious of their dependency. Regionalism was decidedly anticentralist and anti-Franco but not anti-imperialist in the supranational sense. Nor, it might be argued, were they anti-imperialist in an infranational sense; for once the demands for territorialized cultural sovereignty materialized as a commercial cultural institution, regionalism became part of a system that by its nature seeks to trespass sovereign cultural borders—modern imperialism by postmodern means? In practice, then, a truly autonomous regional broadcast system would seem an impossibility.

Thus expansion across space to achieve audience maximization ensures protection of investments in a place, but at the expense of other regional firms. If an audience is not produced for the firm located in a politically bounded region (which in theory could be the national state, autonomous community, or the EU), then it is possible that it can be produced for a firm located outside that region—the nationwide broadcasts being the primary beneficiary of this system as shown by the register of state and private TV revenues. When this occurs—given the right political, linguistic, technical, and economic conditions—then it becomes feasible for the value embodied in the audience commodity form to be realized outside that audience's home region. Again, this constitutes the basis for interregional factional struggle over audiences. Such a conflict occurred in practice when TV-3, the Catalan channel, had achieved territorial coverage over the entire Valencian community, reaching (by some estimates) as far south as Murcia, east to the Balearic Islands, west into parts of Aragon, and north across the French border. This coverage was established rather surreptitiously with power increases and fortuitous topography, linguistic commonality, and the help of viewer clubs in Valencia.[42] However, a struggle erupted when executives of Radiotelevisión de Andalucía (RTVA) sought to reduce TV-3's power by excluding the Catalan radiotelevision company from initial agreements made with FORTA. The Andalusians have the largest potential viewing population, and RTVA executives wanted to increase their power through the federation and beat down their rivals for leadership within FORTA. The plan failed, and the Andalusian plotters were dismissed on charges of corruption. In the end, the Catalan company achieved the leading position in FORTA, serving as the principle force among autonomous regional broadcasters.[43] Although Andalusians and Catalans do not share the broadcast space, the fight over the commanding position within the national federation was won by a company whose advertising income was almost four times greater than the Andalusians'. The Catalans have far greater economic might than all the rest and have always been much more aggressively commercial.

In theory, the power held by the Catalan radio and television network is based on their ability to realize the greatest value in the regionalized audience commodity. In large part this is due to the concentration of relatively high per capita incomes in their broadcast region, but it is also in part due to their aggressive audience maximization strategy that has made their coverage transregional. I want to suggest tentatively that they prosper because of a geographical transfer of value achieved through their transregionalism. The geographical transfer of value is the mechanism that reproduces the conditions for uneven development, or what Costis Hadjimichalis calls differentially localized accumulation.[44] The extent to which this difference in accumulation can contribute to the differential growth of broadcasting firms still needs to be examined empirically in further research. As a corollary, it would be important to identify and analyze the impact that asymmetrical development of the regional forces of cultural production might have on inconstancies in regional economies where media firms are located.

To summarize, it seems useful to conceive of the expansion of television systems at any spatial scale as also an expansion of audience commodification. Such a conceptualization at least shows how the cultural politics of regional resistance, institutionalized in a media practice such as television, can be reincorporated into the systemic processes of capital accumulation. Notably, we find that the defense of investments made by regional TV firms provides a material basis for interregional factional struggle over exchange of the audience commodity. This occurs because the occupation of a geographical space by a regionalist social movement also requires that investments immobilized in that space be protected or devalued. When this happens, the cultural institutions tied to regional mobilizations attempt to direct spatial flows of capital, labor, and values (embodied in the audience commodity form) to their firms and affiliated industries. This process of accumulation brings a public audiovisual industry—one built on an oppositional politics of regionalism—systemically closer to a global corporate logic whose first principle is the expansion of profit. It is at this moment that TV for the autonomous cultural community shows its double profile, becoming the cultural merchant both at home and beyond its political borders. This is, in my assessment, the most troublesome aspect of "mediatized" identity politics in the international television market.

Notes

Earlier versions of this essay were presented to the 1991 Conference of the Society for Cinema Studies in Los Angeles and to the Political Economy

Section of the 1993 Conference of the International Association for Mass Communication Research in Dublin. For more on issues discussed here, see Richard Maxwell, *The Spectacle of Democracy: Spanish Television, Nationalism and Political Transition* (Minneapolis: U of Minnesota P, 1995).

1. Kevin Robins, "Reimagined Communities? European Image Spaces, Beyond Fordism," *Cultural Studies,* 3 no. 2 (1989). David Morley and Kevin Robins, "Spaces of Identity: Communications Technologies and the Reconfiguration of Europe," *Screen* 30, no. 4 (1989): 145–65.

2. Christopher Dandecker, *Surveillance, Power, and Modernity* (New York: St. Martin's, 1990); Anthony Giddens, *The Nation-State and Violence* Vol. 2 of *A Contemporary Critique of Historical Materialism* (Berkeley and Los Angeles: U of California P, 1987). See also Oscar Gandy, *The Panoptic Sort: A Political Economy of Personal Information* (Boulder, Colo.: Westview, 1993).

3. Quoted in Justino Sinova, *La Gran Mentira* (The Great Lie) (Madrid: Planeta, 1983), 30.

4. Rather than abide by the letter of the Third Channel Law, which established the norm of one network within each autonomous region, the authorities in these three regions built independent networks that function, in their words, "alegally." That is, they contend that the Third Channel Law only pertains to the central state allotments and not to their own independent allotments, which have been guaranteed by their Statutes of Autonomy and the national Constitution but which correspond to no existing regulation. The result is that the Basques and Catalans operate two channels but argue, along with the Galician parliament, which operates only one channel, that these are independent of existing law. Thus they maintain that they are still guaranteed one additional channel within the framework of the Third Channel Law, raising the potential number of land-based channels to eight (three private, two state, and three regional).

5. Transmission for which there is no explicit law is considered alegal, rather than illegal, unregulated, or pirated.

6. The six were in the Basque country, Catalonia, Galicia, Madrid, Valencia, and Andalusia; the remaining autonomous broadcasters were in the Canary and Balearic islands, Navarra, Aragon, and Murcia.

7. Law 10 1988, May 3, of Private Television established the following limits: (1) three privately owned television networks with local, regional, and national reach, (2) two publicly owned networks with local, regional, and national reach, (3) one regional network for each of the seventeen autonomous regions, and (4) the potential for sixteen satellite channels.

8. José María Villagrasa, "Spain: the Emergence of Commercial Television," in *The New Television in Europe,* ed. Alessandro Silj (London: John Libbey, 1992), 425.

9. Cornel West, "The New Cultural Politics of Difference," *October* 53 (1990): 93–109.

10. Stuart Hall, "The Emergence of Cultural Studies and the Crisis of the Humanities," *October* 53 (1990): 22; emphasis added.

11. Among the many "unofficial" dialects, it will be remembered that there are four officially recognized languages in Spain: Castilian, Basque, Catalan, and Galician.

12. F. Braudel, *Civilization and Capitalism, 15th–18th Century: The Perspective of the World,* vol. 3, trans. Sian Reynolds (New York: Harper & Row, 1986), 288. The periodization of Spain's administrative unity as a nation-state, although still a matter of historiographical debate, can reasonably be tied to the first national census under the reign of Felipe II in the latter part of the sixteenth century.

13. Eric J. Hobsbawm, *Nations and Nationalism Since 1780: Programme, Myth, Reality* (New York: Cambridge UP, 1990).

14. I'm referring to the challenge of feminists, local grassroots media activism, and other social movements opposed to the dominance of the primarily male political elites who head state agencies and policy formation. This includes regionalist resistance based in linguistic, ethnic, and religio-cultural difference, which, it goes without saying, has its own inherent problematics of gender, race, and class.

15. Cf. Enrique Bustamante, "TV and public service in Spain: A difficult encounter," *Media, Culture and Society* 11 (1989): 78. Also see J. MacLaughlin, "Reflections on Nations as 'Imagined Communities,'" *Journal of Multilingual and Multicultural Development* 9, no. 5 (1988): 449–57.

16. Hobsbawm, 191.

17. Tom Nairn, *The Break-up of Britain* (London: Verso, 1981); Hobsbawm, 191; Eric Hobsbawm and Terence Ranger, *The Invention of Tradition* (Cambridge: Polity, 1983).

18. Phillip Cooke, *Back to the Future* (London: Unwin Hyman, 1990), 20.

19. J. R. Cuadrado Roura, V. Granados, and J. Aurioles, "Technological Dependency in a Mediterranean Economy: The Case of Spain," in *Technological Change and Regional Development,* ed. A. Gilespie (London: Pion, 1983), 118–24.

20. José Casanova, "The Modernization of Spain," *Telos* (U.S.) no. 53 (fall): 33.

21. I am indebted to Daniel Jones, of the Autonomous University of Barcelona, for this data.

22. R. L. Fregoso, "The PEIN in Spain: Telecommunications and Government Policy," *Journal of Communication* 38, no. 1 (1988): 85–95.

23. Ibid.

24. *El País anuario* (Madrid, El País, 1986), 366.

25. "Opus Dei. A lay brotherhood of committed Catholics, aimed at influencing university and political life. Nursery of the 'technocrats' of the 1960s. Fell from influence in 1973." R. Carr and J. P. Fusi, *Spain: Dictatorship to Democracy*

(London: Allen & Unwin, 1984), xvi. The Opus technocrats were largely responsible for the economic policies of the last two decades of Franco's regime and, through the influence of Admiral Carrero Blanco, Franco's number-two man, they were able to extend their power to TVE between 1969 and 1973. Today the Opus is active throughout Latin America and, despite what some may see as the withering away of its influence in Spain, has left a legacy of technocratic rationalism that marks the current behavior of policymakers, especially around issues concerning the so-called information society.

26. Enrique Bustamante, *Los amos de la información en España* (Madrid: Akal, 1982), 64.

27. Ibid, 66.

28. Enrique Bustamante and Ramón Zallo, coordinators, *Las industrias culturales en España: Grupos multimedia y transnacionales* (Madrid: Akal, 1988), 123.

29. Ibid, 152.

30. *American Demographics,* a publication of Dow Jones & Co. Inc., promoted its eleventh annual conference on consumer trends and markets with such slogans.

31. This kind of *post*-modern alliance will perhaps come to typify the emerging European television economy, especially if public service principles are not rediscovered and redeployed with an adequate knowledge of political economy of international media.

32. Kevin Robins, "Global Times," *Marxism Today* December 1989, 21.

33. Despite their often narrow technological determinism and purported concerns with national policy, the scope of national-state collusion with transnationalization is well documented in K. Dyson and P. Humphreys, *The Politics of the Communication Revolution in Europe* (London: Frank Cass, 1986). See also their *The Political Economy of Communications: International and European Dimensions* (London: Routledge, 1990).

34. David Nogueira, "Unrelated Diversity," *The Business of Film,* January/February 1991, 9.

35. Figures from Unesco, cited in Bustamante and Zallo, 124–25. Other figures for 1979 provide a telling contrast: France: 35.4 percent; Finland: 24.3, including private TV; Greece: 29.2; Ireland: 48.9; Holland: 25; Portugal: 38; Sweden: 0; Switzerland: 26.8; and Britain: 55.2, including commercial TV.

36. J. Walter Thompson, *La inversión publicitaria en España, 1987* (The Publicity Investment in Spain) (Madrid: JWT, 1988). Figures exclude Canary Islands. These figures are based on an exchange rate of 1 dollar to 100 pesetas, the 1982 average.

37. Enrique Bustamante, "TV and Public Service in Spain: A difficult encounter," *Media Culture and Society* 11 (1989): 71–72.

38. Thompson.

39. "Regionals Play Wildcard," *Television Business International,* December/January 1990–91, 46.

40. Bustamante and Zallo, 155–56.

41. On the audience commodity see my "The Image is Gold: Value, the Audience Commodity, and Fetishism," *Journal of Film and Video* 43 (spring/summer 1991): 29–45; for more detail on the spatial application of audience commodity theory to the Spanish case, see my *Spectacle of Democracy.*

42. This is another story that is basically about alegal retransmission systems set up by TV clubs in Valencia prior to the establishment of regional radio-television in that autonomous community. These systems were ordered to be dismantled and brought under more systematic regulation.

43. Villagrasa, 374.

44. Costis Hadjimichalis, *Uneven Development and Regionalism: State, Territory and Class in Southern Europe* (London: Croom Helm, 1987).

IÑAKI ZABALETA

Private Commercial Television versus Political

Diversity: The Case of Spain's 1993

General Elections

In 1492, Elio Antonio de Nebrija wrote to Queen Isabel of Castile concerning his *Gramática* (work on Spanish grammar), observing that "language always had been a companion of the empire" and (we might add) an instrument for unifying the nation-state. Today in Spain that linguistic function is primarily fulfilled by mass media, which perform a unifying function both through language and content. This essay will explore the role that television coverage (and to a lesser degree newspapers) played in Spain's 1993 General Parliament elections, in which the issues of national unity and diversity were crucial. It will argue that rather than being represented as a choice among the full spectrum of diverse political parties participating in the process, the election was presented by the mass media as essentially a two-party race.

The 1993 General Parliament Elections

Spain's General Parliament elections of 1993 were prompted by a profound political, social, and economic crisis ("annus horribilis"), which was brought on partly by the extravagant expenditures of 1992 that funded the splendor of the Olympic Games in Barcelona and the Expo (world's fair) in Seville. A few of the telling danger signs were an unemployment rate of 22 percent, a 22 percent devaluation of the peseta, numerous political scandals and charges of corruption leveled against figures who were close to the government and its party (Partido Socialista Obrero Español, PSOE), and a growing disappointment in the moves toward European unity.[1] According to Raúl Heras, Felipe Gon-

Table 1

Votes for Spain's Parliament Seats

Party	1993 (%)	1989 (%)	% Difference	Vote difference	Geography
PSOE	38.79	39.6	−0.81	988,146	Spain
PP	34.77	25.8	+8.97	2,886,708	Spain
IU	9.24	9.23	+0.01	395,027	Spain
CDS	1.76	7.91	−6.15	−1,203,891	Spain
CiU	4.94	5.14	−0.20	132,058	Catalonia
PNV	1.24	1.26	−0.02	36,617	Basque country

Source: Yearbooks *Anuario El País 1994*, ed. José Manuel Revuelta (Madrid: Ediciones El País, 1994) and *Anuario El Mundo 1994*, ed. Ramón Tamames (Madrid: El Mundo, 1994), and personal elaboration.
Note: Total valid votes for Spain in 1993: 23,590,801 (100%).

zález was impelled to promise "the change of the change in politics," for Spain's 1993 elections threatened to bring "the end of an era."[2]

For the past fifteen years Spain had managed to maintain a delicate balance between a centralized and decentralized system: on the one hand, a democratic nation-state parliament and government were running the country from Madrid; on the other hand, there were three historical nationalities (Basques, Catalans, Galicians) and fourteen other regions, each with its own autonomous parliament and government. The political and economic crisis of 1992 threatened to upset this balance, and it was evident that the cohesion of the nation-state might be challenged in the 1993 general election.

This election was to fill 350 seats in Parliament plus 208 more in the Senate, which resulted in the need for different ballots in fifty-one provinces. This diversity plus the general tone of dissatisfaction would seem to hold some promise for the Basque and Catalan nationalist parties. Nevertheless, for several months before the election, there were forecasts of a close tie between the ruling Socialist Party (PSOE) and the conservative center-right Partido Popular (PP); some even predicted victory for the latter. But the polls proved to be wrong: for the fourth time in a row, the PSOE claimed victory, this time by a small, 4 percent margin (representing 900,000 votes).

The election results can be briefly summarized as follows (see also table 1):

—The ruling, socialist party, the PSOE, received 9.1 million votes; though losing its absolute majority in the Parliament, it won the election.

—The main opposition party, the center-right PP, received 8.1 million votes. Though losing the elections, it gained almost 3 million more votes than in 1989, breaking its former 5.5-million-vote ceiling and achieving its highest count in history.

—The leftist party Izquierda Unida (IU) received 2.1 million votes. Although this result represented almost 0.4 million more votes than in 1989, it did not fulfill the party's expectations and was considered a failure.

—The centrist party, Centro Democrático Social (CDS), received 0.42 million votes, 1.2 million fewer than it received in 1989. Although the polls predicted a loss for this party, the results were even worse than expected.

—The Basque moderate nationalist party, Partido Nacionalista Vasco (PNV), received only 0.29 million votes, barely keeping its constituency and declining slightly (0.02 percent) from its 1989 performance. This result was particularly disappointing when one considers that there was a 3.5 percent increase in voting participation within the Basque country.

—The Catalan moderate nationalist party, Convergencia i Unió (CiU), received 1.1 million votes, which represented a 0.2 percent decrease over 1989. As in the case of the PNV performance within the Basque country, this outcome was considered a failure because there was a notable gain in voter participation within Catalonia.

After the election, analysts tried to explain the results by pointing to the last-minute uncertainty of many voters, a substantial number of whom were reluctant to vote. Yet there was actually a 7 percent increase in the voters turnout: 77 percent in 1993 as opposed to 70 percent in 1989 and 1986. With respect to the results in the Basque country, a number of "Spanish voters" (that is, Basque citizens who put their Spanish nation-state identity before their regional identity) finally voted in 1993 after having remained silent and inactive in previous elections. Although their votes increased the participation rate within the Basque country, these gains went not to the Basque nationalists but primarily to three Spanish parties: the ruling socialists (PSOE), the center-right opposition (PP), and the leftist opposition (IU). Several

Table 2

Distribution of Votes in the Basque Country

Party	1993 votes	1989 votes	Class ideology	National ideology
PSOE	401,747	320,327	Social-Democrat	Spanish
PP	287,986	195,913	Conservative	Spanish
IU	102,615	49,302	Leftist	Spanish
PNV	291,448	254,681	Conservative	Moderate Basque nationalist
EA	129,293	136,955	Social-Democrat	Less moderate Basque nationalist
HB	206,876	217,278	Leftist	Radical Basque nationalist

Note: For the purpose of clarifying the political spectrum for an international readership, we simplified the character of the parties in the Basque country (including Navarra).

political analysts argue that the television debates among candidates from the two leading parties had much to do with these results and with the homogenization of the Basque electorate toward the Spanish model (see table 2).[3]

The rest of this essay will analyze to what extent the media coverage of the elections affected these outcomes. But before turning to this topic, we need briefly to review the broadcasting system in Europe and in Spain.

The European Television Landscape

Presently there are many television channels serving Western European countries and (in the more populated ones) even a dual public and private ownership system, but these conditions do not necessarily guarantee plurality of content.[4] Although a plurality of channels inevitably leads to a multiplicity of programs, it is not clear that this always means a meaningful diversity in content and approach. Although one might have expected the emergence of a dual ownership system to increase diversity, the reverse may be the case. According to Elsa DeBens, Mary Kelly, and Marit Bakke, "public service broadcasters [PSB] have traditionally defined their programming responsibilities in terms of offering a wide and 'balanced' range of entertainment and information programs."[5] Because many of the new terrestrial private commercial TV channels (PrTV) have general programming with a broad appeal, they directly compete with PSB stations. As PrTV stations have moved toward popular entertainment programming, the PSB channels have tended to follow. In this competition for higher audience ratings, both increasingly seek a common denominator, which leads to a low-grade similarity in the contents of programming. This situation is particularly problematic in the TV coverage of news.

As Wilbur Schramm has argued, television is a medium that tends to pursue concreteness on political issues and a low level of abstraction and complexity.[6] In Europe and elsewhere, the content of TV news is increasingly being packaged in a personalized, dramatized, fragmented, and normalized form; it is transformed into a consumer good to be sold to audiences purely for profit.[7] Because of the commercial nature of these dynamics, one might expect them to be more pronounced on PrTV than on PSB stations. Yet in the face of competition for higher ratings, this duality may be more apparent than real. Like any other social institution, broadcast media prosper in a climate of stability and are threatened by change, but paradoxically (as Marc Raboy and Bernard Dagenais have argued) they also need to seek out (or possibly even fabricate) crisis or disruption in order to maintain that sense of high drama and action that is so appealing to viewers.[8]

As changes occur in the media environment and in politics throughout Europe, the reliance on television for election coverage becomes increasingly heavy. Around election time the need for sensationalism and spectacle in the representation of public life is frequently fulfilled by a "spectacular" staging of debates between candidates, who are encouraged to rely on the same persuasion techniques that are used to sell consumer goods. As several analysts have noted, elections become ritualized conflicts and, as in the United States, "face-to-face debates between party leaders . . . further reduce the possibilities of selective exposure."[9] Thus, the dramatization and personalization of the news may tend to reduce an election to a duality, that is, a dramatic struggle between two elements (two characters, two people, two parties). Such dualities frequently tend to be more apparent than real, for a "real" opposition might threaten the normalcy of the system and thereby endanger the salability of the news.

Although commonplace in the United States, this reduction of political diversity to a false dualism is particularly problematic in Europe, where national identities are now in great turmoil. National identities may not necessarily mean nation-state identities, for there may be several national identities within a nation-state, as is the case in Spain and France. The creation and shaping of national identity is an ongoing, dynamic cultural process, in which media can function either to define the cultural distinctiveness of historic nationalities (such as the Basque country, Catalonia, and Galicia) or to unify the nation-state.

The Broadcasting System in Spain

Spanish television was a public service broadcast (PSB) monopoly with two state-owned stations, TVE-1 and TVE-2, until 1988, when the Private Television Law was passed. By 1990 three private channel licenses for terrestrial state coverage transmission were granted. Two of these private licensees, Telecinco (owned by Silvio Berlusconi) and Antena 3 (owned by the Z Publishing Group), are free access channels with general programming, which obtain profits through advertising. The third, Canal Plus (owned by the French Canal+ and the Spanish Prisa Publishing group, which also owns the newspaper *El País*), is a coded channel whose profits come from monthly fees. There are also eight autonomous PSB channels with regional coverage,[10] whose funding comes from their autonomous parliaments and from advertising revenues; more than twenty local, alegal low-power television stations; and some DBS Spanish and imported channels.

Thus, Spain has a dual private and public TV system with four main state-level stations: two public (TVE-1 and TVE-2) and two private (Telecinco and Antena 3). According to the statute provisions, public broadcaster TVE is expected to encourage viewers to identify with the values of freedom, justice, equality, and political pluralism, promoting these values not merely passively but actively to maintain the health of Spain's democracy. Yet TVE is frequently criticized for favoring the party in power, the centrist ruling party UCD in the past, and the socialist PSOE through 1996. According to López-Escobar, with the advent of PCTV other parties have had better and more frequent access to the screen.[11] In June 1993, when the general elections took place, the two public commercial TV stations covered the practical totality of the population, whereas the two private television stations covered 86 percent of the Basque population.[12] More specifically, during 1993 the total highest audience percentages of these channels were: TVE-1 56.65 percent; TVE-2 17.69 percent; Antena 3 36.01 percent; and Telecinco 37.50 percent.[13]

What we were interested in exploring was whether any significant differences could be observed in the way the elections were covered by the private television stations in contrast to the public stations and whether this coverage could help account for the results of the election. We hypothesized first that the dramatization and personalization of the television news coverage tended to reduce this election to a duality between two parties, the ruling party (PSOE) and the right-center opposition (PP), and their respective candidates, Felipe González and José María Aznar, and second that although these tendencies could be found both on private and public stations, they would be more pronounced on the former than on the latter.

Television and Spain's 1993 General Elections

The television coverage of the 1993 elections could be broken down into three categories:

1. *Regular election-coverage,* which refers to the daily coverage of election information on regularly scheduled news broadcasts.

2. *Special election-coverage,* which refers to special programming (such as debates, interviews, and round-table discussions) staged and organized by the TV station around the elections. The station's editorial line (i.e., the image or identity it wants to communicate) would be seen in this kind of coverage.

3. *Free time-slots,* which the TV station offered to all parties according to the rules of equal proportion set by the Central and Regional Election Boards.

Our research focused on the second category (special election-coverage), since from an ethnomethodological point of view it seemed more important than regular election news coverage in creating or reinforcing the personality, identity, credibility, and image of the TV channel.[14] To assess this coverage, we examined three research areas:

1. The special election-coverage (SEC) organized and broadcast during the campaign.

2. The newspaper ads that referred to the SEC and that were commissioned by the TV stations. We assumed they might work in conjunction with the SEC as an electoral campaign factor, favoring the advertised parties and as an image/identity shaper, showcase, or reinforcement for the TV channel.

3. Newspaper information items and Op-Ed articles that referred to the SEC. We assumed they would provide feedback on the perceptions the SEC generated in the print press as well as (through inference) in public opinion.

Within the first research area, we hypothesized that private TV channels would have placed more emphasis on state-level party dualism, stressing nation-state identity and homogenization, reducing political diversity and the presence of peripheral nationalist forces, and perhaps refiguring the event as a two-horse-race-style "presidential election." We also hypothesized that the debates might have benefited the two leading parties (the PSOE and PP) and damaged the vote turnout for the rest of the state-level parties (IU, CDS) and for the peripheral nationalist forces (PNV and CiU).

Within the second research area, we hypothesized that private TV channels would have placed more newspaper ads with higher visibility and taking up more space than those placed by public TV and that the majority of the electoral ads would have referred to dual debates—more precisely, to the debates between the two main leaders, Felipe González (PSOE) and José María Aznar (PP).

Finally, in the third research area, we wanted to assess the amount and kind of information published in the newspapers about the SEC.

For a period of thirty-nine days (from April 28, 1993, to June 6, 1993, which included twenty-four days of precampaign and the entire fifteen days of the official campaign), we analyzed the special election-coverage of four television stations: the two public state-level stations (TVE-1 and TVE-2) and the two free-access state-level private commercial channels (Antena 3 and Telecinco). For TV ads and information items about these SEC, we analyzed one newspaper, *El País,* the main newspaper of Spain (which is edited in Madrid) and the prestige paper for reference and record. In 1993 it had 1.4 million readers, which is the largest circulation of general information papers in Spain. As for our units of analysis, in the first research area they were SEC TV programs (interviews, debates, round tables),[15] each of which had to be a minimum of thirty minutes long to be included; in the second area, they were newspaper ads in *El País* paid by TV channels, which we measured by space (i.e., the portion of page occupied by the item), interval, and ratio; in the third area, they were information and Op-Ed articles published in *El País,* also measured by space, interval, and ratio.[16]

Research Results[17]

In the first research area, the special election-coverage on television, we found significant differences between the private and public stations. Of the eight debates in the two-candidate format, all were broadcast on the private television channels. They included two American-style "presidential debates" between González and Aznar, the first in the history of Spain. Organized by the private TV channels—Antena 3 and Telecinco—these highly dramatized debates were presented as face-to-face, two-man fights. Having tremendous impact, they ranked second and third in the year-round top TV audience ratings (being outdrawn only by the televised soccer game between Spain and Denmark on November 17, 1993). The first of these debates took place on Monday, May 24, on Antena 3 in prime time, garnering an audience of 9.7 million viewers (out of a total 1993 TV audience of 28.8 million and a total Spanish population of 39.4 million people). The second debate took place on May 31 on Telecinco, only six days before election day, drawing 10.9 million viewers. For days before and after these debates, Spaniards talked of little else.

Several other results in this research area supported our basic hypothesis about the differences between private versus public television election coverage. The private stations put more than twice as much effort into the SEC programming (69 percent) as the public stations (31 percent). Whereas the private channels featured only two-candidate debates, the public stations presented four-candidate debates exclusively. (See table 3.) Moreover, whereas the two-person debates broad-

Table 3
SEC Programming Format (in %)

Media	1-interview	2-debate	4-debate	5-rt	10-rt	Total
Public TV	18	0	13	0	0	31
Private TV	28	29	0	3	9	69
Total	46	29	13	3	9	100

Note: N = 33 programs. The number before the category name means "the number of candidates" taking part in that program (e.g., 5-rt means a 5-candidate round-table).

Table 4
2- and 4-Candidate Debate Programs (in %)

Media	2-debate PSOE, PP	4-debate PSOE, PP + CDS, PNV	4-debate PSOE, PP + IU, CDS	4-debate PSOE, PP + IU, CiU	4-debate PSOE, PP + IU, PNV	Total	Grand total
Public TV	0	3	3	3	4	13	13
Private TV	29	0	0	0	0	0	29
Total	29	3	3	3	4	13	42

cast by private TV (29 percent) were held solely between PSOE and PP candidates, the four-candidate debates broadcast on public TV kept a balanced approach by granting participation to the PSOE in all cases and to the rest of the parties proportionately. (See table 4.)

The data in table 5 clearly show that both private and public television channels maintained a balanced approach in the interview programs, keeping the one-candidate format and including all major parties and even the peripheral nationalist parties (Basque PNV and Catalan CiU). Perhaps because of its "individuality," this programming format was not considered as potentially dramatic or spectacular as the debates.

In the second research area, the newspaper ads paid by TV stations, we found for the public stations no significant difference in advertising percentages between elections (10 percent) and entertainment (13 percent). This was not the case on the private channels: whereas Antena 3 offered a much higher percentage to election ads (20 percent) than to

Table 5

Interviews in SEC (in %)

Media	CDS	CiU	IU	PNV	PP	PSOE	Total
Public TV	3	3	3	3	3	3	18
Private TV	3	6	6	3	4	6	28
Total	6	9	9	6	7	9	46

Table 6

Newspaper Ads Paid by TV Stations (in %)

Media	Elections	Entertainment	Information	Total
TVE-1	9	11	0	20
TVE-2	1	3	0	4
Public TV	10	13	0	23
Antena-3	20	2	1	23
Tele-5	12	41	0	54
Private TV	32	43	1	77
Total	42	56	2	100

Note: N = 86.57 pages.

entertainment (2 percent), Telecinco offered 41 percent of its ads to entertainment and only 12 percent to the elections. (See table 6.)

The majority of the private TV ads were about the debates (49 percent), followed by the category of TV-elections (33 percent), which addressed the relationship between the TV station and the elections and which therefore was significant in portraying the image of the station. In contrast, public TV showed the same proportion of interviews and TV-election ads (11 percent in both cases) and devoted only 3 percent to the debates. (See table 7.)

In contrast to the ad campaign for public television, which was balanced among the various parties, the ads for private TV overwhelmingly emphasized only two, the PSOE and PP. More specifically, 74 percent of their ads featured the PSOE, 71 percent the PP, 4 percent the PNV, and 0 percent for the IU, and CDS, and the CiU. They also emphasized the two-man horse race by devoting 69 percent of their ads to the PSOE-PP debates, as opposed to only 11 percent to the more

Table 7
Newspaper Ads Referring to Elections (in %)

Media	Debates	Interviews	TV-elections	Total
Public TV	3	11	11	25
Private TV	46	7	22	75
Total	49	18	33	100

Note: N = 36.68 pages.

Table 8
Newspaper Ads Referring to Political Parties (in %)

Media	Interviews					2-debate	4-debate		Total
	CiU	IU	PNV	PP	PSOE	PSOE, PP	PSOE, PP + 2	PSOE, PP + 2	
Public TV	4	4	0	4	4	0	2	2	20
Private TV	0	0	4	2	5	69	0	0	80
Total %	4	4	4	6	9	69	2	2	100

Note: N = 24.68 pages.

inclusive interviews. Out of that 69 percent, 61 percent focused exclusively on the two dramatic "presidential" debates mentioned above whereas only 8 percent concerned the other six debates. (See table 8.) Following these presidential debates, the PrTV channels ran large ads displaying the journalists and candidates, as if the events were being memorialized in these majestic historical images.

From a marketing viewpoint, the majority of the TV ads published in the newspapers (83 percent) emphasized *personalization* by including pictures of the journalists and/or candidates, but here again there was a significant difference between public and private stations. Whereas the ads for private TV show a strong tendency toward personalization (71 out of 77 percent), those for public TV are evenly divided between personalized and nonpersonalized ads. (See table 9.)

There were other key differences in the inferred contents of the ads for public and private television. Within the 26 percent of ads that contained inferred concepts, 20 percent related to the nation-state identity

Table 9

Personalization of Newspaper Ads (in %)

Media	Yes	No	Total
Public TV	12	11	23
Private TV	71	6	77
Total	83	17	100

Note: N = 35.67 pages. Public TV sum: 9 pages; Private TV: 25.67 pages.

Table 10

Inferred Concepts from Newspaper Ads (in %)

Media	Drama.	Spain ID	Winner	Credi.	History	Freedom	Nat. diver.	Other	Total
Public TV	3	20	3	0	0	0	0	0	26
Private TV	30	3	19	8	6	2	3	3	74
Total	33	23	22	8	6	2	3	3	100

Note: N = 35.67 pages.

(Spain ID) and 3 percent respectively to the concepts of dramatization (drama.) and winners (winner). In contrast, 70 percent of the private TV ads had inferred content: 30 percent related to dramatization, 19 percent to winners, 8 percent to credibility (credi.), 6 percent to the history of Spain (history), 3 percent to national diversity (nat. diver.), and 2 percent to the concept of freedom. Although the percentages for the history of Spain and freedom are relatively small, they are still significant in a qualitative sense because of the strong connotative resonance of these terms. (See table 10.)

The results in the third area of research, the information and Op-Ed articles published in *El País,* yielded 105 items (comprising 36.16 pages of newspaper space) devoted to the SEC on television. An overwhelming 91 percent of the items referred to the debates held between the PSOE and PP candidates, suggesting that in the journalistic judgment of *El País* only these two-candidate debates warranted their press coverage. Moreover, the two dramatic "presidential" debates accounted for 88 percent of the paper's coverage of the elections on TV. Only 3 percent

Table 11

Info. and Op-Ed Articles about TV and Parties Involved (in %)

Media	Interviews 1 party	2-debates PSOE, PP	4-debates 4 parties	Round tables 5 + parties	TV-elections	Total
Public TV	0	0	4	0	1	5
Private TV	1	91	0	1	1	94
Other TV	0	0	1	0	0	1
Total	1	91	5	1	2	100

Note: N = 36.16 pages.

of *El País*'s coverage dealt with the other two-candidate debates. (See table 11.)

Conclusions

During the Spanish Parliament's elections of 1993, the private commercial TV channels strongly supported the reduction of the elections into a dualistic race between two parties, the PSOE and PP, and even more narrowly between two men, Felipe González and José María Aznar. This dualism created the false perception of a presidential election and reduced political diversity, which possibly had a negative effect on the results of the other parties. These private stations organized and broadcast 8 two-candidate debates, all of which exclusively featured the PSOE and PP. Since both are national parties that are defenders of the nation-state identity, this coverage could have favored state-level centralism, identity, and homogenization at the expense of nationalities and national diversity. The nationalist vote turnouts might have been negatively affected in the Basque country and Catalonia. In the Basque country, the main nationalist parties (PNV, EA, HB) declined in the percentage of votes they received and two of them (EA and HB) even experienced a loss in the actual number of votes.

In contrast, public TV stations organized and broadcast four-candidate debates. In this way, they avoided the dualization of the election and presented a higher degree of political pluralism, which included the peripheral nationalist parties.[18] These conclusions are even more evident when we consider that both private and public TV channels kept a fair balance regarding the participation of the political and peripheral nationality parties in their SEC (one-candidate-format) interviews.

As far as the newspaper advertising campaigns are concerned, the private TV channels put much more emphasis on the PSOE-PP two-candidate, face-to-face fighting debates (69 out of 80 percent) than on the interviews or round tables. Even more specifically, the two presidential debates absorbed 61 percent of the ads out of the 69 percent total devoted to the two-man debate format. Thus the private TV channels favored these two parties and their leading candidates not only through their election programming but also in their newspaper advertising campaign.

The public TV stations kept a low and balanced profile in their newspaper ad campaign through their choice of program categories and through their inclusion of all parties, including the Basque and Catalan nationalists. Despite this diversity, the theme of Spanish national identity was strongly present.

The personalization of the ads was very strong in those of the private TV channels and evenly divided in those of the public stations. Private television stations also tended to highlight dramatization and victory and tried to link their own identity to freedom and credibility. Because it was the first time that such televised debates were broadcast in Spain, the private channels advertised them as historical events ("going into History"), which reinforced the nation-state identity. In this way, they tried to change their own image from a simple commercial company to a "Spanish institution" with historical significance.

The Op-Ed articles and information on the elections published in *El País*, Spain's most important newspaper, reflected the same atmosphere of personalization, dramatization, dualism, and polarization featured in the television coverage of the private channels. In fact, 91 percent of their articles on the TV coverage of the elections were dedicated to the debates between PSOE and PP, and 88 out of the 91 percent to the two "presidential" debates between González and Aznar. What the rest of the parties and candidates said on television apparently did not count.

Working together as well as with other political forces, the three factors we have studied (special election TV coverage, ad campaigns, and newspaper coverage) seem very likely to have influenced how the public perceived the elections—the campaigns, the atmosphere, the issues, the expectations and fears, and, ultimately, the outcome. In any case, further analyses and research are needed to confirm these results.

Notes

This essay is based on a paper presented at an international conference "Turbulent Europe: Conflict, Identity and Culture," held in London in July 1994.

1. Joaquín Prieto, "Elecciones de transición," *Anuario El País 1994,* ed. José Manuel Revuelta (Madrid: Ediciones El País, 1994), 78.

2. Raúl Heras, "La mutación del año negro," *Anuario El Mundo 1994,* ed. Ramón Tamames (Madrid: El Mundo, 1994), 22–23.

3. Such analysts include Iñaki Iriondo, "El olvidado nuevo alzamiento del voto españolista," *EGIN,* December 21, 1993, Euskadi '93), 4–5; José I. Ruiz-de-Olabuenaga, "Los resultados del 6-J y la inexistente singularidad vasca," *El Mundo,* June 9, 1993, 9; and Jabier Salutregi, "El Español, cuando vota, vota de verdad," *EGIN,* June 9, 1993, 2–3.

4. For a typology of national television systems in Western European countries between 1980 to 1990, see Kees Brants and Karen Siune, "Public Broadcasting in a State of Flux," in *Dynamics of Media Politics: Broadcast and Electronic Media in Western Europe,* ed. Karen Siune and Wolfgang Truetzschler (London: Sage, 1992), 104. In 1990 there were eleven countries, the most populated ones, with a dual broadcasting system—private and public.

5. Elsa DeBens, Mary Kelly, and Marit Bakke, "Television Content: Dallasification of Culture," in Karen Siune and Wolfgang Truetzchler, eds.

6. Wilbur Schramm, "Channels and Audiences," in *Inter/media: Interpersonal Communication in a Media World,* ed. Gary Gumpert and Robert Cathcart (New York: Oxford UP, 1979): 78–92.

7. See W. Lance Bennet, *News: The Politics of Illusion* (London: Longman, 1983) and Gianpetro Mazzoleni and Michael Palmer, "The Building of Media Empires," in *Dynamics of Media Politics: Broadcast and Electronic Media in Western Europe* (London: Sage, 1992), 26–41.

8. Marc Raboy and Bernard Dagenais, ed., *Media, Crisis and Democracy: Mass Communication and the Disruption of Social Order* (London: Sage, 1992).

9. Jay G. Blumler and Michael Gurevitch, "The Political Effects of Mass Communication," in *Culture, Society and the Media,* ed. Michael Gurevitch, Tony Bennett, James Curran, and Janet Woollacott (London: Methuen, 1982), 247. See also Hans-Bernd Brosius and Hans Mathias Kepplinger, "Beyond Agenda-Setting: The Influence of Partisanship and Television Reporting on the Electorate's Voting Intentions," *Journalism Quarterly* 69 (April 1992): 893–

901, and H. M. Kepplinger, H. B. Brosius, and J. F. Staab, "Opinion Formation in Mediated Conflicts and Crises: A Model of Cognitive-Affective Media Effects," *International Journal of Public Opinion Research* 3 (1991): 132–56.

10. The regional PSB channels include two in the Basque country (ETB-1, which broadcasts totally in Basque language, and ETB-2, in Spanish); two in Catalonia (TV-3 and Canal 33, both in Catalan); one in Galicia (TV Galicia, in Galician language); one in Valencia (Canal 9); one in Andalusia (Canal Sur, in Spanish); and one in Madrid (Telemadrid, in Spanish).

11. Esteban López-Escobar, "Spanish Media Law: Changes in the Landscape," *European Journal of Communication* 7 (1992): 241–59 and "Vulnerable Values in Spanish Multichannel Television," in *Television and the Public Interest: Vulnerable Values in West European Broadcasting,* ed. Jay G. Blumler (London: Sage, 1992), 161–72.

12. Retevisión, report by J. A. Tartajo, Ref. RS/201/94, Madrid, April 26, 1994.

13. Tamames, *Anuario El Mundo 1994,* 351. Because these figures represent highest percentages during the year, their sum exceeds 100 percent. The total audience mean value of the autonomous channels was 3.07 percent; foreign TV, 0.44 percent; local TV, 0.44 percent.

14. Ethnomethodology is the study of commonsense knowledge glossed by three phenomena: (1) the stock of knowledge at hand; (2) the practices of commonsense reasoning; and (3) the commonsense reality or attitude of everyday life. See Kenneth Leiter, *A Primer on Ethnomethodology* (Oxford: Oxford UP, 1980), v–vi.

15. We adopted the following definitions for these programs. *Interviews (i)* are programs in which only one candidate participated and was questioned by journalists. *Debates (d)* are programs that have two or more candidates debating against/with each other in a direct way; there might also be one or more journalists posing questions and issues to candidates. *Round table (rt)* are programs consisting of generally more than five candidates and several journalists or specialists engaged in an open, free discussion of issues without direct confrontation among them.

16. We followed the standard procedures of content research methodology, including the correction notes published by Stephen R. Lacy and Daniel Riffe in "Sins of Omission and Commission in Mass Communication Quantitative Research," *Journalism Quarterly* 70, no. 1 (1993): 126–32.

17. All data and tables are at the disposal of the research community upon request.

18. Since our argument compares PSOE and PP with the other parties, these conclusions do not contradict López-Escobar's statement that PSOE's losses in votes were proportionately greater in cities with access to PCTV. In his test case, there is insufficient evidence as to which party received those votes.

SELMA REUBEN HOLO

The Art Museum as a Means of

Refiguring Regional Identity in

Democratic Spain

Regional art museums form one of the most important constellations within the universe of Spanish museums. Beyond displaying the masterworks of a particular place, they have assumed an active role in refiguring Spain. Whereas the powerful state museums, especially those located in Madrid—the Prado, the Reina Sofía, and the Thyssen-Bornemisza—are intended to impress with their "Spanishness" by exhibiting the cultural patrimony in which all Spaniards presumably would claim a share, the regional museums ostensibly exist to strengthen and define local identities. However, it is only when these smaller institutions are understood as playing a metaphorical role (willingly or unwillingly, consciously or unconsciously) in the perpetuation of Spain as a nation-state that their valuable contributions to the constructive tension between local and national forces become evident. Furthermore, it is in the degree to which this tension is perceived as genuine and not merely a political stratagem that one finds the key to the general acceptance of the notion that individual citizens can, in contemporary Spanish society, "patriotically" possess contradictory, conflicting, and overlapping state, regional, and municipal identities.

Traveling throughout Spain one cannot help but be surprised by the liveliness and sophistication of these small- to medium-sized regional art museums. After visiting a number of them it becomes clear that even within their own constellation, they convey a wide range of messages—not only about who their constituencies are, but also about how these constituencies should best relate to Spain, to Europe, and to the larger world. Each message is distinguished by the choices, interpretations, and juxtapositions of works of art and artifacts in the galleries; by the blatant or subtle employment of resonant architectural forms in rich urbanistic settings; by the decisions about which language or languages will appear on the wall labels and in scholarly or general publications; and, of course, by the explicit and implicit museological programs.

What follows are the stories of three regional Spanish museums: the Museum of Fine Arts of Asturias in Oviedo, the Extremaduran and Ibero-American Museum of Contemporary Art in Badajoz, and the Valencian Institute of Modern Art. (Museums in the Basque country and Catalonia are so complex that they need to be discussed separately.) Each one of these regional museums is a model of clarity and focus; each one is unique. They do, however, have in common a fundamental acceptance, differing only in degree, of the obligation to showcase regional art. They also assume a responsibility to advance the construction of the identity of the local citizenry in the direction of greater and greater cultural confidence. Beyond this there is very little that would relate any one of these three museums to the other two—or to any other museum in Spain. To comprehend them as functioning merely as formulaic elements within a static and predictable situation would be to miss their special relationship to that dynamic and kaleidoscopic concept of a nation-state as invented by Spain in the first years of the last quarter of the twentieth century. Studying their evolving roles in the construction of an already vastly changed social identity in post-Franco Spain allows us to come to grips with the fact that although museums are first and foremost vessels for the protection, exhibition, and accumulation of works of art, they are not only that. Museums in Spain, like museums in any democratic country, are open and critical testing-grounds for some of the most advanced ideas and best hopes of the civil society in which they are called upon to function.[1]

Museum of Fine Arts of Asturias

One of the most complete, museologically sound, self-confident, and successful regional museums in all of Spain has taken root in Oviedo, the capital of the autonomous region of Asturias. The Museo de Bellas Artes de Asturias, the Museum of Fine Arts of Asturias, is one of the fruits of the first post-Franco democratic elections in Spain, in 1979. It is an institution brimming with regional pride, yet, because of the sophistication of the professionals who run it, devoid of provincialism. The founders of the approximately fifteen-year-old museum, in conceiving of their project, were conscious that they were undertaking a significant role in the construction of the identity of post-Franco Asturians, residents of a region that most Spaniards (including the Asturians themselves) have always appreciated for its stunning landscape but have seldom taken seriously for its cultural contributions. With a sympathetic understanding of the pervasive sense of cultural inferiority emanating from within the region and of the condescension coming from outside, a museological program was developed in 1979 whereby the museum would unashamedly display, first and foremost Asturias's own artistic patrimony, secondarily Spain's, and finally Europe's, insofar as it related to Asturias's own history and social evolution. Wise leaders saw the importance of highlighting local artists in a nonpatronizing manner so as to immediately enlist the support of their own citizens. Paintings with recognizable images of nature, husbandry, industry, and even of the political upheavals Asturians had suffered were to be put on display so as to make the museum relevant and nonthreatening to the average visitor. At the same time, the curators exhibited less accessible, unknown, or unappreciated Asturian art of the highest tier, from the Golden Age up to and including the present day. Beyond the overriding goal of preserving and displaying the cultural patrimony, the challenge from the start was to elevate the self-image and self-confidence of the Asturian visitors, the museum's primary audience, by educating them to the reality that they had never been as one-dimensional as the rest of Spain (and they themselves) had assumed before the existence of their museum. It was hoped that the non-Asturian visitor would absorb a similar message about a region that he or she most likely had stereotyped as merely agricultural, industrial, or politically plagued.

Energy, elegance, connoisseurship, and clarity of purpose are the hallmarks of the Museum of Fine Arts of Asturias as it appears today. One would like to attribute these qualities only to professional acumen, yet without Spain's change in government from a dictatorship to a participatory democracy, it is unlikely that this museum would ever have come into being. Previous commitments to the preservation, collection, and interpretation of the cultural patrimony had been sporadic, diffuse, clumsily handled, and listlessly pursued. It was only with the challenges, attitudes, and opportunities accompanying the transition to home rule that it became possible for responsible, proactive, and independent citizens to create their own museum.

By all accounts the history of the Museum of Fine Arts of Asturias can be said to have begun by Royal Order on June 13, 1844. According to that decree, all of the provinces of Spain were henceforth required to protect their cultural monuments. Although too little and too late, coming as it did after many of the convents and monasteries that had owned uncountable works of painting and sculptures had fallen into ruin or been dismantled, that order was, nevertheless, the first legal obligation that the provinces care for their own cultural patrimony. It is a sad fact that only fifteen paintings were gathered together in 1844 as a result of that decree, so many others having been lost either by malice or neglect. Ten still could be accounted for (although in a lamentable state) in 1980, when the new museum finally opened. Those ten were supplemented by other Old Master works that had been discovered or recovered since the Royal Order. These were found in Spain's Royal Academy, the Academy of Fine Arts of San Salvador of Oviedo, and other artistic-holding areas in Asturias. In addition, paintings by the finest of Asturias's twentieth-century artists were gathered together piece by piece. All in all, this material, plus additional works of art scattered hither and yon, formed the core collection of seventy-eight works of art—seventy-three paintings and five sculptures—on May 19, 1980, the day the Museum of Fine Arts was inaugurated.

All of the murky and aborted plans between 1844 and 1979 to build a museum did yield one lasting achievement: the purchase of the Palacio de Velarde in the center of Oviedo, which would eventually serve as the core of the museum itself. Superbly located in the historical downtown, an area both picturesque and filled with businesses and crowds of people of all classes, the Velarde Palace would be integrated into the life of the region's capital. The palace was built in 1767 by the Asturian architect Manuel Reguera González, a disciple of Ventura Rodríguez, and was renovated by another native son, Florencio Muñiz Uribe, between 1973 and 1976. Uribe was considerably hampered at this stage of the museum's renovation by the weak museological plan, one which did not recognize the need for conservation laboratories, storage, and study spaces. At this moment, in those early years immediately after Franco died, there was no sustained political will to develop a well-thought-out plan for a serious regional institution of fine arts. It was not until the preautonomic political structures that led to a full democracy were put into place several years after Franco's death that the plans could progress. Not until 1979, when local elections put new people in charge, did the Asturian Ministry of Culture see fit to support aggressively the proper construction of the museum. In 1980 the necessary replanning had been accomplished, the work had been done, and the museum could open its doors.

In 1979, at that crossroads for democracy in Spanish history, the duly elected Conservative Party (the UCD, Unión de Centro Democrático, at that time) recognized the urgent need to start building a powerful sense of self in the Asturian populace. These public servants were willing to work toward that abstract end in the belief that their constituency would show their appreciation concretely at the polls, come the next election. The museum, therefore, was finally completed because politicians were convinced, by Asturian citizens committed to the idea of a museum of fine arts, that being responsible for the construction of the region's major art museum was good for the party. They were led to believe that insofar as the project was successful, it would be seen to reflect the values of the party that created it. And so the museum was designated as one of the UCD's flagship projects. Old ideas were scrapped; fresh goals were set; and finally the museum was unambiguously supported, launched, and protected by an enthusiastic political will.[2]

The professionals could do their work and a respectable museological plan was crystallized. According to that plan, galleries on the main floor were to be dedicated to temporary exhibitions of young Asturian artists in conjunction with Asturian art of the nineteenth century. Upstairs, the plan was to exhibit Renaissance and Mannerist, European and Spanish works. Additional galleries were to be reserved for Asturian artists, especially for the most accomplished among them. Great care was to be taken in remodeling the palace, to lighting, to security, and to storage. Time and money were to be lavished on conservation of the works of art, many by now quite deteriorated. Funds were also to be supplied for public education so that the museum could interpret its rich but unknown past to the hordes of schoolchildren and interested adults who needed to know more about who they were. Moneys were also set aside to buy exceptional works of art that would help to fill in the immense gaps of the lost, depleted artistic patrimony, and the collection grew by

Asturias: The Fine
Arts Museum,
exterior. (Photo
courtesy: the Museo
de Bellas Artes de
Asturias)

leaps and bounds. Donations were encouraged. Scholarly libraries were purchased, and publications both of an academic and popular nature were produced. Although the language of communication remains Spanish, there is an occasional but meaningful nod to the Asturian language/dialect in some brochures and in the founding documents. Collections management, including storage and conservation, is world class. Conferences, meetings, lectures, and concerts explore the regional culture and related issues. But perhaps the most experimental and expansive testing ground for refiguration of Asturian identity is in the sphere of the museum's relationships with other art museums. It is here that one can best discern the consolidation of the museum's sense of itself and of its aspirations, its growing prestige, and self-confidence in the world around it.

On the state level, Asturias's Museum of Fine Arts has consolidated its connections to Madrid by nurturing and enhancing the region's long association with the Prado. For many years Asturias was the recipient of an unheralded loan program with the Prado Museum. As long ago as

Asturias: The Fine Arts Museum, interior. (Photo courtesy: the Museo de Bellas Artes de Asturias)

1900, again by Royal Order, the Prado started sending works from their storage vaults out on long-term loan to Oviedo. Although much of the work was lost or ruined during the years preceding the formation of the museum, some of the pictures were recently rediscovered and restored, and they now hang in the galleries. This loan program with the Prado, now a point of pride, enables the Asturian Museum to fill gaps in its own collection and, sotto voce, to demonstrate that there are active and constructive cultural linkages with Madrid. The spirit of cooperation extended by Madrid is further fostered behind the scenes by the conservation work Asturias has done on its paintings at the National Restoration Center. For a region that, during so much of its modern history, suffered a highly adversarial and often painful relationship with Madrid, the Museum of Fine Arts of Asturias has become a symbol of a new reality. It is the very manifestation of the positive results of a select and harmonious collaboration between the periphery and the center. Yet more significant, it demonstrates to the Asturian citizens concrete civic benefits associated with the ever more expansive, if essentially abstract, ideal of the complex identity they have been donning throughout the new democracy. Since 1979 the Museum of Fine Arts' visitors have been encouraged to become more and more comfortable with Asturias's place in the historical and current Spanish cultural landscape. Visitors constantly receive subtle messages that the region was never as marginalized as it was during the years of the dictatorship. This is accomplished on the public level by the thoughtful and imaginative exhibitions the Museum of Fine Arts regularly mounts wherein Asturias's own artistic past and its rich creative present are elegantly displayed. It is also accomplished by the ongoing acquisitions of works of art that give powerful evidence to the truth of that message: a great Juan Carreño portrait of King Carlos II proves that during the Golden Age an Asturian painter was in the first rank of Spanish court painters, and a powerful Picasso canvas confirms that the most influential artist of the modern age belongs to Asturias as much as to any other region of Spain.

On the regional level, the Museum of Fine Arts organizes traveling exhibitions throughout Asturias and has assumed some responsibility for helping to educate the rest of the region by means of such events. With respect to Europe, there are modest exchange-programs including other museums of similar type, mission, and size in France and Germany. There have even been loan shows coming from the United States. Although the professional staff of the Museum of Fine Arts of Asturias, in its attempt to enhance the cultural confidence of the citizen of the region, consciously stresses the need to first know "who we are," it also sends out signals that it is not wise to spend all of one's energy, as codirector Emilio Marcos says, "looking at our own navels." With all of this, the Asturian museum has become a model of center/periphery cooperation, relating appropriately to Europe and to the United States, as well as to Madrid. It has matured into one of the vehicles whereby its primary constituents can become comfortable with the constantly shifting definition of that which is considered the center in today's world. Usually their center is Asturias, but sometimes it is Madrid, and occasionally it is Europe or America. No doubt in future years we will see, if it is called for, an acknowledgment of other centers such as Asia or Africa. In the museum Asturians learn to shed their old sense of isolation; to enhance their understanding of who they are; and, perhaps most intriguingly, to try on those new and complex identities that they would have never thought possible a mere twenty years ago.

The Museum of Fine Arts has been run since its opening days by two men, Emilio Marcos Vallaure and José A. Fernández-Castañón, who can be described as cultural visionaries. They assumed the responsibility of turning the infirm idea of the museum into a healthy state-of-the-art reality, without having had the benefit of specialized training for directing art museums, without having been able to travel and network internationally, and without up-to-date models of museological standards at hand. Still, Marcos and Castañón not only gave the museum its healthy structure, but have also overseen a subsequent expansion of what has metamorphosed into a truly glorious project. After completing "part 1" of their museum, they spearheaded the purchase of another palace adjacent to the Velarde in 1982. Called the Casa de Oviedo-Portal, this adjacent structure was destined to be the next wing for the museum. As splendid as the Palacio Velarde became, the second renovation, also in the hands of an Asturian architect, is even more beautiful. Like the Palacio Velarde, the Casa de Oviedo-Portal is a metaphor for the marriage of past and present, is dynamic and imposing while remaining inviting. Although quite generous in its interior spaces, the scale remains suited to the medium-sized city and region it serves. The new wing allows the museum to better fulfill its mission, as its regional audiences have come to take its success for granted and to expect ever more ambitious programming where they previously had expected nothing.

The Museum of Fine Arts of Asturias does, however, suffer from one extremely serious weakness common to Spanish museums. Surprisingly, this vulnerability does not spring from a lack of money, even though that is the most often and certainly the most vociferous complaint heard throughout the land. Rather, it is a by-product of the ongoing conflation in Spain of the cultural and political spheres in the name of the democratic process. Politics and democracy may well be conflated with other functions in society, but when the conflation affects museum management and leadership it becomes the enemy of continuity and integrity. The most obvious manifestation of this weakness is the tendency to change directors of Spanish museums with every change in government. Because the government supports almost all of the Spanish museums financially and because of an ancient administrative system dating back to Napoleonic times, it claims the right to name and fire museum directors (along, of course, with innumerable other posts throughout all of Spain) whenever there is a political reversal. That is bad enough, but these dismissals also happen when there is a geo-political difference or even a matter of embarrassment between the director and the party in charge.[3] This, obviously, is a threat not only to the directors themselves, but, much more important, to responsibly developed plans and projects. It also effectively halts decision making around election time, slowing down progress for reasons that have nothing to do with the projects themselves. Excessive politicization is a shadow that looms over cultural life in Spain. And so, Marcos and Castañón, two of Spain's most effective artistic leaders, worry about the inevitable changes of party, changes that could capriciously dismantle all of their hard-won achievements for no professional reason. They worry about an enormous issue, what they term the *indefensión jurídica,* the lack of legal structural protection for Spanish museums.

Marcos wrote, in unpublished letters to the author in 1994 and 1995, that this lack of legal protection causes all of the museums in Spain to be so weak that they ultimately fall prey to self-serving politicians. He wrote further about the benefits of creating a national coordinating museum law, something perhaps like the one France adopted years ago. He is convinced that because of that law, the French museums are significantly safer than their counterparts are in Spain.[4] At the same time Marcos certainly recognizes that a centralist law like France's would be impossible in present-day Spain, precisely because of the fiercely guarded home-rule granted by the democratic structure to the regions—the very same home-rule that finally permitted the building of the Asturias Museum after so many years of paralysis. Still, there are solutions to this paradoxical problem. But these solutions will only be found if the professional leadership of museums can be disentangled somewhat from immediate political fortune, and not destructively linked to democratic process. It is probably only a matter of time before that begins to happen, but meanwhile it must be deemed a serious problem.

Nevertheless, as much as Marcos and Castañón worry about the fissures in the overall museum system (or lack of system) in Spain, the cultural life in Asturias, especially with respect to their own museum, is being better served than those who live and fight for it realize. *From the outside looking in,* the lack of legal protection is more than balanced by the government support the museum does attract. Since the birth of

Spanish contemporary democracy the UCD, and the Socialists who followed, have construed it in their best interests to continue to financially underwrite their stunning fine arts museum. Even though the museum will perpetually need more funds than it receives, thousands of Asturian citizens stream through its doors and are gradually absorbing the lesson that they are a part of a significant region of Spain and that this region is now both autonomous *and* linked with Madrid. Through the art on display at the museum, these visitors acquire credible evidence that they, too, have been contributors to Spain's genius. The Museum of Fine Arts of Asturias, by means of the exhibition, interpretation, conservation, and acquisition of increasingly numerous and important works of art, is one of those institutions in Spain's civil society that helps its regional citizens to picture themselves as participants in a fine and flexible, modern, and benignly balanced democracy. It is one of the triumphs of post-Franco Spain that Asturias can fit so comfortably into the nation-state. And it is one of the triumphs of the region itself that the institution of the museum was understood to be a key partner in that important achievement.

The Extremaduran and Ibero-American Museum of Contemporary Art (MEIAC)

Our next museum is in Badajoz, a city bordering Portugal, on the main road to Lisbon, and the inheritor, even in severe Extremadura, of an unusually tormented past. Perpetually fighting for its existence against aggressors; seemingly forever building, repairing, and tearing down walls, the city endured a succession of violent battles from the Middle Ages on. Badajoz added another level of tragedy to its urban history during the Spanish Civil War. On August 15, 1936, Badajoz became a symbol of suffering for the whole country, and in order to understand the moral force of the museum in that city, one must be made aware of what happened there.

The old bullring in Badajoz was the site of one of the first massacres in the Spanish Civil War. Franco's Nationalist forces had taken the city, which was on the side of the legitimate government, the Spanish Republic. In order to extract revenge against citizens they insisted had supported that government and who, they believed, had perpetuated crimes against them, the Nationalists rounded up men and women and massacred them in front of the already shattered populace. So profound was the shame and dread of this event that there has, not surprisingly, been an attempt to minimize the number of the slaughtered. Some eyewitnesses counted the dead at 1,800; later, others attempted to minimize it by counting around 400. Recently, Paul Preston in his respected 1994 biography of Franco wrote: "After the heat of battle had cooled, two thousand prisoners were rounded up and herded to the bullring, and any with the bruise of a rifle recoil on their shoulders were shot. The shootings went on for weeks thereafter."[5] James Michener, who wrote *Iberia* a full thirty years after the event, tried to talk to the townspeople about it, and reported: "I have never spoken to a man who would admit that he had been in the bullring that day, but once at a café in Sevilla I was shown a man who admitted to having been there. I asked if I could speak with him, and friends approached him, but he stared at me across the tables and shook his head no. Men in the bar said, 'He told us it was the worst thing a man could see on earth.' "[6]

The Museo Extremeño e Iberoamericano de Arte Contemporáneo in Badajoz, inaugurated in 1994 in a former prison built during the earliest years of the dictatorship in the neighborhood of the infamous bullring, has become one of the most powerfully emotional and eccentric of the regional museums in Spain. To build the city's museum in that place was a far-sighted decision, a recognition of the necessity to strike a healthy balance between a society's need to remember and its simultaneous and understandable wish to forget.[7] Planners and politicians were confident that such a balance could be achieved by turning the pain of the communal past into the basis for a renewed future. MEIAC, as the museum would be informally called, was the vehicle for the desired transformation because its physical presence and its impact were unavoidable. Whether or not the people of Badajoz passed through the museum's doors, they would all be confronted by it as it loomed over the cityscape. A clear reminder of one of the main events of the Civil War and the oppression, repression, and punishment that followed it, MEIAC would be simultaneously a memorial and a clarion call to reconciliation.

The idea behind MEIAC, as described by its founders, is in itself a manifestation of Extremadura's cultural maturity. In all of their writings, the founders bring to mind an Extremaduran past with its back always to Spain, with the search for adventure in places far away from home. Miguel Logroño, for example, speaks of the failure to recognize that true adventure either exists where we are, internally, or that it does not exist at all. He alludes to the possibility of transforming Extremadura, not by continued reference to the old, outmoded discourse around overseas explorations (those feats for which the region is mostly nostalgically recalled) but rather by the world of intelligence, of imagination, of culture.[8] Furthermore, the founders did not want to design yet another pseudouniversalist imitation of Paris's Pompidou Center. That is what Madrid undertook to do when it conceived of the Reina Sofía, Spain's national Museum of Modern and Contemporary Art, sometimes referred to as "Sofidu." Nor did they want to import another location's artistic legacy, such as the Basque country is doing by importing a foreign architect and "renting" important works from the Guggenheim in New York for its core collection in Bilbao. And the last thing they wished to do was to try to paint a picture of an increasingly intimate relationship with Madrid. That picture was a true one for Asturias, but such a regional cultural vision would not have resonated for Extremeñans.

Rather, the new museum was visualized as a dramatic means of coming to grips with and reversing entrenched historical associations that had always been crippling for Extremadura: emigration, isolation, and marginalization. It was additionally envisioned that the museum could honor Extremadura's special allegiances to Portugal and Latin America. Naturally, the planners and politicians were also optimistic that MEIAC would contribute to a progressive, urbanistic renewal in the run-down neighborhood near the prison. The more idealistic among them wanted to use the museum to motivate all of Extremadura, not just Badajoz, to reconceptualize the idea of exploration (whether it be cultural or economic) as one based on self-confidence, creativity, and success instead of the poverty and its concomitant humiliations that forced Balboa and Pizarro to abandon their homes in search of betterment so many centuries ago.

Normally, the tale of a museum begins, as the story of the Asturias museum began, with its collections of works of art. MEIAC is unusual in that its tale needs to begin, as we began it here, with Badajoz's modern history. It then continues with the building, one that commands attention today, not only for its beauty but also for its having been reborn from the city's old and abandoned Francoist prison. Planned in 1941 and built in 1942, the original purpose of the prison was undoubtedly to house political prisoners along with common criminals in Spain's postwar period, the "years of misery." Why the prison was only formally inaugurated twelve years after it was built is mysterious, but in 1958 when the event finally took place, it was adorned with all of the civic-religious regalia, the emblems and symbols of the dictatorship. The visibility and the nature of the architecture and its *mobilier* were intended to continually remind the citizens of who the victors were, who the vanquished had been, and who was in charge. By the end of its effective life, as the dictatorship weakened and died, the prison housed only common criminals.

Inspired by the panopticon of Jeremy Bentham, the Badajoz prison tower was based on the notion of the all-seeing eye of central inspection. Although Bentham's panopticon had utopian objectives linked to matters of hygiene and security, at the prison in Badajoz it devolved into a reminder of the most severe, absolute, and authoritarian power. "An abstract and eloquent paradigm, the Bentham-type prison is an authentic machine for guarding and watching, an *ad hoc* apparatus for the custodianship and punishment of prisoners. . . . The omnipresent eye of power was able to produce the fear and respect necessary so as to assure proper behavior and respect."[9] Certainly the purpose of the prison was not only to exercise its power over the prisoners within its walls; it also must have been intended to make an overwhelming impression on passersby. As a perversion of the medieval castle form, the prison on the hill dominated the city. With its blank eye-hole windows it would have also hinted that the city as well as the incarcerated were under constant surveillance. Therefore, first by its explicit function, then by its implicit one, and ultimately by its progressive deterioration and abandonment, the prison made Badajoz (already ugly from decades of indiscriminate expansion and speculation) uglier still. It was a prison that echoed the Franco regime at its most unbeautiful and its most regressive. No doubt, its continued presence was a depressing reminder of days shrouded in pain and denial.

Given that past, it is remarkable that the contemporary city planners possessed the foresight to retain the prison as the core structure of the new museum, and furthermore, to make, as an absolute requirement for that museum, the retention of the tower of the penitentiary. Rather than

Badajoz, The Old
Prison. (Photo courtesy:
MEIAC)

destroy it, they chose as their chief visual reference the very form that
could trigger the worst memories of the past. Optimistic as it may have
seemed, it was their hope that this form would be transformed into a
shape that would become the city's most prominent, forward-looking,
and visible representation of its aspirations. This was not a simple
metamorphosis to effect; but it seems that José Antonio Galea, the
Extremaduran architect of the project, found the challenge to his liking.
He met it by doing intensive research into nineteenth-century museums. There he found that the required elements could be recuperated
from the prison and could be made to serve as valid historical and
museological references. In Galea's research he discovered intellectual
material that would allow him, in good aesthetic conscience, to adapt
the old prison to the new urbanistic needs. He also found reasons that
enabled him to justify disposing of nonessential elements of the old
building such as the radial naves. The essential goals being achievable, it
was then no problem to add a service annex, a huge sub-basement to

Badajoz, The Old Prison. (Photo courtesy: MEIAC)

hang the collections, and elaborate gardens and terraces. The result is a splendid, complex, poeticized museum/ex-prison, a haunting and paradoxical reminder of the potential for liberation that can still be unearthed within the history of battered modern humanity.

It is proclaimed in MEIAC's first publication that "to create a new Museum in the location where a prison previously existed is to bring to completion an act of social transformation. . . . The space for punishment is transformed thus into a space of freedom. Even if art and delinquency are two parallel forms of transgression and for many the avant-garde is an authentic crime against good taste, nevertheless such an act of transformation is to oppose the repulsive with the beauty of aesthetic creation, to make both acts, the artistic and the criminal, antithetical concepts."[10]

The final chapter of the story of the museum in Badajoz segues to the story of the art they have chosen to collect. It may be the last chapter, but it is the one that will endow the story with its future life. The immediate acquisition policy was to recuperate and preserve those parts of the modern art history of the Extremaduran past that were still salvageable, most of it having been lost or destroyed due to exile, migration, poverty, neglect, and war. Thus the collection dates from the first third of this century and focuses on artists from the region who are notable for their

Badajoz, The New Museum: MEIAC Model. (Photo courtesy: MEIAC)

affinities to significant trends of Spanish modern art. The second goal was to collect the paintings and sculpture of the Extremadurans working today. Third, the collection is meant to encourage and pay homage to the relationship with Portugal, a complex relationship that over the years has been fraught with both desire and disdain. Portugal is the natural neighbor of Extremadura, and many residents claim to feel closer to the Portuguese than they do to the rest of Spain. It should be noted here that all publications and wall labels are bilingual, in Spanish and Portuguese. Fourth, the collections also actively include Latin American art because of Extremadura's conviction that it is one of the regions where Spain can most fruitfully expand its relationship to Latin America. Although throughout all of Spain there is a reawakened sense of affinity with and obligation to Latin America, none is as strong, has been as continuous, or is as poignant as Extremadura's. Extremadurans feel as if they, having been the most marginalized of Spaniards, have the ability to empathize with those they describe as the most marginalized of Americans. They believe that because they have never lost contact with Latin America over the centuries, they have something to teach other Spaniards about how they might overcome some of the many obstacles, the roadblocks to understanding between Spain and the "New World." Thus there is already a significant amount of high-quality Latin American art in MEIAC's permanent collection, and there will be serious intellectual dialogue about the painful and positive impact their cultures have had on each other. And, finally, Extremadura hopes to expand and enrich its relationship to Spain itself by collecting contemporary Spanish art. It speaks well for the politicians who are supporting the museum and the professionals who guided them in their efforts that the art being collected is of very high quality and that, at least in the beginning, there was more than sufficient budget to achieve MEIAC's goals. MEIAC is off to an excellent start and, of course the challenge will be, in the event of political change, to sustain those goals by sustaining the investment in the art itself.

The museum in Badajoz is another example of a spectacular regional Spanish museum ostensibly in the service of a specific locale, but profoundly in the service of a sovereign Spain by virtue of its elevation of the role of differences in the society as a whole. MEIAC is quite frankly in the business of identity construction, of educating so-called ideal democratic Extremaduran citizens for the postmodern age so that they can not only tolerate but also enjoy their new role in the kaleidoscope of today's Spain. At the end of the twentieth century, the average citizen of what may still be the poorest, most provincial area of Spain, has become infinitely more prosperous and hopeful about Extremadura's potential for positive contributions to the larger world. The museum in Badajoz, transformed as it was from a symbol of oppression into one of freedom, is a convincing confirmation of the power of art and architecture to validate, test, and even expand the best and most ambitious dreams of a democratic and pluralistic society into the general population.

Valencian Institute of Modern Art (IVAM)

There are more than seventy museums in Valencia, and more are being built each year. Archaeological, ecclesiastical, maritime, fine arts, natural sciences, ethnology, historic, military, medical, agricultural, and monographic museums all contribute their fragments of meaning to the evolving identity of the Valencian citizen. Neither battered nor alienated, Valencia entered the post-Franco period anxious to claim its place in modern Spain (they might now describe it as postmodern) while protecting its well-established historical identity. Autonomous and proud of it, Valencia's main cultural issue, mirrored in its political life as well, continues to be the appropriate balance that ought to be struck between the local and the global, the old and the new. The museums that have emerged since Franco's demise reflect efforts to find that balance. Indeed, so much political/cultural faith has been put into the idea of museums as vessels of identity and tools for its enhancement that it sometimes strikes the visitor to Valencia that there are more museums than necessary. They seem to have sprung up without planning and, sometimes (as in the case of the new science museum), without collections. Even the former director general of the Cultural Patrimony of Valencia, the official whose business included museums, wrote that this growth could be described as a "veritable museological bulimia."[11] But, granting that there has been a binge, there is among Valencian museums one so serious and at the same time so daring, so willing to experiment, so able to highlight the multilayered and contradictory meanings implicit and explicit in the new Spain, that it has emerged as the embodiment of the best aspirations of the postdictatorship years. It is such a fine institution that it was considered as a model in some respects for the Reina Sofía, the State museum of modern and contemporary art, when the Reina evolved into its maturity as an institution in 1994. That the State would follow a region is an indication of how much attitudes had, indeed, changed in the two decades following Franco's death.

This museum is known as IVAM, and is formally referred to as the Instituto Valenciano de Arte Moderno (or Institut Valencia d'Art Modern). What is IVAM and why has it become so prominent in Spain and throughout Europe? IVAM is the concretization of the Valencian ideal of selfhood as the twentieth century draws to its close. With its two stunning buildings, it mediates between past and present and the local and international, and it points to the future by means of art. IVAM has co-opted every means at its disposal to position itself as a leading participant in the shifting temporal and spatial realities of the city in which it sits. The first of these was the decision to have two distinct sites make up the museum complex. The original site for IVAM is an example of adaptive reuse, just as were the Asturias and Badajoz museums, but with very different results. A gorgeous 700-year-old convent, the Centre del Carmé, was and remains one of the most evocative buildings in the Old Quarter of Valencia. The Carmé, as it is called today, was one of the first monasteries to be erected in the city. Its remodeling in the seventeenth century was the transformation that gave it its current appearance. Although parish activities and the Gothic cloister still continue to function, these religious activities are not obviously part of the museum. The zone of the convent that does correspond to IVAM is comprised of three adjacent areas: the Renaissance cloister, dating from the first half of the sixteenth century; the old refectory and the chapter room, now called the "Gallery of Ambassador Vich"; and the "Ala Goerlich," built in the earlier years of this century to complement the installations of the provincial museum of fine arts that was located on this property, together with the Royal Academy of Fine Arts of San Carlos, from 1838–1946. The Carmé is now the site of IVAM's changing exhibitions and is recognized as one of the most striking examples of adaptive reuse of ancient buildings in Europe.

Across a narrow street and down from the Carmé is a modern structure built by a team of Valencian architects, Ximo Sanchis, José Murcia, Vicent Martínez, and Carles Salvadores Navarro, directed by Emilio Jiménez. This, the Centre Julio González, is named for the Catalan creator of modern iron sculpture whose work forms the core collection of IVAM. The building is modernist, pure, attractive, and impressive as well as stylish, confident, cool, and unpretentious. But it, too, is laden with significance. Its location corresponds to the perimeter of the old city walls, only torn down in 1865. With 15,000 square meters, 4,800 of them dedicated to exhibition, and the balance to museum services such as offices, reception, storage, restoration, security, education, and so on, it conforms to the highest international standards. Nine classically laid out galleries for painting and sculpture display the works of art. Not accidentally, the last of the nine galleries is in the sub-basement of IVAM and dramatically reveals the remains of Valencia's ancient walls. In 1994 an exhibition of local medieval ceramics in that gallery reminded any visitor to IVAM that avant-garde as the museum might appear, its very foundations were deeply imbedded in the past.

As evocative as are the buildings, art is at the heart of IVAM and is its raison d'être. The artistic founder of IVAM and its first director, Tomás Llorens, insisted that for this new museum to have lasting impact and heft within the museum world, it would need to own a permanent collection of painting and sculpture capable of projecting the meaning

IVAM: The Carmé,
interior. (Photo courtesy:
IVAM)

of the project as a whole. Hence IVAM immediately acquired a major
collection of the works of the modernist master Julio González and
dedicated itself to purchasing the paintings, prints, and sculpture of
other major Spanish modern masters. The curators thus took upon
themselves the preservation of that portion of the national patrimony
known in Spain as the First Avant-Garde. They then went on to collect
works of other less well-known artists such as Ignacio Pinazo Camar-
lench, whose art bore witness to the beginnings of modernism in Valencia. The permanent collection also consists of international art from
outside Spain's borders beginning in the sixties and continuing until the
present, as well as important objects from the "Second Avant-Garde."
These postwar artists include Antonio Saura, Manuel Millares, Eduardo
Chillida, and Antoni Tapies. Finally, there is a subset of collections of
outstanding abstract works from the thirties including works by Joaquim Torres García, Jean Arp, Moholy-Nagy, and Kurt Schwitters.

Works by contemporary international artists are regularly added to the permanent holdings. It should also be stressed that there is a strong core of Valencian artists working today who are represented in the permanent collections. Such figures as Miguel Navarro, Carmen Calvo, Joaquín Michavila, Grupo Parpallo, Andreu Alfaro, Joaquim Armengol, and the Equipo 57 stand out among them.

The temporary exhibitions at IVAM pay tribute to both the local arts community and to international artists. Of the latter, Cildo Mireiles, from Brazil; Henri Michaux, from France; Markus Raetz, from Switzerland; Andy Warhol, Josef Albers, Mark di Suvero, and James Lee Byars, from the United States; and Sigmar Polke, from Germany have been on the roster of shows. The curators, under the guidance of a succession of gifted directors and, until 1996, with the ongoing artistic vision of chief curator Vicente Todoli, have guaranteed that there will be an open and reciprocal dialogue between the international avant-garde and the city of Valencia. Because of its prestige, IVAM has been able to travel a number of the exhibitions it has organized throughout the world, further enlarging Valencia's sense of itself as a leader in modern life.

Not content only to present objects, IVAM has initiated sophisticated public education and outreach programs so as to affect the citizens at large and to better communicate its vision to them. It has developed a very large audience, due not only to its acquisition and exhibition policy, but also to these programs. Interactive workshops and projects bring children and adults close to the creative process, transferring some of art-making's excitement to them. IVAM has also become a magnet for intellectual and general cultural debate that is of interest to and linked to its local and its international audiences. It produces publications that are both scholarly and popular in nature. Labels and didactic materials are presented both in Spanish and in the local language/dialect, Valencian. Audiovisual and bibliographical material are made available to schools. Scholars use a fine library and documentation center, and IVAM has organized valuable conferences and symposia. It has even offered courses for the training of museum professionals. IVAM has lived up to its name as an institute for research, as a modern art museum, and as a vehicle for the construction of a richer and broader international identity for its already profoundly rooted citizens. Valencians are very proud of IVAM and of the light it casts upon them as they look forward and plan their future.

The Piu Quinto Museum, the city's traditional museum of fine arts, and the National Ceramics Museum highlight the past, lending enormous depth to Valencia's desired identity. But the politicians of the early eighties, along with the citizens who elected them, realized that it was contemporary art that had emerged as one of the most effective international symbols of engagement in the world. IVAM is Valencia's unequivocal, celebratory statement that its citizens are full participants in that reality. At the same time the forces behind IVAM understand that to continue to be supported by its populace, it must not neglect its roots. It is in the conscious balancing of the global and the local, the past and the present, that this remarkable region has created IVAM, hoping that it would be a powerful arena for playing out new rituals of citizenship. Now, if IVAM could only figure out a way whereby it could exist without the hand of politics at its throat!

One would think that because of its success, IVAM might be free of the threat of political evisceration that haunts every other museum at election time in Spain. But that is not the case. The sudden and capricious shifting of museological course by the removal of top personnel is an ever-present threat at IVAM. Indeed, in the 1995 elections, when Valencia swung to the right, the brilliant director of many years was forced to resign simply because he was not a member of the victorious party.[12] In spite of strong pre-election rhetoric proclaiming IVAM to be an unqualified success, Conservative Party (Partido Popular) candidate Eduardo Zaplana could only conceive of IVAM as prime political booty once he had been elected head of the Valencian government.[13] The directorship was deemed to be one of the political plums, and there was simply no serious consideration given to continuing the incumbent in his position based on his universally acknowledged merit. Valencia was looking terribly provincial as politicians wrangled over who would take the helm at IVAM. Finally, the National Conservative Party leadership stepped in to save Valencia further embarrassment. Advice was taken from art world professionals and a compromise reached. In that compromise, the decision to oust the former director was sustained, but the leadership of IVAM was awarded to a highly esteemed Conservative art critic. Tension over the change in power at IVAM was thus diffused, and the subject more or less closed.

One must acknowledge that the 1995 compromise was a sign of progress in a country accustomed to carelessly using its cultural institutions for political ends. In 1996, only a year after the election, IVAM was certainly a more conservative museum than it had been before. Additional weight was being given to the local and less to the global—in both exhibition programming and art collecting. The chief curator, Vicente Todoli, had left for another institution. The Conservative agenda was in place. Still, one had to admit that despite dire warnings from the Left, the museum had not been destroyed. Indeed, it had probably been strengthened for the long run! Why? Because all parties had been taught the lesson that Valencia's contemporary identity and its reputation for integrity are, in important ways, connected to the protection of IVAM's identity and integrity. As a result, even though IVAM's direction remains overly determined by politics, its prominence has taught the region's leadership to be more sensitive to the underlying significance of the museum: IVAM is the mark of Valencia's sophistication. It will never again be mistaken as solely a place to hang art or as merely a vehicle for political patronage.[14]

The museums of Asturias, Extremadura, and Valencia demonstrate only three of the numerous variations on the role that regional museums in Spain play in the refiguration of the complex identities of the democratic Spanish citizen. They showcase the heterogeneity of the country and its many histories and attitudes, as well as the variety of relationships Spain's regions are developing with Madrid and with the rest of the world. Spanish regional museums form an impressive constellation of critical civic institutions. They serve to encourage each citizen to envision him or herself as a participant in a purposefully fragmented and multivocal nation-state whose continuity is founded on the vitality and diversity of its component parts.

Notes

This essay is a version of a chapter in the author's forthcoming book on the role of the museum in the construction of the identity of the "new Spaniard." It will be published by the Smithsonian Institution Press in 1997.

1. According to Carol Duncan: "Exhibitions in art museums do not of themselves change the world. Nor should they have to. But, as a form of public space, they constitute an arena in which a community may test, examine, and imaginatively live both older truths and possibilities for new ones. It is often

said that without a sense of past, we cannot envisage a future. The reverse is also true: without a vision of the future, we cannot construct and access a usable past. Art museums are at the center of this process in which past and future intersect. Above all, they are spaces in which communities can work out the values that identify them as communities." *Civilizing Rituals inside Public Art Museums* (London and New York: Routledge, 1995), 133.

2. The UCD ceased to be a party after the next election. Still, the museum was such a success that the victorious Socialist Party (PSOE), remained supportive of the Asturias Museum and donned the mantle of its success.

3. For example, the director of the Prado, Dr. Alfonso-Pérez Sánchez, was relieved of his position when he signed a petition protesting Spain's support of the Persian Gulf War. Between 1993 and 1994 the Prado saw two more directors come and go. Felipe Garín was ostensibly dismissed because of the embarrassment of leaks in the Prado ceiling that occurred during his tenure, and his successor, Francisco Calvo-Serraller, resigned supposedly because of the scandal resulting from his allowing the use of designer chairs inside the Prado for a photo spread in a magazine managed by his wife. In all three cases the firings were casualties of internal politics.

4. Letter from Emilio Marcos Vallaure to the author, November 29, 1995: "El Sistema español de museos es un organismo que vale para muy poco, no existiendo conexión entre los diferentes museos que lo constituyen. En este aspecto, creo que debemos aprender mucho de Francia; especialmente porque la política museológica francesa ha apostado por una coordinación que permite conservar el patrimonio entendido muy ampliamente." (The Spanish museum system is an entity with little value, as there is no connection between the different museums that comprise it. In this respect, I believe we could learn a lot from France, especially because the French policy has opted for coordination that allows for preservation of the common patrimony.)

5. Paul Preston, *Franco: A Biography* (New York: Basic Books, 1994), 166.

6. James Michener, *Iberia* (New York: Random House, 1968), 91.

7. I had a conversation with a staff member in the Badajoz tourist office in the first days of 1996. When I asked her to locate on the map the exact location of the museum in relation to the bullring, she made a point of telling me that the old bullring was closed and a new one a little farther from the museum was functioning now. She said a garden would be built where the old bullring was because of its history. I wondered whether it would be a memorial, and she said that it would not be—people just wanted to forget. This response further suggested the dynamic balance between remembering and forgetting that needs to be struck in the regions of Spain.

8. Miguel Logroño, "Geografía del Arte: Centro y periferia," in *Museo Extremeño Iberoamericano de Arte Contemporáneo* (Badajoz: Consejería de Cultura y Patrimonio, 1995), 246 ff.

9. Antonio Bonet Correa, "Perennidad del panóptico," in *Museo Extremeño e Iberoamericano de Arte Contemporáneo,* 226.

10. Ibid., 233.

11. Evangelina Rodríguez Cuadros, *Guía de museos de la Comunidad Valencia* (Conselleria de Cultura, Educació i Ciència, 1991), 15.

12. Francisco Yvars, director, letter to the author, September 11, 1995: "As a result of the recently held elections, the Conservative party has taken over Valencia's regional government, and changes have taken place in the departments of cultural policies. In consequence, I have resigned from my position as Director of IVAM."

13. *Eduardo Zaplana, Un liberal para el cambio en la comunidad valenciana* interviews with Rafa Marí (Barcelona: Ediciones B, S.A., 1995), 104.

14. It should be stressed that this vulnerability of the institution of the museum to political fortune is not exclusively a Conservative problem or a Socialist problem in Spain. It is a Spanish problem. Socialists have behaved equally cynically in the past and probably expect to do so again when the tables are inevitably turned. But perhaps, due to the exposure of this essential flaw in Spain's museum structure through what occurred at high-profile IVAM, new safeguards will be developed for other museums in the future. There might yet be a heightened consciousness of those in power with regard to the need to protect Spain's cultural patrimony from the maw of transient political careerism. On the national level, after the 1996 elections, the Conservative Party took steps to protect the Prado Museum from political vulnerability. This issue will be discussed at length in my book.

HILARY L. NERONI

Annotated Bibliography of English-Language

Works on Spanish Film

Amell, Samuel, ed. *Literature, the Arts, and Democracy: Spain in the Eighties.* London: Associated University Presses, 1990. This collection contains essays by Amell, José Carlos Mainer, Pilar Miró, Ignacio Soldevila Durante, Randolph D. Pope, Philip W. Silver, Stephen J. Summerhill, Francisco Ruiz Ramón, José María Rodríguez Méndez, Vicente Cantarino, and Carlos Rojas. The essays deal with Spanish history, poetry, novels, theater, and cinema from the eighties. There is only one essay on film: it is by Pilar Miró and is entitled "Ten Years of Spanish Cinema." (See Miró in this bibliography.)

Aranda, Francisco. *Luis Buñuel: A Critical Biography.* Trans. David Robinson. New York: Dacapo, 1976. This book details most of the events and films in Buñuel's life as well as Aranda's admiration for Buñuel. Aranda also provides an anthology of Buñuel's surrealist and other literary texts from 1922 to 1933, as well as an extensive filmography from 1929 to 1974.

Arata, Louis O. "'I am Ana': The Play of the Imagination in *The Spirit of the Beehive.*" *Quarterly Review of Film Studies* 8, no. 2 (1983): 26–33. Arata discusses the way Víctor Erice, in his film *El espíritu de la colmena* (1993), brilliantly succeeds in portraying the world from the point of view and spirit of a child. After giving a short summary of the plot, Arata contends that the real substance of the film is not the plot but instead the play between the extraordinariness of the child's imagination and the desolateness of the world she lives in. Arata concludes that it is this open-ended play between perception and imagination that allows the most essential question in the film— that of identity as a child understands it—to be fully explored.

Bartholomew, Gail. "The Development of Carlos Saura." *Journal of the University Film and Video Association* 35, no. 3 (1983): 15–33. Bartholomew argues that Carlos Saura has been able to make expressive and personal films because of the Spanish desire for a national cinema that is a real alternative to Hollywood film. She traces this idea through a discussion of the production and reception of Saura's early films.

Besas, Peter. *Behind the Spanish Lens: Spanish Cinema under Fascism and Democracy.* Denver: Arden, 1985. Besas gives the history of Spanish cinema from its beginning in 1897 to the present and even offers predictions for the future. He describes the social situation and production history of the major Spanish films, providing a detailed, and often personal, account of the Spanish milieu.

——. "Spain." In *Variety International Film Guide, 1990,* ed. Peter Cowie. Hollywood: Samuel French, 1989, 325–36. In this special edition of *Variety,* Besas has the task of representing the year of 1989 in Spanish cinema. He discusses the current state of production, the films that opened, the box-office information about those films, and the films currently in production. He also gives a list of producers' names and addresses, distributors' names and addresses, and other useful addresses.

Borau, José Luis. "Without Weapons." *Quarterly Review of Film Studies* 8, no. 2 (1983): 85–90. Well-known filmmaker Borau examines the plight of the Spanish filmmaker in a world that views the Spanish Civil War as the "dress rehearsal" for all that happened later in Europe and always evaluates young filmmakers with such adjectives as "quixotic," "goyesque," and "buñuelesque." Borau discusses international distribution, audience reception, filmmakers' struggle with their heritage and loyalty to their roots, and how a filmmaker attempts to survive all this.

——. "A Woman without a Piano, A Book without a Mark." *Quarterly Review of Film and Video* 13, no. 4 (1991): 9–16. This article is a more in-depth version of a prologue Borau wrote for the memoirs of Don Luis Buñuel's widow, Jeanne Rucar. Borau discusses the disparate sides of Buñuel—his public versus his private—that this book reveals and the artistic contradictions they embody. Borau also discusses Jeanne Rucar's decision to write these memoirs and concludes that rather than being a "stab in the back," these revealing memoirs are from a woman who dedicated herself and her love to this great, controversial director.

Buñuel, Luis. *My Last Sigh.* Trans. Abigail Israel. New York: Vintage, 1984. Most of Buñuel's autobiography is spent recounting his formative years, including his encounters with surrealism, France, and Hollywood. In addition, Buñuel offers his feeling about not only his own films, but also other directors and their films.

Cabello-Castellet, George, Jaume Martí-Olivella, and Guy H. Wood, eds. *Cine-Lit: Essays on Peninsular Film and Fiction.* Portland, Oreg.: Portland State UP, Oregon State U., and Reed C., 1992. This collection of essays is from the First International Conference on Hispanic Cinema and Literature, which focused on the multicultural reality of contemporary Spanish cinema and brought together Basque, Catalan, Galician, and Castilian cultures. The essays deal with "Cinema as an Institutional Challenge," "From Text to

Screen: Translation and Adaptation," "Feminine Voice and/in Cinema," "Peninsular Micro-Cinemas," and "Ideology, Sexuality and Intertextuality in Almodóvar." Half the collection of essays in this book are written in English and half in Spanish.

——. *Cine-Lit II: Essays on Peninsular Film and Fiction.* Portland, Oreg.: Portland State UP, 1995. This is a collection of working papers from the Second International Conference on Hispanic Cinema and Literature, held in Portland, Oregon, in 1994.

Caparrós-Lera, J. M., and Rafael de España. *The Spanish Cinema: An Historical Approach.* Madrid: Film Historia, 1987. This work was published in conjunction with the Retrospective on Spanish Cinema held at the University of New Mexico, September 1987. The first half of this book provides a general introductory history of Spanish film from 1896 to 1975. The second half of the book is a "dictionary of Spanish movies" from 1939 to 1975, which is not complete: the authors have picked those films they felt are most important. The dictionary provides basic production information—but no cast lists—and a brief plot summary.

Cobos, Juan. "Spanish Heroism." *Films and Filming,* November 1960, 9, 41. This article was written before the end of Franco's rule and thus heralds the heroism of Marco Ferreri's *The Wheelchair* in its sheer ability to get through economic and political restraints.

Colmeiro, José, Christina Duplóa, Patricia Greene, and Juana Sabadell, eds. *Spain Today: Essays on Literature, Culture, Society.* Hanover, N.H.: Dartmouth College, Department of Spanish and Portuguese, 1995. This collection of essays is a result of the international symposium "Spain Today: Literature, Culture, Society," which took place at Dartmouth College, November 10–12, 1994. This symposium was meant to address "contemporary cultural forces and critical currents that have completely redefined Spain in the last two decades." The essays are concerned with new critical perspectives in Spanish literature and cinema. There are three essays on film, written by Jaume Martí-Olivella, Marvin D'Lugo, and Paul Julian Smith. (See their entries in this bibliography.)

De España, Rafael, ed. *Directory of Spanish and Portuguese Film-Makers and Films.* Westport, Conn.: Greenwood, 1994. The directory provides a listing of all Spanish and Portuguese filmmakers. The entry for each filmmaker includes a brief biographical sketch and a listing (by year) of all short and feature-length films.

De la Colina, José, and Tomás Pérez Turrent. *Objects of Desire: Conversations with Luis Buñuel.* Ed. and trans. Paul Lenti. New York: Morsilio, 1992. These interviews, each of which focuses on a particular film, represent the only occasions in which Buñuel offered a film-by-film examination of his own films. The interviews were conducted from 1975 to 1977, and the interviewers question Buñuel about his imagery, which characters speak for him, and other filmic choices.

De Stefano, George. "Post-Franco Frankness." *Film Comment* 22, no. 3 (1986): 58–60. De Stefano explores the role Eloy de la Iglesia and his films played in Post-Franco Spain, emphasizing the legacy of Francoist repression in terms of both politics and sexuality. He discusses the political connection between leftist politics and gay rights movements as represented in de la Iglesia's films.

Deveny, Thomas G. *Cain On Screen: Contemporary Spanish Cinema.* London: Scarecrow, 1993. Deveny analyzes the theme of *cainismo* (a conflict between brothers) in Spanish films between 1965 and 1986. He feels that this conflict within Spanish society, and people's awareness of and cultural work about it, has greatly influenced contemporary Spanish cinema, and he examines the political and cultural world of contemporary Spanish cinema from this perspective. In the course of his study, he discusses many films and filmmakers such as Luis Alcoriza, Vicente Aranda, Juan Antonio Bardem, Jaime Camino, Mario Camus, Ricardo Franco, Raphael Gil, Pedro Lazaga, and Carlos Saura.

D'Lugo, Marvin. "Almodóvar's City of Desire." *Quarterly Review of Film and Video* 13, no. 4 (1991): 47–66. Reprinted in Vernon, Kathleen M., and Barbara Morris, eds., 125–44. In this article, D'Lugo investigates the importance of the city, particularly Madrid, in Pedro Almodóvar's films. This city represents a new cultural force that tears down the traditional values of family, the church, and the law. D'Lugo also explains the position of the city during Franco's dictatorship and the way in which other filmmakers have dealt with the city, approaches he then compares to Almodóvar's films. D'Lugo discusses each of Almodóvar's films in terms of its positioning of the city and the way in which the city is mythologized as the site that liberates all desire.

——. "Bigas Luna's *Jamón, jamón:* Remaking the National in Spanish Cinema." In Colmeiro, José, et al., eds., 67–82. D'Lugo argues that in *Jamón, jamón* (1992) Bigas Luna attempts to renegotiate Spanishness and the Spanish sense of national culture. Often this renegotiation results in an allegorical postmodern landscape in which the traditional and the technological exist side by side.

——. "Carlos Saura: Constructive Imagination in Post-Franco Cinema." *Quarterly Review of Film Studies* 8, no. 2 (1983): 34–47. Marvin D'Lugo discusses a cycle of Carlos Saura's films that make up a single conceptual project: *Cría Cuervos* (Raise Ravens, 1975), *Elisa vida mía* (Elisa, My Love, 1977), *Los ojos vendados* (Blindfolded Eyes, 1978), and *Mamá cumple cien años* (Mama Turns 100, 1979). He analyzes each film and reveals their similarities and how one film picks up and explores further the subject of a previous film; for example, the theme of the family as a form of "psychic bondage," and the contemplation of death as a link to maturity. D'Lugo reveals that the spectator of a Saura film gains certain perceptual knowledge that allows contemplation of a future separate from the illusions of the past.

——. "Catalan Cinema: Historical Experience and Cinematic Practice." *Quarterly Review of Film and Video* 13, nos. 1–3 (1991): 131–47. D'Lugo argues that Catalan cinema expresses the distinctive cultural identity of Catalonia and challenges the idea of a "homogeneous Spanish nation." Jaime Camino's *Dragón rapide* (1986), and other Catalan films, challenge earlier films about Catalonia, which tended to submerge the area's distinctive identity within that of Spain as a whole or to accuse Catalonia of regionalism. While resisting homogenization, Catalan cinema works to break down the existing cultural barriers.

——. *The Films of Carlos Saura: The Practice of Seeing.* Princeton, N.J.: Princeton UP, 1991. Following Saura's career of more than three decades, D'Lugo explores each of Saura's films, contextualizing them politically and historically as well as illustrating Saura's style: his "defiant and, at times, renegade" way of looking at the world. D'Lugo discusses Saura's use of personal memory to suggest national history, a method that reveals the "gaps and ruptures" existing in the seamlessness of the *official* Spanish history. More than just an auteur study, this book penetrates the depths of Spanish culture and history.

——. "Historical Reflexicity: Saura's Anti-Carmen," *Wide Angle* 9, no. 3 (1986): 53–61. D'Lugo argues that Carlos Saura's *Carmen* (1983) attacks the stereotypes of an exotic Spain that have been created and perpetuated by the Carmen narrative itself. Saura does this through the reflexive final sequence, which reveals the ideology of art—that which constructs the "Spanish" subject position.

Durgnat, Raymond. *Luis Buñuel.* Los Angeles: U of California P, 1967. Providing plots, stills, and interpretation, Durgnat discusses most of Buñuel's films. He also provides a filmography in this book, which is part of a series, edited by Ian Cameron, designed to provide "readable" books on important directors.

Edwards, Gwynne. *The Discreet Art of Luis Buñuel: A Rereading of His Films.* Boston: Marion Boyars, 1982. Within the framework of what Gwynne calls Buñuel's "remarkable unity of theme and vision," Gwynne provides close analysis of nine of Buñuel's films. The book begins with a biography about Buñuel's life and recounts formative events and the development of his filmmaking career. Gwynne includes cast and plot information as well as his own insights into the films he "rereads."

Eidsvik, Charles. "Dark Laughter: Buñuel's *Tristana* (1970)." In *Modern European Filmmakers and the Art of Adaptation,* ed. Andrew Horton and Joan

Magretta. New York: Frederick Ungar, 1981, 173–87. Working from a premise that Luis Buñuel's sense of humor is critical to understanding his handling of important social and political issues, Eidsvik shows the way in which Buñuel changes—the narrative of Benito Pérez Galdós's 1892 *Tristana* into his 1970 film version and thus reveals his social critiques.

Epps, Brad. "Figuring Hysteria: Disorder and Desire in Three Films of Pedro Almodóvar." In Vernon, Kathleen M., and Barbara Morris, eds., 99–124. Linking *Mujeres al borde de un ataque de nervios* (Women on the Verge of a Nervous Breakdown, 1988), *Laberinto de Pasiones* (Labyrinth of Passions, 1982), and *¿Qué he hecho yo para merecer esto!* (What Have I Done to Deserve This?, 1984), Epps explores how there may be more to these films than meets the eye. He points out traces of hysteria's "crisis of signification" that exist on the films' deceptively mainstream surface; this brings together tensions between the body and image, language and desire, and class and gender.

Evans, Peter Williams. *The Films of Luis Buñuel: Subjectivity and Desire.* Oxford: Clarendon, 1995. Although acknowledging the great auteurship of Buñuel, Evans grounds his detailed analysis of Buñuel's films in the contexts of history, culture, and especially in the context of sexual theory. He privileges questions on subjectivity and desire as they arise in Buñuel's films. The book has four chapters: "Roads to and from the Abyss," "Family Romance: Buñuel's Mexican Melodramas," "Male Desire," and "Female Desire." A detailed filmography is also provided.

———. *Women on the Verge of a Nervous Breakdown.* London: British Film Institute, 1996. Evans provides a multifaceted analysis of Pedro Almodóvar's *Women on the Verge of a Nervous Breakdown.* He draws on a wide range of psychoanalytic and critical concepts to investigate gender, sexuality, and subjectivity in the film, as well as discussing Spain's recent history as it relates to the film. Evans believes that ultimately the film is a dramatization of the nature of sexual desire, and the associated anxieties in relationships and families, but also of the possibility for personal liberation.

Fiddian, Robin W. "The Role and Representation of Women in Two Films by José Luis Borau." In *Essays on Hispanic Themes,* ed. Jennifer Lowe and Philip Swanson. Edinburgh: Department of Hispanic Studies, University of Edinburgh, 1989. Fiddian discusses the position of women in Borau's *Furtivos* (Poachers, 1975) and *La sabina* (1979). He concludes that both films are attacks on the Spanish patriarchal traditions and their creation of dissatisfied individuals.

Fiddian, Robin W., and Peter W. Evans. *Challenges to Authority: Fiction and Film in Contemporary Spain.* London: Tamesis, 1988. Concerned with the interrelations between history and art in mid-twentieth-century Spain, Fiddian and Evans examine Luis Buñuel's *Viridiana* (1961), Carlos Saura's *Stress es tres, tres*

(Stress Is Three, Three, 1968), and Saura's *Carmen* 1983, along with three Spanish novels: José Manuel Caballero's *Dos días de setiembre* (Two Days in September, 1962), Luis Martín Santos's *Tiempo de silencio* (Time of Silence, 1962), and Juan Marsé's *Si te dicen que caí* (If They Tell You I Fell, 1973). The three films are significant because they express, beyond the director's conscious intentions, the cultural mood of Spain at key moments in its history.

Fuentes, Victor. "Almodóvar's Postmodern Cinema: A Work in Progress . . ." In Vernon, Kathleen M., and Barbara Morris, eds., 155–70. Fuentes examines Pedro Almodóvar's later films, in order to evaluate the contribution of Almodóvar—who is seen as a product and promoter of postmodernity—to Spanish and international film. Fuentes also discusses the limitations of Almodóvar's work and how these limitations might expose the limitations of postmodernity itself.

Garland, David. "A Ms-Take in the making? Transsexualism Post-Franco, Post-Modern, Post-Haste." *Quarterly Review of Film and Video* 13, no. 4 (1991): 95–102. Concentrating on Antonio Giménez Rico's *Vestida de azul* (Dressed in Blue), a 1983 documentary, Garland discusses Spanish transsexualism in contemporary films as a symbolic representation of the changing state of religion and class in post-Franco Spain. Garland considers different theories of transsexualism as he explores his own understanding of transsexualism as a mode of constantly calling attention to the transformation of the body. Garland concludes that *Vestida de azul* reveals that although transsexualism might have come from the oppressive environment of Catholicism, it can also co-opt Catholicism and function as a "potentially liberating refuge."

Gubern, Román. "The Civil War: Inquest or Exorcism?" *Quarterly Review of Film and Video* 13, no. 4 (1991): 103–12. Gubern discusses Spanish films about the Civil War and the lack of personal memories contained in them. He feels that this is due primarily to the fact that these filmmakers were generally too young to have vibrant memories of the war. Gubern writes about the exile returning home, a theme that appears in post-Franco films, and about films that deal directly with Franco. Gubern concludes with an analysis of Jaime Camino's *La Vieja Memoria* (Old Memory, 1977), which he feels is the ultimate testimony on the Civil War.

Hanson, Ellis. "Technology, paranoia and the queer voice." *Screen* 34, no. 2 (1993): 137–61. By comparing Stanley Kubrick's *2001: A Space Odyssey* (1968) and Pedro Almodóvar's *La ley del deseo* (Law of Desire, 1987), Hanson investigates the way in which eroticization of technology destabilizes the narrative. Almodóvar's use of the telephone, television, typewriter, and so on, to project disembodied gay voices through machines works to undermine any attempts at repression or closure. Hanson performs a close textual analysis of both films throughout his discussion.

Higginbotham, Virginia. *Luis Buñuel.* Boston: Twayne, 1979. Higginbotham provides a general introduction to the films of Buñuel and discusses his filmmaking style and major themes. She also situates Buñuel's emergence in terms of Spanish history and his own childhood.

——. *Spanish Film under Franco.* Austin: U of Texas P, 1988. In analyzing film both as a "national art form and as a form of national discourse," Higginbotham reveals how Spanish film under Franco dealt with social and political issues. Higginbotham's book begins with prewar Spanish film, then discusses censorship and the influential directors—Juan Antonio Barden, Luis García Berlanga, Luis Buñuel and Carlos Saura—and ends by covering the transition from dictatorship to democracy.

Hopewell, John. "Art and a Lack of Money: The Crises of the Spanish Film Industry, 1977–1990." *Quarterly Review of Film and Video* 13, no. 4 (1991): 113–22. Hopewell scrutinizes the statistics of Spanish audience attendance of Spanish films. Since 1983, attendance has dropped tremendously. Hopewell reveals why this drop has occurred by delving into the history of Spanish filmgoers. After giving a detailed summary of reasons for such a fast decline, Hopewell suggests that young Spanish producers of today have a better understanding of audiences and markets and that this might not be "entirely for the bad," for a reversal in the trend might transpire.

——. *Out of the Past: Spanish Cinema after Franco.* London: British Film Institute, 1986. Hopewell argues that due to the fragmenting effects of Franco's repression, Spanish filmmakers today lack a "sense of identity." In the first half of his book, he describes the effect of Spanish history on Spanish filmmaking, and in the second half he describes the new directions that Spanish cinema has taken, including a renewed influence of Luis Buñuel.

——. "Spotlight Spain," *Variety,* September 23–29, 1996, 58, 85–124. A dossier of articles (most of which are written by Hopewell) on current strategies of Spain's film and television industries both at home and in the global market. Details the current boom in Spanish cinema with its "new wave of talent," new independent distributors, and expanding conglomerates. Particularly informative on new developments in television and previews of forthcoming projects.

Kinder, Marsha. *Blood Cinema: The Reconstruction of National Identity in Spain.* Berkeley and Los Angeles: U of California P, 1993. Neither presenting a strict historical survey nor an auteur study, Kinder uses Spain as a "case study . . . to explore and problematize the concept of a national cinema" (7). Kinder investigates "transcultural reinscriptions," "the representation of violence in the Spanish oedipal narrative," the challenge that the exile and the émigre pose to national unity, and the tensions between regionalism and nationality. Kinder explores these issues through her discussions of Spanish television and Spanish political and cultural issues and through detailed analysis of many films from such filmmakers as Luis Buñuel, Carlos Saura,

Víctor Erice, and Pedro Almodóvar. A companion bilingual CD-ROM titled *Blood Cinema: Exploring Spanish Film and Culture* (1994) is also available, containing seventeen excerpts from fifteen films with audio and printed commentary in English and Spanish.

——. "Carlos Saura: The Political Development of Individual Consciousness." *Film Quarterly* 32 no. 2 (1979): 14–25. Relying on recent interviews with Carlos Saura, Kinder gives a history of his filmmaking, describing in detail *El jardín de las delicias* (Garden of Delights, 1970), *La prima Angélica* (Cousin Angelica, 1973), and *Cría cuervos* (Raise Ravens, 1975). After the death of Franco, Saura anticipates his films becoming more personal and less political.

——. "The Children of Franco in the New Spanish Cinema." *Quarterly Review of Film Studies* 8, no. 2 (1983): 57–76. Kinder deals with those Spanish filmmakers who were in Spain's school of cinematography during the later part of Franco's rule and who, thus, constantly defined themselves in opposition to Franco. Discussing José Luis Borau's and Carlos Saura's comments about their development as filmmakers, Kinder reveals the political struggles and personal decisions that filmmakers from that era had to make and how these considerations affected their work. Kinder then goes on to explore exactly how these struggles manifested themselves artistically—in films by Víctor Erice, Carlos Saura, Jaime de Armiñán, Jaime Chávarri, Manuel Gutiérrez Aragón, and José Luis Borau.

——. "The Disastrous Escape." In *Contemporary Literary Scene, II,* ed. Frank N. Magill. Englewood Cliffs, N.J.: Salem, 1976. This article discusses Luis Buñuel's *El angel exterminador* (The Exterminating Angel, 1962) as a proleptic parody of the disaster film genre.

——. "*El nido.*" *Film Quarterly* 35, no. 1 (1981): 34–41. Though de Armiñán is virtually unknown in the United States, Kinder see him as a sophisticated and original filmmaker. She provides a detailed discussion of his *El nido* (The Nest, 1980), and its intertextual allusions to *Don Quixote* and *Macbeth.*

——. "High Heels." *Film Quarterly* 45, no. 3 (1992): 39–44. In her review of Pedro Almodóvar's *Tacones lejanos* (High Heels, 1991), Kinder notes that this film departs from his earlier films because it attempts to "liberate the maternal from the dreaded image of the repressive patriarchal mother" (39). Kinder reveals how this inverted oedipal narrative works in the film to provide a space in which an alliance among "straight women, lesbians, gay men, transvestites, transsexuals and all other forms of non-patriarchal androgynes" (44) can be formed.

——. "*Jamón, jamón.*" *Film Quarterly* 47, no. 1 (1993): 30–35. Reviewing José Juan Bigas Luna's *Jamón, jamón* (1992), Kinder examines the way in which female desire drives the plot of this film whose scenery and props are often outrageously phallocentric.

——. "José Luis Borau *On the Line* of the National/International Interface in the Post-Franco Cinema." *Film Quarterly* 40 (winter 1986–87): 35–48. Kinder sees Borau's *Río abajo* (On the Line, 1984) as a border film in both senses: on the level of its overt content and in the fact that it displays elements of Hollywood while retaining a strong Spanish outlook. With its international flavor and almost wholly Spanish production, the film challenges the boundaries of Spanish cinema and of Hollywood.

——. "From Matricide to Mother Love in Almodóvar's *High Heels.*" In Vernon, Kathleen M., and Barbara Morris, 145–54. In this essay about Almodóvar's *Tacones lejanos* (High Heels, 1991), Kinder explores the way in which the daughter's passionate love for her mother pulls apart the societal restrictions of the patriarchal law. This challenge occurs within the system: the story takes place in public spaces controlled by patriarchal institutions—a television station, a courthouse, and a jail.

——. "Pleasure and the New Spanish Mentality: A Conversation with Pedro Almodóvar." *Film Quarterly* 41, no. 1 (1987): 34–41. After describing Almodóvar's films and offering a brief bio, Marsha Kinder interviews the filmmaker. The interview took place May 25, 1987, in Madrid. Kinder questions Almodóvar on the international success of his most recent films, "the new Spanish mentality," the unique tone of his films, his ability to make the main character sympathetic even within outrageous events and circumstances, his film's self-reflexive qualities, and the position of the figure of the Mother in Spain and in Almodóvar's films.

——. "Remapping the Post-Franco Cinema: An Overview of the Terrain." *Quarterly Review of Film and Video* 13, no. 4 (1991): 1–7. In this introduction to her special issue, Marsha Kinder describes the articles included and explains that all are attempts to remap the post-Franco cinema from a 1990s vantage point. Kinder also gives historical background on Spain and Spanish cinema in the last ten years.

——. "Review of John Hopewell's *Out of the Past: Spanish Cinema after Franco.*" *Film Quarterly* 41 (spring 1988): 49–51. Describing Hopewell's book as "the best book on Spanish cinema" published in English thus far, Kinder covers the topics Hopewell includes and suggests that his book takes one step further toward demarginalizing Spanish cinema.

——. *Spanish Cinema: The Politics of Family and Gender.* Los Angeles: Spanish Ministry of Culture and the USC School of Cinema-Television, 1989. A catalog for a film series organized by Katherine Singer Kovács and Marsha Kinder.

——. "The Spanish Oedipal Narrative from *Raza* to *Bilbao.*" *Quarterly Review of Film and Video* 13, no. 4 (1991): 67–94. In Spanish film the oedipal narrative is used to represent and to explore political issues. Kinder discusses this important aspect of the Spanish narrative and how it was used during the Francoist era as a way of getting across political beliefs that would have been repressed if represented in their true form. She also describes how current Spanish film, although released from Francoist control, still and with greater "flamboyancy," speaks through this oedipal narrative. Kinder analyses such films as Carlos Saura's *Cría cuervos* (Raise Ravens, 1975), Jaime de Armiñán's *El nido* (The Nest, 1980), Jaime Chávarri's *Dedicatoria* (Dedication, 1980), Pedro Almodóvar's *Laberinto de pasiones* (Labyrinth of Passions, 1982), Imanol Uribe's *Adiós pequeña* (Good-Bye Little One, 1986), and José Juan Bigas Luna's *Bilbao* (1978), and Franco's *Raza* (Race, 1941) and reveals the symbols that have been employed by Spanish filmmakers in their oedipal stories.

——. "The Tyranny of Convention on *The Phantom of Liberty*." *Film Quarterly* 29 (summer 1975): 20–25. Kinder praises Luis Buñuel's *Le Fantôme de la liberté* (The Phantom of Liberty, 1974) which is usually seen as simply rehashing the themes dealt with better in *Le charme discret de la bourgeoisie* (The Discreet Charm of the Bourgeoisie, 1972). Neither the audience nor the artist, Buñuel shows, in *Le Fantôme de la liberté*, ever breaks from the tyranny of convention.

——, ed. Special issue, "Remapping the Post-Franco Cinema." *Quarterly Review of Film and Video* 13, no. 4 (1991). Included in this issue are articles by Marsha Kinder, José Luis Borau, Katherine Kovács, Marvin D'Lugo, David Garland, Román Gubern, and John Hopewell (see this bibliography).

Kovács, Katherine S. "Berlanga Life Size: An Interview with Luis García Berlanga." *Quarterly Review of Film Studies* (spring 1983): 7–13. This interview with Luis García Berlanga took place in Madrid in August 1981. Kovács questions him about the "crisis in Spanish film" at that time, how the cinema has changed since the death of Franco, what young directors Berlanga finds interesting, and how he got started in filmmaking.

——. "Berlanga Retrospective at U.S.C." *Spectator* 3, no. 1 (1983): 1, 9. Kovács details the evolution of Luis García Berlanga's career as a filmmaker, including a summary of his most famous film, *El verdugo* (The Executioner, 1962).

——. "Demarginalizing Spanish Film." *Quarterly Review of Film and Video* 11, no. 4 (1990): 73–82. Kovács reviews four books on Spanish cinema—Peter Besas's *Behind the Spanish Lens*, Ronald Shwartz's *Spanish Film Directors (1950–1985)*, John Hopewell's *Out of the Past*, and Virginia Higginbotham's *Spanish Film under Franco*—and stresses the importance of these four authors in celebrating the uniqueness of Spanish cinema and bringing it into a wider circulation, despite some deficiencies that all the books share: primarily, a tendency to simplify and overgeneralize.

——. "Half of Heaven." *Film Quarterly* 41, no. 3 (1988): 34–37. In this article, Kovács reviews Manuel Gutiérrez Aragón's *La mitad del cielo* (Half of

Heaven, 1986). Kovács gives a bio on Aragón, describes the plot of the film, and suggests that with this great film Aragón goes back to the traditions of Duedo, Goya, and Buñuel.

———. "Introduction: Background on the New Spanish Cinema." *Quarterly Review of Film Studies* 8, no. 2 (1983): 1–6. Introducing her groundbreaking issue on Spanish cinema, Kovács gives a detailed history of how Spain's political events affected film before and after the lifting of censorship. Kovács also discusses who the important filmmakers of that time were and the topics covered by the other contributors to this issue.

———. "José Luis Borau Retrospective." *Spectator* 3, no. 2 (1984): 1–2. Kovács describes José Luis Borau's history as a filmmaker, summarizing his major films: *Mi querida señorita* (My Dearest Señorita, 1971), *Camada negra* (Black Brood, 1977), *Furtivos* (Poachers, 1975), *La sabina* (1979), and *Río abajo* (On the Line, 1984).

———. "The Last Word." *Quarterly Review of Film Studies* 8, no. 2 (1983): 94–98. In this article, Kovács reviews Luis Buñuel's autobiography, *Mon dernier soupir* (My Last Breath, 1982). She describes the book as done in a conversational tone and says that it doesn't actually reveal any new facts. Instead, she feels the importance of the book lies in its style and insights that reveal the dreams and memories of Buñuel that influenced his filmmaking.

———. "Loss and Recuperation in *The Garden of Delights*." *Cine-Tracts* 4, nos. 2–3, 45–54. Kovács first situates Carlos Saura and his film career within the historical events that led to the "New Spanish Cinema" movement. Moving to a more specific subject, Kovács then discusses Saura's film *El jardín de las delicias* (Garden of Delights, 1970) and the film's protagonist, Antonio Cano. Through this character and by using difficult symbolism and complex narrative structure, Saura is able to get around the censorship while he powerfully comments on Spanish history, specifically the Civil War.

———. "Parody as 'Countersong' in Saura and Godard." *Quarterly Review of Film and Video* 12, nos. 1–2 (1990): 105–24. Kovács notes there have been many film versions made of the opera *Carmen* but she chooses to discuss two films that feature *Carmen* in contemporary settings: Carlos Saura's *Carmen* (1983) and Jean-Luc Godard's *Prénom Carmen* (1983). Kovács detailed analysis provides great insight into these two films, their use of music, cultural motifs, and political settings.

———. "Pierre Louÿs and Luis Buñuel: Two Visions of Obscure Objects." *Cinema Journal* 19, no. 1 (1979): 86–98. Reprinted in *Cinema Examined,* ed. Richard Dyer MacCann and Jack C. Ellis. New York: E. P. Dutton, 1982, 282–333. In this article, Kovács looks at Buñuel's *Cet obscur objet du désire* (That Obscure Object of Desire, 1977) and the book upon which it was based, French novelist Pierre Louÿs's *La femme et le pantin* (The Woman and the Puppet), which has a Spanish setting. Louÿs's portrait of Spain is that of the tourist and of Carmen (named Concha in this film), but Buñuel takes these qualities and twists them into his own surrealist vision that comments on romance and on the decadence of modern life and which undermines any nostalgic vision of Spain.

———. "The Plain in Spain: Geography and National Identity in Spanish Cinema." *Quarterly Review of Film and Video* 13, no. 4 (1991): 17–46. In Spanish film, Kovács contends in this article, landscapes and locations are as important, or more important, than character and plot. She gives a detailed historical explanation about why land and geography have played such an important role in shaping Spanish identity and therefore exist as an extremely important characteristic of Spanish film. Investigating films, such as Luis Buñuel's *Las Hurdes/Tierra sin pan* (Lard without Bread, 1932), Carlos Saura's *La caza* (The Hunt, 1965), Ricardo Franco's *Pascual Duarte* (1976), and Víctor Erice's *El espíritu de la colmena* (The Spirit of the Beehive, 1973), Kovács reveals how landscapes and location work in each. In the last section of the article she delves into the importance of "the rain-drenched mist-shrouded woods and mountains of Northern Spain" as they achieved the status of a different Spain—a Spain of freedom—in the films of such directors as José Luis Borau, Manuel Gutiérrez Aragón and Jaime de Armiñán.

———, ed. Special issue, "The New Spanish Cinema." *Quarterly Review of Film Studies* 8, no. 2 (1983). This issue includes essays by Katherine S. Kovács, Román Gubern, Luis O. Arata, Marvin D'Lugo, Annette Insdorf, Marsha Kinder, Mario Vargas Llosa, and José Luis Borau (see this bibliography).

Lev, Leora. "Tauromachy as a Spectacle of Gender Revision in *Matador*." In Vernon, Kathleen M., and Barbara Morris, eds., 73–86. Lev explores the way in which Pedro Almodóvar rewrites the social, aesthetic, and sexual iconography of the bullfight in his film *Matador,* thus reconstituting that which was so fetishized by the Franco-endorsed tourist industry.

Lewis, Carolyn. "*Furtivos.*" *Monthly Film Bulletin* 43, no. 507 (1976), 80–81. Lewis reviews this film by José Luis Borau through a detailed description of the plot.

López, Silvia L., and Jenaro Talens, and Darío Villanueva, eds. *Critical Practices in Post-France Spain.* Minneapolis: U of Minnesota P, 1994. This collection of essays explores Spanish writers investigating poststructuralist narrative theory. The essays include the following: "The Politics of Theory in Post-Franco Spain," Silvia L. López, Jenaro Talens, and Darío Villanueva; "Making Sense after Babel," Jenero Talens; "The Television Newscast: A Postmodern discourse," Jesús González-Requena; "Architectures of the Gaze," Santos Zunzunegui; "The Immutability of the Text, the Freedom of the Reader, and Aesthetic Experience," Rafael Núñez-Ramos; "Phenomenology and Pragmatics of Literary Realism," Darío Villanueva; "The Pragmatics of Lyric Poetry," José María Pozuelo-Yvancos; "Reading in Process, the Antitext, and the Definition of Literature," Manuel Asensi; "Subjectivity and Temporality in Narrative," Cristina Peña-Marín; "Subject and Language: Reflection on Lacan and Jinkins," Juan Miguel Company-Ramón; and "Aesthetics and Politics," Tom Lewis.

Mandrell, James. "Sense and Sensibility, or Latent Heterosexuality and *Labyrinth of Passions.*" In Vernon, Kathleen M., and Barbara Morris, eds., 41–58. Mandrell investigates Pedro Almodóvar's relationship with his international identity as a gay filmmaker. Mandrell then reads the film *Laberinto de las pasiones* (Labyrinth of Passions, 1982) as an allegory "of Almodóvar's career and aspirations." Mandrell believes that this film illustrates (in allegorical terms) Almodóvar's integration into mainstream cinema and its compulsory heterosexuality.

Martí-Olivella, Jaume. "Towards a New Transcultural Dialogue in Spanish Film." In Colmeiro, José, et al., eds., 47–66. Martí-Olivella discusses the need to rethink the concepts of nationalism and feminism in order to enter a truly "democratic culture." First, Martí-Olivella discusses "the nation" as a viable theoretical quilting point by investigating the ideas of Rubert de Ventós, Alonso de los Ríos, and Benedict Anderson and cinema's role in the shaping of an "imagined community." Martí-Olivella then goes on to compare Arantxa Lazcano's *Urte ilunack* (The Dark Years, 1992) and Pilar Miró's *Es pájaro de la felicidad* (Bird of Happiness, 1992) because they are examples of films whose gendered discourses are extremely personal as well as politically relevant and challenging.

Maxwell, Richard. *The Spectacle of Democracy: Spanish Television, Nationalism, and Political Transition.* Minneapolis: U of Minnesota P, 1995. Looking at the influence the media had on the political transition to democracy and vice versa, Maxwell investigates "Political Transitions, Media Transitions," "The Politics of Privatization," and "The Geography of Television in Spain." In these different sections, Maxwell carefully details Spain's cultural, political, and economic history as a way to open the door for theorizing the role of television in shaping regional and national identity.

Miró, Pilar. "Ten Years of Spanish Cinema." In *Literature, the Arts, and Democracy: Spain in the Eighties,* ed. Samuel Amell, trans. Alma Amell. Madison: Fairleigh Dickinson UP, 1990, 38–46. Starting from Franco's death in 1975, Miró—a well-known filmmaker—traces the development of Spanish film in the 1980s. Miró investigates the political and economic events and how they influenced filmmaking during this time.

Molina-Foix, Vincente. *New Cinema in Spain.* London: British Film Institute, 1977. Molina-Foix describes the repressive effect of Franco's rule on Spanish cinema, and argues that alternative cinema in Spain was realized, despite many failed attempts, after the death of Franco in 1975.

Monteath, Peter. *The Spanish Civil War in Literature, Film, and Art: An Interna-*

tional Bibliography of Secondary Literature. London: Greenwood, 1994. This bibliography gathers together a comprehensive and international list of titles dealing with the Spanish Civil War in literature, film, and art. It includes books, articles, and chapters in a wide range of languages, including Spanish, English, Russian, French, German, and Italian.

Morris, Barbara. "Almodóvar's Laws of Subjectivity and Desire." In Vernon, Kathleen M., and Barbara Morris, eds., 87–98. Morris analyzes Pedro Almodóvar's *La ley del deseo* (The Law of Desire, 1987) and concludes that Almodóvar reconstructs the family romance as a "masochistic camp" in his complex web of dialogue and imagery.

Morris, Cyril Brian. *This Loving Darkness: The Cinema and Spanish Writers (1920–1936).* New York: Oxford UP, 1980. Looking at the influence that early cinema had on writers of that time, Morris discusses the reception of early film and the enthusiasm and hostility that it met. Morris investigates the mark left by cinema on Spanish poets (specifically Rafael Alberti, Luis Cernuda, and Frederico García Lorca) and on prose fiction. Morris concludes that writers of Spanish literature in the 1920s and 1930s, a fertile period of imagination, picked up their pens to write in reaction to what they saw at the cinema.

Mortimore, Roger. "Buñuel, Sáenz de Heredia, and Filmófono." *Sight and Sound* 44 (summer 1975): 180–82. Mortimer writes on four films that Luis Buñuel would just as soon forget, but which nonetheless he anonymously co-directed: *Don Quintín el Amargao* (Don Quintín, Embittered, 1935), *La hija de Juan Simón* (Juan Simón's Daughter, 1935), *¿Quién me quiere a mí?* (Who Loves Me?, 1936), and *¡Centinela, Alerta!* (Look out, Sentry!, 1936). Buñuel directed these films with Ricardo Maríade Urgoiti and José Luis Sáenz de Heredia. Mortimer details each of these films and looks at how they represent those few years before the Civil War and the state of film at this time, as well as Buñuel's struggles in desiring to reach a wider audience than his films usually could attract in Spain.

Nandorfy, Martha J. "*Tie Me Up! Tie Me Down!:* Subverting the Glazed Gaze of American Melodrama and Film Theory." *Cineaction* 31 (1993): 50–61. Nandorfy argues that to read *Átame* (Tie Me Up! Tie Me Down!, 1989) as antifeminist is to be submitting to an impoverished notion of spectatorship.

Packer, Peter. "I.F.G. Dossier: Spanish Cinema Now." In *Variety International Film Guide 1990,* ed. Peter Cowie. Hollywood: Samuel French, 1989, 29–65. In this special edition by *Variety,* Packer provides the I.F.G.'s dossier on Spanish cinema. In these thirty-six pages, Packer gives a short history of Spanish cinema from Franco to the present, paying special attention to certain filmmakers (Carlos Saura, Vicente Aranda, and Pilar Miró), certain producers (Elías Querejeta and Andrés Vicente Gómez), and certain actors and actresses (Antonio Banderas, Imanol Arias, Fernando Fernán Gómez,

Victoria Abril, Ana Belén, and Carmen Maura). He also discusses a wide array of other aspects of Spanish cinema and lists the films that did the best at the box office.

Peña, Richard, ed. Special issue, "Spanish and Portuguese Cinema." *Journal of the University of Film and Video Association* 35, no. 3 (1983). This issue includes essays by Peña, Gail Bartholomew, Bruce Austin, Len Masterman, Robert W. Wagner, and others. Bartholomew's article is the only one solely about Spanish cinema (see Bartholomew).

Perkins, Ted. "Spain's Villaronga rebounds with *Moonchild.*" *The Hollywood Reporter* 11 (May 1989): 8. This article discusses Agustí Villaronga's two films, *Tras el cristal* (Behind the Glass, 1986) and *El niño de la luna* (Moonchild, 1989), as offbeat productions. An interesting comparison is made by Villaronga between Pedro Almodóvar's films of the street and his own films of the mind.

Rolph, Wendy. "Afterword: From Rough Trade to Free Trade: Toward a Contextual Analysis of Audience Response to the Films of Pedro Almodóvar." In Vernon, Kathleen M., and Barbara Morris, eds., 171–78. Rolph details the commercial problems and successes of Almodóvar's films, specifically the issues of marketing, where the films played, and audience reception.

Sandro, Paul. *Diversions of Pleasure: Luis Buñuel and the Crises of Desire.* Columbus: Ohio State UP, 1987. Sandro examines Buñuel's *Un chien andalou* (An Andalusian Dog, 1928), *L'âge d'or* (The Golden Age, 1930), *El angel exterminador* (The Exterminating Angel, 1962), *Le charm descret de la bourgeoisie* (The Discreet Charm of the Bourgeoisie, 1972), *Belle de Jour* (Beauty of the Day, 1966), and *Cet obscur objet du désir* (That Obscure Object of Desire, 1977) and investigates how desire and pleasure work in these texts. In the process of these discussions, Sandro deals with subjects such as subjectivity, narrative consumption, and excess. Sandro concludes that Buñuel forces spectators to step aside from their normal classical narrative position and "learn from an ironic distance the lessons of desire."

Schwartz, Ronald. *The Great Spanish Films: 1950–1990.* Metuchen, N.J., and London: Scarecrow, 1991. Begun as a sequel to his book on Spanish directors, Schwartz's work summarizes and comments on a selection of Spanish films that are meant to reflect Spanish society.

——. *Spanish Film Directors, 1950–1985: 21 Profiles.* Metuchen, N.J.: Scarecrow, 1986. Excluding Luis Buñuel (who is termed "more international than Spanish"), Schwartz offers brief histories of the most important Spanish directors from 1950–85, including summaries of their films. He analyzes each director as an auteur, focusing on the individual personalities of the directors.

Smith, Paul Julian. *Desire Unlimited: The Cinema of Pedro Almodóvar.* New York: Verso, 1994. Investigating the issues of gender, nationality, and homosexuality in nine separate chapters, one on each of Almodóvar's feature films to date. Smith lays out Almodóvar's attempt to see "truth in travesty" and the ways in which audiences have reacted to Almodóvar's use of frivolity as a political posture. Smith feels this frivolity can be as tremendously potent as a political stance, as it is "uncontrollable." Smith analyzes each film in light of theoretical, political, and cultural issues that arise in the film itself and in the reactions to the film.

——. "*Kika*: Vision Machine." In Colmeiro, José, et al., eds., 83–92. Smith gives a detailed analysis of Pedro Almodóvar's *Kika* (1993) while he argues that *Kika* is a good example of Paul Virilia's "vision machine," in which "a regime of ever increasing visibility" leads "paradoxically to an aesthetics of disappearance or of blindness" (83).

——. *Laws of Desire: Questions of Homosexuality in Spanish Writing and Film, 1960–1990.* Oxford: Clarendon; New York: Oxford UP, 1992. Smith discusses Spanish films and novels that raise the "question of homosexuality in more or less direct fashion." Thus, Smith's book is not a history of Spanish lesbian and gay life, but instead an investigation that leads to radically new readings of major novelists (Juan Goytisolo and Esther Tusquet) and close textual analysis of two gay auteurs of Spanish films (Eloy de la Iglesia and Pedro Almodóvar). Smith also pursues the question of how lesbian and gay cultures are intricately intertwined with Spanish nationality.

——. "*Pepi, Luci, Bom* and *Dark Habits:* Lesbian Comedy, Lesbian Tragedy." In Vernon, Kathleen M., and Barbara Morris, eds., 25–40. Through detailed analyses of Almodóvar's first film, *Pepi, Luci, Bom y otra chicas del montón* (Pepi, Luci, Bom and Other Ordinary Girls, 1980), and his third, *Entre tinieblas* (Dark Habits, 1983), Smith discusses the way in which Almodóvar breaks societal and cinematic sexual taboos—by foregrounding "the spectacle of lesbian desire."

Suleiman, Susan. "Freedom and Necessity: Narrative Structure in *The Phantom of Liberty.*" *Quarterly Review of Film Studies* 3, no. 3 (1978), 277–95. Attempting to bring to bear the works of Ferdinand de Saussure (specifically the opposition between syntagmatic and associative relationships in language) and the works of Roman Jakobson (specifically the opposition between the axis of combination and the axis of selection) on the analysis of a specific text, Luis Buñuel's *La Fantôme de la liberté* (The Phantom of Liberty, 1974), Suleiman engages with Buñuel's film from the perspective of a general theory of narrative rather than of film semiotics. She concludes that this chaotic-seeming narrative actually has an excess of structural continuity, though semantically it is absurd.

Tate, S. "Carlos Saura, Spain and Mama Turns 100." *Cinéma P,* no. 37 (April 1982): 125–27. After giving a quick history of Spanish film during Saura's lifetime and a bio on Saura, Tate launches into a discussion of Saura's film

Mamá cumple cien años (Mama Turns 100, 1979). Tate also reveals the inter-connectedness of Saura's films.

Valleau, Majorie A. *The Spanish Civil War in American and European Films.* Ann Arbor: UMI Research Press, 1982. Valleau investigates and compares the representation of the Spanish Civil War in American and European films, highlighting the differences in their ideological content and methods of representation. The American films that Valleau discusses are *The Last Train from Madrid* (James Hogan, 1937), *Blockade* (William Dieterle, 1938), *For Whom the Bell Tolls* (Sam Wood, 1943), *The Confidential Agent* (Herman Shumlin, 1945), *The Angel Wore Red* (Nunnally Johnson, 1960), and *Behold a Pale Horse* (Fred Zinnemann, 1964), and the European films are *Sierra de Teruel* (André Malraux, 1938), *El Alcázar* (Augusto Genina, 1940), *La guerre est finie* (The War Is Over; Alain Resnais, 1966), *Le mur* (The Wall; Sergio Roullet, 1967), *El jardín de las delicias* (The Garden of Delights; Carlos Saura, 1970), and *Viva la muerte* (Long Live Death; Fernando Arrabal, 1970). Valleau details the aesthetic and political differences between these films and discusses how their different countries of origin influence these attributes.

Vargas Llosa, Mario. *"Furtivos."* *Quarterly Review of Film Studies* 8, no. 2 (1983). Vargas begins by discussing the crumbling of censorship in Spain and the positive and negative effects this process will have on the film industry and audiences. José Luis Borau, Vargas feels, is among the handful of filmmakers who can overcome the difficulties of making this transition. Vargas then launches into a lengthy discussion of Borau's film *Los Furtivos* (The Poachers, 1975) as an important example of an auteur film that can appeal to main-stream audiences.

Vernon, Kathleen M. "Melodrama Against Itself: Pedro Almodóvar's *What Have I Done to Deserve This?*" *Film Quarterly* 46, no. 3 (1993): 28–40. Reprinted in Vernon, Kathleen M. and Barbara Morris, eds., 59–72. After discussing Almodóvar, his relationship to Franco, Hollywood, and melo-drama, Vernon launches into detailing Almodóvar's film *¿Qué he hecho yo para merecer esto!* (What Have I Done to Deserve This? 1984). She contends that the feminine is repressed in favor of the masculine in this melodrama grounded in sexual difference. Vernon reveals the way the film works to challenge the hold that history, that is, Franco, has over future stories.

——. "Re-viewing the Spanish Civil War: Franco's Film *Raza.*" *Film and History* 16, no. 2 (1986): 26–34. Vernon begins her article by giving a brief plot summary that emphasizes both the positive and negative sources of the novel/film's "genesis in the author's life history." She then suggests three possible ways for reading *Raza* (Race, 1941) as a filmic text: through a kind of psychobiography, by examining *Raza* as a type of historical study, or by undertaking an aesthetic analysis. Vernon engages in each of these inter-pretations as she discusses its possibilities.

———. "The Third Wave." *Quarterly Review of Film and Video* 13, no. 4 (1991), 123–27. Kathleen Vernon reviews J. M. Caparrós Lera and Rafael de España's *The Spanish Cinema: An Historical Approach,* Nuria Vidal's *The Films of Pedro Almodóvar,* and Robin W. Fiddian and Peter Evans's *Challenges to Authority: Fiction and Film in Contemporary Spain,* three books she feels are the third wave of books about Spanish film to be directed at a broad and nonspecialist readership. Out of all three of these books, Vernon feels that Fiddian and Evans' book is the most interesting. However, she points out that by and large a critical language about Spanish cinema has not yet been developed.

Vernon, Kathleen M., and Barbara Morris. "Introduction: Pedro Almodóvar, Postmodern *Auteur.*" In Vernon, Kathleen M., and Barbara Morris, eds., 1–9. Vernon and Morris introduce their book and trace the history of Almodóvar as a postmodern filmmaker.

———, eds. *Post-Franco, Postmodern: The Films of Pedro Almodóvar.* London: Greenwood, 1995. This collection of ten essays investigates Almodóvar's films within the larger context of their social, historical, technological, national, and international impact. The contributors are Paul Julian Smith, James Mandrell, Kathleen M. Vernon, Leora Lev, Barbara Morris, Brad Epps, Marvin D'Lugo, Marsha Kinder, Victor Fuentes, and Wendy Rolph.

Vidal, Nuria. *The Films of Pedro Almodóvar.* Madrid: Ministerio de Cultura, 1988. The first section of this book about Pedro Almodóvar and his nine feature films is a collection of interviews Vidal conducted with Pedro Almodóvar, Carmen Maura, Julieta Serrano, and Agustín Almodóvar. The majority of the interviews are with Pedro Almodóvar, who also shares his notes that he wrote while filming each film. Thus, the reader gets a more complete feeling for the process before and during the creation of these films. Vidal calls the second section of his book a "thematic dictionary" because it critically outlines the stylistic development of "props, places and characters" in six of Almodóvar's films. The last section of the book is a filmography, which includes Almodóvar's credits of his "professional work and projects, synopses and various articles that show how the critics have reacted to his work."

Williams, Linda. *Figures of Desire: A Theory and Analysis of Surrealist Film.* London: U of Illinois P, 1981. The main project of Williams's book is to discover how the early "pre-Surrealist poetic theory of the image and the later Freudian influences on this theory in Surrealism proper combined to form a new concept of film art." Williams does a close analysis of four of Buñuel's films—*Un chien andalou* (An Andalusian Dog, 1928), *L'Âge d'or* (The Golden Age, 1930), *Le fantôme de la liberté* (The Phatom of Liberty, 1974) and *Cet obscur objet du désir* (That Obscure Object of Desire, 1977)—paying close attention to the way in which metaphoric and metonymic figures become more important than the plot or diegesis.

Wood, Michael. "The Corruption of Accidents: Buñuel's *That Obscure Object of Desire* (1977)." In *Modern European Filmmakers and the Art of Adaptation,* ed. Andrew Horton and Joan Magretta. New York: Frederick Ungar, 1981, 329–40. Wood compares Buñuel's film *Cet obscur objet du désir* (1977), to Pierre Louÿs's novel *La Femme et le pantin* (The Woman and the Puppet), from which it was adapted. Wood investigates the main female character of Concha as she existed in Louÿs's novel and in Buñuel's film—Buñuel creates two Concha's for his very distinctive version of this story.

CONTRIBUTORS

PETER BESAS has been the Madrid bureau chief and film critic for *Variety* since 1969. He has lived in Spain since 1965 and is the author of *Behind the Spanish Lens: Spanish Cinema under Fascism and Democracy* (1985), the first book-length study of Spanish film published in English. He has produced several short films in Spain, one of which, *Pipe Dreams,* won the top prize at the Madrid Film Festival in 1989.

MARVIN D'LUGO is professor of foreign languages and literatures at Clark University and has also been a visiting professor in Spanish cinema and literature at Iowa University and Dartmouth College. He is the author of *The Films of Carlos Saura: The Practice of Seeing* (1991) as well as several seminal articles on Spanish, Catalan, and Latin American film. He is also the co-author (with Marcia Butzel and Philip Rosen) of *The Concept of National Cinema* (forthcoming). In June 1992 he co-directed (with Marsha Kinder) the Spanish Film Institute at Clark University, a rigorous training program for teaching Spanish language film at the college level.

SELMA REUBEN HOLO is director of the Fisher Gallery and the Museum Studies Program at the University of Southern California in Los Angeles. She has published many scholarly articles on Spanish painting, particularly on the etchings and drawings of Goya. Holo's latest work focuses on museological issues. One of her recent articles appeared in *Kallias,* the journal of the Institut Valencia d'Art Modern (IVAM), and dealt with problems and issues surrounding authenticity in the exhibition of contemporary art. Her forthcoming book, *Museums and Their Role in the Construction of Identity in Democratic Spain,* will be published by the Smithsonian Institution Press.

DONA M. KERCHER is an associate professor of Spanish at Assumption College in Worcester, Massachusetts, where she teaches Spanish language, peninsular literature, and international film. Her publications have focused primarily on Spanish Golden Age literature and on the representation of the

Golden Age in contemporary Spanish culture. She is currently working on a book on Spanish cinema and the visual arts tradition.

MARSHA KINDER is professor of critical studies in the School of Cinema-Television at the University of Southern California in Los Angeles, where she received the 1995 Associates Award for Creativity in Research and Scholarship. Her publications on Spanish cinema include *Spanish Cinema: The Politics of Family and Gender* (1989); "Remapping the Post-Franco Cinema" (a special issue of *Quarterly Review of Film Studies,* 1991); *Blood Cinema: The Reconstruction of National Identity in Spain* (1993), which has a companion bilingual CD-ROM *Blood Cinema: Exploring Spanish Film and Culture* (1994); and *Revisiting "The Discreet Charm of the Bourgeoisie"* (forthcoming from Cambridge University Press). She has been a contributing member of the editorial board of *Film Quarterly* since 1977 and the co-editor of the *Console-ing Passions* book series on television, video, and cultural power for Duke University Press. She has also been co-curator of the annual American Cinematheque series "Recent Spanish Cinema" in Los Angeles and is currently the general editor of a CD-ROM series on national media and culture.

JAUME MARTÍ-OLIVELLA holds degrees in English philology and Catalan literature from the University of Barcelona and in comparative literature from the University of Illinois. He is a founding member of NACS (North American Catalan Society). Currently an associate professor of Spanish at Allegheny College, Martí-Olivella has published extensively on Catalan narrative, Peninsular film, and literary theory. He has edited two special issues of *Catalan Review:* "Homage to Mercè Rodoreda" (Barcelona, 1987) and "Women, History and Nation in the Fiction of Maria Aurèlia Capmany and Montserrat Roig" (Barcelona, 1993). He has also co-organized Cine-Lit I, II, and III (First, Second, and Third International Conference on Hispanic Cinema and Literature, Portland, 1991, 1994, and 1997). He is now at work on a book-length study, *Spanish Cinema in the Classroom.*

RICHARD MAXWELL teaches international communication and political economy of media and culture in the Department of Radio-TV-Film at Northwestern University. He is the author of *The Spectacle of Democracy: Spanish Television, Nationalism, and Political Transition* (1995).

HILARY L. NERONI is a doctoral candidate in the Critical Studies Program in the School of Cinema Television at the University of Southern California in Los Angeles. She is writing a dissertation on violence in contemporary American cinema, specifically on how violence intersects with gender and race in American society.

PAUL JULIAN SMITH is professor of Spanish and head of the Department of Spanish and Portuguese at Cambridge University. His books include *Writing in* *the Margin: Spanish Literature of the Golden Age* (1988); *The Body Hispanic: Gender and Sexuality in Spanish and Spanish American Literature* (1989); *Laws of Desire: Questions of Homosexuality in Contemporary Spanish Writing and Film 1960–1990* (1992); *Desire Unlimited: The Cinema of Pedro Almodóvar* (1994), and *Vision Machines: Cinema, Literature, and Sexuality in Spain and Cuba, 1983–1993* (1996). He is also the general editor of the Oxford Hispanic Studies series.

ROLAND B. TOLENTINO is an instructor in the Department of Humanities at the University of the Philippines in Manila. Born in the Philippines, he has a B.A. in economics and an M.A. in Philippine studies, and a Ph.D. in Critical Studies. His dissertation was on the use of cinema in refiguring postcolonial Filipino identity. He is a writer of fiction, a journalist, and a film reviewer, and he has edited a number of journals, including *Kultura Magazine: A Forum for Artist, Critic, and Audience, Balani,* and *Habilin.* He has published several scholarly articles on Filipino culture and has curated film and video programs for the Filipino American Arts Exposition in San Francisco and the Festival of Philippine Arts and Culture in Los Angeles.

STEPHEN TROPIANO is the director of Ithaca College's Communications Program in Los Angeles, where he teaches film theory and international cinema. He was the editor of *The Spectator* and has published a number of essays on the representation of homosexuality in European film. His book titled *Out of the Margins: The Construction of Homosexuality in Spanish, German, and Italian Cinema* is forthcoming from University of Texas Press.

KATHLEEN M. VERNON teaches Hispanic film and literature at the State University of New York, Stony Brook. Her publications on Spanish cinema include *Post-Franco, Postmodern: The Films of Pedro Almodóvar* (1995) and *The Spanish Civil War and the Visual Arts* (1990) as well as essays in *Film Quarterly, Film and History, Hispania,* and *Quarterly Review of Film and Video.* She is currently completing a book on the representation of history and memory in post–Civil War Spanish narrative, novel, and film.

IÑAKI ZABALETA is co-director of the Masters Degree Program (Communicators in Radio and Television) and from 1989 to 1994 was director of the Department of Journalism at the University of the Basque Country. From 1991 to 1993 he was director of the Annual International Conference on Radio and Television in Bilbao. He also was a visiting professor at the School of Journalism and Mass Communication at the University of Iowa in 1992. His books include *Innovaciones en programas de radio y televisión* (1993), *Innovaciones tecnológicas en radio y televisión* (1994), and *El factor humano en radio y televisión* (1995). As a journalist he has been CNN's correspondent in the Basque country, has produced fifteen documentaries for the Basque TV network, and has published a novel, a volume of short stories, and two collections of poetry.

INDEX

Library of Congress Cataloging-in-Publication Data

Refiguring Spain : cinema, media, representation / Marsha Kinder, editor.
p. cm.
Includes bibliographical references and index.
ISBN 0-8223-1932-2 (alk. paper).—ISBN 0-8223-1938-1 (pbk. : alk. paper)
1. Motion pictures—Political aspects—Spain. 2. Motion pictures—Social aspects—Spain. 3. Television broadcasting—Social aspects—Spain. 4. Television and politics—Spain.
PN1993.5.S7R35 1997
791.45'0946—dc21   96-39967
CIP